A-LEVEL
AND AS-LEVEL

LONGMAN
REVISE
GUIDES

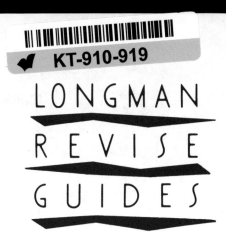

GERMAN

Alasdair McKeane

Longman

LONGMAN A AND AS-LEVEL REVISE GUIDES

Series editors:
Geoff Black and Stuart Wall

Titles available:
Accounting
Art and Design
Biology
Business Studies
Chemistry
Computer Science
Economics
English
French
Geography
General Studies
German
Modern History
Mathematics
Physics
Psychology
Sociology

Longman Group Limited,
Longman House, Burnt Mill, Harlow,
Essex CM20 2JE, England
and Associated Companies throughout the world

First published 1994

British Library Cataloguing in Publication Data

A catalogue record for this book is available from the British Library.

ISBN 0-582-22653-8

Set by 6QQ in 10/12pt Century Old Style

Printed in Great Britain by William Clowes Ltd., Beccles and London

CONTENTS

	Editor's preface	iv
	Acknowledgements	iv
1	Study skills and assessment	1
2	Reading	15
3	Listening	49
4	Speaking	73
5	Writing	85
6	Literature, Civilisation and Coursework	99
7	Grammar: 1	120
8	Grammar: 2	155
9	Vocabulary	201
	Appendix: Board-by-board syllabus details	262
	Index	268

EDITORS' PREFACE

Longman Revise Guides are written by experienced examiners and teachers, and aim to give you the best possible foundation for success in your course. Each book in the series encourages thorough study and a full understanding of the concepts involved, and is designed as a subject companion and study aid to be used throughout the course.

Many candidates fail to achieve the grades which their ability deserves, owing to such problems as the lack of a structured revision strategy, or unsound examination technique. This series aims to remedy such deficiencies, by encouraging a realistic and disciplined approach in preparing for and taking the examinations.

The largely self-contained nature of each chapter gives the book a flexibility which you can use to your advantage. After starting with the background to the A, AS-Level and Scottish Higher Courses and details of the syllabus coverage, you can read all other chapters selectively, in any order appropriate to the stage you have reached in your course.

Geoff Black and Stuart Wall

DEDICATION

für Elisabeth Becker

ACKNOWLEDGEMENTS

To the Examination Boards for providing liberal quantities of advice, materials and encouragement, and permission to reproduce questions:

The Associated Examining Board (AEB), Stag Hill House, Guildford, Surrey, GU2 5XJ

The University of Cambridge Local Examinations Syndicate (UCLES), 1, Hills Road, Cambridge, CB1 2EU

University of London Examinations and Assessment Council (ULEAC), Stewart House, 32 Russell Square, London, WC1B 5DN

Northern Ireland Schools Examination and Assessment Council (NISEAC), Beechill House, 42 Beechill Rd, Belfast, BT8 4RS

The Oxford Delegacy of Local Examinations (ODLE), Ewert House, Ewert Place, Summertown, Oxford, OX2 7BZ

Northern Examinations and Assessment Board (NEAB), Devas Street, Manchester, M15 6EU

Oxford and Cambridge Schools Examination Board (OCSEB), Elsfield Way, Oxford, OX2 8EP *and* Purbeck House, Purbeck Road, Cambridge, CB2 2PU

Scottish Examinations Board (SEB), Ironmills Rd, Dalkeith, Midlothian, EH22 1LE

Welsh Joint Education Committee (WJEC) Cwd-Bwyllgor Addysg Cymru, 245 Western Avenue, Cardiff, CF5 2YX

To my wife Anne for her unstinting support, for research, and for her many suggestions. To my sons, John George, Andrew and James for their patience and understanding. To Geoff Black and Eleanor and Stuart Wall for judicious encouragement. To Elizabeth Norris for advice and guidance, and the elimination of errors from the manuscript. To Alex Reich for the Vocabulary, and for proof-reading the German language content. To Gail Wilson and Glenise Radford for reading the Grammar Chapters and making valuable suggestions. To Karen Hilton for researching Exam Board materials, for many of the transcripts of listening exercise, and for proof-reading. To Wendy Wood and Patsy Perry for permission to use their work as examples. To Martin Durrell's *Hammer's German Grammar and Usage (Second Edition)* (Edward Arnold) which proved an invaluable reference source. To Brian Keighley who taught me. To all my A Level students over the years.

NOTE

The suggested answers provided in this book, while in accordance with Examination Boards' guidelines, are the author's own and are not 'official answers'. The Examination Boards are unable to enter into any correspondence concerning the suggested answers.

Alasdair McKeane

STUDY SKILLS AND ASSESSMENT

GETTING STARTED

This chapter gives many hints on study skills – i.e. on how to study effectively. The section below will apply to virtually any A Level or AS Level subject, while the next section looks in turn at each of the study skills which are especially relevant to learning German. You will find advice on using dictionaries, learning vocabulary, speaking, listening, writing and reading.

1. Materials. Make sure you have everything you need for lessons and for study. You should always turn up for lessons with a pen (and a spare, possibly coloured, one to provide a contrast), paper, the books, work and notes required for the session, and probably a dictionary. This is such an obvious point that it is too often overlooked.

2. Assignments. You will have many more assignments to complete than when you were doing your GCSE German course. There will probably be texts to prepare, regular language work to be done, notes to be written up, vocabulary to be learnt, and listening exercises to be done. An A Level in a modern language differs from other subjects in that students obtain the greatest value from work which is short-term. So the assignment to prepare a text is of most value before the lesson in which that text is discussed, and this week's language assignment is most valuable to you this week. While not all German assignments and activities fall into this category, the majority do. So the important message about assignments is: *do it NOW!*

3. Places. You will need to have a regular place for study, preferably one which is undisturbed. You will be able to have a dictionary and your notes to hand. There will be good lighting, and a steady table or desk to write at.

4. Times. Regular study is an important aim. You will have timetabled lessons, of course, and you should make certain that other matters such as dental appointments and driving lessons do not clash with them. As well as timetabled sessions, you will also have rather more private study time than in Year 11. This is necessary to allow you to complete the greater burden of preparation and assignments. What is vital is that it should not be wasted.

5. Notes and files. Efficient organisation of teaching and learning materials is a key to success at A Level. It is unlikely that teachers will proceed using just one textbook as a source, and you are likely to receive a good quantity of photocopied material during your two-year course. It is essential to keep this in good order if you are to be able to revise at all well, and you will need to arm yourself with an A4 lever-arch file, some section separators (you can make good ones out of cereal boxes) and a hole punch, preferably portable.

DICTIONARY WORK

VOCABULARY LEARNING

SPEAKING

LISTENING

WRITING

READING

PREPARING FOR THE EXAMINATION

ESSENTIAL PRINCIPLES

We now consider a variety of study skills for learners of foreign languages, including the following:

- dictionary use
- vocabulary learning
- speaking
- listening
- writing
- reading

DICTIONARY WORK

Although it is possible to do A Level German without *owning* a **dictionary**, it is certainly not possible to do the course without consulting one. You should really make sure you own one. Fond relatives might like to make you a present of one, or you could write to Santa! It is important to have one which is big enough to contain the majority of words you need, but which is not so big that you are discouraged from bringing it to lessons. As a rough guide, aim to pay between £10 and £20 for an English–German dictionary, slightly more for a German–German one.

💬💬 Choose an appropriate dictionary 💬💬

Before taking the plunge, check with your teacher whether your examination board allows you to take dictionaries into the examination, and if so, whether they allow English–German or insist on German–German. It may be that your teacher recommends a particular dictionary, or would prefer you to have one type rather than the other. If you are not given any specific advice, go for a dictionary which shows the plurals of German nouns, and which has been out for a relatively short length of time, say, less than 10 years since its last revision.

(a) German–English dictionaries

The main part of the dictionary is taken up with two alphabetical lists of words. It is important to take the time to get to know the other information in the entries, and to learn how to use the information given.

In particular you need to be familiar with the majority of abbreviations commonly used in the text. These might include, using my own venerable German–English Dictionary as a source, the following:

Acc	accusative	irr	irregular
adj	adjective	m	masculine
art	article	n	neuter
coll	colloquial	Nom	nominative
comp	comparative	pass	passive
conj	conjunction	pl	plural
Dat	Dative	p.p.	past participle
dial	dialect	poss	possessive
dim	diminutive	prep	preposition
esp	especially	pres	present
f	feminine	pron	pronoun
Gen	Genitive	reg	regular
h.	haben	s	substantive (= noun)
imp	impersonal	s.	sein
imper	imperative	sing	singular
imperf	imperfect	sl	slang
indic	indicative	subj	subjunctive
inf	infinitive	v.tr	transitive verb
insep	inseparable	v. intr	intransitive verb
inv	invariable	v. refl	reflexive verb

💬💬 Some useful abbreviations 💬💬

Practice varies a little concerning the way irregular verbs are presented. Some dictionaries give all the parts of irregular verbs in the text, others merely the vowel changes, others confine themselves to having a table of irregular verbs. Make sure you understand the system your dictionary uses.

💬💬 Common sense can help 💬💬

When you look up a *German word*, you may find a number of possible English translations, listed with the most common first. You will then have to apply common sense to work out which meaning is most likely in the context.

You may find that a word is not listed. This may mean that it is a past participle. Check if it begins with *ge-*, or one of the inseparable prefixes such as *be-, emp- ent-*, or *ver-*, or if it ends in *-en*. Then use either the rules for formation of regular verbs to deduce the infinitive, or consult a table of strong (irregular) verbs. Alternatively, it may be an irregular imperfect form. Again, consult the strong verb table.

Looking up an *English word* to find the German equivalent is more tricky. To be sure of having chosen the right word, follow some or all of the following steps:

(a) Make sure you know if you want a noun, adjective, verb, etc.

(b) After finding the German word, look that up in the German-English section. You should get the word you started with, or one which means the same thing in the same context.

Some hints on finding the correct word

(c) Beware of choosing from a list *Fremdwörter* which seem the same as the English word in preference to a German-root word. Often the *Fremdwörter* have a more specialised meaning and usage than their English equivalent.

(d) If the English verb is followed by a preposition, make sure you have found the exact equivalent usage in German, and that you know which case follows the German preposition.

You can see some of the major features of German–English dictionaries in Fig. 1.1.

phonetic script — **di-vulge** [daɪˈvʌldʒ] *v/t. Geheimnis etc.* enthüllen. preisgeben

dix-ie[1] [ˈdɪksɪ] *s. sl.* **1.** Kochgeschirr *n;* **2.** , 'Gulaschka,none' *f.*

transitive verb — Dix-ie [ˈdɪksɪ] → *Dixieland;*

D-mark [ˈdiːmaːk] *s.* Deutsche Mark. (f)

slang — **do** [duː;dʊ] **I** *v/t. [irr.]* **1.** tun, machen: *what can I ~ for you?* womit kann ich dienen?; *what does he ~ for a living?* womit verdient er sein Brot?; *~ right* recht tun; → *done* 1; **2.** tan, ausführen, sich

gender of noun — beschäftigen mit. verrichten. voll-bringen. eriedigen. *business* Geschäfte machen; *~ one's duty* s-e Pflicht tun; *~German* Deutsch lernen; *~ Shakespeare* Shakespeare durchnehmen *od.* behandeln;

noun (substantive) — *my work is done* m-e Arbeit ist getan *od.* fertig; *~ 60 miles per hour* 60 Meilen die Stunde fahren; *It can't be done* es geht nicht; *~ one's best* sein Bestes tun, sich alle Mühe geben; *~ better* **a)** (et.)

different meanings — Besseres tun *od.* leisten, **b)** sich verbessern; → *done;* **3.** herstellen, anfertigen: *~ a translation* e-e Übersetzung machen; *~ a portrait* ein Porträt malen; **4.** *j-m et.* tun, zufügen, erweisen, gewähren: *~*

examples of idioms — *s.o. harm* j-m schaden; *~ s.o. an injustice* j-m ein Unrecht zufügen, j-m unrecht tun; *three pills ~ me (no) good* diese Pillen hefen mir (nicht); **5.** bewirken, erreichen: *I did it* ich habe es geschafft;

phonetic script — **tuberkul ös** [-kuˈløːs] *adj.* tuberculous, tubercular; **~ ose** [-kuˈløːzə] *f* (-; -n) tuberculosis; **~ osenverdächtig** *adj.* suspected of tuberculosis.

optional e in Genitive singular — **Tuch** [tuːx] *n* (-[e]s; -e) cloth; fabric; (-[e]s, -er) shawl; scarf, neckerchief, duster; rag; *das wirkt auf ihn wie ein rotes ~* that's a red rag to him; *~* **ballen** *m* bale of cloth; *~* **fabrik** *f* cloth factory; *~* **handel** *m*

neuter noun — cloth trade, drapery; *~* **handler** *m* (wool(l)en) draper; *~* **handlung** *f,* *~* **laden** *m* draper's shop; *~* **macher** *m* cloth-maker.

adjective — **tüchtig** [ˈtʏçtɪç] **I.** *adj.* able, fit; (cap)able, competent, qualified; efficient; clever, skil(l)ful; proficient, experienced; excellent; good, considerable; powerful, strong; thorough; *~ in (dat.)* good

adverb — at, proficient (*or* well versed) in; *~er Esser* hearty eater; **II.** *adv.* vigorously, with a vengeance, like mad, thoroughly, well; *coilog* really *~arbeiten* work hard; *~ essen* eat heartily; *~ verprügeln* give a sound thrashing; *~* **keit** *f* (-) ability, efficiency; cleverness; proficiency; excellence *sportliche ~* sporting prowess.

Tuch...: ~ waren *flpl.* cloths, drapery *sg.;* *~* **zeichen** *aer. n* ground panel.

Tückje [ˈtʏkə] *f* (-; -n) malice, spite; perfidy, insidiousness; trick (*of fate, memory*); **oisch** *adj.*

plural — malicious, spiteful; insidious (*a. disease* = malignant); vicious (*a. animal, blow*); treacherous (*a. ice, road, etc.*)

feminine noun — **Tugend** [ˈtuːɡənt] *f* (-; -en) virtue; *es sich zur ~ machen, zu inf.* make a virtue of *doing a th.,* → *Not;* **ohaft** *adj.* virtuous; **oreich** *adj.* most virtuous; **osam** *adj.* virtuous; chaste.

genitive singular — **Tüll** [tʏl] *m* (-s; -e) tulle; *~e* [ˈtʏlə] *f* (-; -n) socket; spout; *~* **spitzen** *flpl.* net lace.

Tulpe [ˈtʊlpə] *f* (-; -n) *bot.* tulip; *~* **nzwiebel** *f* tulipbulb.

Tumor [ˈtuːmɔr] *med. m* (-s; -moren) tumour.

Tumult [tuˈmult] *m* (-;[e]s; -e) tumult; riot, uproar; row.

medical — **tun** [tuːn] *v/t. (irr., h.)* do; perform, make; → *machen;* put (*to school, into the bag, etc.*); make

masculine noun — (*remark, request*); take (*jump, oath*); *nichts ~ do nothing;* so *~, als ob* make *or* act as if, pretend to *inf.;* *würdig, etc., ~ assume* an air of dignity, *etc.;* *~ Sie ganz, als ob Sie zu Hause wären* make

range of — yourself quite at home!; *was hat er dir getan?* what has he done to you?; *damit ist es nicht getan*

translations of contexts — that's not enough; *es tut nichts* it doesn't matter, never mind; *es tut sich (et)was* something is going on (*or* is in the wind *or* is brewing); *es tut nichts zur Sache* it is of no significance, that is neither here nor there; *das tut man nicht!* that is not done!; *tu doch nicht so!* don't make a fuss!, *was ist zu ~?*

Fig. 1.1 — what is to be done?;

(b) German–German dictionaries

Using one of these is quite challenging, but is certainly good for your German if you stick at it. You need to remember that the dictionary is intended for native speakers, and not for learners of the language. This means that there are no holds barred on the examples which are chosen to illustrate various aspects of usage. The most common entry will be a definition, with examples to illustrate the finer points.

In general, the abbreviations used will be similar to those used in German–English dictionaries.

Useful German – German dictionaries

One German–German dictionary which is very useful is the *Duden Stilwörterbuch*. It lists words in context, and is invaluable for working out which prepositions to use and which cases to use with them. Most school or college libraries will have a copy. There are other volumes in the series which can sometimes be useful, notably the *Bildwörterbuch*, which has hundreds of labelled drawings, and the more tricky *Hauptschwierigkeiten der deutschen Sprache*, which concentrates on the finer points of German.

VOCABULARY LEARNING

Much of a good student's success at A Level depends on his or her breadth of **vocabulary**. That knowledge may be of three kinds:

Types of vocabulary

(a) **active** – the student can readily use words accurately in context
(b) **passive** – the student would not necessarily use a word personally, but knows what it means
(c) **deductive** – the student does not know for sure what the word means, but can work out from the context, from the form of the word and from the root words, prefixes and suffixes it contains pretty well what it means.

Be regular

Vocabulary learning is a gradual process which can only be done on a regular basis. It is hopeless to attempt to acquire the 3000 or so words of active vocabulary in the last few weeks before the final examination. And it is utterly hopeless to attempt to learn an additional 5000 or so words for recognition purposes in the same short period.

The only logical solution is to have a regular method of noting, classifying and learning new vocabulary as you come across it. The maintenance of a personal vocabulary notebook or file is a good activity for private study sessions. But you should always be ready to note down new words and expressions. The act of writing them down, and perhaps transferring them to a more permanent record will help you to remember them. So, when preparing new material, note down what you have had to look up. When doing listening work, make a rough note of key expressions and check them in a dictionary afterwards. And if you have had to look up words to complete a written assignment, add them to your list.

Probably the most useful way of keeping notes is by *topic*. They can then be filed with the topic and used in conjunction with the teaching material for revision. The vocabulary in this book has been arranged that way, too.

By systematic

You should also decide at the outset in what form you are going to keep your notes. Because German plurals are often awkward to work out, you would be well-advised to note them for each noun you come across, like this:

der Mann (-"er)	*man*
die Frau (en)	*woman*
das Kind (-er)	*child*
der Lehrer (-)	*teacher*
das Glück (no pl)	*luck*

Similarly, there is something to be said for noting whether verbs are weak (regular) or strong (irregular), and, if strong, what the imperfect and perfect tense are, and whether the verb takes 'sein' as its auxiliary in the perfect and other compound tenses. An entry might look like this:

A sample entry for verbs

spielen (wk)	*to play*
gehen, ging, *gegangen	*to go*
singen, sang, gesungen	*to sing*

The asterisk denotes verbs which take 'sein'.

As well as noting vocabulary as a matter of habit, you should actively learn it. Various techniques are effective, including merely writing new material out 5 or 10 times on scrap paper, writing yourself tests to be done a day or two later, making a game of it with a friend, carrying your 'words for the day' on a scrap of paper in a pocket and consulting it at idle moments, designing crosswords for fellow-students, memorising lists, etc. Try some or all of these, and remember that a little but often is the key to a broad vocabulary.

SPEAKING

Knowledge of a foreign language is commonly described as 'speaking' it. And, as at GCSE, **Speaking** remains a major element in assessment of your performance at A Level (about 20%), and is even more important at AS, where it may account for up to 40% of the marks.

◖◖ Be bold ◗◗

The British often feel that speaking a foreign language is a matter for considerable embarrassment, and avoid doing so where they can. This is really foolish. Nothing pleases people more than meeting foreigners who speak German well, or who are making a reasonable attempt at it. Particularly in Germany, there are large numbers of foreigners resident, so Germans are well used to the efforts of learners.

There is no doubt that, in the course of your A Level studies, you will come across a large amount of vocabulary and you will improve your knowledge of grammar. This really means that you ought to be speaking better German at the end of the two years. For many students, however, this is not so. The main reason is quite simply lack of practice. There are, however, many ways of ensuring that you use the language.

(a) Many teachers will run their classroom using German as the primary means of communication. The sort of things you, as a student, have to do, will be to ask simple questions. Some of the phrases you might need include the following:

■ Ich verstehe das nicht.
 I don't understand.
■ Können Sie das bitte wiederholen?
 Can you repeat that, please?
■ Wie schreibt man das?
 How do you spell that?

◖◖ Some useful phrases ◗◗

■ Was bedeutet 'Umweltschutz' auf deutsch/auf englisch?
 What does 'Umweltschutz' mean in German/in English?
■ Ich habe leider meinen Kuli zu Hause liegenlassen.
 I'm afraid I have left my pen at home.
■ Bis wann müssen wir die Aufgabe gemacht haben?
 When does the assignment have to be done by?
■ Wann ist der Vokabeltest?
 When is the vocabulary test?

If your teacher does not automatically encourage the use of German, ask him/her if your class could try it.

(b) Some teachers may ask you to *define* things in German, or to give *examples* or *opposites* in German. This is another opportunity for you to practise, and you should make sure you join in.

◖◖ Take every opportunity to practise ◗◗

(c) There may even be a *warm-up* spot to the lesson where students say what they have been doing over the weekend, or what they have seen on TV and what they thought of it. Again, take advantage of the chance to practise.

(d) Some A Level syllabuses require you to write about *literary works* in German. Where this is so – and even if it isn't required in the examination – you may find yourself discussing what happened in a text, the motives of characters, and your opinions of them in German. Of course this is quite tricky at first. But you can soon build a repertoire of suitable phrases to support your efforts, and you can often prepare what you have to say in advance.

(e) You may also find that your teacher asks you to discuss *language topics* in German. Many of these may be at least slightly controversial, and you will need to build a repertoire of debating phrases. These will come in handy when writing essays. As in discussing literary works, you may well be able to prepare some of your remarks in advance.

◖◖ You can prepare some things in advance ◗◗

(f) Many schools and colleges have a *German Assistant*. Although untrained, the majority of them are intending to be teachers, and they are often keen to do a good job. The use made of them varies from one Sixth Form to another. But you should be sure to make the most of any time you have with them. If you are lucky enough to have a half-hour a week with the Assistant alone or with a small group, do make every effort to make the most of the privilege. It really should be treated as a serious part of your course, and you should aim to gain as much benefit as you can from your sessions.

> 🗨️ Make good use of any German assistant 🗨️

It may well be that the Assistant is not vastly different in age from A Level students and may welcome being included in social activities. This may provide additional opportunities to practise German.

(g) Because Germans cannot get far in life without a knowledge of English, there are often young Germans about in Britain, perhaps on exchange. They are often only too pleased to chat briefly in German – they may be feeling homesick. On the other hand, you might volunteer to show a group of younger German visitors round your school or town. But beware – you will need to prepare what you say carefully.

> 🗨️ Look out for German visitors 🗨️

(h) Your school may run a German exchange. If you have already made contacts when younger, you might be able to arrange a return visit if your teacher is happy about it. Alternatively, there may be a programme specially designed for Sixth Formers, perhaps incorporating some work experience. You should think twice before missing this most valuable of all opportunities to speak German.

> 🗨️ Are there exchange opportunities? 🗨️

(i) Even if your school or college doesn't run an exchange scheme, there may be a nearby town which has a twinning arrangement. Don't be put off participating in their activities by the fact that you live a short distance away. Usually the organisers are pleased to have some extra participants to spread the costs further. Twinning associations often allow you to share your own sporting or cultural interests with Germans, and their activities may have a less 'schooly' feel to them.

(j) There are also various organisations which operate exchange schemes. The government one is:

CBEVE (Central Bureau)
Seymour House
Seymour Mews
London
W1H 9PE

> 🗨️ Some useful organisations 🗨️

It also publishes *Working Holidays*, and is the link organisation for the EC Lingua scheme.

The Anglo-Austrian Society operates a variety of schemes, including hosting in Britain, as well as travel to Austria, and it offers some bursaries for language courses in Austria.

The Anglo-Austrian Society
46 Queen Anne's Gate
Westminster
London
SW1H 9AU

A commercial organisation which has proved reliable in the past is:

Dragons International
The Old Rectory
South Newington
Banbury
OX15 4JN
Tel: 0295 721717

(k) It is possible for groups of friends to spend a 'German morning' speaking nothing but German – strange at first, but effective if tolerance is exercised.

(l) You may wish to exchange *taped letters* with a German correspondent, perhaps agreeing how often to swop cassettes, and perhaps what themes to tackle. If the taped letter is 50/50 German/English, it is useful to both sides.

(m) The German-speaking world is well-supplied with youth hostels, and campsites, and, while travelling alone is not perhaps advisable nowadays, both allow inexpensive opportunities to meet people, and will oblige you to polish your survival vocabulary. If you need a compact reminder of the survival German you are supposed to have known for GCSE, try *GCSE German – Your Speaking Test Guide*, £2.00 by mail order only from Malvern Language Guides, PO Box 76, Malvern, WR14 2YP. Student Interrail cards, too, are a good buy, and Germans are often very sociable on trains.

(n) Even speaking to the goldfish in German will improve your fluency. NB - This is not as good as practice with a human!

❝❝ Keep trying to get your message across in German ❞❞

Whatever means you use of ensuring that you get practice in German, be prepared to have a go at communicating. Of course accuracy matters at A Level. But there are always marks to be gained for keeping going or getting the message across, and, in the adult world, these are the skills which will in fact be most useful to you when using a foreign language.

LISTENING

Like Speaking, your abilities in **Listening** will have been assessed at GCSE. And at A Level, too, there will be a test of Listening comprehension, worth about 20% of the marks. At AS Level, it may be up to a third of the marks.

So clearly you need to spend some time on improving your listening comprehension skills. At first, 'real' German, that is to say, spoken by native speakers to other native speakers, will seem impossibly fast. But with practice you ought to be able to follow a standard radio broadcast without too much difficulty by the end of your A Level or AS course, provided you give Listening its fair share of your attention.

❝❝ Radio broadcasts can help ❞❞

The following are a few suggestions for Listening activities and sources of material in German. But of course any of the activities suggested above for practising Speaking involve listening, too.

❝❝ Some useful listening activities ❞❞

(a) In class, you will hear your teacher, probably the German Assistant, and almost certainly material recorded on audio cassette. As ever, listening with a pen in the hand is the most productive. The spelling of German is not tricky for non-native speakers and with practice you will be able to write unknown words down well enough to ask about them afterwards, or to look them up in a dictionary. It is particularly worth cultivating this skill if your exam board allows the use of dictionaries in the A Level Listening exam.

❝❝ Listen to cassettes ❞❞

(b) You may be able to ask your teacher if you can borrow or make a copy of any audio-cassette material you have heard in class. It will probably only be a few minutes long, and you will be able to make up a personal course tape which will help your consolidation of material during private study and during revision.

❝❝ Make your own transcripts, if one is not available ❞❞

(c) With any recording, take a minute or so, and make a *transcript*, using the review and pause buttons on your cassette machine or walkman. Get someone competent to check it. You can do this yourself if you can find material which has a transcript provided. Many of the more modern course books and materials do have transcripts. Your teacher might be able to let you have a copy of the relevant page of the teacher's book.

❝❝ Make use of any transcripts ❞❞

(d) If you *can* find material with a transcript, use a photocopier to enlarge it, and correction fluid to blank out occasional words. You might ask someone else to use the correction fluid for you. Then play the tape and use it to fill in the blanks.

(e) The publication *Authentik* (for details see below under Reading) has a cassette which accompanies each issue, together with listening activities and a key. Although the cassette is quite expensive, your school or college library or the German department may be able to make a copy available to you. The activities are constructed with the variety of exercises found at A Level in mind.

❝❝ Look out for TV programmes in German ❞❞

(f) Although rare, there are occasional TV broadcasts of German series in German, often with English subtitles. This is really helpful, as well as being entertaining. Recent offerings have included *Heimat* and *Das Boot*.

(g) Less rare are occasional TV screenings of classic films in German, again with subtitles. Channel 4 and BBC2 are the likely channels, and, unless you are a night owl, you might need to video them to view at more social hours.

(h) Satellite dish owners and cable users can receive several Eurochannels in German, providing daily news, as well as a variety of other programmes. As the offer of satellite programmes changes frequently, you should consult the press or specialist magazines for details of what is currently on offer. Watching the news does, however, have the advantage that you can find out what is being said by listening to a UK station. Incidentally, it is possible to make audio recordings of TV material via a video recorder so that you can work on them as in (c) above.

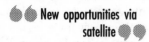 New opportunities via satellite

(i) In Germany itself, if where you are staying has cable TV, you can probably view programmes in English or German at will. This could, of course, be useful to you. Nicam stereo sets have the same facility.

(j) As well as 'real' TV programmes, there is quite a good range of schools broadcasts available. Schools and colleges will have recorded series, and may be able to make them available to you. Even if the material is intended for beginners or near beginners, it will be beneficial in that it will reinforce what you already know, and will contain some language which is more complex.

TV titles to look for include:

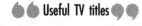 Useful TV titles

■ Lernexpress
■ Kontakte
■ Treffpunkt Deutschland
■ Treffpunkt Österreich

(k) The BBC has also broadcast material on radio over the years, for example *Deutsch für die Oberstufe*.

German music can help

(l) Many German songs (Schubert), operas (Mozart, Wagner), oratorios (Händel) and much sacred music (J.S. Bach) are available on record with transcripts, and in many cases English versions. If you enjoy the music, you will enjoy it more as listening practice.

(m) If one or more of your set texts is a *play*, it is likely to be available on cassette from:

The Goethe-Institut
50 Princes Gate
(Exhibition Rd)
London
SW7 2PG

Regular listening in small doses is the best way

The important thing about listening is to make sure that you do plenty, frequently, but in very small doses. You should try to cover a range of situations – news broadcasts, weather forecasts, traffic reports, interviews, stories, historical items, and even humour, and to 're-visit' them often during your course. If you can do so, you will find that your competence increases steadily.

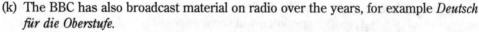

WRITING

Writing correct German is the most demanding skill at A Level. Many (but not all) AS syllabuses require very little writing in German, and the little they do require is marked mainly for 'getting the message across'. However, AS students should not get out of the habit of writing correct German, as it is the basis of linguistic progress at this level. In any case, they may well share their lessons with A Level students.

Writing is very important at A level

The main difference between GCSE and A Level is that, while a top grade at GCSE is obtainable without being more than reasonably good at writing, the same is not true of A Level. So improving the absolute quality of Writing can be a real struggle for many A Level students after their GCSE experience. But it is a necessary one if you are ambitious, and knowing how to go about it is vital.

First of all, you need to be frank with yourself about your competence. Are you really quite good at writing a Higher Level GCSE essay, and able to obtain close to full marks on it, or are you really struggling to write correctly in the perfect tense? Are you able to operate the cases after the common prepositions with 90% accuracy, or do you just guess? Is your grasp of adjective endings faultless, or do you just add *-en* and hope for the best?

If you fall into the 'really quite good' category at the start of your course, all you need to do is to make absolutely sure of any difficulties which arise, and concentrate on absorbing new material as your course progresses.

On the other hand, if you are one who often 'guesses and hopes', then you have some work to do. As a minimum before the end of the first term of the A Level course you must be absolutely sure of the following:

A self-check early in your course

- 40 strong verbs in present, perfect and imperfect
- weak verbs in present, perfect and imperfect
- adjective endings after *der* and *ein*
- the uses of the Nominative, Accusative, Dative and Genitive
- the common prepositions which
  (i) always take Dative
  (ii) always take Accusative
  (iii) always take Genitive
  (iv) take either Dative or Accusative

All of the above can be looked up in the Grammar section of this book (Ch. 7). Relatively painless practice can be had in Rogers and Long: *Alles Klar* (Nelson Harrap).

Once that is done, you can begin on the new grammar and material for A Level with confidence. But it is futile to attempt to master the more complicated grammar without being quite sure of the basic material.

The strategies given below will help you to improve your written work over your course, or may provide ideas for revision activities.

Useful strategies for improving your writing

(a) Write in German using alternate lines. This makes it easier for you to change things legibly after checking, and it is easier for you or your teacher to write in corrections and alternative versions.

(b) Prepare written work in rough, check it systematically, and hand in a neat version that you believe to be correct. If the first draft, checking, and writing up can be done on separate occasions, you will eliminate more errors and produce better work.

(c) Checking is best done systematically with reference material to hand. One possible mode of proceeding is:

Be systematic

(i) **Check genders**
 - by applying gender rules
 - by looking up individual words

(ii) **Check cases**
 - is there an Accusative after each verb?
 - if not, do you know why?
 - are they right after each pre-position?

(iii) **Check adjectives**
 - if they are not followed by a noun, they should not have an ending
 - if they are followed by a noun, do they have the correct ending for
   - following *der, ein*, or nothing
   - the case of the noun
   - the gender of the noun
   - singular or plural?

(iv) **Check verbs**
 - is the tense right in each instance?
 - is it weak or strong?
 - is the form of the verb right?
 - does it need *haben* or *sein*?
 - does it agree with its subject?

(v) **Check word order**
 - is the verb in the right place? (second idea or at end of clause)
 - are time, manner, place in that order?
 - are DAN and PAD right? (order of direct and indirect objects – see Grammar Chs. 7 and 8)

(vi) **Check spelling**
 - capital letters on nouns?
 - e and i always the right way round?
 - Umlauts where needed?
 - no Umlauts over the letters e or i?
 - no words hyphenated over line ends?
 - ß and ss correct?
 - Sch- always with a c?

(vii) **Check punctuation**
 - commas only for subordinate clauses and lists?
 - speech marks in the right places?

(d) When corrected work is returned, write out a fair copy incorporating the corrections and suggestions made, then file it carefully with the original. This only takes a few minutes, but does draw your attention to the shortcomings.

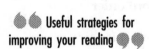 **Learn from your mistakes**

(e) In addition, you could analyse the mistakes, note them, and act on preventing recurrence by looking up the point. Give the most frequent errors the most urgent attention. You could also compare notes week by week and see where your weaknesses lie.

(f) Most importantly, if you can establish *what* it is that is causing you trouble, you are in a much better position to ask your teacher for help in dealing with it. You should certainly make the most of what are often relatively small teaching groups to get the individual help *you* require. So – don't be shy – ask!

So, while practice certainly makes perfect in writing, analysis before, during and after writing 'makes perfect' even more quickly!

READING

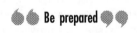 **Reading is important**

 **Read in a constructive way**

Finding German to read is not really a problem. And, given that **Reading** accounts for 20% of many A Level syllabuses, (more if you include the set texts in Literature/ Civilization options and the fact that some syllabuses set their Listening and Reading comprehension questions in German), and up to a third of AS syllabuses, you will certainly need to read a great deal of authentic German before your two years are over.

Of course, merely reading the German and letting the words roll over you will not help very much. What is needed is *constructive* reading, with something to show for it afterwards, following a programme of varied material.

By the end of the A Level course you should be in a position to read a regional newspaper without too much need to consult a dictionary. You should also be able to tackle more straightforward fictional and factual writers without undue difficulty.

But to achieve this standard you will need to be *systematic* in your approach to Reading. The following hints are likely to prove beneficial, both for locating a variety of material in addition to what your teacher provides, and for suggesting ways of deriving maximum benefit from your reading.

Useful strategies for improving your reading

(a) Always read with a pen and paper handy. You will approach reading more seriously on an upright chair seated at a desk. You should aim to note any vocabulary or phrase you had to look up, and anything which you understood readily, but which you might not perhaps have produced yourself.

Beware, however, of noting obscure phrases which are pretty unlikely to crop up again. I remember noting – religiously – *der Wipfel (n)* (= the crown of a tree), and I am certain I have never used it since!

Be prepared

Constructive reading is particularly important when your teacher has asked the class to 'prepare' a passage. Too often students will not really look at the passage, and they waste nearly a whole lesson in going over matters which they could perfectly easily have found out for themselves. It is much more helpful to arrive at a lesson with a list of half a dozen things you weren't sure of, but a reasonable knowledge of the text. That way, the finer points can also be worked on, and much more benefit is derived from discussion of the text.

(b) File the notes you generate carefully, with good references to what text (and what part of a longer text) they refer to, and perhaps the date you read the text.

(c) You could – particularly with journalism – list synonyms which the writer has inserted to avoid repetition. This is a very useful way of making newspaper articles less tricky to understand.

Make lists

(d) You could also decide to make a list of the adverbs, say, in a particular article, to extend your knowledge of them.

(e) Every subject has its specialised vocabulary. Try listing what you have found on, for example, *die Umwelt*, and then compare it with a list prepared by someone else, or with the one provided in the vocabulary chapter of this book.

(f) For magazine articles, try to discover the plan to which the article was written. Many will have an introduction, arguments pro and contra, and then a conclusion. Others may be more narrative. But try to find where the writer has moved to another point in his/her plan, and how the joins have been made. Many points will have a number of sub-points. Learning how to find them will make doing summaries easier.

(g) Try to be alive to nuances such as the use of the subjunctive to allow the writer to distance him or herself from the opinions being expressed, or the use of adverbs such as *mutmaßlich* and *angeblich* to get round the libel laws.

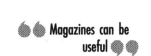 **Keep a record of your reading**

(h) Keep a record of your reading on a single sheet of paper. You will then be able to see how many texts of a particular type you have read. You need to include all newspaper sections, including crime, politics, scandal, magazine, adverts, travel, reviews, human stories, from a variety of papers. You should also work through general interest articles in magazines such as *Brigitte* and teenage ones such as *Freundin*.

German newspapers will help

(i) Obtaining German newspapers in Britain is not as difficult as you might think. No ordinary A Level student needs a daily German paper, though some schools and colleges provide one in the library. But in most large towns there will be a newsagent who stocks foreign newspapers. It is often a trader near the railway station. Your German teacher is the person most likely to know where you can buy an occasional newspaper without having to order it.

Although often somewhat salacious, *Bildzeitung* and *Bild am Sonntag* is probably the easiest to read and the most widely available. But you should also be able to manage much of what is printed in a good-quality regional paper such as the *Kölner Stadtanzeiger*, the *Rheinische Merkur* or the *Berliner Morgenpost*. Although fairly widely available in UK, the *Frankfurter Allgemeine Zeitung* and *Die Zeit* are quite tricky. As well as newspapers, the news magazine *Neue Revue* is quite widely available and easy to read. *Stern* and *Der Spiegel* are more serious news magazines, but not impossible to tackle.

(j) As well as buying newspapers in Britain, you could perhaps ask someone who is travelling to Germany to pick some up for you. Frequently the contents of the pile of newsprint waiting to go to the *Altpapiersammlung* in most German households provide varied reading at no cost. After all, the date of the newspapers you practice on hardly matters.

Magazines can be useful

(k) One very good source of more structured journalistic material is the magazine *Authentik*. Published by Trinity College Dublin, it is a digest of a variety of sources, often with exercises, and fairly up to date. It represents a really good buy for A Level students. Their address is:

Authentik Language Learning Resources Ltd
27 Westland Square
Dublin 2
Ireland
Tel: 353-1-77152

As mentioned above, a cassette containing linked audio material is available with each issue.

(l) If your teacher uses a textbook, it will have selected passages on a variety of topics. But there are half a dozen modern A Level textbooks available, and any of them published since about 1980 will have a good range of modern materials. Ask your local public library which ones they can obtain for you to read. If your teacher does not use a textbook, there is even more reason to try and get hold of a couple of collections of texts for a while as an alternative source of information.

(m) The German government publishes a glossy magazine, *Scala*, and a youth version, *Jugendscala*, several times a year. These are available free to schools. Ask your teacher to obtain copies for you. Both magazines are well-produced and both their content and level of difficulty are very suitable for A Level students.

(n) The Goethe-Institut has a library which is free. Their address is:

Goethe-Institut
50 Princes Gate
(Exhibition Rd)
London
SE21 8EL

(o) Finally, do not forget to read the material which your teacher sets when and as it is due. That way you will gain maximum benefit from lesson time.

Be active

So finding German to read is not difficult, and *active* reading ensures that none of the effort involved is wasted. Do not be put off if you find reading longer passages of

German tricky early in your course. If you stick at it, it will be amongst the first areas of the course where you can really feel the progress you are making.

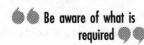

The most important thing to do about dealing with anything very unfamiliar – like an A Level or AS examination – is to make sure you know as much as possible about what you are up against. It is very motivating to have worked out what exactly is going to face you in the examination room, and to have worked out what you are going to do beforehand and during the examination to make sure that you can do what the examiners want you to do.

Similarly, it is very important to know some good ways of planning revision and to be sure of good techniques for the examination papers themselves. It is amazing how often people are ignorant of the most obvious things to do to be sure of giving their peak performance. Don't be one of them – read on!

The detailed syllabuses of each board (you need only check your own), are presented as an appendix to the book. We now look at the aims of your course, some useful hints on **revision** and on what you should do in the **examination** itself.

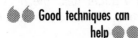

AIMS OF A LEVEL AND AS LEVEL GERMAN

The aims of the A Level and AS syllabuses are broadly as follows:

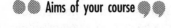

- to enable students to communicate confidently in German in speech and writing,
- to enable students to understand written and spoken German from a variety of contemporary registers and sources; the materials used will eventually be unabridged and at natural speed,
- to encourage a knowledge of how languages (including German) are best learnt, and to develop an increased linguistic awareness,
- to provide enjoyment and intellectual stimulation,
- to develop an awareness of the culture and civilisation of the German-speaking countries, including contemporary issues.

REVISION PLANNING

As I have already suggested, being *organised* produces better results. This applies, of course, to **revision** as well as normal study. Here are some tips about efficient revision:

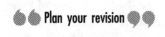

1. **Count the weeks.** Work out how many weeks there are left before the A or AS Level examination. For A Level German, the various examinations are spread over several weeks, so time the run-up to each one individually. There is little point in slaving over your Writing the day before your Speaking Test, for example.
2. **Make a revision planner, week by week.** Write in the topics you wish to revise, week by week and skill by skill. Allow a week near the end for 'slippage' – time to catch up on what you have missed. Make sure you have sufficient variety, and don't be over-ambitious about what you can get done. You may need to decide what is top priority for you.
3. **Know what the Examinations involve.** Check the details for each type of test given in this book. Knowing what to expect gives direction and urgency to your revision and prevents you wasting time on irrelevant material.
4. **Check that you personally can do what is required.** The Vocabulary chapter of this book has lists of words and phrases for most topics you are expected to have covered, as laid down in the various Examination Board syllabuses. Make sure you know them!
5. **Question-spot.** Use mock and past papers, either ordering them from the Examination Board, or asking to see copies in school or college: careful reading of them makes it possible to work out fairly accurately the sort of question that might be asked. For example, there is a limited range of things which can be asked about weather forecasts. If you know them, you needn't worry about them if they crop up, say, in the Listening test.
6. **Analyse your own performance.** If you have done a mock examination, work out where your weaknesses are, and do something about them. If you are uncertain

where to begin, consult your teacher who, after all, knows your abilities best. Even if you haven't yet done a mock examination, you can still give direction to your revision by honestly pinpointing things you don't do well.

Directed revision pays off. **Revise early**, and **revise often**!

REVISION TECHNIQUES

The most difficult thing about revision is overcoming boredom. By definition, you have seen things you are revising before, so you need to find ways of compensating for the lack of novelty.

Many students revise ineffectively because they merely read through notes and chapters in the text-book and let the information wash over them. This is almost always a waste of time, certainly after the first half-hour or so. The key is to **do something**. Activity is an aid to concentration. In a skill-based subject like German, where your performance is measured, you will improve your performance by practice.

Try some or all of the following techniques:

1. **Write notes**. When reading, say, grammar rules again, make yourself skeleton notes which are sufficiently detailed to jog your memory. Some students do this on small pieces of card (index cards or chopped up pieces of cereal packet) which they carry about with them and consult in odd moments. The same goes for vocabulary. Writing a word down with its gender and meaning will help to fix it in your memory. Another hint is to write down a phrase which contains the word and its gender and plural. When reading texts, make a note of every word you had to look up. As time goes on, you will have to look up fewer and fewer.

2. **Work with a friend**. This can relieve the boredom. Pick a friend who is about the same standard as you are. Working with someone a lot better can be good for their ego, but not for yours! Similarly, working with someone a lot weaker doesn't teach you anything new. Testing each other is a good idea. But don't forget to include written testing, which is the ultimate proof of whether you know things. Because of the danger of being side-tracked, don't rely on this method of revision alone.

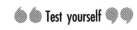

3. **Set yourself tests**. While learning, make a note of things you found hard, and test yourself later – at the end of your session, then the following day, then the following week. You have to be honest with yourself about how you got on! Keep a chart of your marks as a rough guide to progress.

4. **Tick off what you've done**. Using the revision planner you have made, tick off the topics you have dealt with. Do NOT tick off ones you have missed out! The more you have dealt with, the better you will feel.

5. **Set realistic targets**. Don't try to do too much in one session – you'll end up frustrated and become more and more depressed. Far better to learn, say, 10 irregular verbs and succeed than to try to learn 56 and fail miserably.

6. **Reward yourself**. If you have done a reasonable stint of revision, or done well in a test, give yourself a treat – a sweet, or a coffee break, or the chance to watch a favourite soap opera. Having something to look forward to is a great incentive.

7. **Don't go too long without a break.** 45–50 minutes is probably the longest session most people can concentrate for without a break – even if it's only to stretch you legs for 5 minutes.

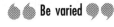

8. **Give yourself variety.** Vary what you look at – revise different skills in German. Also, vary the subjects you do in any one session – 3 spells of 45–50 minutes on three different subjects will be more productive than a 3-hour 'slog' on one area.

9. **Don't be fooled by other students.** During the examination season, some fellow-students will be loudly proclaiming either that they 'never do any revision' or that they are 'up till 2 a.m. every evening working'. Ignore them. They are being hysterical, and may well not be telling the truth anyway. What matters to you is not how much or how little revision your friends do, but how much *you* do.

Most important of all, don't kid yourself that you are working when you aren't. You can't revise at all while watching TV, chatting to friends, washing your hair or eating a meal. So don't even attempt it. Instead, use these activities to reward yourself after a revision session.

EXAMINATION TECHNIQUES

The best cure for examination nerves is the knowledge that you have done all the preparation that can reasonably be expected. There are also various practical things you can do to make sure you can concentrate during the examination itself.

The evening before an examination:

- Put everything you need the following morning, ready packed, by the front door to eliminate last-minute panic. Include spare pens, pencils and rubbers, and a silent watch.
- At the end of the evening, do something *other than work* to relax yourself. If you can manage to take the whole evening off, that's even better.
- Go to bed at a reasonable hour so you have enough sleep.
- Be very moderate with alcohol; the after-effects definitely impair performance!

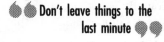
Don't leave things to the last minute

The morning before an examination:

- Get up in good time to avoid rush and panic.
- Dress carefully, possibly even smartly (to take your mind off the examination).
- Eat breakfast so that you aren't hungry during the examination.

Start the day well

Just before the examination:

- Be there in good time, but not too early.
- Read or listen to something EASY and familiar in German.

In the examination room:

- Sit as comfortably as possible. Use folded paper to stop your desk rocking.
- Check the number of questions you have to answer and the time available.
- Read the questions carefully. Often the wording of a question can indicate a good way of going about answering it.
- Decide which order to tackle the questions in. Don't leave your strongest topic to the end.
- Pace yourself so you have enough time to answer the questions at the end of the paper. If you can't do a question early in the paper inside the time it deserves, leave it and come back to it later.
- Don't leave blanks – make a sensible guess. This applies especially to multiple-choice questions.
- Use your common-sense in *Listening* and *Reading* papers; if you don't know what happened, think what a sane and rational person might do in identical circumstances. Check also that you have given enough details in Listening and Reading papers.
- In *Writing* examinations, check verbs, genders and agreements.
- Ignore the behaviour of other candidates. Many poor candidates demonstratively sit back or go to sleep having 'finished', or even walk out early. Don't be tempted to imitate them.
- When you have finished, check your work *systematically.*

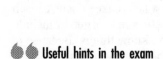
Useful hints in the exam room itself

After the Speaking Test

Avoid panicking others by saying how terrible it was, etc. Smile sweetly and wish them good luck.

When it's all over

Celebrate moderately. And try to forget about it until results day. Worrying is an unproductive waste of time. What isn't a waste of time, though, is having strategies prepared for what you will do *if* the results are not as good as you had hoped.

READING

GETTING STARTED

Reading is one of the skills which is easiest to practice. The majority of your German lessons will involve reading something or other, journalism, literature, background information, or comprehension questions in German. There are many sources of Reading material listed in the study skills chapter (Ch. 1).

However, it is important to make reading an *active* experience, where you are involved in actually *doing* something. My tutor at college used to say that reading without making notes is reading lost, and there is much truth in that. You should be making sure you are improving your knowledge of vocabulary, genders, word families, and structures every time you sit down to read a piece of German. Most important, be sure that you never turn up at a lesson where the text has been given to you beforehand without having had a good look at it, using a dictionary where necessary. That really is the best way to be sure of getting the best out of any discussion of a text.

Finally, remember to feed your reading into your written and oral work. Your teacher will expect you to re-use phrases and vocabulary you have come across. That is, after all, the way we all learnt our native language!

WORD FORMATION

ROOT WORDS, SUFFIXES, PREFIXES

COMPOUND WORDS

WORDS FROM OTHER LANGUAGES

FEATURES OF JOURNALISM

COMPREHENSION QUESTIONS

TRANSLATION INTO ENGLISH

SUMMARIES

ESSENTIAL PRINCIPLES

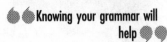
WORD FORMATION

Getting the best out of reading involves an understanding of the way in which German is put together. Clearly, knowing how the *grammar* works (Chs. 7 and 8) will help with such obvious matters as knowing when something occurred, and in deciphering who did what to whom. However, a special feature of German is its wealth of *long words*. If you can understand what might be termed the 'Lego building system' of German, your understanding of new and unfamiliar texts will be that much quicker.

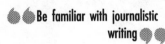
❝❝Knowing your grammar will help❞❞

It is also important to be aware of the way in which journalism is written. Most of the pieces in the Reading Comprehension paper will have been written for magazines and newspapers, and it is really helpful to understand how such articles are put together.

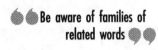
❝❝Be familiar with journalistic writing❞❞

Finally, a number of boards (but not all – check *your* syllabus details in the Appendix) require candidates to translate into English. There is no doubt that practice improves your performance at this skill. The important thing is that the finished result reads like English.

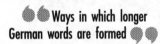
❝❝Be aware of families of related words❞❞

German, in common with other languages, has **families** of related words. The common perception of German is that it contains large numbers of very long words. This is in fact true, but really, in most cases, the problem is not the absolute length of the words, but the fact that understanding is much easier when the words have been analysed into their *components*. A knowledge of how longer words are formed is very useful here. They fall into three categories:

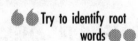
❝❝Ways in which longer German words are formed❞❞

(1) – words which have a root plus prefixes and suffixes
(2) – words which are made up of several shorter words
(3) – words which have been borrowed from other languages.

WORDS WITH A ROOT AND PREFIXES OR SUFFIXES

Many long words contain a **root word**, often a modifying *prefix* (= syllable at the beginning), and often a *suffix* (= syllable at the end) which indicates whether it is a noun, adjective, or verb. In the case of nouns, the suffix often indicates the gender, too.

❝❝Try to identify root words❞❞

It is therefore worth spending time training yourself to identify the root words, and making sure that you have reasonable knowledge of the effect of various prefixes on meaning, and (a much easier job) that you know which suffixes indicate nouns, adjectives and verbs, and the gender rules which are implied.

(i) NOUNS WITH SUFFIXES

(a) *-chen* and *-lein* (always neuter)

❝❝Be familiar with the effect of suffixes❞❞

These **suffixes** are attached to form diminutives (= forms showing that something is small.) The vowel of the word being diminished normally gains an Umlaut if possible.

Examples:
das Haus – *das Häuschen*
die Frau – *das Fräulein*
der Mann – *das Männchen*

This method of forming words accounts for the confusing gender of das Mädchen.

(b) *-e* (always feminine)

From verbs, a noun may be formed by removing the *n* from the infinitive to form a noun which describes an instrument or an action.

Examples:
bremsen – *die Bremse*
pflegen – *die Pflege*

From adjectives, an abstract noun can be formed, with an Umlaut over the main vowel if possible:

Example:
groß - *die Größe*

(c) -ei, -erei (always feminine)

They often describe the places things are done in.

Example:
der Bäcker – *die Bäckerei*

Sometimes they express disapproval.

schreiben – *die Schreiberei* (annoying writing)
der Sklave – *die Sklaverei*

(d) -er, -ner,-ler (always masculine)

These are used to form nouns from verbs or other nouns. They often indicate a job or an activity.

Example:
lehren – *der Lehrer*
betteln – *der Bettler*
die Wissenschaft – *der Wissenschaftler*
die Kunst – *der Künstler*

Some items of technical equipment which perform a function are formed in the same way.

Examples:
Staub saugen – *der Staubsauger*
hören – *der Hörer*

And the inhabitants of towns are usually referred to by adding -er to the name of the town.

Examples:
Wien – *der Wiener*
Köln – *der Kölner*

Some town names have a secondary meaning

It is perhaps worth mentioning that some of these town names have secondary meanings. As well as the obvious *Hamburger* and *Frankfurter*, which refer to foodstuffs, *der Berliner* is a doughnut or a type of beer, while *der Pariser* is a condom. So President Kennedy actually said: 'Ich bin ein Berliner' (= I am a doughnut).

(e) -heit, -keit, -igkeit (always feminine)

These are added to adjectives concerning a quality to form abstract nouns.

Examples:
schön – *die Schönheit* (beauty)
einsam – *die Einsamkeit* (loneliness)
geschwind – *die Geschwindigkeit* (speed)

(f) -in (always feminine)

This can be added to most masculine persons and many masculine animals to give a female version. Usually the vowel gains an Umlaut in the process, if possible.

Examples:
der Zahnarzt – *die Zahnärztin*
der Hund – *die Hündin* (bitch)

(g) *-ling* (always masculine)

From verbs, it is used to show people who are the object of some action.

Example:
lehren – *der Lehrling* (apprentice)

Added to nouns, it shows possession of an (often undesirable) characteristic.

Example:
feige – *der Feigling* (coward)

(h) *-nis* (neuter or feminine)

This is used on abstract nouns formed from verbs or adjectives. Those from verbs often show the result of some verbal action.

Examples:
finster – *die Finsternis* (darkness)
erleben – *das Erlebnis* (experience)

(i) *-schaft* (always feminine)

This usually shows a state or something collective.

Examples:
der Freund – *die Freundschaft* (friendship)
der Lehrer – *die Lehrerschaft* (the staff)

(j) *-tum* (always neuter)

This is usually used to show collective bodies or characteristics.

Examples:
der Deutsche – *das Deutschtum* (German-ness)
der Papst – *das Papsttum* (papacy)

(k) *-ung* (always feminine)

This is used to make nouns which show the action suggested by a verb.

Examples:
verschmutzen – *die Verschmutzung* (pollution)
landen – *die Landung* (landing)

(ii) NOUNS WITH PREFIXES

The gender of nouns with suffixes is the same as that of the root noun in virtually all cases.

(a) *Erz-* = arch, thorough-going

Examples:
der Bischof – *der Erzbischof* (Archbishop)
der Gauner – *der Erzgauner* (thorough-going scoundrel)

(b) *Ge-*

This is often added to a root word to show repeated or long-running activity. Sometimes it is used to show disapproval.

Example:
reden – *das Gerede* (idle chatter)

Ge- is also added to show a collective sense

Example:
der Berg – *das Gebirge* (mountain range)

(c) *Fehl-* = mistaken

Example:
die Einschätzung – *die Fehleinschätzung* (mistaken calculation)

(d) *Grund-* = basic, fundamental, essential

Example:
die Bedeutung – *die Grundbedeutung* (basic meaning)

(e) *Haupt-* = main

Example:
der Grund – *der Hauptgrund* (main reason)

(f) *Miß-* is used to show an opposite or a negative

Example:
der Brauch – *der Mißbrauch* (misuse)

(g) *Mit-* = co-, fellow-

Examples:
der Arbeiter – *der Mitarbeiter* (collaborator)
der Bürger – *der Mitbürger* (fellow-citizen)

(h) *Nicht-* = non

Example:
der Raucher – *der Nichtraucher* (non-smoker)

(i) *Riesen-* = enormous

Example:
der Spaß – *der Riesenspaß* (enormous fun)

A number of other prefixes have the same effect and are common in speech:
Super- , *Spitzen-* , *Bomben-, Heiden-* , *Höllen* , *Mords-, Top-*.

(j) *Rück-* = backwards

This is often found with nons which are connected with verbs using zurück.

Example:
die Fahrt – *die Rückfahrt* (return journey).

(k) *Un-* = opposite, unusual

Examples:
die Ruhe – *die Unruhe* (unrest)
der Mensch – *der Unmensch* (inhuman person)
das Wetter – *das Unwetter* (appalling weather)

(l) *Ur-* = original; great- (as in generations)

Examples:
der Wald – *der Urwald* (the primeval forest)
der Großvater – *der Ururgroßvater* (great, great grandfather)

(iii) ADJECTIVES FORMED USING SUFFIXES

(a) *-bar* = the English -able, -ible

Examples:
trinken – *trinkbar* (drinkable)
fahren – *fahrbar* (driveable)

(b) *-en, -ern*

These are added to nouns to show the materail something is made of. In most cases, the main vowel gains an Umlaut.

Examples:
das Holz – *hölzern* (wooden)
das Silber – *silbern* (silver)

(c) *-haft*

This shows a quality similar to that possessed by the original noun. -haft is related to haben.

Example:
der Grauen – *grauenhaft* (scary)

(d) *-ig*

In many cases this approximates to the English -y.

Examples:
haarig (hairy)
milchig (milky)

It is also found with longer adjectives formed from complete phrases:

Examples:
notdürftig (scanty)
braunäugig (blue-eyed)

A small number of adjectives are formed in -ig from certain adverbs.

dort – *dortig*
morgen – *morgig*
hier – *hiesig*
ehemals – *ehemalig*
heute – *heutig*
sonst – *sonstig*

(e) *-isch* = ish, -ic, -ous

It is used to form adjectives from proper names.

Examples:
Europa – *europaisch*
der Brite – *britisch*

It also shows characteristics similar to that of the original noun.

Example:
das Kind – *kindisch*

And it is used to form adjectives from words borrowed from other languages.

Examples:
die Biologie – *biologisch*
die Mode – *modisch*

(f) *-lich*

Adjectives in *-lich* often have an Umlaut.
   It shows possession of the quality implied by the root noun.

Examples:
der Arzt – *ärztlich* (medical)
der Tod – *tödlich* (fatal)

If derived from expressions of time, *-lich* conveys frequency.

Example:
vierstündlich (every 4 hours)

Adjectives ending in *-lich* also indicate ability.

Example:
unverkäuflich (unsaleable)

-lich can also render a less clear possession of the characteristics of another adjective.

Examples:
arm – *ärmlich* (poorish)
rot – *rötlich* (reddish)

(g) *-los* = English *-less*

Examples:
nutzlos – useless
hoffnungslos – hopeless

(h) *-mäßig*

This often means 'in accordance with'.

Example:
der Plan – *planmäßig* (according to plan)

It can mean 'in respect of', or 'as far as ... is concerned'.

Example:
Schule – *schulmäßig* (as far as school is concerned)

(i) *-sam*

This usually expresses an ability or tendency.

Examples:
arbeiten – *arbeitsam* (industrious)
sich biegen – *biegsam* (flexible, bendable)

(iv) ADJECTIVES FORMED BY PREFIXES

(a) *erz-, grund-* and *hoch-*

The first two of these have the same meanings as for nouns, *hoch-* renders 'highly'.

Examples:
reaktionär – *erzreaktionär* (thoroughly reactionary)
verschieden – *grundverschieden* (totally different)
intelligent – *hochintelligent* (highly intelligent)

(b) *un-* = English 'un-', etc.

Examples:
höflich – *unhöflich* (impolite)
glücklich – *unglücklich* (unlucky)

(c) *ur-* intensifies the sense

Examples:
alt – *uralt* (as old as the hills)
deutsch – *urdeutsch* (typically German)

(v) VERBS FORMED WITH SEPARABLE PREFIXES

For the rules about the positioning of separable prefixes, see Chapters 7 and 8.

(a) *ab-* normally means 'away', 'down' or 'off' (i.e. finishing something)

Examples:
abfahren – to depart, leave, drive away
absetzen – to put down
abdrehen – to switch off

(b) *an-* convey either the idea of approaching, or the start of an action

Examples:
ankommen – to arrive
anmachen – to switch on

(c) *auf-* conveys the idea of 'up' or 'on'

Examples:
aufbleiben – to stay up
aufsetzen – to put on (e.g. hat)

(d) *aus-* conveys 'out'

Example:
ausgehen – to go out

(e) *ein-* refers to getting used to something

Example:
sich **ein**arbeiten – to get used to a new job

(f) *los-* usually refers to the start of something as in: Achtung, fertig, los!

Example:
losgehen – to start

(g) *mit-* usually conveys accompanying or co-operation

Examples:
mitfahren – to travel with someone
mitarbeiten – to co-operate, work together with someone

(h) *nach-* to follow

Examples:
nachmachen – to imitate
nachgehen – to pursue

(i) *vor-* either means to do something in advance, or to demonstrate something

Examples:
vorbereiten – to prepare
vorlesen – to read aloud

(j) *weg-* = away

Example:
weggehen – to go away

(k) There are also a number of compound separable prefixes the most frequent of which are given below:

●● Some compound
seperable prefixes ●●

dabei-	**dabei**stehen – to stand close by
daneben-	**daneben**schießen – to miss a shot
davon-	**davon**laufen – to run away
dazu-	**dazu**kommen – to be an additional factor
empor-	**empor**streben – to strive upwards
entgegen-	**entgegen**kommen – to come towards
überein-	**überein**stimmen – to agree
voraus-	**voraus**sagen – to predict
vorbei-	**vorbei**gehen – to go past
zurück-	**zurück**gehen – to go back
zusammen-	**zusammen**brechen – to collapse

(vi) VERBS FORMED WITH INSEPARABLE PREFIXES

(a) *be-* is used to indicate providing something with something else

Examples:
Wasser – *bewässern* (to provide with water)
frei – *befreien* (to liberate)
die Antwort – *beantworten* (to answer)

(b) *ent-* conveys either: escaping or going away or: removing something (= English 'dis-', etc.)

Examples:
laufen – *entlaufen* (to run away from)
der Mut – *entmutigen* (to discourage)
das Gift – *entgiften* (to decontaminate)

(c) *er-* often expresses a change of state, or great thoroughness

Examples:
blind – *erblinden* (become blind)
schießen – *erschießen* (shoot dead)

(d) *ver-* has a variety of strands of meaning

(i) finishing, or 'away'

Examples:
hungern – *verhungern* (starve to death)
brauchen – *verbrauchen* (consume, use up)

(ii) wrongly, or excessively

Examples:
salzen – *versalzen* (to over-salt)
fahren – *sich verfahren* (to take a wrong turning)

(iii) to express opposites

Examples:
kaufen (buy) – *verkaufen* (sell)
achten (respect) – *verachten* (despise)

(iv) to express a change of state

Examples:
einfach – *vereinfachen* (simplify)
länger – *verlängern* (extend)
das Unglück – *verunglücken* (to have an accident)
das Glas – *verglasen* (to glaze)
der Körper – *verkörpern* (to embody)

(e) *zer-* conveys the notion of 'in pieces'

Examples:
splittern – *zersplittern* (to splinter)
fallen – *zerfallen* (to fall to pieces, into ruin)

(vii) VERBS WITH PREFIXES WHICH MAY BE SEPARABLE OR INSEPARABLE

The prefixes are separable if the stress is on them, and inseparable if unstressed in pronunciation.

(a) *durch-* means 'through'

inseparable: durchleben – experience
           durchdenken – think through
           durchlöchern – make holes in
separable: **durch**blicken – see or look through
           durchfallen – fall through; fail an exam
           durchführen – carry out
           durchhalten – hold out, survive
           durchkommen – get through
           durchsehen – see or look through

There are very slight differences of meaning between the separable and inseparable versions of many compounds using *durch*. The separable versions generally mean all the way through, while the inseparable ones emphasise entry.

Pairs include:
durcheilen/**durch**eilen – to hurry through
durchbrechen/**durch**brechen – to break through
durchsetzen/sich **durch**setzen – to carry through/get your own way

(b) *hinter-* means 'behind' and is usually inseparable

Examples:
hintergehen – to deceive, go behind someone's back
hinterlassen – to leave behind
hinterlegen – to deposit

(c) *miß-* is usually inseparable and means either 'mis-', etc. or implies doing something wrongly

Examples:
mißtrauen – to distrust
mißhandeln – to mistreat

(d) *über-* generally means 'over'

Inseparable are:
überkochen – to boil over
überhangen – to overhang

Separable are:
überarbeiten – to overwork
überhören – to fail to hear
übertreiben – to exaggerate
überfallen – to attack

There are also pairs of words which change their meaning depending on whether they are separable or inseparable.

Pairs of words which change their meaning

Separable		Inseparable	
überfahren	to cross over	überfahren	to run over
überführen	to transfer	überführen	to convict
überlegen	to put something over something	überlegen	to consider
übersetzen	to ferry over	übersetzen	to translate
überziehen	to put (clothes) on	überziehen	to overdraw

(e) um- generally means 'round'

Inseparable are those which express surrounding.

Examples:
umarmen – to embrace
umgeben – to surround
umfassen – contain, encircle

Separable are those which express turning round or changing state.

Examples:
(sich) **um**blicken – to look round
(sich) **um**drehen – to turn round
umsteigen – to change (trains)
sich **um**ziehen – to change (clothes)
umbringen – to kill

There are also pairs of words which change their meaning depending on whether they are separable or inseparable.

Separable		Inseparable	
umfahren	to run over	umfahren	to drive round
umstellen	to rearrange	umstellen	to surround

(f) unter-

Separable are verbs with a more literal meaning of 'under' for unter.

Examples:
unterkommen – to find accommodation
untergehen – to go down (sun), decline, sink
untersetzen – to put underneath

Inseparable are verbs which have a more abstract meaning.

unterschätzen – to underestimate
untersteuern – to understeer
unterdrücken – to oppress
unterrichten – to teach
untersagen – to forbid
unterschreiben – to sign
unterstützen – to support

There are also pairs of words which change their meaning depending on whether they are separable or inseparable.

Separable		Inseparable	
unterbinden	to tie underneath	unterbinden	to prevent
unterstellen	to store	unterstellen	to assume
unterziehen	to wear underneath	unterziehen	to undergo

(g) *voll-* expresses completeness

Inseparable are more abstract words meaning 'finish', 'complete', etc.

Examples:
vollbringen   – to complete
vollenden   – to complete
vollstrecken   – to carry out (a sentence)

Separable are words which have the more literal meaning of 'full'.

Examples:
vollstopfen – to cram full
volltanken – to fill with petrol

(h) *wider-* means 'against', it usually forms inseparable verbs such as

widerstehen – to resist

There are only two separable verbs using *wider-*

widerhallen – to echo
widerspiegeln – to reflect

(i) *wieder-* = again

Only wiederholen – to repeat – is inseparable. All other compounds are separable.

Examples:
wiederkehren – to return home
wiedersehen - to see again

(vii) VERBS FORMED WITH SUFFIXES

(a) *-eln* is added to verbs to express a weak version of another action. Often an Umlaut is added.

Examples:
lachen – to laugh   lächeln – to smile
streichen – to stroke   streicheln – to caress, stroke gently

(b) *-ieren* is added to verbs borrowed from other (usually Latin-based) languages. No ge- is used in forming the past participle

Examples:
spazieren – to go for a walk
gratulieren(+D) – to congratulate

WORDS WHICH ARE MADE UP OF SEVERAL SHORTER WORDS

❝❝ Be familiar with compound words ❞❞

There are very large numbers of **compound words**, mainly nouns, which are composed of *shorter words* joined together. It would probably be fair to say that the higher the level of discussion, the greater the number of compound words which will be found. It is probably worth knowing how compounds are formed in order to make your own writing in German better. The habit of saying things over in your head as you read them can also help with understanding.

In their simplest forms compound nouns are formed merely of the juxtaposition of two words to express a more complex notion. Compound nouns always take the gender of the last element and form their plural like it.

Simple examples include:
dunkel + grün = dunkelgrün
Rat + Haus   = Rathaus
Rad + Weg   = Radweg

CHAPTER 2 **ESSENTIAL PRINCIPLES** 27

Occasionally several elements combine:

Funkel + Nagel + neu = funkelnagelneu

Splitting a long compound into different parts is relatively easy, as with such words as:

der Donaudampfschiffahrtsgesellschaftskapitänsuniformknopf

a button for the uniform of a captain of the Danube Steam Navigation Company.

The only difficulty in forming such long words concerns whether extra letters such as *-s-*, or *-en* are added at the joins. Experience, or *Sprachgefühl* will help. But broadly, the rules are as follows:

(a) *-s-* is added where an element ends in

-tum – Altertumskunde – knowledge about antiquity
-ion – Informationslücke – information gap
-ing – Heringssalat – herring salad
-ling – Frühlingssturm – spring storm
-heit – Schönheitskönigin – beauty queen
-keit – Heiterkeitserfolg – comic success
-schaft – Mannschaftsbus – team bus
-tät – Universitätsstadt – university town
-ung – hoffnungsvoll – hopeful

(b) *-s-* is also added where an infinitive has been used as a noun

Examples:
die Schlafenszeit – sleeping time
sehenswürdig – worth seeing

(c) *-s-* is also added to compounds of *Armut* (poverty) *Liebe* (love) *Hilfe* (help) *Geschichte* (history)

Examples:
Armutszustand – state of poverty
Liebeslied – love song
Hilfsarbeiter – unskilled worker
Geschichtsbuch – history book

(d) No *-s-* is added where an element ends in

-s – Preisliste – price list
-sch – Fleischsorte – type of meat
-z – Platzkarte – seat reservation ticket
-ß – flußaufwärts – upstream
-st – Herbstwetter – autumn weather

This is because the *s* sound is already present.

(e) In general, no *-s-* is added where the element ends in

-er – Fleischerladen – butcher's shop
-el – engelschön – as beautiful as an angel

(f) Feminine nouns ending in *-ik* and *-ur* have no *-s-*

Examples:
Kulturfilm – art film
Musikladen – music shop

(g) One-syllable feminine nouns and two-syllable feminine nouns ending in -e compound without an -s-

Examples:
Bahnhof – railway station
Wärmeflasche – hot water bottle

(h) -en- is added to nouns (weak nouns) which have a genitive form ending in -en

Examples include:
Hirtengruppe – group of shepherds
Sonnenschein – sunshine (using an obsolete Genitive of *Sonne*)

(i) -es- is sometimes added in preference to a plain -s-

Examples:
Bundeskanzler – Federal Chancellor
Bundespost – Federal Post Office

❝❝ Find the root meaning and use linguistic clues ❞❞

So, if faced with a long word, try and find the *root meaning*, and use the *linguistic clues* to find out the nuances of meaning which are expressed. Practice makes perfect, so you should note down additional examples of each kind of compound as you come across them. Alternatively, you could analyse a passage you have already read, classifying the different sorts of compound as you come across them.

WORDS WHICH HAVE BEEN BORROWED FROM OTHER LANGUAGES (FREMDWÖRTER)

❝❝ German uses many borrowed words ❞❞

One factor which is often helpful to foreign learners of German is that, in more educated writing and speech, Germans often use a large number of words which have been borrowed from other languages, notably English, French, Italian, Latin and Ancient Greek. Grammatical terms provide a clear example of this. *Das Adjektiv* for example, comes from Latin, but is instantly recognisable to English speakers. There is also a 'German' equivalent, *das Eigenschaftswort*, more comprehensible to less educated German native speakers.

Clearly the use of *Fremdwörter* is especially helpful to native speakers of English, as our language has many elements from Latin-based languages, and from Greek. However, exactly how useful these concepts are to you is a function, sadly, of your word-power in English.

One word of caution: sometimes what looks like a direct equivalent of an English word has a much more restricted meaning in German. For example, *die Kaution* does not mean 'caution' in the English sense, but is the word for a deposit on a rented flat which will be returned if the flat is in good condition at the end of the rental period. So, although it is connected with 'caution', its actual meaning is much more specific. So, although many *Fremdwörter* are helpful, unfamiliar ones should be treated with caution.(!)

Sometimes, too, the German root words are more illuminating than the high-falluting classically-based equivalents. This applies particularly to medical terms and conditions. For example, *Durchfall* is more graphic than diahorrea, although less so than the widespread dialect equivalent *Dünnschiß*! More seriously, it is easy to understand what is involved in pneumonia if you know it is *eine Lungenentzündung* (lung infection), and meningitis is clearly explained as *eine Gehirnhautentzündung* (a brain skin infection).

FEATURES OF JOURNALISM

❝❝ Be familiar with how journalists write ❞❞

Journalists, like all writers, plan their work. As a person trying to work out the message of an article, you will find it helpful to be aware of the structure of what they have written, of the re-phrasing they indulge in, and of the use of the special phraseology they employ.

(a) STRUCTURE

Most articles start with an introduction of some sort. However, many articles from magazines and newspapers will try to catch the reader's eye with some startling fact of a sensational piece of information. This may be an echo of the headline. For the non-native speaker reader this sometimes presents difficulties as it often refers to matters

Look for the structure
behind the writing
which you may not be fully aware of. Don't be put off, merely move on to the next paragraph which will contain the actual introduction or scene-setting.

Many articles are organised on the principle of: tell them what you're going to tell them; tell them; tell them what you've told them. This means you get a summary of what is to be discussed or an introduction to a problem, followed by the meat of the discussion or event, finishing with a conclusion or a summary of the main argument or a list of unresolved matters.

As well as the three-part structure for the sections of the article, journalists often work with three examples of any point made, often with one made more fully than the other two. And many writers prefer sentences with three clauses.

Finally, many writers 'telegraph' their structure by using words such as *auf der einen Seite .... , im Gegenteil, erstens, schließlich etc.* Be on the lookout for evidence of 'visible structure'.

(b) JOURNALISTIC PARAPHRASING

Paraphrase is often
used
As mentioned in the chapter on Listening, it is worth knowing is that journalists try to avoid using the same phrase twice in a piece. So their work is littered with re-phrasing of what turns out to be the same thing or person. The more highbrow the publication, the more obscure the **paraphrases** used. So a simple policeman will be, in turn, *der Polizeibeamte, der Ordnungshüter, der Wachtmeister* and *der Kriminalbeamte.* And President Clinton will become, on his second mention in a piece, *der USA-Staatsoberhaupt* and subsequently *Little Rocks berühmtester Bürger, der amtierende demokratischer Parteichef* and so on. It is therefore useful to keep a list of suitable paraphrases for famous people and others, and add to it. This is particularly difficult to do for German public figures, as your level of general knowledge about them may be on the low side. But it is worth persevering, and those who take the trouble to do so will find their efforts repaid.

(c) CLICHÉS

German-speaking journalists are not immune to the use of **clichés** (well-worn turns of phrases which have all but lost their original impact). This might in part be due to the fact that politicians use them, too! A few of the more frequent ones are given below:

in Anbetracht der Tatsachen	in view of the circumstances
in angetrunkenem Zustand	drunk
im Anschluß daran	after that
der Auftakt zu + D	the signal for
die Frage aufwerfen	to raise the question
sich übereinstimmend aussprechen für + A	to vote unanimously for
auf die lange Bank schieben	to put off
Bedenken hegen	to harbour doubts
Begleiterscheinungen	side effects
in groben Zügen darstellen	to outline in broad terms
die derzeitige Lage	the current situation
sich distanzieren von + D	to dissociate oneself from
eine Einigung erzielen	to reach an agreement
einen Gesetzentwurf einbringen	to introduce a Bill (to parliament)
ein Gesetz verabschieden	to pass an Act of parliament
von einer erheblichen Größenordnung	big
jüngsten Nachrichten zufolge	according to latest reports
es kam zu einer Kundgebung	there was a demonstration-
es kam zu Auseinandersetzungen mit der Polizei	there was fighting against the police
der Männer wurden handgreiflich	there was hand to hand fighting
die Lage hat sich entspannt	the situation has become calm
die Lage hat sich versch?rft	the situation has become tense
in zunehmendem Maße	increasingly
Maßnahmen zur Sanierung der Wirtschaft	measures to cure the economy
der (heftige) Meinungsaustausch	a (heated) exchange of views

Some useful clichés

in Mitleidenschaft ziehen	to affect
mitunter	including
der mutmaßliche Täter	the probable culprit
der angebliche Verantwortliche	the alleged culprit
der Plan scheiterte	the plan failed
ein heiß umstrittener Punkt	a hotly disputed point
die Möglichkeiten sondieren	to sound out the possibilities
die Stellungnahme	statement
Stellung nehmen zu + D	to comment on
der Tatort	the scene of the crime
die Übergangsregelung	temporary measures
die Meinungsumfrage	opinion poll

There are many more phrases and items of vocabulary in the vocabulary chapter, particularly under **Politics and Social Affairs**. Add to your own list as you come across new examples.

Also worth knowing are the many alternatives for 'sagte'. These include:

Ein Sprecher...	*gab zu verstehen*
meinte	*wies darauf hin*
erklärte	*beteuerte*
betonte	*versicherte*
behauptete	*verkündete*
	etc.

Again, add to this list as you come across them.

COMPREHENSION QUESTIONS

💧💧 Read the passage through more than once 💧💧

💧💧 There is usually one mark for one piece of information 💧💧

💧💧 The order of the questions can help 💧💧

All boards set these, but you should check whether you can expect to answer questions in German or English. On the day, answer questions in the language the question is set in.

As with other **reading comprehension** exercises, it is important to read the whole passage through a couple of times to benefit from any internal evidence contained in the passage.

When answering the questions, it is a waste of time to write an answer which 'contains the question' of the kind favoured by some primary teachers. Merely make sure that you have conveyed the necessary information. And you can be sure that, if there are four marks, that four pieces of information will be required. If there are gap-filling or multiple-choice questions, be sure not to leave a blank. Even if you haven't a clue you could just be lucky.

Normally, comprehension questions are set in the order in which their answers are to be found in the passage. So the answer to question 1 is NOT in the last sentence! On the other hand, there are sometimes questions which sum up the mood of the passage.

If you are struggling with a question, don't give it more than its fair share of time. If necessary, leave it and come back to it later.

Finally, check your work carefully, preferably some time after completing it. It is surprising what you notice with a fresh look at something.

TRANSLATION INTO ENGLISH

💧💧 Translation is an important skill 💧💧

💧💧 Some useful techniques for translating 💧💧

Many of the A Level boards require you to **translate** a passage of a couple of hundred words or so into English. On the face of it, this sounds simple enough, but it is important to understand why the exercise is set, what distinguishes a good from a poor performance, and how to go about making a good job of it. Many candidates feel, consciously or subconsciously, that translation into English is an easy exercise not worthy of much of their attention. They overlook the fact that it is a very useful skill and that it does prove whether or not you have understood the German in every detail.

What, then, is the best way to tackle a translation into English? First of all, read the passage all the way through. Sometimes there is internal evidence which helps you to understand parts of the text which weren't clear on first reading. The next step is to have a first go at translating the passage. I would personally use pencil, but in an examination where time is short you might be best advised to use pen. Space it out well so that there is plenty of room for re-drafts so that the work is legible even before you write up a fair copy.

When the first draft is ready, subject it to a *systematic* check, using the following list:

■ Have you got an equivalent for every phrase in the original?
■ Have you made sure that you have spotted whether verbs are in the equivalent tenses? Most frequently, the pluperfect is overlooked.

 A useful checklist for your first draft

■ Having decided the tenses, have you chosen the English simple form (e.g. I went) or the continuous form (e.g. I was going?). Are you happy about the choices you have made?
■ German sentences usually have time before manner before place, and the general before the particular. In English sentences, time often comes last. Does the order you have chosen read nicely and sound English enough?
■ Have you found equivalents for all the little adverbs such as *doch, eben, ja, bloß*?
■ Have you found reasonable English equivalents for words you have had to work out? Or does your work still contain heavily germanicised renditions such as 'auto track' for *Autobahn*?
■ Where the original German uses an idiom, have you either (a) made sure that you have found a close equivalent (e.g. 'she was in trouble' for *sie saß in der Tinte*) or (b) that you have not blindly translated the German idiom even when it is meaningless in English (e.g. 'she was sitting in the ink').
■ Have you left proper names in their German form? There is no point in translating Friederich as Frederick; people do not re-christen themselves every time they cross a border, and, anyway, you might get it wrong.
■ Have you considered that mystery words might be names of places or surnames?
■ Have you tried to eliminate errors caused by taking over German word order?
■ Have you re-punctuated the work making sure that you use commas and speech marks in the English way?
■ When copying up your final draft – highly recommended – have you checked off each sentence in your draft against the fair copy and against the original? I always think it wise to write on the 'write a line, miss a line' principle even for the final copy; you might notice something during a final check.
■ Finally, if possible, read the finished product through a little while after completing it. Sometimes things become clearer when your mind has been working on something else in the interim.
■ The ultimate test of a translation is the 'Granny test' – would your Granny recognise it as English?

SUMMARY

Some boards require you to **summarise** a piece of German in either English or German. Whichever language you are asked to write in, the object is the same: to test whether you can demonstrate your understanding by producing a more concise version of what has been written. The comments made above about the structure of newspaper and magazine articles are of use here.

A suggested method is as follows:

■ Read the passage through at least twice to make sure you have understood the main points. Do not attempt to make a complete translation – you haven't time.
■ Make skeleton notes, paragraph by paragraph. These form the basis for your summary.

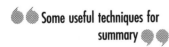 Some useful techniques for summary

■ Re-write them as prose, having decided which are the main points, and which are merely illustrative material which could be reduced to a passing reference. Main points often come early in a paragraph. There is much to be said for writing on alternate lines for ease of editing.
■ Look out for words and phrases which introduce counter-arguments of different strands. These betray the writer's original structure.
■ Check the length of what you have written against the length you have been asked to write. It if is too long, prune it!
■ When the pruning has been done, check your final version against the original German for any errors or omissions.
■ Remember that most mark schemes for summary award full marks to a candidate who makes, say, 30 out of a possible 40 points. So there is no need to worry unduly about missing the odd fine detail out.

READING: EXAMPLES OF TEXTS

SAMPLE QUESTIONS WITH STUDENT'S ANSWERS AND EXAMINER'S COMMENTS

Please note that the answers and markschemes given are NOT official ones but are the author's own. The Examination Boards are not able to enter into any correspondence about them.

(a) COMPREHENSION QUESTIONS

Text 1:

Bei einem nur vermuteten Unfall:

Dürfen Ärzte im Stau vorfahren?

Amtsgericht stellt Bußgeldverfahren gegen Mediziner ein

Von Ekkehard Müller-Jentsch

Der Münchner Frauenarzt Hans-Peter Becker mußte seinen Wagen auf der Autobahn wegen eines Staus plötzlich abbremsen. Weil der Mediziner Sauerstoff- und Wiederbellebungsgeräte ebenzo wie seinen Notarztkoffer—wie immer—bei sich hatte, schaltete er am Auto das schwarz-gelbe Schild 'Arzt Notfalleinsatz' ein und fuhr kurzerhand über den Seitenstreifen an den stehenden Fahrzeugen vorbei. Der Doktor hatte nach eigenen Angaben angenommen, daß der unerwartete Stau auf einen Unfall zurückzuführen sei und wollte nachsehen, ob es Verletzte gegeben hat.

Doch es gab überhaupt keinen Unfall. Vielmehr handelte sich der Arzt eine Anzeige wegen verkehrswidrigen Verhaltens ein. Fahren auf dem Stanstreifen wird genauso wie Rechtsüberholen geahndet, es kostet 100 Mark und bringtr drei Strafpunkte.

Nach einigem Hin und Her stellte die zuständige Amtsrichterin das Verfahren zwar ein. Doch Hans-Peter Becker ist völlig verunsichert: 'In Zukunft traut man sich als Notarzt gar nicht mehr, an den Unfallort zu fahren. Dabei leiste ich so shcon seit 20 Jahren Hilfe und habe einigen Menschen das Leben gerettet.' Die SZ fragte den Verkehrsrechtsexperten des Innenministeriums, Wolfgang Bouska, was ein Arzt generell in solch einer Situation tun darf.

'Jeder Arzt, der sich zur Hilfeleistung befähight fühlt, kann bei der Zulassungsstelle die Berechtigung für ein ‚Arzt-Notfalleinsatz'-Schild bekommen. Und wir sind froh über jeden Arzt, der helfen will', sagt Bouska.

10. What did Dr Becker do when he had to stop because of a traffic jam on the motorway? *(3)*
11. Why did he decide to take this course of action? *(2)*
12. What could have been the legal consequences of his action? *(3)*
13. What in fact happened when the case came to court? *(1)*
14. What effect has this affair had on him? *(1)*
15. What advice does Herr Bouska give to doctors? *(1)*

TOTAL 30 marks

(USLEB, AS, 1992)

Student's answer:

1. What did Dr Becker do when he had to stop because of a traffic jam on the motorway? *(3)*

   He drove on the hard shoulder past the stopped traffic.

   ❝❝ 2 out of 3. You could also have mentioned that he switched on his sign and that it read Emergency Medical Service. In this case, any three out of four possible points would have gained full marks. ❞❞

2. Why did he decide to take this course of action? *(2)*

   He thought the jam had been caused by an accident and that he could help the injured.

   ❝❝ Excellent. 2 marks. ❞❞

3. What could have been the legal consequences of his action? *(3)*
   He could have been done for dangerous driving.

   👎👎 This is too vague, and certainly does not deserve three marks. The three points needed were: – could have been guilty of driving on the hard shoulder – fined DM100 – given three penalty points. I think the candidate was guessing! 👎👎

4. What in fact happened when the case came to court? *(1)*
   The case was dismissed.

   👍👍 Correct. 👍👍

5. What effect has this affair had on him? *(1)*
   He can't get insurance.

   👎👎 The candidate has misunderstood 'verunsichert' (= made unsure of himself) and confused it with insurance (Versicherung). No mark. 👎👎

6. What advice does Herr Bouska give to doctors? *(1)*
   To get a sign saying 'Emergency Medical Service'

   👍👍 Correct. 👍👍

   👍👍 Overall: this candidate has understood the text well. However, it is worth remembering that the papers are designed not to be do-able by those who indulge in guesswork. 👍👍

(b) TRANSLATION INTO ENGLISH

Text 2:

Englands Schulsystem dient der britischen Wirtschaft schlecht. Es bereitet die Jugendlichen ungenügend auf das Berufsleben vor. Der Schwerpunkt des Unterrichts liegt zu sehr auf den "theoretischen" Fächern, also der Muttersprache, Literatur, Fremdsprachen und Kunstfächern. Zu sehr vernachlässigt werden die "praktischen" Fächer wie Naturwissenschaften, einfache Mathematik, arbeits- und berufsbezogenes Wissen. Das deutsche Schulsystem ist besser, weil es auch denjenigen Jugendlichen eine brauchbare Grundbildung vermittelt, die nicht zur Universität gehen wollen und mehr praktisch veranlagt sind. Die deutsche Real-* und die Hauptschule* werden den Bedürfnissen dieser vielen Kinder besser gerecht als die britische Gesamtschule.
* *Do not translate.*

(NISEAC, 1992)

Student's answer

England's school system serves the british pub(1) badly. It does in no way(2) prepare boys (3) for a (4) working life. The main emphasis in lessons is on the 'theoretical' subjects, also (5) the mother tongue (6), Literature, (6a) foreign languages and arts subjects (7). The 'practical' subjects like science, simple maths and knowledge (8) related to work and jobs will be (9) too left behind. The German system is better, (10) because it gives those youths (11) a real basic education, who (12) do not want to go onto (13) university and have more practical skills (14). The German Realschule and Hauptschule will be the right thing (15) for these children, rather than the British comprehensive school.

Examiner's comments

1. *Die Wirtschaft* can, of course mean a pub. But its most common meaning is 'economy'.
2. 'In no way' is a very weak and over-colloquial version of 'ungenügend' (= inadequately).
3. *Jugendliche'* are young people of both sexes!
4. Surely 'for working life' reads better.
5. and 6. 'The mother tongue' could be improved on by using either 'their mother tongue' or 'English'.

6a. Why has Literature suddenly got a capital letter, alone of all the proper nouns there? Be consistent!

7. 'Kunstfächern' sadly means art as opposed to arts subjects. Again, precision is called for.

8. Well done – a tricky bit to translate done well.

9. 'Werden' is not future here, but passive. So it should read: the 'practical' subjects are too greatly neglected.

10. The comma here is not needed in English. Check punctuation has been done English-style.

11. see 3. – it includes girls, too!

12. This relative clause belongs with the young people. Remember to check that what you have written sounds natural to the ear of an English-speaker.

13. Careless: should read: on to

14. This is an example of a successful intelligent guess. The precise translation reads: 'and are more practically inclined' but this version is quite acceptable.

15. In this case, the intelligent guess has fallen a little wider of the mark. It should read: The Realschule and Hauptschule suit the needs of these children better than the English comprehensive school.

"Overall: A number of points have been overlooked, especially the passive. On the other hand, the candidate has clearly understood the majority of the passage and has rendered most of it reasonably."

(c) SUMMARY

Text 3:

Study the newspaper report below and then answer the question which follows it.

Spinne irritierte Fahrer: Wagen überschlug sich

Bad Honnef. Eine kleine Spinne war die Ursache eines schweren Verkehrsunfalls am Samstag in Bad Honnef. Ein Autofahrer bemerkte plötzlich das Tier auf seiner Hand, erschrak und versuchte mit einer heftigen Bewegung, es abzuschütteln.

Dabei riß er das Steuer nach rechts, der Wagen prallte gegen die seitliche Böschung, wurde zurück auf die Straße geschleudert und rutschte über die Gegenfahrbahn links von der Straße. Dort überschlug er sich mehrfach und geriet in ein Waldstück hinein. Der Wagen schlitterte an zehn Bäumen vorbei und blieb schließlich völlig zerstört auf dem Dach liegen. Fahrer und Spinne krochen unverletzt aus dem Autowrack.

(JMB, 1992, AS)

Summarise the main sequence of events outlined in the report and describe the final outcome.

Student's answer

A spider caused a road accident in Bad Honnef on Saturday (1) A driver found it on his hand and caused the accident while trying to shake it off. (2)

The car went off the road on the right, hit a bush (3) and went onto the left (4) landing in a wood (5) on its roof. Both the driver and the spider were uninjured. (6)

Examiner's comments

1. Nice and concise.
2. Skilful combination of phrases to get the maximum information in the minimum space.
3. An unlucky guess. Böschung means 'bank'.
4. More could have been made of 'Gegenfahrbahn', for example by using 'the wrong side of the road'.
5. Again, this understates the events – the car skidded past ten trees.
6. Nicely captures the punchline of the the article.

EXAMINATION QUESTIONS

Here are some questions on each of the three types for further practice. Outline answers are provided at the end of the chapter.

(a) READING COMPREHENSION

Text 4:

Erster Teil

Lesen Sie zuerst den untenstehenden Text.

Immer noch Probleme für Karrierefrauen

Obwohl der Anteil von Frauen in Führungspositionen in der deutschen Wirtschaft auf zwischenzeitlich vier Prozent gestiegen ist, sind die Arbeitsstrukturen noch immer weitgehend auf den Mann zugeschnitten. Stellenausschreibungen, die sich exklusiv an männliche Bewerber richten, sind nur die ersten Stolpersteine auf dem steinigen Weg karrierewilliger Frauen nach oben.

Weitere Nachteile erwachsen ihnen nicht selten aus dem überlieferten familiären Rollenbild, das sich hartnäckig behauptet und in der Praxis häufig so aussieht: Für jede anspruchsvolle Position, die der Arbeitgeber mit einem Mann besetzt, 'kauft' er im Grunde eineinhalb Personen: den voll belastbaren, dynamischen Mann und die dazugehörige Ehefrau, die ihm den Alltagsärger vom Hals hält. Entscheidet sich der Personalchef hingegen für eine Frau, kauft er quasi nur eine 'halbe Person', weil die Frau auch als Managerin ihre häuslichen Verpflichtungen kaum vernachlässigen kann. Und das schon gar nicht, wenn sie Kinder hat oder sich welche wünscht. Da nur sehr wenig Ehemänner zu einem Rollentausch bereit sind, sehen sich viele Frauen gezwungen, zwischen ehelicher Partnerschaft und beruflicher Laufbahn zu entscheiden, während Männer alles haben können!

Selbst wenn es einer Frau gelingt, Mann, Mutterschaft und Management unter einen Hut zu bringen, hat sie doch die größte berufliche Hürde noch vor sich: den Umgang mit der Macht. Selbst eine erfolgreiche Managerin gibt zu, daß sie als erste Frau in einer Männerdomäne Startschwierigkeiten hatte. Am Anfang war sie bei den Kongressen richtiggehend schüchtern und saß ohne Selbstbewußtsein zwischen den gutgekleideten älteren Herren. Die Reaktionen reichten von wohlwollender Duldung bis zu offener Ablehnung und augenzwinkernder Galanterie unter dem Motto: 'Was haben wir denn da für ein hübsches Mäuschen am Tisch?'

Unter solchen Umständen wächst der Anreiz, eigenhändig neue Strategien zur Selbstbehauptung zu entwickeln. Denn Unterstützung aus den Reihen derer, die die Managerin auf dem Weg nach oben hinter sich ließ, ist kaum zu erwarten.

1. Suchen Sie im Text Wörter, die den folgenden Ausdrücken entsprechen.
   - (a) zum großen Teil *(1)*
   - (b) traditionell *(1)*
   - (c) viel verlangend *(1)*
   - (d) fähig, viel Arbeit auf sich zu nehmen *(1)*
   - (e) Aufgaben, die man machen muß *(1)*

   (Total 5)

2. Referring to the passage, but without translating, explain in **English** the following points:
   - (a) why an employer may prefer to employ a man rather than a woman in a high-level post, *(4)*
   - (b) why the writer claims that men can have everything, *(4)*
   - (c) at what stage career women face the greatest hurdle, and what it is, *(4)*
   - (d) how the successful manageress was treated at conferences, *(4)*
   - (e) why such women have to take matters into their own hands. *(4)*

   (Total 20)

Text 5:

In the following extract the author, a descendant of Baron Münchhausen, explains the operation of the farm that he has designed for his cousin, Robert.

Study the extract and then answer the questions which follow it.

Münchhausens Roboterfarm

In aller Frühe zog man die Kühe auf. Das genügte für den ganzen Tag. Sie trotteten dann allein über den Hof, zum Tor hinaus auf die Weide und begannen zu fressen. Mittags ließen sie sich dann auf ihren Aluminiumbäuchen zum Wiederkäuen nieder, ein Bild des tiefsten Friedens. Abends genügte ein Elektronenpfiff, und sie trotteten wieder zurück, unter die bollautomatische Melkmaschine. Aus dem Gras war inzwischen in ihrem Innern bereits pasteurisierte Milch geworden. Durch eine unterirdische Pipeline stand die Melkmaschine direkt mit der Molkerei in Verbindung. Nach dem Melken standen die Kühe in ihren stählernen Boxen und warteten geduldig darauf, daß man ihre Gelenke ein wenig ölte oder hier und da mit dem Schraubenschlüssel an ihnen etwas nachzog. Sonst machten sie keine Arbeit.

Noch weniger Arbeit hatte man mit meinen Hühnern. Sie bestanden aus unverwüstlichem Kunstharz. Sie mußten nur von Zeit zu Zeit abgestaubt werden. Man konnte die Größe der Eier, die sie automatisch legten, je nach der Marktlage einstellen. Es gab einige Spezialisten darunter, die nur Sonderklasse legten. Andere lieferten nur billige Knickeier. Eine Stempeleinrichtung am Hinterteil sorgte dafür, daß Eier auch gleich den richtigen Stempel erhielten. Zum Legen zogen sich die Hühner über eine Rolltrepe in ihr Hühnerhaus zurück; auf einem Förderband rollten von dort die Eier direkt in die Kisten in einem Verpackungsraum. Ich sagte euch ja, vollautomatisch!

Das Glanzstück des Hofes aber waren die Schweine. Bei all meiner Bescheidenheit muß ich doch sagen, daß mir bein ihnen ein Glanzstück der Robotertechnik geglückt war. Es war mir nämlich auf sehr kniffligen Umwegen gelungen, künstlich Schweine herzustellen, die aus echtem Schweinefleisch bestanden! Der Hof hatte seine eigene Schweineschlächterei. Auf der einen Seite kamen die Schweine auf einem Fließband an, auf der anderen verließen sie die Anlage als Würste und Schinken.

Meine Roboterfarm machte, abgesehen von einigen Handgriffen wie Ölen, Schraubenanziehen und Messingputzen, keinerlei Arbeit. Robert mußte nur am Abend die Hebel an einer Schalttafel einstellen. Dann konnte er beruhigt schlafen gehen. Am nächsten Tage würde alles vom ersten Hahnenschrei an allein ablaufen, während Robert auf der Bank in der Sonne saß und die Daumen drehte. Es war wie ein neues Märchen vom Paradies.

Ich überließ Robert seinem jungen Farmerglück und fuhr nach Hause. Ich glaubte, daß alles in Ordnung sei. Aber ach, ich hatte etwas vergessen, eine Kleinigkeit nur, aber man muß bei den Robotern an alles denken. Es sollte sich bitter rächen.

Einige Tage später rief mich Robert an. Er sprach ganz verwirrt und ich verstand nur, daß ich sofort kommen sollte. Ich fuhr eilig hin. Als ich mich der Farm näherte, sah ich eine einzelne Aluminiumkuh auf der Weide stehen. Sie öffnete ihr Maul und stieß ein langgezogenes 'Kikeriki' aus! Donnerwetter, was war da los?

Ich stürzte in den Hof. ein entsetzlicher Lärm! Robert stand kreidebleich neben der großen Schalttafel und hielt sich die Ohren zu. Ein Blick überzeugte mich, daß alle Hebel richtig saßen. Aber das war auch das einzige, was auf meiner Musterfarm in Ordnung war.

Stellt euch nur vor: Die Kühe standen in ihren Boxen und krähten. Die Schweine gaben Milch und muhten. Die Milch lief nicht durch die unterirdische Pipeline, sondern sie strömte das Förderband hinunter und überschwemmte die Eierkisten. Dafür schossen die Eier, die jetzt die Kühe legten, wie Kanonenkugeln durch die Pipeline in die Molkerei. Die schönen Kunstharzhühner wurden in der Schlächterei zerlegt und gepökelt. Das war das Ende meines schönen Traumes!

Nun ja, ich habe die Ursache der Katastrophe gefunden. Hinter der Schalttafel entdeckte ich ein Mäusenest. Die Mäuse hatten die Drähte zernagt und unentwirrbar durcheinander gebracht. Und das war's, was ich übersehen hatte: Auf den Roboterhof hätte unbedingt noch eine automatische Katze gehört. Es hätte vollauf genügt, wenn ich für sie Schaumgummi genommen hätte . . .

(JMB; AS 1990)

(a) Summarise the daily routine followed by the cows on the farm. *(4)*

(b) Explain how the laying pattern of the hens was regulated and describe the types of egg available. *(3)*

(c) Which farm animal did the author feel particularly proud of, and why? *(2)*

(d) What work was Robert required to do on the farm? *(2)*

(e) Describe four of the mistakes witnessed by the author when he was called to the farm. *(4)*

(f) What explanation is given for the problems? *(2)*

(g) How did the author think he could have avoided this situation? *(1)*

Text 6:

Study the article below and then answer the questions which follow it.

Ihr habt sicher schon gehört, daß auch in Österreich das Washingtoner Artenschutz-abkommen in Kraft getreten ist. Dieses Übereinkommen regelt den internationalen Handel mit gefährdeten Arten freilebender Tiere und Pflanzen. Der Zweck des Übereinkommens ist es, den innerhalb der letzten Jahrzehnte sprunghaft angestie-genen weltweiten Handel mit Wildtieren und Pflanzen in den Griff zu bekommen. Dies geschieht, indem:

1. der Handel mit lebenden und toten Exemplaren von unmittelbar von der Ausrottung bedrohten Tier- und Pflanzenarten weitgehendst unterbunden und

2. der Handel mit gefährdeten Arten einer Kontrolle unterworfen werden.

1700 Tierarten sowie rund 30 000 Pflanzenarten werden in den Anhanglisten I bis III des Übereinkommens angeführt. Die Arten in Anhang I gelten als unmittelbar bedroht, diejenigen in Anhang II und III als mittelbar bedroht bzw, nur in einzelnen Ländern ihres Verbreitungsgebietes gefährdet.

Wenn also jetzt bei einer Auslandsreise exotische Waren zum Einkauf locken, so sollte man daran denken, daß viele der angebotenen Sachen unter Umständen bei der Einreise nach Österreich durch den Zoll beschlagnahmt werden. Dies gilt nicht nur für lebende Tiere wie z. B. die herzige griechische Landschildkröte, die man einfach am Strand eingesammelt hat, sondern auch für tote (ausgestopfte) Tiere oder Teile von ihnen (das sind Felle, Schildpatt, Reptilleder und -waren, Elfenbein usw.). Auch bei

Pflanzen wie Orchideen und Kakteen, Palmen und Farnen dürfen ohne Bewilligung weder tote noch lebende Exemplare eingeführt werden.

Der Handel mit Tieren und/oder ihren Teilen brachte zahlreiche Tierarten unmittelbar an den Rand der Ausrottung. Das Verschwinden einer jeden Tier- oder Pflanzenart aber bedeutet einen unersetzlichen Verlust mit nicht voraussehbaren Folgen für das betroffene Ökosystem. Die Schuld am Ausverkauf der Natur tragen mehrere Beteiligte. Der weltweite Tourismus trägt ebenfalls zu diesem Raubbau bei. Deshalb beim Souvenirkauf daran denken:

Hände weg von Produkten, die Wildtieren den Tod brachten. Selbst wenn es sich 'nur' um die Schwanzhaare eines Elefanten handelt. Solange ein Markt für solche Produkte besteht, haben die Wilderer einen Grund für ihre ruchlosen Nachstellungen. Es gibt Alternativen zum Kauf von Souvenirs, die der Tier- und Pflanzenwelt eines Urlaubsortes keinen Schaden zufügen und vielleicht sogar das lokale Handwerk fördern. Etwa Textilien, Metallwaren, Schnitzereien oder Steinschmuck.

Wir kommen mit einem 'grünen Gewissen' aus den Ferien zurück.

(JMB, AS 1990)

(a) What, according to this article, is the main aim of the Washington agreement?
(2)

(b) Explain the differences between the three 'lists' mentioned. *(3)*

(c) List any **three** of the items identified which may be confiscated by Customs officers.
(3)

(d) Summarise the advice given to tourists in the final paragraph. *(4)*

(12)

Text 7:

Beim Langlauf die Stille der Landschaft genießen

Winterurlaub, so schwören Kenner, kann nirgends schöner sein als in dem 'Geburtsland' des Winters, in Norwegen also. Wer noch nie die Einsamkeit und Einmaligkeit dieses nordischen Winterparadieses erlebt hat, dem fehlt wirklich etwas. Das sagen alle, die immer wieder hierher zurückkehren. Und das sind in jedem Jahr mehr.

Wintersport-Gebiete erkennt man hier nicht an riesigen Liftanlagen, großen Hotels und Hüttenzauber wie in Tirol und im Engadin. Nur vereinzelte Spuren im Schnee weisen darauf hin, daß der Tourenlauf, wie die Norweger den Langlauf nennen, hier zu Hause ist. Die Loipen sind auch keine einfachen Rundkurse von 10 oder 15 Kilometern Länge – Skilanglauf hat hier andere Dimensionen: Über Hunderte von Kilometern ziehen sich die Loipen im leichten Auf und Ab über die Hochflächen und durch die Wälder hin. Da kann man tagelang unterwegs sein, ohne auch nur ein Stück zweimal spuren zu müssen. Die einsam in der Winterlandschaft verstreuten kleinen Hotels sind da die eigentlichen 'Zentren' des Wintersports. Einige wenige, wie in Fefor, Wadahl oder Sjusjöen, haben aber auch ein Herz für alpine Skifahrer – sie haben einige Skilifte und Pisten.

Doch es gibt auch Alternativen, die die schmalen Bretter schnell vergessen lassen: Ausritte hoch zu Roß fern von Streß und Hektik, Ausflüge mit Pferdeschlitten oder hinter dem Rentiergespann lassen die stille Natur in einem ganz anderen Licht erscheinen.

Manchmal geht's aber auch laut und abenteuerlich zu: Dann werden die Schneeskooter, die Motorschlitten, angeworfen. Ein Heidenspaß, so über die verschneiten Flächen zu flitzen! Und wenn der eisige Fahrtwind schließlich doch an den Kräften zehrt – auf dem Picknickplatz wartet der Wirt mit einem Büfett und heißem Punsch zum Auftauen . . .

Wer da unterwegs auch an einem der kleinen Holzhäuschen klopfen möchte, die verstreut in der Landschaft liegen, wird von der Gastfreundschaft der Norweger überrascht sein. Wenn sie gerade zu Hause sind – man erkennt es an der auffälligen roten norwegischen Flagge über dem Dach. Gastlichkeit wird aber auch in den Hotels großgeschrieben – und die üppigen Büfetts sind nicht umsonst ein 'Wahrzeichen' der skandinavischen Länder. Einziger Wermutstropfen: Jegliche Art von Alkohol ist sehr teuer. Dafür ist aber der Winterurlaub insgesamt nicht kostspieliger als in Österreich oder der Schweiz. Und man kann einfach keinen Reinfall erleben: Der Bilderbuchwinter hier oben kennt keine Schneesorgen. Und nicht zu vergessen: Von Mitte Februar an sind in Südnorwegen die Tage schon deutlich länger als in Deutschland . . .

Nähere Auskünfte erteilt das Norwegische Fremdenverkehrsamt, Hermannstr. 32, 2000 Hamburg 1, Telefon: 0 40/32 76 51.

(WJEC, A Level, 1991)

(i) How do we know that Norway is becoming ever more popular as a winter resort? (1)

(ii) Name two ways in which skiing resorts there differ from those in the Tyrol and Engadin. (2)

(iii) Describe what is understood by 'Loipen' in Norway. (3)

(iv) Name one other leisure pursuit on offer. (1)

(v) What would be offered at a typical winter picnic? (1)

(vi) Some wooden lodges fly red flags. What does it mean? (1)

(vii) What is said about food and drink? (2)

(viii) What three comparisons are drawn between winter holidays in Norway and in Austria, Switzerland or Germany? (3)

Text 8:

Türkischer Abend

Volkshochschul-Fest in Laichingen

Einen 'türkischen Abend' gibt es am Samstag, 6. Juli, ab 19 Uhr im evangelischen Gemeindehaus Laichingen. Veranstalter ist die Volkshochschule Laichingen–Blaubeuren, die ihn zusammen mit Eltern türkischer Schulkinder und mit ihrem Lehrer Necip Ylmaz vorbereitet hat. Der Abend ist als Einstimmung auf die bevorstehende Urlaubszeit gedacht, auf Fremdes und Faszinierendes, und soll gleichzeitig zeigen, daß die Türkei neben sonnigen Stränden auch eine schöne Landschaft, eine reiche alte Kultur und freundliche und gastfreundliche Menschen zu bieten hat.

Einen Schwerpunkt bilden ,Volkstänze der Türkei', ein Film aus verschiedenen Regionen des riesigen Landes. Danach sollen die deutschen Gäste die Tänze live erleben: Türkische Kinder in farbenprächtigben Trachten werden sie vorführen. Im zweiten Teil des Abends gibt es wieder einen Film zu sehen. Gezeigt werden die bisher vom Tourismus unberührten Landschaften Mittelanatoliens, der rituelle Tanz der Derwische und die Kunst des Tepichknüpfens. Zum Schluß wird eine türkische Geschichte in beiden Sprachen vorgelsen.

Im Rahmenprogramm werden türkische Handarbeiten ausgestellt; natürlich gibt es auch allerlei Kulinarisches zu probieren – schließlich gilt die türkische Küche als eine der besten der Welt. Zur Vorbereitung bittet die Volkshochschule um unverbindliche Anmeldung unter Telefon (07333) 3535.

(WJEC, A Level, 1992)

Study the text and answer the following questions.
(i) Who is involved in the organisation of the Turkish Evening? *(2)*
(ii) What, according to the article, does Turkey have to offer? Mention **four** attractions. *(2)*
(iii) How are the visitors going to learn about Turkish folk dancing? *(2)*
(iv) What cultural aspects will be shown in the second film? *(2)*
(v) What is the final event going to be? *(2)*

Text 9:

Study the advertisement below and then answer the questions which follow it.

Haben Sie wirklich schon alles probiert, um Lehrlinge zu finden?

Weil die Zahl der Schulabgänger zurückgegangen ist, sind die Lehrlinge knapp geworden. Tratzdem können manche Betriebe problemlos ihre Ausbildungsplätze besetzen. Wie machen sie das?

Sie reagieren flexible und mit neuen Ideen auf die Marktsituation. Und sie fragen sich ganz pragmatisch, wer alles für eine Ausbildung in Frage kommt.

Muß es unbedingt ein einserschüler sein? Ist nur ein Junge geeignet? Muß es ein Deutscher sein? Ist die körperliche Unversehrheit Eine unabdingbare Voraussetzung?

Wenn Sie auf die veränderte Marktlage geschickt eingehen, können sie Ausbildungs-engpässe vermeiden.

Sprechen Sie auch mit Jugendlichen,. die eine Ausbildung abgebrochen ader bisher ganz dorauf verzichtet haben. Geben Sie auch Mädchen in angeblichen Männerberufen eine Chance.

Nutzen Sie die große Motivation von Aussiedlern und Übersiedlern. Sehen Sie Sprachprobleme von Ausländern nicht als Hindernis an – die jungen Leute sprechen bald fließend deutsch.

Nehmen Sie auch etwas ältere Bewerber. Und bieten Sie auch ungelernten Kräften, die schon in Ihrem Betrieb arbeiten, einen Ausbildungsplatz an – mit einer verkürzten Ausbildungszeit und angemessenen Konditionen.

In jedem Fall lohnt sich ein Gespräch mit dem Arbeitsamt.

Arbeitsamt

(JMB, AS Level, 1991)

(a) What, do you believe, is the purpose of this advertisement? *(1)*
(b) State any **two** of the questions which prospective employers should ask themselves, according to the third paragraph. *(2)*
(c) What advice is given about people from countries other than Germany? *(2)*
(d) Give details of any other **two** categories of people who could be considered. *(2)*
(7)

(b) TRANSLATION INTO ENGLISH

Text 10:

Translate into English:

Sie öffnete die Pforte, ging durch den Vorgarten, läutete an der Haustür. Lüdeck öffnete ihr. Er sah gut aus: graue Flanellhose, dunkelblauer Schifferpullover, weiße Schuhe; ein gebräuntes, glattes Gesicht, dazu volles eisgraues Haar und ein Hauch von 'Eau Sauvage'.

Er bat sie herein, gab ihr die Hand. Sie zuckte zurück, so sehr erschreckte sie der Kontakt mit seiner deformierten Rechten, von der sie gewußt, an die sie aber nicht gedacht hatte.

Ein Unfall, sagte er. Er sprach sehr laut, und da fiel ihr das kleine Hörgerät ein, das sie in seinem Hotelzimmer entdeckt hatte. Aber ein kurzer verstohlener Blick genügte ihr, um festzustellen, daß er es nicht trug. Hoffentlich ist es auch nicht so schlimm mit seiner Schwerhörigkeit, dachte sie; sonst könnte es mit der Unterhaltung mühselig werden.

Lüdeck führte seinen Gast in ein großes Wohnzimmer, in dem ein Tisch für zwei Personen gedeckt war. Sie sah Lachs, Aal und Kaviar, Brot und Butter und ein kleines silbernes Tablett mit 'Petits Fours', auch einen Eiskkkübel mit einer Flasche Sekt.

Sie sagte: So viel Feierlichkeit für einen kleinen Nachbarschaftsbesuch?

Es kommt immer darauf an, erwiderte er, wie hoch man seinen Nachbarn einschätzt, und für Sie schien es mir gerade so recht.

Sie setzten sich, doch gleich darauf stand der Hausherr schon wieder auf, öffnete die Flasche und schenkte ein.
(50 marks)
(USLEB, A Level, 1991)

Text 11:

Translate the following passage, including the title, into English. Candidates should understand that their work will be judged by its style as well as by its accuracy.

»DAS KANN MAN NOCH GEBRAUCHEN – !«

Es dürfte ja wohl die gewitzten Amerikaner gewesen sein, die die verschiedenen »Wochen« erfunden haben: die Bade-Woche, die Unfallverhütungswoche und die Mutter-Woche und die Zähnefletsch-Woche . . . und was man noch so hat. Und einmal war auch die »Bodenaufräumungs-Woche« dabei. Gar kein schlechter Gedanke . . .

Denn nur bei einem Umzug oder, was dem nahe kommt, bei einem Brandunglück entdeckt die Familie, was sie alles besitzt, was sich da alles angesammelt hat, wieviel man »aussortieren« muß, müßte . . .

Auf dem Boden, im Keller und in heimtückisch verklemmten Schubladen ruht der irdische Tand. Als da ist:

Fünf Handschuhe (Stück, nicht Paar, und immer eine ungerade Zahl); acht Bleistiftstummel; ein Porzellanschäfer ohne Kopf; ein Kopf ohne Porzellanschäfer; eine durchlöcherte Blechbadewanne, eine wacklige Petroleumlampe; und dergleichen mehr.

Manchmal sucht die Hausfrau etwas – dann stößt sie auf einen Haufen Unglück. Sie verliert sich darin, taucht unter, kommt erst spät zu Mittag wieder hervorgekrochen, staubbedeckt, mit rotem Kopf und abwesenden Augen, wie von einer Reise in fremde Länder . . . »Denk mal, was ich da gefunden habe! Paulchens ersten Schuh!«

Warum heben die Leute das alles auf–?

Sie heben es gar nicht auf. Sie können nur nicht übers Herz bringen, es wegzuwerfen.

Wenn es so weit ist: wenn der Porzellanschäfer den Kopf verliert, wenn die Handschuhe nicht mehr schön sind:- dann wiegen die Menschen einen Augenblick den Kopf nachdenklich hin und her. Da steht der Papierkorb und sperrt höhnisch das Maul auf, hier sicht ihn der oft gebrauchte Gegenstand traurig an, der Invalide – was nun? Da kann er sich nicht entschließen – vor allem: da kann sie sich nicht entschließen. Manner sind roh und werfen wohl manches fort. Aber Frauen . . .

(50 marks)
(OCSEB, A Level, 1992)

(c) SUMMARY

Text 12:

Zwei Männer wie durch ein Wunder vor dem Erfrieren gerettet.

Bergsteiger war Stunden in Schneeloch gefangen

Gleich zweimal wurden Männer in den Bergen wie durch ein Wunder gerettet: Im Rechgraben bei Mariazell wurde der 46jährige Bergwanderer Roland Pötzelberger aus Linz schwerverletzt aus einem Bach geborgen, nachdem er zwei Tage lang um Hilfe gerufen hatte. Nach erfolglosen Suchaktionen hatten Bewohner des Rechgrabens Dienstag nachmittag die verzweifelten Rufe des Wanderers gehört und ihn im Bach liegend entdeckt. Er war bereits stark unterkühlt.

Mehr als drei Stunden war Dienstag der 52 Jahre alte Pensonist Huber Lechner aus Mürzzuschlag in einem drei Meter tiefen Schneeloch auf der Schneealpe bei Neuberg an der Mürz 'gefangen'. Als der Mann bereits zu erfrieren drohte, wurden seine Hilferufe von einer zufällig vorbeikommenden Alpinistengruppe gehört, kurze Zeit später konnte er von Alpingendarmen gerettet werden. Wegen der extremen Unterkühlung mußte der Mann aber mit einem Hubschrauber in die Intensivstation des LKH Graz geflogen werden.

Hubert Lechner befand sich allein auf dem Abstieg vom Schneealpenhaus nach Neuberg. Dabei kam er in einer Seehöhe von 1000 Meter nur wenige Schritte vom Wanderweg ab und stürzte in das Schnelloch, dessen Wände von Schmelzwasser glattgeschliffen worden waren.

Der Mann hatte nicht die geringste Chance, sich daraus zu befreien, er stand zeitweise fast knietief im Schmelzwasser und hatte sich bereits aufgegeben, als dann seine Hilferufe doch noch gehört wurden.

Der Mann erlitt neben schwersten Erfrierungen einen schweren Schock.

Seine Rettung wird in Neuberg als 'kleines Wunder' bezeichnet.
LKH = Landeskrankenhaus

(ODLE, A Level, 1990)

Fassen Sie den Artikel auf englisch kurz zusammen. Erwähnen Sie alle wichtigen Punkte. *(14 Punkte)*

OUTLINE ANSWERS TO PAST EXAMINATION QUESTIONS

(a) READING COMPREHENSION

Please note that these answers are the author's own and are not official ones. The Examination Boards are unable to enter into any correspondence concerning them.

Text 4:

1. (a) weitgehend (1)
    (b) überliefert (1)
    (c) anspruchsvoll (1)
    (d) belastbar (1)
    (e) Verpflichtungen (1)
2. (a) He gets one and a half people (1)
    the totally committed, dynamic man (1)

and the wife who goes with him (1)
and spares him everyday worries (1)
(b) women are not able to neglect their household duties (1)
especially not if they have or want children (1)
few men are prepared to swap roles (1)
so many women have to choose between family and career (1)
(c) women find dealing with power difficult (1)
even a sucessful female manager admits (1)
that she had intial difficulties (1)
as the first women in a male domain (1)
(d) Any four of: reactions varied (1)
from well-meaning tolerance (1)
to open hostility (1)
to gallantry inspired by the attitude: (1)
Who's the pretty lady at the table, then? (1)
(e) because of such circumstances (1)
they have to become more assertive (1)
those who have overtaken women managers on the way up the promotion ladder (1)
are hardly likely to help them (1)

Text 5:

(a) Any four of:
they are released early in the morning (1)
they go alone to the field (1)
at midday they lie down to chew the cud (1)
on their aluminium bellies (1)
in the evening, at an electronic whistle, (1)
they trot back to the automatic milking machine (1)
after milking they require oiling (1)
or having a screw tightened (1)
(b) size of eggs was regulated according to market conditions (1)
some laid only extra-large (1)
others cheap small eggs (1)
(c) pigs (1)
made of real pig-meat (1)
(d) in the evenings he had to adjust the levers on a switchboard (1)
in the daytime he would sit on a bench in the sun and twiddle his thumbs (1)
(e) the cows were crowing in their stalls (1)
the milk was running down the egg conveyor belt (1)
eggs were being shot like canonballs out of the milk pipeline (1)
the fibreglass hens were being chopped up in the slaughterhouse (1)
(f) behind the control panel was a mouse's nest (1)
the mice had gnawed through the cables and mixed everything up (1)
(g) he should have installed an automatic cat (1)

Text 6:

(a) to get a grip on the world-wide trade in wild animals and plants (1)
which has taken off enormously in the last 10 years (1)
(b) List I is under immediate threat (1)
List II is under less immediate threat (1)
List III is under threat in only some countries within its range (1)
(c) Any three of: living animals like Greek tortoises you can collect on the beach (1)
dead or stuffed animals or parts of animals (1)
including skins, shells, reptilian leather and leather goods ivory, etc (1 mark per detail)
plants like orchids, cactus, palms and ferns, living or dead (1 mark per detail)
(d) Any four of: hands off products which have caused the death of wild animals (1)
even 'only' elephant's tail hair (1)
as long as there is a market for such products, poachers will be at work (1)

there are alternative souvenirs which don't harm local flora and fauna (1)
e.g. textiles, metalwork, carving, or stone jewellery (1)

Text 7:

(i)   More people return there every year (1)

(ii)   No large hotels (1)
No large ski lifts (1)

(iii) long ski routes several hundred km long (1)
go gently up and down (1)
over the high plateaux and through the woods (1)

(iv) Any one of: excursions on horeseback (1)
excursions by horse-drawn sleigh (1)
excursions by reindeer-drawn sleigh (1)

(v)   hot punch (1)

(vi) that there is someone at home (1)

(vii) the Scandinavian hotel buffets are justly famous (1)
alcohol of any sort is very expensive (1)

(viii) a Norwegian winter sport holiday is no more expensive (1)
there is never any worry about a lack of snow (1)
from mid-February on the days are longer than in Germany (1)

Text 8:

(i)   the Volkshochschule (evening institute) (1)
the Turkish parents and the Turkish teacher (1)

(ii)   sunny beaches (1)
beautiful scenery (1)
rich, ancient culture (1)
friendly and hospitable people (1)

(iii) they will see a film entitled 'Folk Dance in Turkey' (1)
they will see a live performance by Turkish children (1)

(iv) the ritual Dervish dance (1)
the art of carpet-making (1)

(v)   a Turkish story will be read out (1)
in Turkish and in German (1)

Text 9:

(a)   to encourage employers to recruit apprentices from a wider range of young people (1)

(b)   any two of: Does it have to be a student with 1 in his report? (1)
Is the job only suitable for a boy? (1)
Does it have to be a German? (1)
Is the lack of physical handicap an absolute necessity? (1)

(c)   Employers should use the extra motivation of those who have come from other countries or from the East (1)
language problems will quickly disappear (1)

(d)   Any 2 of: older applicants (1)
unskilled workers your already employ (1)
they can be offered a reduced-length training (1)

(b) TRANSLATION INTO ENGLISH

Text 10:

She opened the gate, went through the front garden and rang the doorbell. Lüdeck opened the door to her. He looked good: grey flannel trousers, a dark blue nautical pullover, white shoes; a bronzed, smooth face with a full head of silver grey hair and a whiff of 'Eau Sauvage'.

He asked her in and shook her hand. She pulled back, so startled was she by the contact with his deformed right hand; she had known about it, but hadn't thought of it.

'An accident', he said. He spoke very loudly, and then the tiny hearing aid she had discovered in his hotel room occurred to her. But a brief, discreet glance was enough for her to establish that he wasn't wearing it. I hope his hardness of hearing isn't too bad, she thought; otherwise conversation could become heavy going.

Lüdeck led his guest into a large living room in which a table was laid for two. She saw salmon, eel and caviar, bread and butter and a small silver tray with 'Petits Fours', as well as an ice bucket with a bottle of German champagne.

She said, 'So much pomp for a little neighbourly visit?'

'It depends,' he replied, 'on how highly one regards one's neighbours, and for you it seemed right like this.'

They sat down, but straight away the host stood up again, opened the bottle and served its contents.

Text 11:

'That's all you needed!'

It must have been the Americans who invented the various 'weeks' – the Bathing Week, the Accident Prevention Week, and Mothers' Week and Teeth-Baring Week . . . and all the rest of them. And once there was also a Loft-Clearing Week amongst them. Not a bad idea . . .

For only when moving house or (an event which comes close to it) after a house fire, does a family discover everything it possesses, what has accumulated up there, how much needs to be 'sorted out', or really ought to be . . .

In the loft, in the cellar and in obstinately jammed drawers resides the earthly bric-à-brac.

To be found there are:

Five gloves (singles, not pairs, and always an odd number); eight pencil stubs; a porcelain shepherd without a head; a head without a porcelain shepherd; a tin bath with holes in; a wobbly paraffin lamp; and more such items.

Sometimes the housewife is looking for something – then she stumbles on a heap of trouble. She loses herself in it, disappears, only crawls out again late in the morning, covered in dust, with a red face and absent eyes, as if she had been on a journey to foreign parts . . . 'Imagine what I found there! Little Paul's first shoe!'

Why do people keep all this stuff?

They don't keep it. They just can't bear to throw it away.

When it happens, when the porcelain shepherd loses his head, when the gloves are no longer smart, – then people move their head thoughtfully hither and thither. Here stands the waste paper basket and mockingly holds its mouth open, there the much-used object gazes sadly at him, an invalid. What now? He cannot decide - above all, she cannot decide. Men are hard and throw many a thing away. But women . . .

(c) SUMMARY

Text 12:

One mark each for up to 14 of the following points:
two men have been saved in the mountains
by a miracle
the 46-year old hiker Roland Pötzelberger
was rescued from a stream
badly injured
after calling for help for two days
after fruitless searching
his desperate cries were eventually heard
he was already suffering from hypothermia

52-year old pensioner Hubert Lechner
was in a 3 metre deep snow hole
for more than 3 hours
He was about to freeze to death
when his cries were heard by a party of climbers
who happened to be passing
he was rescued by Alpine Patrol
Because of his extreme hypothermia

he was taken by helicopter
to the Graz regional hospital
He had been descending alone from the Schneealp hut to Neuberg
about 1000 metres above sea level
he was a few metres of the path
and fell into a snow hole
whose sides had been worn smooth by melting snow
he had absolutely no chance of getting out
had been up to his knees in water
had already given himself up when his shouts were heard
was suffering from shock as well as exposure

REVIEW SHEET

In this Review Sheet we further practice translation and summary.

Translation into English

■ Look back to Text 8 (p. 39). Now translate the passage into English.

_____

_____

_____

_____

_____

_____

_____

_____

_____

_____

_____

_____

_____

NB. You can check the general meaning of your translation by looking at the answers to the comprehension questions set on the passage (p. 44).

■ Look back to Text 12 (p. 42). Now translate the passage into English.

_____

_____

_____

_____

_____

_____

_____

_____

_____

_____

_____

_____

_____

_____

NB. You can check the general meaning of your translation by looking at the answer to the summary question set on the passage (p. 45).

Summary

■ Look back to Text 2 (p. 33). Now summarise, in less than 50 words, the main problems with the English School system.

_____

_____

_____

_____

NB. You can look back to the Student _translation_ and examiner comments on p. 33 and 34 to check the general meaning of your summary.

■ Look back to Text 10 (p. 41). Now Summarise, in less than 50 words, the appearance and other personal characteristics of Lüdeck.

_____

_____

_____

_____

_____

NB. You can look back to the _translation_ on p. 44 to check your summary.

CHAPTER 3

LISTENING

GETTING STARTED

Listening is one of the skills which proves very useful in real life. Let's face it, even the most proficient speaker of a foreign language has to listen to other people sometimes! Getting over the hurdle of being able to follow what is going on is one of the really important stages in language learning. Once you have some idea of the main points, you then begin to discover the joys of working out the subtleties and nuances of language, the humour and irony being expressed, in short, the sub-text as well as the text of the conversation.

Listening can be off-putting at first. The most common complaint about speakers of another language is that they speak too quickly. What you are actually saying is that *you* cannot process the information quickly enough. But it is surprising how, with a little regular practice, you really can make progress. What is absolutely certain is that you will make very little progress if you do not practise.

The examination boards vary very little in the sort of exercise they require you to do for listening. All of them set 'real' passages, that is to say, passages which were designed to be heard, rather than, say, reading out a section of a novel. The passages fall into two kinds:

(a) Shorter passages such as new items, weather forecasts, adverts, announcements and traffic reports.

(b) Longer passages such as interviews, dialogues and information pieces.

Read again the suggestions for approaching the *Listening* assessments considered in Chapter 1 of this book.

LISTENING TECHNIQUES

VOCABULARY AREAS/ LINGUISTIC FEATURES

SHORT PASSAGES

LONG PASSAGES

FIGURES AND SPELLING

ESSENTIAL PRINCIPLES

For the examination, the passages will usually have been re-recorded by professional actors in a studio. This is done so that the quality of the recordings in an examination is consistent, and so that no candidate is disadvantaged by failing to hear clearly what is actually said. The cassettes are played to candidates on a variety of machinery in a variety of locations, and the exam boards really want to do their bit to help candidates. One advantage of the re-recording of passages is that often the speed is a little slower than 'natural'. Not many candidates complain about this!

The passages are recorded twice, and longer ones are often split up, so you should not be under too much pressure to write your answers in a given period of time.

Examiners will be looking for three sorts of skill:

■ the ability to pick out specific details from longer and shorter passages,
■ the ability to render the gist of a passage, summarising its main points,
■ the ability to draw inferences about meaning from the passage, and to find the structure and the relationships between the various parts of a passage.

TECHNIQUES FOR DOING LISTENING EXERCISES

❝❞ **Be aware of what is expected** ❝❞

Although most of the examination boards set questions in English to be answered in English, some require answers in German. Check what you will be facing in the 'Examination requirements' chapter.

Knowing what to expect is very important, so you should make very certain you know exactly what sort of questions will be set. In particular, you should take any mock examination or practice papers you are set very seriously, as they are by definition the nearest thing to the real examination which you could be given. Don't waste the opportunity.

❝❞ **Avoid wasting time** ❝❞

When actually doing the examination, it is a good idea to have a pencil and rubber to hand to write down first impressions, with a biro for writing up the final version. Although it is obvious, it is perhaps worth stating that there is no point in writing answers which 'contain the question' of the sort favoured by some primary teachers. For example, if you have a question which asks: At what time did the robbers attack the bank? there is no point writing an answer such as: The time at which the robbers attacked the bank, according to the tape, was 6.30. You have been wasting time you could usefully have spent on other questions.

❝❞ **Usually one point will gain one mark** ❝❞

On the other hand, there is equally little point in writing down only one detail, when the question paper shows that there are, say, four marks for the question. You can be sure that the examiner will be looking for the right number of points in order to award full marks. It's worth knowing that there are often marks for adverbs such as *ziemlich*, *ausschließlich* and *außerordentlich*, so listen out for them. Precision really is important here.

It is also important to make sure you are listening to the right part of the recording. A certain ruthlessness is required in that you have to forget about what you have written for earlier questions. You must be strict with yourself and not waste time mulling over what you should have written for Question 2 while the recording for Question 5 is being played.

SPECIAL VOCABULARY AREAS AND LINGUISTIC FEATURES

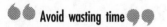

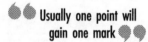

❝❞ **Be familiar with different types of language used in different settings** ❝❞

❝❞ **Look out for re-phrasing or paraphrase** ❝❞

Because items such as new broadcasts, weather forecasts and traffic reports are intrinsically fairly repetitive, they have evolved their *own* linguistic features. Awareness of what these are does, of course, improve your chances of knowing what is going on. The more obvious subjects for news are fully covered in the Vocabulary chapter under Current Affairs, while weather forecasts and traffic reports are covered under Weather and Travel respectively.

What is also worth knowing is that journalists – whether they publish in print or over the radio – try to avoid using the same phrase twice in a piece. So their work is littered with re-phrasing of what turns out to be the same thing or person. The more highbrow the publication, the more obscure the paraphrases used. So a simple policeman will be, in turn, *der Polizeibeamte, der Ordnungshüter, der Wachtmeister* and *der Kriminalbeamte.* And President Clinton will become, on his second mention in a piece, *der USA-Staatsoberhaupt* and subsequently *Little Rocks berühmtester Bürger, der amtierende demokratischer Parteichef* and so on. It is therefore useful to keep a list of suitable paraphrases for famous people and others, and add to it. This is particularly difficult to do for German public figures, as your level of general knowledge about them may be on the low side. But it is worth persevering, and those who take the trouble to do so will find their efforts repaid.

QUESTIONS WITH STUDENT'S ANSWERS AND EXAMINER'S COMMENTS

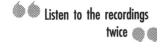
Listen to the recordings twice

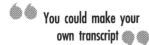
You could make your own transcript

These are recorded on the audio cassette that accompanies this Revise Guide. They are recorded once only for reasons of space. However, you should play them to yourself *twice*, allowing about a minute between playings in order to simulate the examination experience. Transcripts are given at the end of the chapter to allow you to use the tape as a real learning experience. You could, for example, try making your own transcript and comparing it with my version as a check of how well you have done it. Other suggestions of things to do to improve your *listening* skills are given in the 'Study Skills' Section of Chapter 1.

Please note that the answers and mark schemes given here are NOT official ones but are the author's own. The examination boards are not able to enter into any correspondance about them.

SHORTER PASSAGES

EXTRACT 1:

You will hear a weather report.

■ Play Extract 1 (or listen to your friend reading the transcript on page 59).

(a) How has the weather changed in the last 24 hours and who has been especially pleased with the new conditions? *(4)*
(b) (i) What has happened to the air temperature in North Germany? *(1)*
    (ii) How do air and sea temperatures compare with each other? *(1)*
(c) What are we told about conditions in the Mediterranean? *(2)*
(d) What are we told about the weather in the south and west of Germany? *(1)*
(e) In what way are the temperatures expected to change in the next 24 hours? *(1)*
Total: 10 marks
(AEB, 1992)

(a) It has become windier which pleases the surfers.

 2 out of 4. The forecast also mentions that it had become cooler, and that yachtsmen were pleased.

(b) (i) It has got cooler.

 Correct.

(ii) Sorry, Examiner, I don't know this one.

 What a waste of time. Even if you don't know, guess. Or put a dash. But don't waste time writing when you could be listening out for the next answer.

(c) You could bathe in it.

 This is true of all the seas mentioned! The candidate has fallen for a 'distractor', Badewannetemperaturen. Often plausible-sounding but incorrect words find their way into passages to sow a little confusion. In this case, successfully. The correct answer was that it was as warm as having a bath at home.

(d) It will be sunniest there.

 Correct.

(e) They will rise by a couple of degrees.

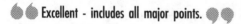 True. It would have been even better to have been as precise as the orginal text and said 'by one or two degrees'. That way you will avoid falling victim to interpretation of what exactly 'a couple' means.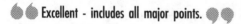

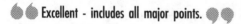 Overall: This candidate has clearly understood the main points of the passage, but could usefully refine technique and precision here and there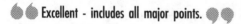

Extract 2:

You will hear a traffic report.

■ Play Extract 2 (or listen to your friend read the transcript on page 59).

What is the advice given to car-drivers and football supporters in Dortmund?   *(2)*
(WJEC, 1992)

Car drivers are advised to park at the university and use the free buses. Football supporters are strongly advised to use public transport.

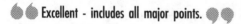 Excellent - includes all major points.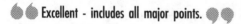

LONGER PASSAGES

Extract 3:

Interview mit Dieter Thoma.

■ Play Extract 3 (or listen to your friend read the transcript on page 59).

(a) Just before a competitive ski-jump, what sort of physical demands must Dieter Thoma's body cope with?   *(2)*
(b) What does he concluded from analysing the falls he has sustained in the last four years?   *(3)*
(c) Describe the single instance of real panic which Thoma witnessed in the case of a fellow competitor.   *(4)*
(d) During this interview, various aspects of Thoma's views on ski-jumping emerge. What are his attitudes to risks and the demands of this sport?   *(4)*
(NISEAC, 1992)

(a) A racing pulse

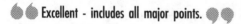 OK as far as it goes. But mentioning the exact pulse rate (160–180) would have earned a second mark.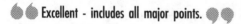

(b) They were never his fault

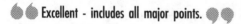 Although this is stated, it is not the whole story. The candidate should have mentioned both faults in the material and the weather to gain all three marks.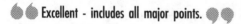

(c) A fellow competitor was sweating with fear. He felt very cold.

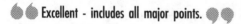 This answer lacks precision. What was really required for 4 marks was: the name of the competitior or the fact that he was British; the fact that it was minus 20 degrees; the competitor (Eddie the Eagle Edwards, actually) was dressed only in a T shirt; and the fact that this was because he was sweating with fear. So only 1 out of 4. Common sense might have suggested that more than a couple of statements were required for four marks.

(d) He really likes it and would jump more often if he could. He deosn't mind the risks.

   ❜❜ This answer contains enough information for full marks. It suffers slightly from imprecise English. 'He really likes it' isn't quite the register which Examiners are looking for. ❛❛

   ❜❜ Overall: this candidate would benefit from more attention to precise detail and precise expression. It is likely that she understood the passage very well. However, she has fallen short of demonstrating that beyond reasonable doubt. ❛❛

FURTHER EXAMPLES FOR PRACTICE

Further extracts have been pre-recorded on the audio cassette to provide extra practice. The questions are given here, and at the end of this *section* you will find possible answers. A transcript of each recording is given at the end of the chapter. At the end of the cassette are some numbers, telephone numbers and prices to write down at dictation, and finally the German alphabet with some exercises in spelling at dictation.

SHORTER PASSAGES

EXTRACT 4:

An announcement at a railway station.

■ Play Extract 4 (or listen to your friend read the transcript on page 60).

When and where is the train for Munich leaving? What sort of train is it?   *(3)*
   (WJEC, 1991)

EXTRACT 5:

A weather forecast.

■ Play Extract 5 (or listen to your friend read the transcript on page 60).

(a) Which two factors determine the weather in Germany on this day?   *(4)*
(b) What is the outlook for the North?   *(3)*
(c) What is the outlook for the South?   *(3)*
(d) What day and night temperatures are forecast for North and South Germany? *(3)*
(e) What is the weather forecast for the following week?   *(2)*
   (NISEAC, June 1990)

EXTRACT 6:

Information zur Verkehrslage.

■ Play Extract 6 (or listen to your friend reading the transcript on page 60).

Auf der Karte an der nächsten Seite notieren Sie mit einem Pfeilchen die Richtung jeder erwähnten Autobahn. Geben Sie die Nummer der Autobahn und die dazu gehörende Information. Die Namen aller Großstädte, die Sie für diese Aufgabe brauchen, stehen schon auf der Karte, und es ist nicht nötig, andere Ortsnamen zu notieren.

Die erste Strecke - A391 BRAUNSCHWEIG RICHTUNG SALZGITTER BAUARBEITEN 4 Km STAU – ist als Beispiel notiert.

Fig. 3.1

(ODLE, 1991)

EXTRACT 7:

Unruhen in der Stadt Nablus im israelischbestezten Westjordanien.

(This passage was recorded before the 1993 Israeli-Palestinian peace moves.)

You will now hear a report of unrest in the town of Nablus on the Israeli-occupied West Bank. Fill in the gaps in **English** on your question paper.

Unruhen in der Stadt Nablus im israelischbestezten Westjordanien.

Füllen Sie die Lücken in dieser Passage auf **englisch** aus.

■ Play Extract 7 (or listen to your friend reading the transcript on page 60).

Now read the passage.

In the town of Nablus on the Israeli-occupied West Bank, four Palestinians have been
(1) .... by soliders and another twenty people injured. According to an
announcement on Israeli (2) .... there had been many violent disturbances
in the area during which demonstrators had thrown (3)................... .
A curfew has been imposed on Nablus and nearby (4) ....
The Israeli army has (5) .... houses in the area around Nablus and several
people have been arrested.

(UCLES, June 1991)

EXTRACT 8:

You will hear a short news item.

■ Play Extract 8 (or listen to your friends reading the transcript on page 61).

What are President Bush's plans regarding space research?   *(2)*

EXTRACT 9:

A news report about floods in the Ottrupp area, near Münster.

■ Play Extract 9 (or listen to your friends reading the transcript on page 61).

(a) What particular task faced the firemen in Langenhorts during the night?   *(2)*
(b) Why was the situation urgent?   *(2)*
(c) How did they manage to control the situation?   *(2)*
(d) What problem did the floods bring for householders, and how was it solved? *(2)*

(AEB)

EXTRACT 10:

Polizeibericht aus Langenhausen.

■ Play Extract 10 (or listen to your friends reading the transcript on page 61).

(a) Give details about the age and circumstances of the young man.   *(3)*
(b) How did he go about robbing the bank?   *(3)*
(c) How do we know that he was very nervous during the robbery?   *(2)*
(d) How did he try to make his getaway, and what happened at this point?   *(4)*
(e) Why did he return to the bank, and what happened to him there?   *(3)*

(NISEAC)

EXTRACT 11:

A report about tennis in Germany.

■ Play Extract 11 (or listen to your friends reading the transcript on page 61).

(a) What general effect have the successes of Graf and Becker had on tennis in
     Germany?   *(2)*

(b) (i) How popular is tennis in Germany? *(1)*
   (ii) What is its standing relative to other sports? *(3)*
(c) What is said to be the most interesting aspect of the statistics provided in the report? *(3)*

(AEB)

EXTRACT 12:

An interview for a job.

■ Play Extract 12 (or listen to your friends reading the transcript on page 61).

(a) Where is this interview taking place? *(1)*
(b) What job is he looking for? *(1)*
(c) How did he bcome interested in that kind of job? *(2)*
(d) Why is Herr Hübner not in a position to employ him? *(2)*
(e) Where does he send Peter Schön? *(3)*

(WJEC)

LONGER PASSAGES

EXTRACT 13:

Wettervorhersagen: Interview mit einem Fachmann.

Background: You are about to hear a radio interview with a metereologist called Dr Horst, foillowed by some brief closing remarks by the interviewer. In these she will quote an old countryman's saying about the weather.

Task: Your task is twofold:

A. To answer in English the questions below on the interview

B. To jot down **in German** the second part of the countryman's saying, and to give an English translation of the whole of it.

■ Play Extract 13 (or listen to your friends reading the transcript on page 62).

A.
1. Where does Dr Horst work? *(1)*
2. What needs to be established as the first step in producing a weather forecast? *(1)*
3. How many stations are involved world-wide in weather observation work, and how often do they take readings? *(2)*
4. How are the data they collect and exchange then processed to produce a forecast of the global situation? *(2)*
5. What, according to Dr Horst, is the **third** step in the forecasting process? *(1)*
6. What is the current success rate of 24-hour forecasts? *(1)*
7. In recent years, Dr Horst claims, great progress has been made. In what kind of forecasts? *(2)*
8. What two examples does the interviewer use in her question about localised weather? *(2)*
9. Why does Dr Horst decline to make any predictions about the Christmas weather? *(2)*

EXTRACT 14:

■ Play Extract 14 (or listen to your friends reading the transcript on page 63).

(a) How had Reinhard Mey been described in a TV Magazine? *(2)*
(b) What reason does Reinhard Mey give for taking up his chosen career? *(2)*
(c) How does he get ideas for texts? *(2)*
(d) How have the texts of Reinhard Mey's songs been used for educational purposes in other countries? *(2)*

(e) What does Reinhard Mey say about his performance in German at school, and what is suggested as a reason for this?   *(2)*
(f) How does Reinhard Mey feel about his texts being used for teaching German, and what is his comment on this?   *(2)*

(ULEAC)

EXTRACT 15:

You will hear in interview with two blind people, Hans-Oskar Baumeister and his wife, Pilar, and with the Robert. You will hear the interview **three** times. There are pauses in the recording, indicated on the questions paper.

■ Play Extract 15 (or listen to your friends read the transcript on page 63).

(a) What do we learn about Hans-Oskar's sight?   *(3)*
(b) What was the post- war situation regarding his schooling?   *(2)*
(Pause)
(c) Why did he have to take a refresher course in Braille?   *(2)*
(d) How long have they been married?   *(1)*
(e) What do we learn about Pilar's nationality?   *(2)*
(Pause)
(f) Why did she first want to make contact with German people?   *(2)*
(g) What prompted Hans-Oskar's visit to Spain?   *(2)*
(Pause)
(h) Why did he send a photograph to his blind wife-to-be?   *(2)*
(i) Where did they meet him?   *(1)*
(j) Describe his reaction when meeting her family and other Spanish people.   *(3)*
(Pause)
(k) How does Pilar describe her relation to nature?   *(2)*
(l) Who is Robert?   *(1)*
(m) Why do the Baumeisters consider themselves luckier than other blind people?   *(1)*
(n) What are Robert's duties?   *(4)*
(o) Why was he surprised when he first met them?   *(2)*

EXTRACT 16:

Sie werden ein Gespräch zwischen Monika und Sonja hören. Sie sprechen über die Vorund Nachteile des Lebens in der Stadt und auf dem Land.

Notieren Sie, was jede zu sagen hat, und dann schreiben Sie auf deutsch eine kurze Zusammenfassung, in der Sie die Gedanken und Meinungen der beiden Sprecher vergleichen. (150–200 Worte).

Sie werden die Kassette zweimal hören.

■ Play Extract 16 (or listen to your friend reading the transcript on page 64).

(SEB)

EXTRACT 17:

Aids: Der Bericht der Enquete-Kommision.

Beantworten Sie die folgenden Fragen.

■ Play Extract 17 (or listen to your friends reading the transcript on page 65).

(a) Wie lange hat die Arbeit der Enquete-Kommission gedauert?   *(1)*
(b) Worum handelt es sich im Bericht und wann wird es fertig sein?   *(1)*
(c) Was erfahren wir über diesen Bericht?   *(3)*
(d) Was wird über die Anzahl der Kranken und Infizierten gesagt?   *(4)*

(e) Was bedauert Dr Vogt? (2)

(f) Was würde ihn glücklich machen? (4)

(g) Was sagt Dr Vogt vom Verhältnis der jüngeren Generation zu AIDS? (4)

(h) Warum ist Dr Vogt optimistisch? – aber mit welchem Vorbehalt? (4)

FIGURES AND SPELLING

EXTRACT 18:

Telefonnummern, Daten, Zahlen Transcript.

■ Play Extract 18 (or listen to your friend reading the transcript on pages 65 and 66).

Telefonnummern

Write down the following three telephone numbers:

(a)

(b)

(c)

Daten

Write down the dates you will hear.

(d)

(e)

(f)

(g)

(h)

Zahlen

Write down the two figures you will hear.

(i)

(j)

EXTRACT 19:

Zeiten.

■ Play Extract 19 (or listen to your friend reading the transcript on page 66).

Write down the times you will hear.

(a)

(b)

(c)

(d)

(e)

(f)

(g)

(h)

(i)

(j)

EXTRACT 20:

Das deutsche Alphabet

■ Play Extract 20 (or listen to your friend reading the transcript on page 66).

TRANSCRIPT OF PASSAGES

EXTRACT 1: TRANSCRIPT

Seit gestern ist es etwas windiger, auch kühler geworden, und darüber freuen sich vor allem die Surfer und Segler, denn bei kräftigem Wind sind in den Nord- und Ostseen ideale Wassersportmöglichkeiten vorhanden. Nachdem sich in Norddeutschland die Luft etwas abgekühlt hat, sind Wasser und Luft jetzt gleich warm, nämlich rund 19 bis 20 Grad. Nur weniger wärmer ist der Atlantik. Ideale Badetemperaturen hat man vor Südspanien mit rund 23 Grad. Der Spitzenreiter mit geradezu Badewannentemperaturen ist das Mittelmeer. Dort hat sich das Wasser auf 25 bis 29 Grad erwärmt.

Gewitter gibt es bei uns heute nicht, aber die Luft bleibt weiterhin kühl. Temperaturen 18 bis 23 Grad - Sonne und Wolken wechseln sich dabei ab. Die meisten Sonnenstrahlen Können Sie auf jeden fall erwischen im westen und im Südwesten Deutschlands. Im Norden an der Küste und am Alpenrand bleibt es bedeckt – es kann auch mal regnen, und so wird es auch morgen fortsetzen – ein bis zwei Grad wird es wärmer werden.

EXTRACT 2: TRANSCRIPT

Und jetzt noch eine Meldung aus Dortmund: Dort sind aufgrund mehrerer Veranstaltungen im Bereich Westfalenhalle und Bundesgartenschau die Parkplätze überlastet. Pkw-Fahrer werden gebeten, den ausgewiesenen Parkplatz 2 an der Universität zu benutzen. Es ist ein kostenloser Bus-Pendelverkehr eingerichtet. Besucher des Fußballspiels Dortmund – St. Pauli werden dringend gebeten, öffentliche Verkehrsmittel zu benutzen.

EXTRACT 3: TRANSCRIPT

Und jetzt hören sie ein Interview mit Weltmeister Dieter Thoma über Gefahren und Geschäfte beim Skispringen. Diester Thoma gilt als Jahrhunderttalent. In der vorigen Saison gewann er die internationale Vier-Schanzen-Tournée und die Skiflug-Weltmeisterschaft.

– Herr Thoma, wie schnell schlägt Ihr Puls im Moment?
– Das weiß ich gar nicht, 50 oder 60 Schläge pro Minute vielleicht.
– Und wie schnell ist er, wenn Sie oben auf der Schanze stehen?
– Da hämmert der Puls im ganzen Körper, 160 bis 180 Schläge – ohne jede körperliche Anstrengung.
– Ist das die nackte Angst?
– Wenn es nur um Weltcup-Punkte geht oder den Gesamtsieg, ist es eher Nervosität. Wenn aber ein Konkurrent einen Supersprung vorgelegt hat und es kaum möglich ist weiterzukommen, ohne über den kritischen Punkt zu springen, dann packt dich die Angst. Du weißt genau wie du dir alle Knochen brechen kannst, wenn du es trotzdem riskierst. Springen ist schön und grausam zugleich.
– In den letzten vier Jahren sind Sie dreimal gestürzt. Ist es da schwierig, sich ein starkes Selbstbewußtsein einzureden?
- Da muß ich mir gar nichts einreden. Wir analysieren jeden Sturz, da wird dann klar, wo der Fehler lag. Bisher lag es am Material oder am Wetter, aber nie an mir.
– Oben auf der Schanze sollen sich einige Ihrer Kollegen Mut antrinken, mit Pillen beruhigen oder sich vor Angst schon mal übergeben.
– Richtige Panik habe ich nur beim Briten Eddie Edwards gesehen. Bei 20 Grad Minus standen wir alle im Daunenanorak da oben, aber er trug nur ein T-Shirt, weil ihm der Angstschweiß ausgebrochen war. Springen ist eben auch eine Art Mutprobe.
– Sie machen 600 Sprünge im Jahr. Wird das nicht mal langweilig?
– Überhaupt nicht. Ich würde noch viel öfter springen. Ich springe, solange die Knochen noch halten. Ein Tennisspieler übt 3000 mal die Rückhand - wenn es nötig ist, noch öfter. Wir können nur ein paar Monate im Winter springen, das reicht eigentlich gar nicht.

EXTRACT 4: TRANSCRIPT

Sie haben Anschluß zum Eilzug nach Regensburg, planmäßige Abfahrt 11.20 Uhr, Gleis 28, zum Eilzug nach Frankfurt, planmäßige Abfahrt 11.22, Gleis 7, zum Schnellzug nach München, planmäßige Abfahrt 11.34 Uhr, Gleis 2.

EXTRACT 5: TRANSCRIPT

Und jetzt der Wetterbericht.
Ein Tief über der Nordsee bestimmt das Wetter im Norddeutschen Raum, während der Süden weiterhin unter dem Einfluß eines Hochs über dem Alpenraum steht.

Die Vorhersage bis morgen Abend:

In der Nordhälfte stark bewölkt und zeitweise Schneefälle, zum Teil in Regen übergehend. Im Süden wolkig mit Aufheiterungen und zunächst kaum Niederschläge. Tageshöchsttemperaturen im Norden ein bis fünf Grad, im Süden um zwei Grad. Tiefstwerte in der Nacht Null bis minus fünf Grad.

Die Aussichten für die kommende Woche:

Weiterhin unbeständig und wieder naßkalt.

EXTRACT 6: TRANSCRIPT

Aus dem Verkehrsstudio hören wir jetzt Informationen zur Verkehrslage.

A 391 Braunschweig Richtung Salzgitter. Bauarbetien für Braunschweig-Gartenstadt. Je Richtung 4 Kilometer Stau.

Autobahn 1 Bremen Richtung Osnabrück zwischen Bremer Kreuz und Brinkum stockender Verkehr.

A2 Hannover Richtung Dortmund zwischen Rehren und Bad Eilsen 3 Kilometer Stau. Umleitungsempfehlung ab Rehren über U44 Auffahrt Bad Eilsen.

Baden-Württemberg. A6 von Nürnberg in Richtung Heilbronn zwischen Ilshofen-Wolpertshausen und Schwäbisch-Hall defektes Fahrzeug. 5 Kilometer Stau.

Und Bayern. A3 von Nürnberg in Richtung Frankfurt zwischen Kitzingen-Schwarach und Wertheim hohes Verkehrsaufkommen und 60 Kilometer Stau.

N1 St Gallen in Richtung Zürich zwischen Oberwinterthur und Winterthur-Wülfingen Baustelle. 2 Kilometer Stau.

EXTRACT 7: TRANSCRIPT

Unruhen in der Stadt Nablus im israelischbestezten Westjordanien.

In der Stadt Nablus im israelibestezten Westjordanien sind Berichten zufolge vier Palestinenser von Soldaten erschossen und 20 weitere Menschen verletzt worden. In einer Meldung des israelischen Rundfunks hieß es, es habe zahlreiche gewalttätige Zwischenfälle in dem Gebiet gegeben, in deren Verlauf die Demonstranten mit Steinen geworfen hätten. Über Nablus und dem nahegelegenen Flüchtlingslager sei eine Ausgangssperre verhängt worden. Die israelische Armee, so die Rundfunkstation weiter, habe im Gebiet um Nablus Hausdurchsuchungen durchgeführt und mehrere Personen verhaftet.

EXTRACT 8: TRANSCRIPT

Ungeachtet aller Sparmaßnahmen will Präsident Bush im Haushaltsjahr 1991 die amerikanische Raumfahrt stärker als bisher finanziell unterstützen. Die Raumfahrtbehörde NASA erhält nach dem Etatentwurf rund 5 Milliarden Dollar, das sind 25% mehr als im laufenden Jahr.

EXTRACT 9: TRANSCRIPT

Gestern gab es Hochwasseralarm im münsterländischen Ottrupp. Zirka hundert Feuerwehrleute waren die Nacht über im Einsatz, um ein Überlaufen eines Flußes in der Ortschaft Langenhorst zu verhindern. Innerhalb weniger Stunden stieg der Fluß um eineinhalb Meter und drohte, den tiefergelegenen Ort zu überfluten. Mit 2000 Sandsäcken wurde der Damm befestigt. Erst gegen Mitternacht blieb das Wasser konstant. Zusätzlich mußten von der Feuerwehr in 20 Häusern Keller leergepumpt werden. Im Laufe des Vormittags entspannte sich die Lage.

EXTRACT 10: TRANSCRIPT

Es folgt ein Polizeibericht aus Langenhausen.

Ein 28 Jahre alter Automechaniker brachte gestern das Geld zurück, das er kurz zuvor bei einem Überfall auf eine Bank in Langenhausen gestohlen hatte. Der völlig mittellose junge Mann hatte in der Stadtsparkasse eine Kundin mit einem Spielzeugrevolver bedroht und den Kassierer gezwungen, ihm 21 400 Mark auszuhändigen. Der Räuber war so nervös, daß er es nicht schaffte, das Geld in einer Plastiktüte zu stopfen. Mit dem Geld in der Hand lief er zum Ausgang und verlor dabei bereits einen Teil. Als er in seinen vor der Bank geparkten Wagen steigen wollte, verlor er weiteres Geld, und wurde so von einem anderen Autofahrer bemerkt und verfolgt. Einige Zeit später erschien der Automechaniker reumütig auf der Bank, um das Geld zurückzubringen. Er händigte das Geld über und sagte: 'Es tut mir leid, ich bin durchgedreht.' Bis zum Eintreffen der Polizei wurde der junge Mann im Zimmer des Direktors eingesperrt.

EXTRACT 11: TRANSCRIPT

Sie hören einen Bericht über Tennis in Deutschland.
Gerade durch die Erfolge von Steffi Graf und Boris Becker hat Tennis in Deutschland immer noch enorme Zuwachsraten, und steht mit 2,1 Millionen eingetragenen Mitgliedern an dritter Stelle, hinter Fußball mit 4,8 und Turnen mit 3,9 Millionen. Interessant is aber auch, daß 55% dieser Mitglieder im Seniorenalter sind, daß heißt also Frauen über 40 und Männer über 45.

EXTRACT 12: TRANSCRIPT

- Ja, guten Tag, Herr Hübner, äh . . . .
- Bitte kommen Sie weiter.
- Ja, danke schön.
- Nehmen Sie Platz.
- Also, ich heiße Peter Schön, und ich wollte mich eigentlich nach einem Job bei Ihnen, in Ihrem Theater erkundigen.
- Sie sind Schauspieler?
- Nein, eben nicht Schauspieler, eben. Mich würde eher die Beleuchtungstechnik reizen.
- Hmm.
- Daran zu arbeiten.
- Was haben Sie denn für eine Ausbildung?
- Ja, ich bin nach dem 10. Schuljahr abgegangen. Ich habe eine Realschulabschluß. Übrigen, wenn Sie mein Zeugnis sehen wollen, das habe ich hier. Aber ich weiß nicht, ob Sie das . . . . Bitte schön.

– Mmmh. Gut Äh . . . . . Sie sind geboren am . . . . ja, das käme in Frage . . . gut
– Und Mein Vater, äh, hat früher auch mal in einem Theater als Beleuchter gearbeitet, und ich habe ihm auch mal ab und zu mal geholfen. Mit macht das also unheimlich Spaß und . . . .
– Was ist Ihr Vater von Beruf?
– Eben auch Beleuchter in einem Theater.
– Beleuchter.
– Ja.
– Also, Elektromeister.
– Elektromeister, ja.
– Ja.
– Und mich würde sowas auch reizen.
– Mmmh, ja, ob eine Vakanz da ist, das muß ich jetzt meinen technischen Direktor fragen. Ich bin eigentlich jetzt für die künstlerischen Engagements zuständig. Wie war Ihr Name gerade?
– Peter Schön heiße ich.
– Herr Schön, wenn Sie gerade zum technischen Direktor hinübergehen würden und sich dann an die Buchhaltung wenden würden, ja.
– Ja, das ist gut.
– Dort können Sie ihr Bankkonto und Lohnsteuerkarte und so weiter hinterlassen.
– Ja, danke schön.
– Bitte sehr.
– Wiedersehen.
– Wiedersehen.

EXTRACT 13: TRANSCRIPT

Wettervorhersagen: Interview mit einem Fachmann.

– Unser Studiogast heute ist Meterologe. Ich begrüße Dr Horst, Leiter des Münchener Wetteramts. Herr Dr Horst, welche Information brauchen die Meterologen heute, um eine Wettervorhersage zu erstellen?
– Für eine Wettervorhersage ist ein erheblicher Aufwand nötig. Ähh, Sie geschieht in drei Schritten. Der erste Schritt ist die Feststellung des Zustands der Atmosphäre. Dazu gibt es ein weltweites Wetterbeobachtungsnetz. Es besteht aus 10 000 Wetterstationen, die alle 3 Stunden eine Wetterbeobachtung anstellen. Der nächste Schritt ist, diese Beobachtungen fließen in einen Computer, in dem, mit Hilfe von mathematischen, und physikalischen Modellen, die, ähhh, zukünftige Großwetterlage errechnet wird. Und zuletzt muß diese Großlage noch umgerechnet werden, in regionales Wetter.
– Die Wahrscheinlichkeit, daß das Wetter so kommt, wie Sie vorausgesagt haben, liegt derzeit bei 80%. Glauben Sie, daß diese Trefferquote noch zu steigern ist?
– Diese 80% beziehen sich auf die 24-Stunden-Vorhersage. Es ist sicher noch eine Steigerung möglich. Man muß sich allerdings vor Augen halten, daß jedes Prozent Verbesserung mit einem erheblichen Aufwand verbunden ist. Aber für die Mittelfristvorhersagen bis zum siebten Tag haben wir in den letzten Jahren große Fortschritte gemacht. Auch hier sind in Zukunft noch Verbesserungen zu erwarten.
– Wie sieht es aus mit lokalen Wetterereignissen, beispielsweise, einem Hagelschlag, oder Nebel auf einem Flughafen?
– Also diese kleinräumigen Ereignisse sind sicherlich sehr schwer zu erfassen. Mit Modellrechnungen geht das im Moment nicht. Jedenfalls nicht routinemäßig.
– Wir haben jetzt einen Fachmann im Studio. Herr Dr Horst, werden wir ein weißes Weihnachten haben?
– Das kann man jetzt nicht sagen. Weihnachten ist noch lange hin. Alles, was über den siebten Tag an Vorhersagen hinausgeht, ist wissenschaftlich nicht vertretbar.
– Vielen Dank, Herr Dr Horst.
   Ob wir also weiße Weihnachten haben, kann uns der Meterologe nicht sagen. Aber vielleicht hilft uns eine alte Bauernregel weiter. Und die lautet: 'Regnet's an Martini noch, liegt der Schnee um Weihnacht hoch.' Und an Martini, also am 11. November, schien in weiten Teilen der Bundesrepublik die Sonne. Also, schlechte Aussichten für Schnee am 24. Dezember.

EXTRACT 14: TRANSCRIPT

- Reinhard Mey, eine Fernsehzeitschrift nannte Sie kürzlich den wohlbekanntesten deutschsprachigen Liedersänger Europas. Wie wurden Sie eigentlich Liedersänger – oder soll man besser sagen, Liedermacher?

- Ja, Liedermacher vielleicht eher, weil es eben auch noch das Schreiben mit einschließt, wo hingegen Liedersänger eben unter Umständen so zu verstehen ist, als daß mit jemand anders die Texte schreibt, was nicht der Fall ist, also ich mache alles selber. Wie ich's geworden bin? Wahrscheinlich aus Unzufriedenheit darüber, daß auf dem Unterhaltungsmusiksektor in Deutschland so wenig geboten wurde, was einen, na ja . . . . wo es Spaß machte, mal auf den Text hinzuhören.

- Und woher nehmen Sie die Ideen für Texte?

- Aus . . . . . ja, aus allen möglichen Begebenheiten. Da ist mir also . . . alles, was mir am Tage passieren kann, ist mir da gerade recht. Es gibt eigentlich auch keine Begebenheit oder keinen Gegenstand, der mir zu gering wäre, als da irgendwann mal ein Lied drüber zu machen. Am meisten natürlich aus Begegnungen mit Leuten.

- Ich komme noch einmal auf die Fernsehzeitschrift zurück. Da heißt es an anderer Stelle: Reinhard Mey ist in letzter Zeit erfolgreich als (in Anführungsstrichen) 'Deutschlehrer für Ausländer'. Die Zeitschrift begründet ihre Aussage damit, daß Texte Ihrer Lieder im ausländischen Rundfunk im Deutschsprachkursus verwandt werden, und auch deutsche und ausländische Verlage sie in ihren Unterrichtswerken 'Deutsch' abdrücken. Welche Note hatte Reinhard Mey in der schule in Deutsch gehabt?

- Tja, ich hatte sehr schlechte Noten in Deutsch und ich bin sogar in der 11. Klasse, wahrscheinlich wegen Meinungsverschiedenheiten mit meinem Deutschlehrer, kleben geblieben. Wegen Deusch '5', damals gab's noch keine '6', sonst hätte ich vielleicht ein '6' gekriegt.

- Hätten Sie je daran gedacht, daß Ihre Lieder oder Texte einmal in deutschen Unterrichtsbüchern stehen?

- Natürlich nicht. Aber ich muß sagen, daß ich sehr stolz bin, und daß es für mich ein kleine, nicht bös gemeint, aber doch eine kleine Rache ist, jetzt in den Deutschbüchern drin zu sein.

EXTRACT 15: TRANSCRIPT

HANS-OSKAR BAUMEISTER: Ich bin als Sehbehinderter auf die Welt gekommen und bin seit circa acht Jahren völlig blind.

INTERVIEWER: Was sind Sie von Beruf?

HANS-OSKAR BAUMEISTER: Ich bin von Beruf Telefonist. Ich sagte, daß ich als Sehbehinderter zur Welt gekommen bin. Nach dem Krieg, da gab's keine Sehbehindertenschulen, da gab's nur Blindenschulen oder Schulen für Normal-sehende. Und weil ich in der Schule nicht mitkam, hat man mich in eine blindenschule gesteckt. Dort habe ich die normale Volksschule durchgemacht. Dann hinterher habe ich einen Handwerk gelernt und zwar Korbmachen, Bürstenmachen, Stuhlflechten und habe in diesen Berufen meine Gesellenprüfung gemacht. Dann wurde mein Sehen plötzlich so gut, daß ich in diesem Beruf unzufrieden wurde. Und dann habe ich Krankenpfleger gelernt.

(Pause)

Kurz bevor ich fertig wurde, bekam ich den grünen Starr. Dann kam ich nach Düren in die Rheinische Umschulungsstätte für Späterblindete und habe dort meine Kenntnisse in Blindenschrift aufgefrischt, die ich total vergessen hatte.

INTERVIEWER: Sie sind verheiratet – wie lange?

HANS-OSKAR BAUMEISTER: Jetzt werden es sechs Jahre sein.

INTERVIEWER: Sie haben sich kennengelernt durch die Blindheit?

PILAR BAUMEISTER: Durch Briefkontakt . . . .

HANS-OSKAR BAUMEISTER: Meine Frau studierte zu der Zeit in Barcelona an der Universität Deutsch.

PILAR BAUMEISTER: Damals war ich Spanierin. Jetzt bin ich Deutsche geworden – durch Einbürgerung.

HANS-OSKAR BAUMEISTER: Und sie suchte Kontakt mit Deutschen, damit ihre Sprache und so ihre Kenntnisse verbessert wurden. Und dann haben wir uns fast ein Jahr geschrieben, beziehungsweise Tonbänder, Cassetten und dergleichen geschickt. Und meine Frau sagte auf irgendeiner Kassette oder Tonband plötzlich mal: 'Mensch, komm mich doch mal besuchen.' Ja, und dann habe ich mich eines Tages in den Zug gesetzt und bin denn nach Spanien gefahren.

(Pause)

Vorher hatte ich ein Foto geschickt gehabt, damit die Eltern wußten, wie ich aussah. Und dann habe sie mich am Bahnhof abgeholt, und so eine Herzlichkeit und so ein Leben habe ich selten kennengelernt wie bei dieser Familie, überhaupt bei den Spaniern. Ganz nett, freundlich, herzlich, als wenn man schon immer da gewesen wäre. Ja, und nachdem ich dann so ein paar Mal dagewesen bin in Spanien, da haben wir dann ausgemacht, daß wir heiraten würden, und daß wir hier in Deutschland leben würden.

(Pause)

INTERVIEWER: Frau Baumeister, Sie haben ja dadurch, daß sie nie sehen konnten, auch nie irgendwelche Eindrücke haben können. Farbeindrücke, Blumen, Bäume, was bedeutet das für Sie?

PILAR BAUMEISTER: Die Natur ist für mich auch wichtig, und ich liebe Blumen sehr und Bäume, jedoch muß ich eingestehen, daß ich natürlich viele Beschränkungen wegen meiner Blindheit in Kauf nehmen muß.

HANS-OSKAR BAUMEISTER: Wir sollten kurz erwähnen, daß wir einen Zivildienstleistenden haben. Leider hat das nicht jedes blinde Ehepaar und leider auch nicht jeder Blinde – einen Zivildienstleistenden, der uns zur Arbeit, zur Universität bringt, der mit uns einkaufen geht, der für uns Briefe vorliest, und das ist unser Robert.

ROBERT: Ich fange morgens um halb sieben an und fahre den Herrn Baumeister zur Arbeit. Wenn sie zur Uni muß, fahr ich Frau Baumeister hin und bringe sie zum Hörsaal. Zwischendurch, wenn sie Bücher braucht aus der Bücherei, gehe ich dann, suche sie 'raus und kopiere sie oder leihe sie aus und fahr' dann nach Hause. Hab' da auch einen Cassettenrecorder. Spreche die Sachen auf Cassette. Ich war eigentlich vom Anfang an sehr erstaunt, wie relativ selbsständig doch so blinde Menschen sind. Wie die ihren Haushalt erledigen und so, das konnte ich mir vorher überhaupt nicht vorstellen.

EXTRACT 16: TRANSCRIPT

– Monika, wohnst du in einer großen Stadt?
– Oh ja, du, ich wohne in München und mir gefällt's da prima.
– Ja?
– Ja. Ich bin mein ganzes Leben lang in einer Großstadt aufgewachsen. Wir haben schon immer, meine ganze Familie, schon immer in der Großstadt gelebt und ich find mich dort eigentlich sehr gut zurecht. Ich genieße es zum Beispiel, ein, ein riesiges Kinoprogramm zu haben, ja: man schlägt die Zeitung auf und es gibt zwanzig verschiedene Programme und ich kann mir, wenn mein Taschengeld es erlaubt, kann ich mir aussuchen, was ich sehen möchte. Oder ich gehe auch sehr gern ins Theater und kann eigentlich drei- oder viermal im Monat verschiedene Theaterprogramme sehen.
Was mir auch tierisch Spaß macht – ich laufe gern durch Fußgängerzonen. Ich schaue mir unwahrscheinlich gern Schaufenster an, und Geschäfte, ich probiere gern Kleider

an - nicht, daß ich mir alle Kleider kaufen könnte, aber ich habe gern die Auswahl. Ich schau mir auch gern.. zum Beispiel in Fußgängerzonen um und schaue mir gern die Leute an. Ich könnte stundenlang auf einem Marktplatz sitzen und die Leute vorbeilaufen sehen. Ich finde das interessant, wie sie alle angezogen sind. Es gibt verschiedene Leute – es gibt Punks, und es gibt ganz vornehm angezogene Yuppies und ich find es toll. Mir macht es Spaß. Ich lebe unwahrscheinlich gern in einer Stadt. Und du, Sonja?
– Naja, ich lebe auch in einer großen Stadt. Ich lebe in Berlin, aber mir gefällt's überhaupt nicht. Ich meine, wenn ich richtig in die Stadt gehe und in der Fußgängerzone herumlaufe, dann, ich weiß nicht, mich werde da unheimlich schnell müde und ich finde es tierisch langweilig, Schaufenster anzugucken und die ganzen Modesachen und die ganzen Leute, die total hektisch durch die Straßen laufen. Ich würde, ich würde unheimlich gern irgendwo auf dem Lande wohnen. Ich meine, im Moment kann ich noch nicht ausziehen von zu Hause aber, wenn meine Eltern auf das Land ziehen würden, das würde mir tierisch gut gefallen.

Und der Gestank in der Stadt. Es stinkt immer nach Autos, die Abgase. Ich fahre unheimlich gern Fahrrad, zum Beispiel, aber es ist einfach viel zu gefährlich, Fahrrad zu fahren in einer großen Stadt, finde ich. Und naja, auch ich kenne einige Leute, die auf dem Land wohnen und die ich schon in den Ferien besucht habe, und mir gefällt das unheimlich gut. Ich hätte sehr gern Tiere, zum Beispiel, Tiere, die man in der Stadt nicht haben kann, wie zum Beispiel große Hunde oder ein Pferd, Pferde oder sogar Kühe. Ich würde unheimlich gern auf dem Bauernhof wohnen.

EXTRACT 17: TRANSCRIPT

Aids: Der Bericht der Enquete-Kommision

Das letzte Thema in den heutigen Funkbildern betrifft die Aids-Problematik. Nach etwa zweieinhalbjähriger Arbeit wird die Aids Enquete-Kommission des deutschen Bundestages Ende Mai ihren Bericht der Bundestagspräsidentin vorlegen können, und danach wird dieser Bericht veröffentlicht. Er wird 1400 Schreibmaschinen-Seiten umfassen und damit der ausführlichste sein, den es zur AIDS-Problematik in der Bundesrepublik bisher gibt. Maite Zeeg führte ein Gespräch mit dem Vorsitzenden dieser Enquete-Kommission, Dr Hans-Peter Vogt, CDU-Bundestagsabgeordneter aus Nordheim.
– Wie ist denn die Entwicklung bei AIDS? Gibt es mehr Krankheiten?
– Es gibt nach wie vor mehr Krankheitsfälle, auch wenn die prozentalen Zuwächse glücklicherweise nicht so dramatisch sind, wie man das noch vor einigen Jahren erwartet hatte. Aber für uns ist es auch nicht der Zuwachs der AIDS-Kranken, denn das sind ja die Kranken, die sich vor 5 bis 10 Jahren angesteckt haben, sondern für uns ist wichtig die Zuwachsrate der Infizierten. Hier gibt es Zuwächse, die im Bereich von 15 Monaten-Verdoppelung liegen, also weniger, als vor einigen Jahren befürchtet, aber es gibt keinen Anlaß zur Entwarnung. Und wir bedauern es, daß das Thema AIDS völlig aus den öffentlichen Diskussionen verschwunden ist. Wir wären glücklich, wenn wir wieder mehr darüber sprechen könnten – allerdings nicht mit Falschmeldungen oder mit Hektik, sondern mit sachlicher Information.
– Ja, und wie sieht es dort aus, beispielsweise bei den jungen Leuten? Sind denn diese bereit, sich nun vorzusehen? Gibt es genügend Schutzmaßnahmen?
– Ich glaube, daß die jüngere Generation die Problematik schon erfaßt hat. Wir können nicht messen, inwieweit die jüngere Generation – vor allem die Jugendlichen, auch die jetzt vor allem nachwachsenden Jugendlichen, die nicht in der ersten AIDS-Welle schon angesprochen worden sind – wie weit sie tatsächlich auch ihr Verhalten ändern. Daß sie die Problematik kennen, das kann man zu weit über 95% annehmen, aber ob sie auch tatsächlich ihr Verhalten dementsprechend einrichten, vermag man im Augenblick nicht zu sagen. Ich habe die Hoffnung, es gibt einige Parameter, aus denen man schliessen kann, daß die Jugendlichen schon die Problematik sehr ernst nehmen. Aber die Evaluationen unsere Maßnahmen sind da noch nicht ausreichend.

EXTRACT 18: TRANSCRIPT

Telefonnummern
(a) 02264/35 41
    Null zwo zwo sechs vier, fünfunddreißig einundvierzig

(b) 01531/ 34 22 11
Null eins fünf drei eins, vierunddreißig zweiundzwanzig elf
(c) 112
Eins eins zwo

Daten

(d) am 13. 6. 1995
am dreizeihnten sechsten fünfundneunzig
(e) am 17.6.
am siebzehnten Juno
(f) am 14.7.
am vierzehnten Juli
(g) 1871
achtzehnhunderteinundsiebzig
(h) im 11. Jahrhundert
im elften Jahrhundert

Zahlen

(i) 5,3%
fünf Komma drei Prozent
(j) 1 351 267
Eine Million
dreihunderteinundfünfzigtausendzweihundertsiebenundsechzig

EXTRACT 19: TRANSCRIPT

(a) elf Uhr dreißig
(b) Viertel vor fünf
(c) halb neun
(d) dreizehn Uhr fünfundvierzig
(e) fünf nach halb zwei
(f) Dreiviertel sechs
(g) dreiundzwanzig Uhr neunundfünfzig
(h) sechzehn Uhr sechs
(i) Mitternacht
(j) eine Minute nach eins

EXTRACT 20: TRANSCRIPT

a b c d e f g h i j k l m n o p q r s t u v w x y z ß ä ö ü é

ANSWERS TO QUESTIONS ON EXTRACTS 4 to 20

Please note that these answers are the author's own, and that the Examining Boards are unable to enter into any correspondence concerning them.

Extract 4: Answers

It leaves at 11.34 (1) platform 7(1), and is an express (1)

Extract 5: Answers

(a) Low pressure (1) Over the North Sea (1) High (1) over the Alps (1)
(b) Clouds(1) Snow showers (1) changing to rain(1)
(c) Clouds (1) Bright intervals (1) hardly any precipitation (1)
(d) North: Daytime 1–5 degrees C South: Daytime around 2 degrees C North and South: Nightime 0–5 degrees C
(e) Unsettled (1) wet *and* cold (1)

Extract 6: Answers

(a) A1 Bremen Richtung Osnabrück stockender Verkehr
(b) A2 Hannover Richtung Dortmund 3Km Stau
(c) A6 Nürnberg Richtung Heilbronn defektes Fahrzeug, 5Km Stau
(d) A3 Nürnberg Richtung Frankfurt hohes Verkehrsaufkommen, 60Km Stau
(e) St Gallen in Richtung Zürich in der Nähe von Winterthur Baustelle, 2Km Stau

Extract 7: Answers

(1) shot
(2) radio
(3) stones
(4) refugee camp
(5) searched

Extract 8: Answers

Bush wants to increase financial support (1) by 25% (1)

Extract 9: Answers

(a) to prevent (1) the river overflowing (1)
(b) because it had risen a metre and a half (1) and was threatening to flood the low-lying village (1)
(c) built a dam(1) with 2000 sandbags (1)
(d) flooded cellars (1) pumped out by firemen (1)

Extract 10: Answers

(a) 28 years old (1) car mechanic (1) without money (1)
(b) threatenend customer (1) with toy pistol (1) forced cashier to hand over money (1)
(c) didn't manage (1) to put money in a plastic bag (1)
(d) Any 4 of: Got into car (1) parked outside the bank(1) dropped more money (1) noticed by another driver (1) chased (1)
(e) he was sorry (1) kept in manager's office (1) until police arrived (1)

Extract 11: Answers

(a) enormous (1) increase in numbers (1)
(b) (i) 2.1 million members of tennis clubs (1)
    (ii) 3rd place (1) behind football (1) and gymnastics (1)
(c) 55% of club players (1) women over 40 (1) or men over 45 (1)

Extract 12: Answers

(a) in a theatre (1)
(b) lighting engineer (1)
(c) father's profession (1) occasionally helped him (1)
(d) Hübner is the artistic director (1) needs to ask technical director (1)
(e) to the office (1) to sort out bank (1) and tax details (1)

Extract 13: Answers

A
1. Munich Weather bureau (1)
2. The state of the atmosphere (1)
3. 10,000; (1) every three hours (1)
4. by computer (1) using physical models (1)
5. global situation re-worked as regioanl weather (1)
6. 80%
7. medium-term (1) up to 7 days (1)
8. hailstorms (1) airport fog (1)
9. it's a long time away (1) forecasts more than 7 days ahead are unreliable (1)

B
1. liegt der Schnee um Weihnacht hoch (3) (deduct 1 per error)
2. If it is still raining on St. Martin's day, there will be deep snow at Christmas (3) (deduct 1 per error)

Extract 14: Answers

(a) best known (1) German-speaking singer (1) in Europe
(b) unhappy that in German popular music sector (1) so few texts which were fun to listen to (1)
(c) things which happen to him daily (1) mainly encounters with people (1)
(d) in radio German courses (1) and in German language textbooks (1)
(e) had to repeat year 11 (1) because of differences of opinion with his German teacher (1)
(f) proud (1) a small revenge (for his treatment at the hands of his German teacher) (1)

Extract 15: Answers

(a) Was visually handicapped (1) from birth (1) has been blind since age 8 (1)
(b) Any two of:
> There were only schools for the blind (1)
> or the sighted (1)
> there were no schools for the partially sighted (1)
(c) Became blind just before completing his training as a nurse (1)
Had forgotten Braille (1)
(d) 6 years (1)
(e) Born a Spaniard (1) Now naturalised German (1)
(f) Pilar was studying German at university (1) Wanted to meet Germans to improve her language (1)
(g) Pilar invited him (1) on a cassette she had sent him (1)
(h) So that her parents (1) would recognise him (1)
(i) at the railway station (1)
(j) He found them friendly (1) lively (1); they treated him as if he had always been there.
(k) it's important to here (1) particularly likes flowers/trees (1)
(l) their young Community Service Worker (1)
(m) not everyone has help like that
(n) Any four of:
> drives Herr Baumeister to work
> takes Frau Baumeister to the university
> into the lecture room
> fetches her books from the library
> copies them
> or borrows them
> records them on cassette   (4)
(o) He was surprised how independent they are (1) and how they manage the housekeeping tasks (1)

Extract 16: Answers

As this is a summary in German, marks would be awarded for gaining up to 20 of the following points. There is no mark for the quality of the German, as long as it is comprehensible.

Monika:
has always lived in a city
so have her family
feels quite at home there
likes the choice of cinema programme
can see what she feels like seeing
can see different theatre shows
three or four a month

likes walking through pedestrian zones
likes window displays
likes trying on clothes
even if she can't afford them
likes looking at the people
punks and yuppies

Sonja:
also lives in a city
doesn't like it
gets tired very quickly
when in a pedestrian zone
finds window displays deadly boring
people running about hectically
would prefer to live in the country
can't leave home yet
but would love it if her parents moved into the country
dislikes the stink
and the car fumes
likes riding a bike
but too dangerous in the city
knows some people who live in the country
has visited them in the holidays
would like animals
of the sort you can't keep in town
e.g. big dogs, horses, cows
would enjoy living on a farm

Extract 17: Answers

The answers to this would need to be in German, but no marks are given for the accuracy of the German, provided that the meaning intended is clear.

(a) two and a half years (1)
(b) AIDS (1) end of May (1)
(c) 1400 sides long (1) typewritten (1) the most comprehensive ever on the subject (1)
(d) not the number originally expected (1) those getting ill now were infected 5–10 years ago (1) doubles every 15 months (1) no grounds for ending the state of alert (1)
(e) the theme of AIDS has disappeared entirely (1) from public discussion (1)
(f) if he could speak about it again (1) not with untrue reports (1) or undue panic (1) but with objective information (1)
(g) the current new adults (1) missed the first AIDS scare (1) one can't say (1) how much they will alter their behaviour (1)
(h) he hopes that some indicators (1) show that young people take the problem seriously. (1) it is difficult to have reliable feedback (1) on the measures which have been taken (1)

Extract 18: Answers

Telefonnummern
(a) 02264/35 41
(b) 01531/ 34 22 11
(c) 112

Daten
(d) am 13. 6. 1995
(e) am 17.6.
(f) am 14.7.
(g) 1871
(h) im 11. Jahrhundert

Zahlen
(i) 5,3%
(j) 1 351 267

Extract 19: Answers

Zeiten

(a) 11.30
(b) 4.45
(c) 8.30
(d) 13.45
(e) 1.35
(f) 5.45
(g) 23.59
(h) 16.06
(i) midnight
(j) 1.01

Extract 20: Answers

Das deutsche Alphabet

a b c d e f g h i j k l m n o p q r s t u v w x y z ß ä ö ü é

REVIEW SHEET

Listen again to each of the first 16 extracts on the tape. Now write down **3** extra questions of your own (with answers). You can then try these extra questions on a friend and/or ask your friend to try 3 extra questions of his/her own on you.

Extract 1

Q1 _____ Ans _____

Q2 _____ Ans _____

Q3 _____ Ans _____

Extract 2

Q1 _____ Ans _____

Q2 _____ Ans _____

Q3 _____ Ans _____

Extract 3

Q1 _____ Ans _____

Q2 _____ Ans _____

Q3 _____ Ans _____

Extract 4

Q1 _____ Ans _____

Q2 _____ Ans _____

Q3 _____ Ans _____

Extract 5

Q1 _____ Ans _____

Q2 _____ Ans _____

Q3 _____ Ans _____

Extract 6

Q1 _____ Ans _____

Q2 _____ Ans _____

Q3 _____ Ans _____

Extract 7

Q1 _____ Ans _____

Q2 _____ Ans _____

Q3 _____ Ans _____

Extract 8

Q1 _____ Ans _____

Q2 _____ Ans _____

Q3 _____ Ans _____

Extract 9

Q1 _____ Ans _____

Q2 _____ Ans _____

Q3 _____ Ans _____

Extract 10

Q1 _____ Ans _____

Q2 _____ Ans _____

Q3 _____ Ans _____

Extract 11

Q1 _____ Ans _____

Q2 _____ Ans _____

Q3 _____ Ans _____

Extract 12

Q1 _____ Ans _____

Q2 _____ Ans _____

Q3 _____ Ans _____

Extract 13

Q1 _____ Ans _____

Q2 _____ Ans _____

Q3 _____ Ans _____

Extract 14

Q1 _____ Ans _____

Q2 _____ Ans _____

Q3 _____ Ans _____

Extract 15

Q1 _____ Ans _____

Q2 _____ Ans _____

Q3 _____ Ans _____

Extract 16

Q1 _____ Ans _____

Q2 _____ Ans _____

Q3 _____ Ans _____

4

SPEAKING

GETTING STARTED

Practising **Speaking** may seem impossible without actually visiting a German-speaking country. But there are all sorts of opportunities which you can take in school or in college to speak German. Your teacher may well use German as a main means of communication in the lesson. If you are lucky, you may have access to time with a German Assistant. But it is possible to develop your own opportunities, for example to arrange a German-speaking evening with friends. You could also use a cassette recorder to help you prepare for the actual Speaking Test.

Preparation for the actual examination is also manageable, by working on role-play situations set in previous years, by careful preparation of the discussion topics you have chosen, and by practising reacting to current affairs articles on the level of 'intelligent dinner party conversation'.

As with every skill at A Level and AS, competence in speaking is built up gradually, almost imperceptibly. Unlike some of the other skills, however, cramming at the last minute has no benefit at all – it just doesn't work. So you really do need to make the most of any chance to practise – beginning with maximum participation in your next German lesson!

NATURE OF THE TEST

COMMUNICATION AND ERROR

MARK SCHEMES

RÔLE-PLAYS AND NEGOTIATIONS

DISCUSSING WRITTEN TEXTS

DISCUSSING LITERARY, CULTURAL OR BACKGROUND TOPICS

ESSENTIAL PRINCIPLES

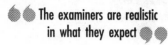

The speaking test is often a source of particular concern to candidates. Students can be apprehensive about meeting a stranger or being recorded talking to their teacher. But in fact, the majority of the examination exercises can be prepared and practised beforehand and need hold no terrors. What the Examiner is looking for is whether you can communicate in German at the level which might be expected from an A Level or AS candidate who is not a native speaker. So a top grade performance is quite possible even for someone who falls short of native speaker competence. Some allowance is made for a slight British accent, or for occasional errors of grammar or choice of vocabulary.

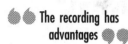 The examiners are realistic in what they expect

The exam is very likely to be recorded on cassette. This is to your benefit, as it means that the standard set by your examiner can be compared fairly to that of other examiners. So see the cassette recorder as a sort of referee – unobtrusive, but there to ensure fair play.

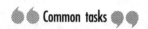 The recording has advantages

The different examination boards have slightly differing tests, so you should check with your teacher exactly what to expect in the year in which you take the exam. Most boards require you to:

- do some kind of rôle-play or negotiation exercise,
- to react to a newspaper or magazine article and discuss the topics suggested by it,
- to discuss a literary, cultural or background topic with the examiner.

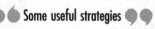 Common tasks

It is therefore clearly possible to prepare much of the material beforehand. The different examination boards vary in the amount of notice you are given of the rôle-play/negotiation tasks. Clearly the longer the notice, the more straightforward the preparation will be.

As far as the *general conversation* or *discussion of a topic* is concerned, again, practice makes perfect. There is plenty of opportunity here in class to develop a stock of debating ploys. But, like everything else, you will get most benefit by adding to a list of phrases and strategies throughout your course, and by making sure that you take every opportunity to take part in oral activities in class, and, if you are fortunate enough to have one, by using your time with the German Assistant wisely.

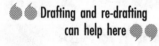 Some useful strategies

In any event, you will be able to choose and prepare a *literary* or *background* topic and work on it in advance. In some ways this topic is a sort of spoken coursework. There is much to be said for using your skills of drafting and re-drafting on this sort of work. While it is not the intention that you should recite a pre-learnt piece, you will find that practising the topic with another person, and listening to a recording of your efforts can be very instructive.

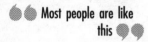 Drafting and re-drafting can help here

Some students are not at all tongue-tied in a foreign langauge, but are quite happy to rattle away as if they had always spoken it, impervious to any errors they might make, but concentrating on the business of **communicating** what they have to communicate. If you are one of these fortunate souls, move on the the next section.

The majority of learners however feel self-conscious about speaking in a foreign language. For some, there is a deep fear – perhaps fuelled by experiences early in the language-learning process – of making a mistake. This can lead to them being unwilling to do very much more than nod in agreement. What they are doing is confusing the message that language needs to be correct on paper with the requirements of speech.

Most people are like this

If you listen to someone who is *not* a professional speaker (such as a newsreader) of English, you will discover that they re-phrase things, re-start sentences, occasionally trip over pronunciation, say 'um' rather a lot, and make the odd mistake of grammar. And this person is a native speaker! The important thing is that they are able to communicate what they need to communicate; and the listener tolerates slight error without comment or without even noticing.

Listeners expect some errors

The same features apply to your German. And it is important to realise that slight errors of, say, adjective ending, do not impede communication in speech. (It is, of course, a more serious matter in writing.) On the other hand, a common fault found in English-speaking learners of German is that the Umlaut is ignored. Germans find this seriously confusing, particulary when *mochte* is used where *möchte* is required, or where *würde* is subsituted for *wurde*.

Pay attention to the Umlaut

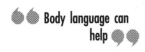
Body language can help

Body language also plays an important part in communication. Good communicators look the person they are talking to in the eye, smile, lean forward and look interested when listening, and often emphasise their meaning by gesture. Anyone who has ever seen two people who hardly speak each other's langauge using 'sign language' to communicate will know how effective this can be on its own.

Some useful hints

So enhance the impression you make on your Speaking examiner (whether it is your own teacher or a visiting examiner) by making sure you maintain eye contact, leaning forward and looking interested. It simply gives a better impression than staring awkwardly at the table. And, as nothing succeeds like success, acting confident will boost your confidence. There is also something to be said for dressing a little smartly for the Speaking test – smartness shows you consider the occasion an important one.

Finally, it is important for both you and for the examiner that you arrive at your appointment in good time, or at least on time. Being flustered will not improve your performance. Being late is hardly an impressive start.

Despite all of the above, the examiner will, of course, be looking to ascertain the actual quality of your German. And (s)he will not be fooled by those who rely too heavily on body language to achieve communication. The cassette recorder does not, of course, record gestures or grimaces.

It is therefore important to develop a range of linguistic strategies to cope with the various exercises and, as always, to consciously keep a record of them as you meet and perfect them.

MARK SCHEMES

Mark schemes are a useful guide

Most examination boards publish their **mark schemes** or guidance for teachers about the Speaking Test, and your teacher should have them available. In the Speaking Test, the mark schemes remain constant from year to year, as they are profiles of how candidates perform. It may be useful to make a a careful study of a typical scheme, which divides candidates into bands by describing their performance. It is fairly easy to see from the scheme what skills are best rewarded. The scheme is for a working total of 25 marks.

A AND AS LEVEL SPEAKING MARK SCHEME

21–25	Considerable amounts of information and clear expression of opinion. The candidates takes the initiative and sustains the flow of the conversation, using a wide range of structure and vocabulary. Very good pronunciation and intonation.
16–20	Plenty of information and expression of opinion, with little hesitation. The candidate takes the initiative sometimes, uses a good range of structure and vocabulary. There are some errors, but these do not normally obstruct comprehension.
11–15	Reasonable amount of information and expression of opinion, but the examiner leads the conversation. Flow not always smooth, and some prompting needed. Use of structure and vocabulary just adequate, with some reliance on phrases which have been obviously 'swotted up'. There are errors which sometimes obscure meaning.
6–10	Small amount of information, very basic expression of opinion. Hesistant, needing much prompting. Inadequate range of structure and vocabulary used, often inaccurate. Meaning often obscured by error.
0–5	Little or no relevant information. Very hesitant. Most of what is said is short factual utterances, and there is no discussion. The range of structure and vocabulary used is totally inadequate, and there are many gross inaccuracies. Meaning frequently quite obscure.

It is therefore clear that the wider the range of structures and vocabulary you use, the better. Equally, the better marks go to candidates who lead the conversation, take the initiative and express opinions. Accuracy is not the prime concern where mistakes do not obstruct meaning, although clearly, candidates who don't make mistakes will do better than candidates who do. And pronunciation is only used to differentiate between the top two levels of performance.

So the most important things to work on are, in order of priority:

- formulation and expression of opinion,
- strategies for leading the conversation,
- maintaining the flow.

EXAMPLE PAPERS

RÔLE-PLAYS AND NEGOTIATIONS

TEXT 1:

Brief: While staying with you, your German exchange partner has had to be rushed into hospital with acute appendicitis.

Task: You are now telephoning his or her parents in Dortmund.

(a) Tell the father or mother, whoever answers, what has happened, explaining that the operation has already taken place and that their son/daughter is being kept in for a few days for rest and observation.

(b) Explain that it will be possible for them to speak briefly to their son/daughter if they ring your local hospital between 7 and 8 p.m. and ask in the first instance for Sister Wheen in Ward 26. You should make sure they get the telephone number to ring, including the area code, and be prepared to spell out the name of the sister, making it clear how it is pronounced.

(c) Say that you and your parents will be making regular visits to the hospital, and ask if there is anything in particular they recommend you to take their son/daughter as a gift.

(d) As you say goodbye, promise to keep them informed and tell them not to worry; their son/daughter is in good hands.   (OCSEB, AS Level, 1991)

TEXT 2:

Brief: You are on a visit to Germany in the Half Term of the Autumn Term. You see a poster for the Munich Oktoberfest sellotaped to a door inside a small railway station in southern Germany. The Fest is over, you would like the poster as a souvenir but do not feel you can simply take it.

Task: Persuade the ticket-seller to let you have it.

(a) Attract the ticket-seller's attention (he/she is busy with some paperwork) and explain what you have seen and what you would like. He/She will be very reluctant.

(b) Ask if you can talk to his/her boss, the station-master for instance, or someone in higher authority. He/She will say there is no-one there.

(c) Explain that the poster is out-of-date, surely no-one else will want it, could he/she simply let you detach it. He/She will be very unsure what to do.

(d) Plead that you have been to the festival, it would be a wonderful souvenir, say how much you like Bavaria, etc. (i.e. appeal to his/her good nature).

(e) If he/she is adamant that it is not possible, ask if you can leave a note for the station-master explaining your request and saying that you will come back tomorrow.

If he/she seems to be weakening, say that you cannot afford to offer him/her money for the poster but that, if he/she would like you to, you could send him/her a poster from Britain in exchange to put up in the office or give to his/her children.

                                                            (OCSEB, A Level, 1992)

TEXT 3:

Communicative task A – report of road accident

Candidate's sheet

Anweisung: Manche Fragen erfordern etwas Phantasie.

Situation: Sie sind mit Ihrer Schwester bei deutschen Freunden in Bonn zu Besuch. Leider hat Ihre Schwester gestern nachmittag einen Verkehrsunfall gehabt: sie ist von einem Fahrrad überfahren worden und wird jetzt im Krankenhaus behandelt. Zum Glück ist sie nicht schwer verletzt und soll morgen entlassen werden.

Aufgabe 1: Ihre Schwester hat einen kurzen Bericht über den Unfall auf englisch geschrieben. Sie werden von einem/r deutschen Polizeibeamten/in gebeten, ihm/ihr zu erklären, was in diesem Bericht steht.

Es ist nicht nötig, den ganzen Text zu übersetzen. Versuchen Sie nur, die Hauptpunkte zusammenzufassen.

Aufgabe 2: Der/die Polizeibeamte/in besteht darauf, daß Sie und Ihre Schwester in Bonn bleiben, bis sich alles geklärt hat. Sie beide wollen aber am nächsten Tag zurück nach England. Versuchen Sie, den/die Beamten/in davon zu überzeugen, daß Sie am nächsten Tag fahren dürfen (zB aus folgenden Gründen: kranke Großmutter zu Hause in England, Reiseversicherung und Fahrkarten nur bis übermorgen gültig, Schwester möchte eigenen Arzt besuchen, nur sehr wenig Geld, usw).

Materialien: Unfallbericht auf englisch.

Accident report

I was walking along the main shopping street with my German friend – we were on a shopping trip before my brother and I left to go home to England. It was getting late (I think it was about 5.30 pm) and it was already quite dark. The street was very crowded because of the winter sales. People were pushing and shoving and we were getting tired. But I still hadn't got all the things I wanted, including some presents to take home to my family and for the friends we were staying with in Bonn. Across the road I saw a big department store – I think it was Kaufhof. In fact it was right over the other side of a huge intersection. I thought this would be a good idea for the presents I wanted to buy. My friend said we should use the underpass, but I come from London, so I'm used to traffic and insisted that it would be quicker to use the crossing. We went down to the traffic lights to cross. The 'green man' had been on for some time. My friend ran across safely to the other side, but I dropped a parcel just as I was crossing. By the time I'd stopped to pick it up, the 'green man' had turned to red. I was just about to run across to join my friend when something hit me from the side. I didn't know what had happened. My friend rushed up to me and said that a bike had knocked me down but that it hadn't stopped. In the meantime all the rest of the traffic was still waiting at the lights. Maybe the bike came straight through the middle of the cars waiting there for the lights to change. I didn't see the cyclist, but my friend said it was definitely a man, and that he was wearing a cap and a dark jacket, possibly with a pair of jeans. He had a bag strapped to the back of his bike – like a briefcase of some kind. Maybe his lights weren't working properly either. My friend isn't sure – it all happened so quickly. We waited by the side of the road for about 10 minutes before the ambulance came and took me to hospital.

Examiner's sheet

Situation: As on Candidate's Sheet.

Task 1: You are a German police officer who doesn't understand much English. You are investigating the road accident in which the candidate's sister has been run over. Ask the candidate to tell you what she (the sister) has written in her English report of the accident.

Allow the candidate to talk without interruption, but if s/he fails to cover the main points adequately, or if the information is not clear, intervene with questions.

Remember that this is NOT a translation exercise, and the candidate should not be expected to cover every detail.

The task should not be allowed to continue for more than 5 minutes.

Up to 10 marks to be awarded for task completion (see below for language marks).

Task 2: You want the two English visitors to stay in the vicinity of Bonn for a few more days until you have made some more enquiries (e.g. interview sister again, and her friend, complete some formalities, possibly also identify cyclist, etc.). You also suspect that her behaviour may have contributed to the accident. Try to persuade the candidate and sister to stay around Bonn – but compromise in the end by allowing them to leave the day their insurance and tickets expire.

The task should not be allowed to continue for more than 5 minutes.

Up to 10 marks to be awarded to fask completion.

The remaining 10 marks are to be awarded globally for the quality of the candidate's language in carrying out the two tasks.

Material supplied: Accident report in English.

(ODLE, 1990, A and AS Level)

Some exam boards provide stimulus in German, some in English. Check carefully with your teacher what you can expect in your examination.

TEXT 4:

Greenpeace

Fig. 4.1 Wie konnten Sie es zulassen, daß unsere Erde in so kurzer Zeit vergiftet wurde?

Die Zeit der Regenbogen-kämpfer

'Es wird eine Zeit kommen, da fallen die Vögel von den Bäumen, die Flüsse sind vergiftet, und die Wölfe sterben in den Wäldern.' So lautet eine alte Prophezeiung der Cree-Indianer in Nordamerika. Heute, so sagen die Cree, leben wir in dieser Zeit. Die Profitgier des weißen Mannes beutet die ganze Erde rücksichtslos aus. Überall ist der natürliche Kreislauf des Lebens angegriffen und gestört.

Doch die Boraussage der Cree endet mit Hoffnung: Ist die schlimme Zeit erst da, dann 'werden die Regenbogen-Kämpfer erscheinen, um die Erde zu retten'. Fast zwölf Jahre ist es heute her, daß ein Medizinmann der Cree-Indianer Frauen und Männer von Greenpeace als die langersehnten Regenbogenkämpfer ausrief. Seitdem versuchen die Mitglieder von Greenpeace weltweit, diesem Namen gerecht zu werden.

Doch eine einzelne Gruppe kann nicht die Erde retten. Viele Menschen aller Nationen müssen mithelfen, die Prophezeiung der Cree-Indianer zu erfüllen.

„Was wir heute für die Umwelt tun, stellt die Weichen für unsere Zukunft und die Zukunft unserer Kinder. Von ihnen haben wir diese Erde nur geliehen. Eines Tages gehört sie ganz der nächsten und übernächsten Generation. Wir tragen Verantwortung für den Zustand, in dem wir unseren Kindern die Erde überlassen. Alle Lebewesen der Erde, Pflanzen, Tiere und Menschen, stehen in Beziehung zueinander. In seiner Rede an den US-Präsidenten im Jahre 1854 sprach der Indianerhäuptling Seattle: 'Alle Dinge teilen denselben Atem – das Tier, der Baum, der Mensch – sie alle teilen denselben Atem." Der Mensch ist nicht die Krone der Schöpfung, sondern ein Teil von ihr. Er kann sich die Natur nicht untertan machen und sie ausbeuten, ohne selbst darunter zu leiden."

Leben und Überleben sind nur möglich, wenn alle Lebewesen in einer ausgewogenen Beziehung zuein-ander stehen. Doch dieses ausgewogene Verhältnis gibt es nicht mehr. Der Mensch hat das ökologische Gleichgewicht durch die Vergiftung von Flüssen. Seen und Meeren, die Verschmutzung der Luft und die Ausrottung vieler Tierarten empfindlich gestört. Jeden Tag stirbt eine Tierart aus, jede

Stunde eine Pflanzenart. Der hemmungslose Raubbau an der Natur macht die Erde immer ärmer und unbewohnbarer.

Darum müssen wir jetzt handeln. Nicht nur jeder für sich im privaten Bereich, sondern auch gemeinsam mit Greenpeace. Gemeinsam mit Greenpeace können wir an den lebensnotwendigen Veröanderungen arbeiten, die wir für eine Zukunft in einer gesunden Welt brauchen.

Was ist Greenpeace?
'Green' bedeuten 'grün', 'Peace' ist auf englisch der Frieden. Greenpeace heißt also 'Grüner Frieden'.

Greenpeace ist eine internationale Umweltschutz-organisation. Sie ist unabhängig und überparteilich. Seit 1971 arbeiten Greenpeace-Grupen in aller Welt, inzwischen in 17 Ländern der Erde. Mit gewaltfreien, direkten Aktionen setzen sich Greenpeacer gegen die weitere Vergiftung und Zerstörung des Lebens auf der Welt ein. 1984 erhielt Greenpeace für sein Wirken den Gustav-Heinemann-Preis.

'Erst wenn der letzte Baum gerodet, der letzte Fluß vergiftet, der letzte Fisch gefangen, werdet ihr feststellen, daß man Geld nicht essen kann!'

(USLEB, 1991)

TEXT 5:
The following advertisement aims to raise money for German sportsmen and sportswomen. Study the material carefully and be prepared to answer questions on its content and issues arising from it.

Spenden Sie dem deutschen Sport mehr als Beifall

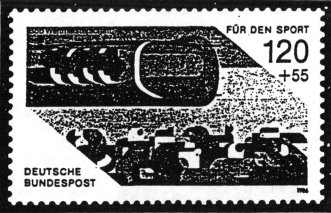

Fig. 4.2

(AEB, June 1991)

Training, Stipendien, Ausrüstung. Spitzenleistung kostet Geld. Nur unter optimalen Voraussetzungen können unsere Sportler gegen die Besten der Welt bestehen. Porto-Zuschläge für die Deutsche Sporthilfe bringen sie weiter.
Sporthilfe-Briefmarken gibt es beim Postamt. Oder direkt von der Stiftung Deutsche Sporthilfe, Otto-Fleck-Schneise 12, 6000 Frankfurt am Main 71.

TEXT 6:

Was Frauen und Männer im Fernsehen begeistert und was sie nicht ausstehen können

Absolut einig sind sich Männer und Frauen nur in einem: Kirchliche Sendungen stehen an erster Stelle – wenn es darum geht, was im Fernsehen wenig Gefallen findet. HÖRZU wollte genau wissen, wie sich die Gunst beim TV-Programm verteilt, und ließ in einer repräsentativen Untersuchung 1087 Männer und Frauen befragen. Ergebnis: Vor dem Bildschirm träumt das starke Geschlecht immer noch davon, die Fäden in der Hand zu halten. 'Männer identifizieren sich mit den Helden, um so ihre Sehnsüchte zu befriedigen', erklärt der Psychologe Dr. Rainer Richter die Vorliebe der Männer für Abenteuerfilme. Ganz traditionell auch die Frauen. Richter: 'Tiere werden oft im Familienverbund gezeigt, und das spricht stark weibliche Wünsche an.'

Frauen

Sensatio-
nen aus
der Natur:
Tierfilmer
Sielmann
mitt Löwe

Beliebt

1. Tierreportagen faszinieren 48 Prozent aller Frauen, weil hier 'so schön anrührende Bilder' gezeigt werden.
2. Reiseberichte lieben 47 Prozent der Zuschauerinnen,. besonders über feme Länder. Grund: 'Im Urlaub bekommt man die Einheimischen ja meistens gar nicht zu sehen. So komme ich ihnen wenigstens mal nah.'
3. Musiksendungen schalten 42 Prozent der Frauen ein, weil 'Musik beruhigt und gute Laune macht' und 'man bei den zärtlichen Liedern so herrlich träumen kann'.
4. Krimis reizen 39 Prozent. Der Nervenkitzel begeistert die Frauen, aber auch, daß 'man bei den dollsten Gaunereien dabei ist, ohne ins Gefängnis zu müssen'.

Langwei-
liges aus
der Kirche:
Bischof
Sterzinsky
zelebreirt

Unbeliebt

1. Kirchliche Sendungen mögen 42 Prozent nicht. Wichtigste argumente gegen religiöse Themen auf dem Bildschirm: 'Moralpredigten' und pastorale 'Weltfremdheit'.
2. Kriegsfilme lehnen 40 Prozent der Frauen ab. Einhelige Meinung: vei zuviel Gewalt, die in vielen Filmen auch noch verherrlicht wird.
3. Sexstreifen verabscheuen 38 Prozent des weiblichen Publikums, weil sie diese Filmchen nicht erotisch, sondern 'widerlich' und 'billig' finden.
4. Fußball – 'die ewige Kickerei ödet mich an', sagen 37 Prozent und verlassen den Raum, wenn der Mann guckt.

Männer

Abenteurer
Cartouche
(Bemondo)
mit
Odile
Versois

Beliebt

1. Abenteuerfilme erinnern 48 Prozent des männlichen Publikums an ihre Kinderträume und an Karl-May-Bücher: 'In jedem Mann steckt die Lust auf Abenteuer.'
2. Fußball begeistert 47 Prozent, weil sie Fans sind und sich vor dem Fernseher 'so herrlich aufregen können'.
3. Krimis lieben 45 Prozent. Aber nicht nur, weil sie spannend sind. Sondern auch, weil die Herren den Bürofrust abschütteln, wenn 'Schimanski so richtig aufräumt'.
4. Nachrichten interessieren 42 Prozent der Zuschauer. Die Gründe: Aus Zeitmangel kommen die meisten nicht zum Zeitunglesen, und das Fernsehen 'geht hautnah an die Geschehnisse heran'.

Undurch-
sichtig:
„Magnum"
Tom
Selleck mit
Ferrari

Unbeliebt

1. Kirchliche Sendungen lehnen auch die Männer ab. 47 Prozent schalten lieber ab, ween das Fernsehen konfessionelle Lebenshilfe bieten will.

2. Amerikanische Serien finden 40 Prozent überflüssig: 'Immer diese Forsetzungen – mal kann ich's sehen, mal nicht. Dann versteh' ich nicht mehr, wer gerade gegen wen intrigiert.'

3. Volkstheater mögen 32 Prozent nicht, weil sie 'die Dialekte nicht verstehen' und 'diese Art von Theater veraltet ist'.

4. Prominenten-Interviews sind langweilig, meinen 31 Prozent der Zuschauer. 'Ob Politiker oder Schauspieler, die sagen doch alle nicht die Wahrheit.'

(OCSEB, 1991)

TEXT 7:

Study the advertisement below and then, in German, explain the main points to the examiner.

You must not translate the advertisement but you may refer to it if you wish.

To the Aztecs, there was nothing quite as good as gold.

With one possible exception. Chocolate.

Consumed almost exclusively by the ruler Emperor Montezuma and his court, it was taken in the form of a cold, sugarless drink called 'cacahuatl'.

A concoction that may seem pretty unappetising to our refined palates, until one is reminded that the Aztecs lived in what is now known as Mexico.

And the only thing hotter than the climate was the food.

In those heady times, chocolate was held in such high esteem it was drunk only from solid gold goblets.

And only on feast days and special occasions at that.

Which, in the case of the Montezuma's court, appears to be about 50 times a day.

(With a goblet of chocolate in the offing, special occasions were not thin on the ground.)

Remarkably, the contents of such a goblet were held to be of greater value than the goblet itself.

Something that's still true of our chocolate today, some 500 years later.

Though to be honest, we do wrap

Cadbury's Bournville rather more modestly in a glittering gold foil.

(Gold leaf at around £4,030 a lb is a little hard to swallow. Even for the likes of Bournville.)

Eating chocolate has only been with us since Victorian times.

And Cadbury's Bournville has changed remarkably little since it

was first introduced in 1908.

Which is why we think we can justifiably claim it to be the original plain chocolate.

TO BE HONEST, THE IDEA OF ENCASING CHOCOLATE IN GOLD WASN'T ONE OF OURS.

Chocolate wrapping courtesy of the Aztecs, 1488.

Chocolate wrapping courtesy of Cadbury's, 1988.

Indulge in a bar.

Notice how the initial crisp clean bite develops into a warm rich sensation you need to take your time over.

Then while you're savouring its luxurious taste, spare a thought for that ancient Aztec ruler, Montezuma.

Had he been asked to choose between a bar of gold and a bar of Bournville, it would have been' no contest.

He'd have settled for the chocolate every time.

Cadbury's **Bournville**
The Original Plain Chocolate.

Fig. 4.4

(JMB, 1990)

DISCUSSING A LITERARY, CULTURAL OR BACKGROUND TOPIC

❛❛ Some useful hints for literary, cultural or background discussions ❜❜

Because the choice of topic is left with the candidate, there are no exam papers for this part of the Speaking Test. However, study of the reports on the examinations does yield some information about pitfalls to avoid in the choice of topic and the presentation of it. In any event, you should be guided by your teacher, who will know exactly what your exam board currently requires, and will steer you in the right direction.

As a guide, though, do:

- Choose a topic which interests you – perhaps one which feeds off another subject you are studying. Enthusiasm is catching.
- Choose a topic on which you have access to source material in German – attempts at translating lengthy pieces of English into German are often unsucessful. And you lose the benefit of seeing how the relevant vocabulary is used in context.
- Consider bringing something related to the topic to show the examiner if this is allowed (an obvious example is to bring pictures of paintings if you have chosen an artistic topic).
- Consider making brief prompt notes on a piece of card if this is allowed.

Some exam boards specifically recommend that you do not use the same topic for more than one A Level language – they cite evidence that candidates seem stale and are led to use English-based sources.

What is also useful is to put yourself in the examiner's shoes. List the questions that you would ask about your chosen topic if you were examining someone, and prepare answers to them. A mock examination can be especially instructive, especially if recorded on cassette. Don't waste the opportunity by being ill-prepared for it.

REVIEW SHEET

1. Here are some further opportunities for you to practise rôle-plays. Imagine that you are visiting your German exchange partner, **Jürgen**, in Dortmund when each of these situations arises. Say what it seems natural to say in each situation.

a) You've just heard that Jurgen's friend has lost his job. What do you say to him?

b) Jurgen is giving a party. You've just notice that one of the guests is standing all alone looking rather lost. What do you say to him?

c) You see a young boy taking photographs, but he's forgotten to take the cap off the lens of his camera. What do you say?

d) Walking home one evening you see a woman trying to push her car off the road. What do you say?

e) A friend of Jürgen tells you that her brother has just been accepted for Cambridge University. What do you say?

f) You see a friend who never has much money geting out of a chauffeur-driven Mercedes. What do you say to him?

g) You see something in the window of an antique shop. You would like to buy it buy you don't know what it's called in English. What do you say?

h) Jürgen's friend has just come back from a holiday abroad. He now has his leg in plaster. What do you say?

i) Your car breaks down on a country road. You walk to a nearby house. Whay do you say to the woman who comes to the door?

j) Some friends of Jürgen have asked you to babysit for them. Their children are not very well-behaved. Say no, but nicely.

k) You are watching television with some friends. You go to the kitchen to make coffee for them. When you come back, they've changed over from the programme you wanted to see. What do you say?

l) You know Jürgen's neighbours are on holiday. In the middle of the night, you hear noises coming from their house. You ring the police. What do you say?

m) You're in a plane travelling from Dortmund to Berlin sitting in a NO SMOKING area. The man in front of you lights a cigarette. What do you say?

2. Look again at Text 3. This time get a friend to play the part of the candidate discussing his sister's report of the accident. *You* play the part of the German police officer (see the Examiner's Sheet).

3. Look again at the advertisement in Text 7. this time explain to a (real or imagined) listener what type of chocolate *you* prefer the most, and why. Also discuss any differences you may have noticed between the types of chocolate on sale in England and those on sale in Germany.

4. Study the advertisement below and then, in German, explain the main points in the advertisement.

Weil die Zahl der Schulabgänger zurückgegangen ist, sind die Lehrlinge knapp geworden. Tratzdem können manche Betriebe problemlos ihre Ausbildungsplätze besetzen. Wie machen sie das?

Sie reagieren flexible und mit neuen Ideen auf die Marktsituation. Und sie fragen sich ganz pragmatisch, wer alles für eine Ausbildung in Frage kommt.

Muß es unbedingt ein einserschüler sein? Ist nur ein Junge geeignet? Muß es ein Deutscher sein? Ist die körperliche Unversehrtheit Eine unabdingbare Voraussetzung?

Wenn Sie auf die veränderte Marktlage geschickt eingehen, können sie Ausbildungs-engpässe vermeiden.

Sprechen Sie auch mit Jugendlichen,. die eine Ausbildung abgebrochen ader bisher ganz dorauf verzichtet haben. Geben Sie auch Mädchen in angeblichen Männerberufen eine Chance.

Nutzen Sie die große Motivation von Aussiedlern und Übersiedlern. Sehen Sie Sprachprobleme von Ausländern nicht als Hindernis an – die jungen Leute sprechen bald fließend deutsch.

Nehmen Sie auch etwas ältere Bewerber. Und bieten Sie auch ungelernten Kräften, die schon in Ihrem Betrieb arbeiten, einen Ausbildungsplatz an – mit einer verkürzten Ausbildungszeit und angemessenen Konditionen.

In jedem Fall lohnt sich ein Gespräch mit dem Arbeitsamt.

5. Imagine that you are *one* of the characters in the story below. Tell the story to your friend (real or imagined) in German.

6. Do the same as in question 5. above, but this time imagine that you are a *different* character in the story.

7. Describe the main points in the newspaper report below to a friend (in German).

Spinne irritierte Fahrer: Wagen überschlug sich
Bad Honnef. Eine kleine Spinne war die Ursache eines schweren Verkehrsunfalls am Samsag in Bad Honnef. Ein Autofahrer bemerkte plötzlich das Tier auf seiner Hand, erschrak und versuchte mit einer heftigen Bewegung, es abzuschütteln.

Dabei riß er das Steuer nach rechts, der Wagen prallte gegen die seitliche Böschung, wurde zurück auf die Straße geschleudert und rutschte über die Gegenfahrbahn links von der Straße. Dort überschlug er sich mehrfach und geriet in ein Waldstück hinein. Der Wagen schlitterte an zehn Bäumen vorbei und blieb schließlich völlig zerstört auf dem Dach liegen. Fahrer und Spinne krochen unverletzt aus dem Autowrack.

8. You have received this letter from your pen friend in Germany. You telephone him at home. Using German develop an appropriate conversation with him.

> Fulda, den 10. Juni
>
> Lieben Michael,
>   vielen Dank für den letzten Brief und für die Einladung. Ich glaube, alles klappt. Du kommst am 28. Juli zu uns hier in Fulda und dann fahren wir im August nach Manchester zusammen.
>   Schreib uns bitte die Flugnummer und wohin Du fliegst – die ganze Familie möchte da sein, wenn Du ankommst!
>   Fliegst Du gern? Ich fahre lieber mit dem Zug. Weißt Du schon jetzt, was Du während Deines Aufenthaltes machen möchtest? Wir haben ja genug Zeit, alles im voraus zu planen, wenn Du uns die Pläne in Deinem nächsten Brief schreiben könntest.
>   Wir freuen uns sehr auf Deinen Besuch.
>   Bis bald,
>   Tschüß
>   Gerd
> P.S. Wie war das Wochenende in Yorkshire?

5

WRITING

GETTING STARTED

Writing accurate German is probably the most difficult skill to master at A Level. The Germans themselves find it difficult to be 100% accurate, and will often tell you Deutsche Sprache, schwere Sprache. However, the more accurate your written German, the higher your final grade is likely to be. Because Writing is the hardest of the skills, those that can do it reasonably well will find it informs and improves their performance in other areas.

As with all other skills, constant practice and review will pay dividends. With Writing as with Speaking, there is no point in attempting to make up for two years' work in the last few days before the examination. Only constant practice will ensure progress!

Written accuracy is, of course, measured at GCSE where it accounts for 25% of the marks. Many courses which preceded the GCSE laid even greater stress on the written word (up to 70%). Older teachers often say that there is a 'bridging exercise' to be done after GCSE for those taking A Level. There is something in that view as far as writing is concerned. But experience (and the rising number and quality of A Level and AS Level results) suggest that the gap is perfectly bridgeable, and that the benefits GCSE brings in candidates' Listening and Speaking skills more than compensate for a few features of the written language which now have to be taught in the Lower Sixth.

If you are taking AS, there is much less writing involved in the final examination. However, it is certainly true that writing things down is amongst the major tools for learning a language, and AS candidates should beware of thinking that they need never write anything!

Of course the Grammar Chapters (7 and 8) will contain many practical suggestions to help you develop your writing skills. The Literature/Civilisation/Culture Chapter (Ch. 6) and the Vocabulary Chapter (Ch. 9) are also highly relevant to improving your writing.

WRITING AS A SKILL

GETTING IT RIGHT

ESSAY WRITING

SAMPLE ESSAY TITLES

TRANSLATION INTO GERMAN

TACKLING TRANSLATIONS

COURSEWORK

ESSENTIAL PRINCIPLES

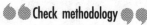

WRITING AS A SKILL

Modern German was the first of the European languages to be printed, and Martin Luther's translation of the Bible into German was the first best-seller. While the language has obviously progressed and developed since the 16th century, Luther's German has shaped the modern forms to a considerable extent.

Writing is a skill which has obvious practical uses, and it deserves an important place in an A Level syllabus. Those who write accurately in a foreign language show:

- that they are quite clear about how all the grammatical rules operate,
- that they have a fair vocabulary,
- that they have a grasp of idiom, and know when direct equivalents are inappropriate,
- that they know what they can say successfully, and have the sense to avoid that which they are not so sure of,
- that they can give sustained attention to detail in progressing from a first draft to a final, polished version.

What you show by your writing skills

No matter which exercise in Writing is being done, the above apply. Because there is wide variation in the sorts of exercise specified by each exam board, you would be particularly well advised to check in detail with your teacher what to expect. This chapter contains hints and advice on Essays in German, Translation into German, and Use of German, as well as a summary of checking strategies.

GETTING IT RIGHT

English-speakers have little difficulty with writing German down at dictation – less, actually, than many Germans – but do need to remember that the Umlaut can be a crucial conveyor of meaning, and that missing it out (or inserting it incorrectly) can be very confusing. This is particularly true of plurals and conditionals/passives. So the first message of this section is: make sure you overcome the 'Umlaut-blindness' of the English-speaker.

Pay attention to the Umlaut

Check methodology

The second message is get methodical about checking. This is particularly true for work done at home or with reference materials to hand. Writing the first draft takes a small fraction of the time needed to produce a decent piece of written work in German. The following scheme has proved helpful, and references are given to the appropriate pages in the Grammar Chapters.

(i) **Check genders**
- by applying gender rules (page 134)
- by looking up individual words

(ii) **Check cases**
- is there an Accusative after each verb?
- if not, do you know why not? (page 129)
- are they right after each preposition? (page 141)

(iii) **Check adjectives**
- if they are not followed by a noun, they should not have an ending (page 123)
- if they are followed by a noun, do they have the correct ending for:
- following der, ein or nothing
- the case of the noun
- the gender of the noun
- singular or plural? (page 124)

A useful checklist when writing German

(iv) **Check verbs**
- is the tense right in each instance? (page 156)
- is it weak or strong? (page 157)
- is the form of the verb right? (page 158)
- does it need haben or sein? (page 160)

(v) **Check word order**
- is the verb in the right place? (second idea or at end of clause) (page 152)
- are time, manner, place in that order? (page 153)
- are DAN and PAD right? (page 154)

(vi) **Check spelling**
- capital letters on nouns?

> – *e* and *i* always the right way round?
> – Umlauts where needed?
> – no Umlauts over *e* or *i*?
> – no words hyphenated over line ends? (rules are complex in German)
> – *ß* and *ss* correct? (page 148)
> – *-sch* always with a *c*?

(vii) **Check punctuation**
> – commas only for subordinate clauses and lists? (page 149)
> – speech marks in the right places? (page 150)

Learn from past mistakes

Finally, remember to review work which has been marked and analyse the errors so you can bear them in mind next time you write. A successful student of mine had a *Fehlerheft* into which all errors, their causes, and the correct version were carefully written. Needless to say, the number of entries soon dwindled to nearly nothing; the Fehlerheft had done its job.

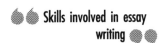
ESSAY WRITING

Skills involved in essay writing

Writing an **essay** of 250–350 words in German is an exercise intended to test three things:

- your ability to write correct and idiomatic German in a formal register,
- your ability, in a fairly short space, to construct an essay in response to a task set using a clear structure,
- your ability to use an appropriate range of vocabulary and structures.

Writing in correct and idiomatic German obviously requires a sound understanding of how to get the German right. But there are several basic strategies which can assist in this.

First, make a distinction between the work you do for your teacher during your A Level course and the work you do in the actual exam. It is clearly stupid to use constructions and vocabulary which you are not sure of in the exam. The time for

Experiment during the course, not the exam

experimentation and linguistic risk-taking is earlier. In work you do for your teacher, it is, however, permissible, to see if something does in fact work. On the other hand, it is even better if you are able to check areas you are not sure of before including them in a finished piece of work.

Pay attention to any stimulus materials you are given on a topic

Second, make sure you use the stimulus material you have been given on a topic as a source of relevant vocabulary and structures. There is no point in starting from scratch and looking up everything you need to say 'cold' in a dictionary. Nevertheless you will need to use the checking strategies you have developed for written work to ensure that, when 'lifting' material you have been able to include it correctly in your writing. In particular you should beware of changed cases, and should note that ein can be either masculine nominative or neuter nominative or accusative.

Thirdly, after receiving back a piece of written work, make sure you do more than just look at the mark on the bottom. Analyse your performance:

- Are the mistakes consistent?
- Are they the result of carelessness or of some point you did not know?

Note the causes of mistakes and determine not to repeat them. Referring to an analysis of previous work can give you useful information next time you write, indicating where your personal weaknesses lie.

Fourthly, make sure you are familiar with a variety of approaches to planning your essay. The principles are exactly the same as for writing Literature or Civilisation/Background essays. The four main types are:

Planning your essay will help

- For and against.
- Analysis of features.
- Development.
- Compare and contrast.

Look also at Chapter 6 for essay planning

See Chapter 6 for a more complete description of the various possible sorts of essay plan. However, given that the amount of space available to you is strictly limited, it is even more important to be quite strict with yourself about how much you write on each topic in the examination.

Finally, you will need to develop a repertoire of 'essay phrases'. A useful set is given in the Vocabulary chapter, but you could also start your own lists.

SAMPLE ESSAY TITLES

The titles set are of several distinct types. They include describing or commenting on a contemporary social problem, tackling a topic in the arts, completing a narrative, or occasionally writing a dialogue. All the examples given are similar to titles which have been set at A Level in the 1990s.

(a) Contemporary social questions

> The types of essay which might be set

- Untersuchen Sie die Rolle der ausländischen Arbeitnehmer in der Bundesrepublik seit 1961.
- Welche Probleme und welche Gelegenheiten bietet die Wiedervereinigung Deutschlands der deutschen Industrie?
- Könnte man heute ohne das Auto leben?
- Wie beinflußen Fernseh- und Videofilme Kinder und Jugendliche?
- Vergleichen Sie das deutsche und das englische Schulsystem. Welches ziehen Sie vor, und warum?
- Die Ossis sind die neuen Gastarbeiter.

(b) A topic in the arts

- Welcher deutschsprachige Komponist der letzten vier Jahrhunderte ist Ihrer Meinung nach der wichtigster?
- Was ist Ihnen in einem guten Drama wichtig?

(c) Completing a narrative

- Wir waren bei unseren Freunden eingeladen, und saßen beim Abendessen, als das Telefon klingelte. Sobald Uschi den Hörer abhob, wurde sie ganz blaß. Etwas Schreckliches war passiert.' Erzählen Sie weiter.

(d) Writing a dialogue

- Schreiben Sie einen Dialog zwischen einem Verkehrspolizisten und einem Motorradfahrer, der sich verkehrswidrig verhalten hat.
- Erfinden Sie ein Streitgespräch zwischen einem Ossi und einem nicht-deutschen Ayslanten.

At this stage it may help to look at an actual student's answer to an essay question, with examiner comments on that answer.

STUDENT'S ANSWER WITH EXAMINER'S COMMENTS

Question

Die Werbung – Fluch oder Segen?

(1) Angeblich ist die Wirtschaftswerbung (daß heißt die Reklame im Gegensatz zur politischer Werbung, die Propaganda heißt) ein Fluch unserer modernen Gesellschaft, weil sie die Menschen veranlaßt, über ihre Verhältnisse zu leben und (2) macht sie habgierig und niedisch. Die Werbung sowohl beinflußt die

sie

Menschen als ihnen (3) zu informieren. Auf der anderen Seite jedoch, stellt der Welt der Werbung die Öffentlichkeit (4) mit vielen Stellen zur Verfügung.

Firmen und Wirtschaftsunternehmen, die ihren Absatz steigern wollen, wollen Menschen durch Reklame zum Kauf ihrer Produkte bewegen. Die Werbung hilft ihnen größeren wirtschaftlichen Erfolg, größere Umsätze und größeren Profit zu erreichen, weil sie sowohl den Verbrauch in bestimmmte Richtungen lenken kann, als auch ganz neue Bedürfnisse wecken. (5)

t   Man finde(6) die Werbung überall – in den
im Werbespots des Werbefunks, ~~am~~ (7) Fernsehen, im Kino, wo Reklamefilme gezeigt werden, und auch in ~~die~~ (8) Zeitungen und Zeitschriften, die wahrscheinlich ohne Anzeigenwerbung gar nicht existieren könnten. Viele
s Menschen zeigen die "T-shirts", (9) die mit einem Werbeslogan oder gar einem längeren Werbetext verziert sind. Ohne Reklamefächen, Neonschilder und erleuchtete Schaufenster, die Tausende von begehrenswerten Produkten zeigen, sähe es in unseren Städten sicher trüber aus.

Ich denke daß (10) das Bild von unmündigen, durch die Werbung manipulierten, überreizten, verwirrten und verunsicherten Menschen wohl übertrieben ist. Außerdem gibt es viele Gesetze, die die Freiheit der Werbung (schränken) ein, (11) damit kann die Werbung psychologische Umweltverschmutzung nicht sein. (12)

Examiner comments

1. Good introduction – states the case for and against clearly.
2. Even though there is an *und* there, the verb macht still depends on the earlier *weil* and therefore goes to the end of the clause. If you write a more complex sentence, have a good look round if you use an *und* for any reason which might nevertheless send the verb to the end of the clause.
3. Accusative pronoun after *informieren*.
4. You had spotted that zur Verfügung stellen requires a Dative, but you had got the Dative and Accusative the wrong way round!
5. Sensible use of stimulus material to generate a paragraph which is virtually error-free.
6. A slip here – correct verb form is *findet*.
7. An idiom which you could be expected to know is *im Fernsehen*. Think of the speakers as sitting inside the box!
8. No definite article needed here. There wouldn't have been one in English either. Remember that ninety-nine times out of a hundred the use of the definite article is the same in English as in German. Forget everything your French teacher told you!
9. English words often retain their -s plural in German.
10. Punctuation: the comma goes before the *daß*.
11. Although *einschränken* is a separable verb, it does of course join together again when it has been sent to the end of the clause.
12. Conclusion sound.

TRANSLATION INTO GERMAN

Overall Comment: This is a very sound essay for one written under examination conditions. It has a very clear structure, a good range of vocabulary, and is, on the whole, accurate. It is free of repetition and cliché and expresses an original line of thought

This exercise is also known as 'prose translation', and is set by some boards in order to test a range of structures in context. For some, it may even become a useful professional skill. From the examiner's point of view, it does provide quite a good measure of exactly how competent you are in dealing with a range of structures. It also shows whether you have been able to learn how to get round certain difficulties of finding direct equivalents in German for English constructions and phrases. Finally, it is a good test of your ability to proof-read your own work for accuracy.

Perhaps the most light-hearted way of approaching translation into German is to treat the exercise as a form of crossword puzzle. During your course you will be able to extend your repertoire of clues you know the answer to, and will, hopefully, be in a position to deal with the examination piece without too much bother.

PITFALLS

The inexperienced translator into German will often fall into one or more of the following traps:

(a) Failing to recognise that, although English has three versions of every tense, German has only one.
So *ich gehe* can translate
(i) I go
(ii) I am going
and even
(iii) I do go
The most common – and crass – error is to translate both the parts of the English continuous form with something like **ich bin gehen* or **ich bin gehend*. Make sure you do not commit this error – it's every examiner's pet hate!!

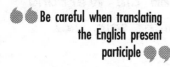
German has only one version of each tense

(b) Clumsy or incorrect translation of the English present participle *-ing*.
There is a variety of ways of doing this explained in the Grammar Chapter page 187. Poor renditions such as: **sehend, daß du da bist* for 'Seeing that you are here' do not impress.

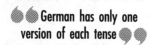
Be careful when translating the English present participle

(c) Mistakes in word order.
Remembering which conjunctions send the verb to the end of the clause is not that difficult if you know that *und, aber, oder, sondern* and *denn* don't, but all others do. Sometimes students are not sure how to deal with a complex sentence with a number of subordinate clauses. What one should try to avoid is a sentence which is like a set of Russian dolls with one clause inside another. A good trick is to look for a point in a longer sentence at which you could split it into two. Finally, the rule that the verb is the second idea in the sentence is often overlooked, especially after speech marks.

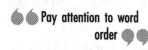
Pay attention to word order

(d) Not knowing if verbs are strong or weak.
Students often make mistakes in verb forms which are caused by them not knowing whether the verb is strong or weak. If you know the 40 or so most common strong verbs, the odds are that new words are weak, most especially if their past participle ends in *-t*. Past participles ending in *-en* are all of strong verbs. And, if you have reference books available, if the verb is not in your strong verb table, then it is almost certainly weak! Remember that the vast majority of weak verbs form their perfect tense with *haben*.

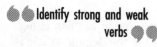
Identify strong and weak verbs

(e) Incorrect choice of tense.
The majority of passages for translation use past tenses, although they may also use present and future and conditional forms, especially inside speech marks. You should be aware that the standard narrative tense in the past is the simple

❝❝ Choose the correct tense ❞❞

past, e.g. *er ging, er kaufte* rather than the perfect tense. However, if the passage should happen to be a letter, then the perfect would be appropriate to express meanings in the past.

Many students overlook the difference between 'she *has* gone' and 'she *had* gone', the second of which requires a pluperfect.

(f) Failure to realise that a subjunctive is needed.

❝❝ Pay attention to the subjunctive ❞❞

Particularly in reported speech, candidates often echo the English choice of tenses in their choice of German tenses, where in fact the complex rules governing the German subjunctive need to be brought into play. Be aware that phrases which start on the lines of: He asked her if.../whether.... may require a subjunctive. See page 161 in Chapter 8.

(g) Failure to realise that a passive is needed.

❝❝ Also be alert to the passive ❞❞

The English construction along the lines of 'hockey was played' can mislead candidates into using the *sein*-passive rather than the *wurde*-passive. For a more detailed explanation, see page 163–73 in Chapter 8.

(h) Choice of words for 'you'.

❝❝ Select the appropriate word for 'you' ❞❞

The translation passage is full of traps for the unwary. First, a decision has to be made as to what the characters would call each other if they were speaking German. This requires a good knowledge of the rules governing the use of *Du* and *Sie*. But quite often a situation occurs in which, say, a parent addresses her two children. The astute candidate spots that the *ihr* form is needed. Sometimes the relationship between characters is only fully apparent later in the passage, so it is worth reading the whole thing through carefully for clues. Once you have made your decision, stick to it. Examiners are not impressed by those who jump randomly between *du, ihr* and *Sie*.

(i) Choice of *das* and *daß* for 'that'.

You should be clear that *daß* is only used as a conjunction, and translates *that* only when *which* could not be subsituted without making nonsense. *Das* can be a pronoun, or can be a relative pronoun (and *which* could be substituted for *that*) introducing a clause. Beware of assuming that the relative pronoun has to be neuter.

(j) Over-reliance on '*sein*' and '*haben*' when used other than as auxiliary verbs.

Just as your English teacher will have persuaded you at a young age to extend the range of your verbs beyond 'has' and 'is', the same is true of German. So make sure you are able to provide a few synonyms for *war* and *hatte* in your translations. Keep and update a list.

❝❝ Use the correct ending for adjectives ❞❞

(k) Incompetence with adjective endings.

This is a weakness which translation into German cruelly exposes.

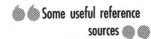

HOW TO TACKLE TRANSLATIONS

For translations you do *during your course*, you should proceed as follows:

❝❝ Some hints for translations tackled during your course ❞❞

- Try a rough version, writing on alternate lines to allow revision later. It is important to be able to attempt an English-German translation without a dictionary if that is how you will have to do it in the final exam.
- Check the rough version using the guidelines on checking given earlier in this chapter on pages 86–7.
- Check again using the guidance given above on pitfalls as a reference
- Check using works of reference. The most useful are:

Any German–English, English–German dictionary of Penguin book size or larger. If you have looked something up, and are not sure you have chosen the right word from list of synoyms, look the German words up in the German-English section.

❝❝ Some useful reference sources ❞❞

Farrell: *Dictionary of German Synonyms* (Cambridge University Press). Words are listed under English head-words, and common confusions between the meanings of similar words are explained with clear examples.

Stern and Novak: *A Handbook of English-German Idioms and Useful Expessions* (Harcourt Brace Jovanovich). Words are listed under English head-words, and very clear examples are given of how they are used.

Cassell's *Advanced Learner's Dictionary of Modern German*. Words are listed under German head-words, with a clear English explanation of their exact usage and meaning.

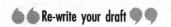 Re-write your draft

Duden Stilwörterbuch. Words are listed under German head-words, with examples in German to show how they are used in a comprehensive range of circumstances. Tricky at first, but fascinating – and addictive – to use, and the standard authority on good contemporary German usage.

■ Re-write your draft as a neat copy, being careful to check that for every sentence in the original you have written an equivalent in German. A good method of preventing the loss of marks by stupid omissions is to tick off each sentence of the original in pencil when checking.

■ If possible, leave your final version for a day or two and re-read it again. It is amazing how many errors you find on a second reading! And parliament reads its legislation at least three times....

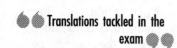 Translations tackled in the exam

In an *exam*, the principles are much the same, except that you do not have the reference material to hand. It may be wise to ensure that your first draft is legible enough to be handed in after you have corrected it in case you get short of time later in the exam. It is also worth knowing how long it takes you to copy up a passage of German of the length your exam board sets (typically a couple of hundred words or so) so that you can allow yourself enough time and a few minutes over for a final check.

In an examination, part of the difficulty is in knowing what to write when you don't know an item of vocabulary. One thing is sure: a blank will definitely score nothing, so you might just as well enter your best guess, perhaps using what you know about word formation to help you. Some candidates give the examiner a choice of words in the hope that one will be right. Sadly, this loses marks, as the exercise is designed to test whether *you* know which one fits.

Finally, although you will not be able to leave an examination translation into German a couple of days before final proof-reading, there is something to be said for tackling it in the early part of the examination and doing some other exercise before giving it a final check. Just because an exercise is number 3 on the paper, that is no absolute reason for doing it third!

STUDENT'S ANSWER WITH EXAMINER'S COMMENTS

Question: Translate into German:

> After walking the streets of Manchester for an hour, Brian came back and collected his old Ford. Then he drove back to his home. He was a puzzled man. He could not understand why he felt so little excitement about his enormous success. If this sort of thing had happened to him last year he would have gone mad with excitement.
>
> What was really odd was that he didn't feel excited at all. He felt melancholy. Somehow it had all been too easy. There was no thrill, no danger of losing. He knew of course that he could now travel the country and make millions. But was he going to have fun?

Student Answer

> *Nachdem(1) er in (2) den Straßen von Manchester seit einer Stunde gebummelt hatte, kam Brian zurück und holte seine (3) alten(4) Ford. Dann fuhr er nach Hause. Er war verwirrt. Er konnte nicht verstehen, warum er sich so wenig über seinen Erfolg freute (5). Vor drei Jahren, wenn ihm so etwas passiert hätte (6), wäre er vor (7) Freude wahnsinnig geworden.*
>
> *Was wirklich komisch war, war die Tatsache (8), das (9) er sich überhaupt nicht aufgeregt fühlte. Er fühlte (10) traurig. Irgendwie war alles zu einfach gewesen. Es gab kein ....(11) keine Gefahr zu verlieren. Er wüßte naturlich (12) daß er jetzt durch die Landschaft (13) fahren könnte und Millionen machen (14). Aber w?rde es ihm Spaß machen?*

Examiner Comments

1. Neat way of doing an after -ing construction.
2. Germans walk on roads, not in them: *auf.*
3. Cars are masculine in German.
4. The adjective ending should at least match the gender the candidate has chosen. It should be: *seinen alten Ford.*
5. A neat rendering of 'felt so little excitement'.
6. The correct tense of the subjunctive to express the correct sort of condition. But, sadly, *passieren* takes *sein* and it should be *passiert wäre.*
7. Correct use of *vor* together with an emotion. Well done!
8. A nice idiomatic insert, entirely appropriate.
9. Wrong *das – daß* is required.
10. 'To feel' is *sich fühlen.* The student got it right in the previous sentence!
11. Gaps never earn marks.
12. Umlaut blindness has led to the wrong tense of *wußte* and a mis-spelling of *natürlich.* And there is a comma missing before *daß*!
13. Wrong word for 'country' – *Landschaft* means 'scenery'; durch *das Land* is required here.
14. A superior version would be the less ambiguous *Millionen verdienen.*

Despite all the errors this is not the work of a poor candidate. Much of it is correct, and some of the errors are honest enough.

COURSEWORK IN GERMAN

Much of what has been said above concerning checking for accuracy is, of course, very applicable to the production of extended essays as coursework. Further hints about coursework are given in the Chapter on Literature, Civilisation and Background (Ch. 6).

REVIEW SHEET

For each of the following, identify the pitfall you must remember to avoid. In other words, what must you check?

1. der Mann kam ✓ der Mann kamen ✗

   Check that
   _____

   _____

2. die Frau sagte ✓ die Frau sagtest ✗

   Check that
   _____

   _____

3. ich bin ✓ nach Bonn gefahren ich habe ✗ nach Bonn gefahren

   Check that
   _____

   _____

4. als ich in die Schule ging ✓ als ich in die schule gehe ✗

   Check that
   _____

   _____

5. die Bücher ✓ das Bücher ✗
   das Mädchen ✓ die Mädchen ✗

   Check that
   _____

   _____

6. der Mann – er ✓
   die Frau – sie ✓
   das Buch – es ✓

   Check that
   _____

   _____

7. Mein Vater <u>fährt</u> am Donnerstag nach Berlin. ✓
   Am Donnerstag <u>fährt</u> mein Vater nach Berlin. ✓

   Check that
   _____

   _____

8. Ich kann dieses Lied nicht <u>leiden</u>. ✓
    Warum hast du die Platte <u>gekauft</u>? ✓

    Check that
    _____
    _____

The following translations into German will help to remind you of some of the key rules and checklists when writing German.

1. i)   We have neither a cat nor a dog. _____
    ii)   Herr Rabowski is a dentist. _____
    iii)   The cars are not here. _____
    iv)   I am brushing my teeth. _____
    v)   She is my sister. _____
    vi)   Our grandpa is at home. _____
    vii)   These people are hungry. _____
    viii)   Which boy can you see? _____
    ix)   He's got toothache. _____
    x)   Switzerland is beautiful. _____

2. i)   He is learning Italian. _____
    ii)   We used to live in Austria. _____
    iii)   I would like some tomatoes, please. _____
    iv)   Have you bought the house? _____
    v)   I had already left. _____
    vi)   Are you reading the paper? _____
    vii)   I would stay at home, if ... _____
    viii)   They are tired. _____
    ix)   We had already eaten. _____
    x)   What did you find? _____

3. i)   Go home! (all three forms) _____
    ii)   Don't drive so fast! (all three forms) _____
    iii)   Wash your hands! (all three forms) _____
    iv)   Let's stay at home! _____
    v)   She's getting changed. _____
    vi)   He's shaving. _____
    vii)   We are chatting. _____
    viii)   I get up at seven o'clock. _____
    ix)   We watched TV last night. _____
    x)   What have you got in mind today? _____

N.B. For these questions you can check yourself against the answers at the end. Think about the rule involved in each answer.

The following will give you the opportunity of practising writing to a stimulus. Remember to use the checklists outlined earlier in the chapter after writing each piece.

1. You are spending a fortnight abroad as a guest of a German-speaking family.
    You are interested in journalism as a career and you decide to write a piece for the local newspaper editor giving your impressions of the area and the way of life there. Write 250–350 words **IN GERMAN**.

    _____
    _____
    _____
    _____
    _____

_____

_____

_____

_____

_____

2. You are staying with your German pen friend, who asks you to write an article for the school newspaper which is produced by him and his friends. He wants you to describe your home town or region, and he wants you to make it sound lively and interesting enough to attract a large group of applicants for next year's exchange visit. Write about 250 words IN GERMAN, including your own suggestion for a title. Remember to make your account appealing to people of your own age.

_____

_____

3. Imagine that you are any one of the characters portrayed in the story below. Tell the story, in the past, IN GERMAN. Write 250–350 words.

_____

_____

_____

_____

_____

_____

_____

_____

_____

_____

_____

_____

Answers to earlier exercises:

1. i) Wir haben weder Katze noch Hund.
   ii) Herr Rabowski ist Zahnarzt.
   iii) Die Autos (Wagen) sind nicht hier.
   9v) Ich putze mir die Zähne.
   v) Sie ist meine Schwester.
   vi) Unser Opa ist zu Hause.
   vii) Diese Leute sind hungrig.
   viii) Welchen Jungen kannst du sehen?
   ix) Er hat Zahnschmerzen.
   x) Die Schweiz ist schön.

2. i) Er lernt Italienisch.
   ii) Wir wohnten in Österreich.
   iii) Ich möchte bitte Tomaten.
   iv) Haben Sie das Haus gekauft?
   v) Ich war schon abgefahren.
   vi) Lesen Sie die Zeitung?
   vii) Ich würde zu Hause bleiben, wenn...
   viii) Sie sind müde.
   ix) Wir hatten schon gegessen.
   x) Was haben Sie gefunden?

3. i) Geh nach Hause! Geht nach Hause! Gehen Sie nach Hause!
   ii) Fahr (Fahrt, Fahren Sie) nicht so schnell!
   iii) Wasch dir (Wascht euch, Waschen Sie sich) die Hände!
   iv) Bleiben wir zu Hause!
   v) Sie zieht sich um.
   vi) Er rasiert sich.
   vii) Wir unterhalten uns.
   viii) Ich stehe um sieben Uhr auf.
   ix) Wir haben gestern abend ferngesehen.
   x) Was haben Sie heute vor?

LITERATURE, CIVILISATION AND COURSEWORK

GETTING STARTED

While the skills of listening, reading, writing and reading comprehension are familiar to students from GCSE, the **Literature and/or Civilisation** component of A Level is new to most of them. Often students are quite apprehensive about this new area of work, but in fact soon realise that there is nothing magical about it. In the main, much of the value of this part of the course is that it extends your skill at reading comprehension, and, where exam candidates have to write their answers in German, your skill at arguing and writing in German.

As far as the Literature is concerned, its study allows you to read good quality writing in German. A majority of the texts set are twentieth-century. The events of the century in the German-speaking world have determined or reflected the trends in world history (the arms race, the Great War, inflation, the failed Weimar Republic, Nazism, the Second World War, the re-construction, the cold war, iron curtain and Berlin Wall, the assimilation of large numbers of foreigners, the collapse of communism, the development of the European Union, etc.). Unsurprisingly, this has produced a rich harvest of literature, much of it deliberately written in relatively simple language.

The civilisation option, which deals largely with social and historical topics, is interesting for the same reasons as the literature. The texts studied are varied, but all of them mean that you are reading German intended to be read by intelligent Germans. You cannot fail to acquire a wide general knowledge of German-speaking countries.

If you elect to do a **Coursework** option, you may often choose either a literary or a civilisation theme. The benefits of either remain equally valid. In addition, you will be able to use your skills of planning, drafting and re-drafting to produce a really polished piece of work, which can be very satisfying.

So the Literature/Civilisation/Coursework component is quite manageable, and many students find it amongst the most enjoyable parts of their course, providing an outlet for personal in-depth study and individual approaches to problems.

ROLE OF LITERATURE

ESSAY WRITING

STUDYING A TEXT OR A TOPIC

READING LITERARY TEXTS

READING NON-LITERARY TEXTS

SAMPLE QUESTIONS

COURSEWORK

ESSENTIAL PRINCIPLE

The study of a modern language is often perceived as learning to 'speak' it. And of course that is a very useful skill. But unless you live in a German-speaking country, reading German is actually likely to be the most frequently encountered contact with German.

The teaching of modern languages developed as a counterpart to the teaching of the Ancient languages (Latin and Greek) and, until relatively recently, a major focus was on the ability to read the **literature** of the language being learned.

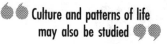

Reasons for studying the literature of the language being learned

The reasoning was that it was important to understand the literature of a country in order to understand what 'made it tick'. In addition, the study of the literature of another country encouraged an appreciation of English literature. And finally, because the literature studied was generally considered to be 'good', the learner of a foreign language learnt it from impeccable sources. This line of reasoning lies behind many of the traditional literature-based available degree courses in Modern Languages. For some students, it certainly does work well.

Culture and patterns of life may also be studied

In more recent times, a reaction to a concentration on literature arose. The reasoning was that there is more to life than literature, and that considerable understanding of the way of life of a foreign country could be gained by studying its history, politics, social arrangements and contemporary fiction and non-fiction writing. Again, the learner is enabled to make comparisons with the state of affairs in his or her own country, and draw conclusions about sensible ways of arranging civilised society. This line of reasoning lies behind many of the non-literary degree courses available.

In practice, at A Level, it makes very little difference to candidates whether literature or civilisation is chosen, provided that it is taught well and authoritatively. What is important is that students should take the opportunity of reading a fair amount of German in context, and should develop skills of analysis. They will also need to be able to perform the sorts of exercise that their examination requires. These will usually include:

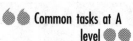

Common tasks at A level

- writing essays,
- responding critically to extracts from literary and non-literary texts,
- for coursework, presenting an extended polished piece of work.

Writing **essays**, whether in English or in German, causes no end of puzzlement amongst students. What are the examiners looking for? And what is the best way of going about providing it?

You develop skills during the course

The first distinction to be made is between essays done *during* the A Level course, which are part of the learning process, and those done in limited time *under examination conditions* and with limited or no reference materials. Essays done during your course are meant to get you to look at particular problems fully. You should expect to spend a good number of hours researching, planning, drafting and writing each one, using a methodical approach, not least so that, come revision time, you have a good class of information available to revise from. When the essay has been marked, some more work is required to see how the notes you have and the conclusions you have reached can be bettered, and to allow you further to polish the quality of your notes and improve your understanding.

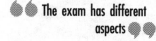

The exam has different aspects

The exam essay is a different animal entirely. Your aim is to communicate in, say, 45 minutes, that you know the text or topic well, can express and justify your opinion, and can muster arguments in response to the problem posed in the title. It will necessarily be much shorter than an essay written while you are 'learning' a topic, but will have a very clear logic which is easy for the examiner to follow. Ideally it should be legible! A useful tip to is get into the habit of writing on alternate lines so that, if you need to change or add something, you have space to do it clearly.

Good preparation for the A Level examination, therefore, will include practice at turning 'learning' essays into timed examination pieces. If this is not done in class, it can most certainly be done at home, and has the merit of being do-able in 45 minutes.

STRUCTURE AND PLANNING

The essentials of a good essay (whether in an examination or as part of the learning process) may be summarised as follows:

It:

Elements of a good essay

- answers the question,
- has a clear structure,
- has evidence proving each assertion made,
- considers other points of view,
- comes to an obvious conclusion or makes it clear why not,
- is written in formal language avoiding errors of style.

The following steps in planning may help. They apply equally to essays on literature or civilisation/background topics.

(a) Read the question carefully

This may seem obvious. But there is much truth in the 'teacher joke': 'if all else fails, read the question'. Questions may include such phrases as:

Common phrases in essay titles

assess the role of...
contrast......with ......
compare.....with .....
discuss the significance of.....
analyse the function of ....
assess the purpose of.....

Put simply, if the question asks you to discuss the significance of something, and you hardly mention it, you are unlikely to score high marks. So there is much to be said for reading questions carefully, especially in the heat of the examination.

If the question consists of a quotation or a statement asking you to discuss it, you have the option of agreeing or disagreeing. Either approach will get the same marks, providing you can prove your view. If, on the other hand, you are asked to write an appreciation of a work of literature or an institution, it is probably more difficult to do a 'demolition job' than to sing its praises. But if you can do a negative critique well it will be well-rewarded by the examiner.

Useful techniques

One technique which can be helpful is to take a phrase or a word out of the title (e.g. is 'unlikely' to) and use it several times in your essay. This helps to keep you from getting off the point. Another technique for preventing 'waffling' is to ask a question and answer it in each paragraph. If the question refers back to the title, so much the better.

The major pitfall to be avoided in literary answers is to re-tell the story of a set book without making any real attempt to answer the particular question. It is safe to assume the examiner has read the book! What is being sought is your ability to analyse the various facets of the topic in the title with reference to the text.

Another feature of weak candidates' literature answers is that they preface their remarks with lengthy details about the author's upbringing and his or her times. For a very few questions this may be relevant. But for most, it simply does not answer the question set. It may be interesting to know the profession of Bertolt Brecht's parents and which day of the week he was born on, but that knowledge hardly adds much to a question about Galileo's motivation in *Das Leben des Galilei*.

(b) Make the structure clear

Many students find planning an essay difficult. The complaint 'I don't know where to begin' is often heard. If you are in that situation, 'brain-storm'. Write down a brief reference to everything you can think of in answer to the essay title on a piece of paper.

Have a clear structure

Then take another piece of paper and re-write them in some kind of order, crossing them off on the original as you go. You may have to have several attempts. But you should be able to determine the best order for the material you have by using this method. Some people find it helpful to use different coloured pens, arrows and diagrams to cheer the whole process up.

Your structure may follow one of the following *patterns*: The suggested percentages of length are for guidance only.

(i) For and against

Introduction	10%
For	40%
Against	40%
Conclusion	10%

(ii) Analysis of features

> **Some patterns you might follow in planning your essay**

Introduction	10%
Feature A	
Feature B	
Feature C	
Feature D (etc.)	
Conclusion	10%

(iii) Compare or contrast

Introduction	10%
X's Feature A compared with Y's Feature A	
X's Feature B compared with Y's Feature B	
X's Feature C compared with Y's Feature C (etc.)	
Conclusion	10%

(iv) Development

Introduction	10%
Change/Event/Development A	
Change/Event/Development B	
Change/Event/Development C	
Change/Event/Development D (etc.)	
Conclusion	10%

It is also good practice to 'flag' the various parts of your structure with such phrases as:

> **Useful phrases for introducing various sections of the essay**

- Let us first consider the arguments in support of the view that....
- So much for arguments in favour of that view. It would also be possible to maintain that .....
- Choice of language is a distinctive feature of X's work.
- Once Y had been established, a demand arose for Z, for the following reasons:
- In conclusion, it seems that the overwhelming weight of evidence suggests that....

(c) Give evidence for assertions

Evidence for the opinions you express must be given. This can be done:

> **Provide evidence wherever possible**

- By alluding to something, e.g. 'as X's hurried return to Berlin by train shows'.
- By relevant quotation, e.g. 'sein übereilter Rückkehr nach Berlin'.
- By referring briefly to something, e.g. 'X's hasty return'.

What is important is to have evidence for every statement. This shows that you have knowledge of the text or the topic, and that you have thought about the significance of each piece of information.

(d) Consider other points of view

Although you may have very clear views on a particular topic, the mark of academic excellence is that the opposite point of view is fully understood, and the reasons for not accepting it are clearly explained.

(e) Come to an obvious conclusion, or make it clear why not

As an academic it is necessary to either come down in favour of one side or other of an argument, or to state clearly that there is no clear decision possible for reasons you give. In some types of essay, especially those following the 'analysis of features' or 'development' models, the conclusion can be a summary of the features and development followed by an expression of opinion.

(g) Use formal language and suitable style

Examiners frequently comment on the following features of candidates' work.

(i) Spelling

Increasingly there is emphasis on the correct spelling of English in examinations, and there is no doubt that those who spell incorrectly create a worse impression than those who spell correctly. Where the answers or coursework are written in German, the same applies, although UCLES overlooks it in its Thematic Studies paper if the content of the answer is comprehensible.

Common mis-spellings include:

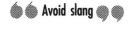
Common spelling errors

argument
attempt
commitment
definite
foregoing
fulfilment
misinterpret
perturbing
turbulent

(ii) Use of slang

The convention is that slang is avoided in formal essays. That means you need to develop an awareness of which expressions from your everyday speech are in fact slang. Indeed some teachers use everyday language when discussing texts or topics with students in order to be sure that students can relate easily to the issues. But the spoken word is not always acceptable when written down.

The sort of thing to be avoided might include:

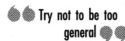
Avoid slang

Dr von Zahnd really *gave* Möbius *a hard time*. She certified him *bonkers* for pretending to see visions of King Solomon and *really put the frighteners on him* after he had *bumped off* Schwester Monika.

A more formal version might read:

Dr von Zahnd really made life difficult for Möbius. She certified him insane for pretending to see visions of King Solomon and seriously intimidated him after he had murdered Schwester Monika.

(iii) Vagueness

Examiners' pet hates are sweeping statements which have no supporting evidence, or which are so imprecise as to be meaningless, for example:

Try not to be too general

- This is a very meaningful book.
- There is a lot of good imagery here.
- A lot of what he says is very deep.
- Bismarck had a big effect.

While on the subject of vagueness, remember that it is always unimpressive to refer to a play as 'the novel' or 'the book'.

So the message is clear – be precise.

(iv) Being over-personal

The convention in writing examination essays is that the style should be impersonal. It is probably best either never to use the word I, or to reserve its use for the conclusion.

(v) Tense

Convention in literary essays when referring to events in the text is to use the present tense.

STUDYING A TEXT OR A TOPIC

Good notes will help

The key to successful study of a **text** or a **topic** is efficient note-taking. That it is necessary to have a clear record of work over a two-year course is obvious – you simply could not be expected to remember in sufficient detail to be useful everything done in, say, the second term of the Lower Sixth when the A Level exam comes.

Several activities are useful in building up a good record of what you have learned and in improving the quality of your learning. Your eventual aim should be to have a concise record of the various aspects of what you are studying so that you are able to answer any of the likely questions without difficulty. If your examination board requires you to write examination answers in German, there is much to be said for doing a goodly portion of your notes in German.

Try some or all of the following strategies:

Useful techniques in preparing for revision

- Write a summary of the text as you read it; be sure to include a note of the page numbers in your copy.
- Write notes on each of the main characters, institutions, or themes.
- Keep a list of quotable quotes, and re-organise it under headings when you have finished reading the text or topic material.
- keep a vocabulary list, with page references, so that you have a 'user dictionary' when you come to revise.
- For literary texts, prepare notes on language, humour, irony, symbols, staging, themes, as appropriate.
- Review your notes after completing a topic and produce skeleton notes while the details are still fresh in your mind; you'll be glad you did it when you come to revise.
- After completing a topic, store the notes safely at home to prevent loss and to reduce the amount of weight you have to carry about with you.

READING LITERARY TEXTS

Translations may not always be best

Many students' first reaction on being presented with a text in German is to ask where they can obtain an English translation. For a majority of literary texts they do exist – although not all of them are easily obtainable. However, there are certain disadvantages to operating with a translation:

- You lose the linguistic benefit of reading a lengthy piece of German in context.
- The translation may have been adjusted to suit a particular purpose or have been based on different version of a work than the one now commonly used (a particularly frequent occurrence with plays).

There is also the matter of your own pride: why study German at all if, when the going gets a little tricky, you immediately opt for an English-based solution?

Other useful helps for reading literary texts

There are a few crutches which are useful, however. Chief amongst them are the schools editions of texts where the German text has been provided with notes and often a German-English vocabulary. These are very useful, and may well be the edition used in your school. If time is short (or you are desperate!), it can sometimes be helpful to have a second-hand copy in which the previous owner has written notes and translations. Be sure to pick one which belonged to a reasonably clever student with clear handwriting!

The editor's preface in schools' editions can be useful. However, it is worth checking on the frontispiece when it was written. Generally, the older it is, the less helpful it will be. You should also note that many prefaces contain a lengthy range of references to other works by the writer or to works by other writers (or, in some extreme cases, a précis of a B.A. course in German Literature!). While of interest, such details should not be taken as a model for your answers about the text in question.

On the other hand, prefaces often contain thoughtful analyses of character, plot, style, etc. But you should not be afraid to supplement the editor's opinions with your own views where there is clear evidence in the text.

Many editions have notes in the back of the book, an asterisk in the text alerting you to the fact that there is one. Again, the older editions are less helpful than more modern ones; they are particularly coy about bad language, innuendo and body language. And quite a number of editions actually omit comments on difficult (or risqué) idiomatic expressions. So you should be aware of the shortcomings of schools editions and be prepared to research some details yourself.

Many excellent answers are written by candidates who have not read any secondary literature (= books about books). However, if you do wish to check what is currently available, the handiest source of information is Grant and Cutler's *Modern Languages catalogue*, available free from:

Grant and Cutler Ltd
55–57 Great Marlborough Street
London W1V 2AY
Tel: 071 734 2012

They will also supply books by mail order, as will:

BH Blackwell Ltd.
Continental Department
Broad Street
Oxford OX1 3BQ
Tel: 0865 249111

Blackwell's are helpful on the phone, and also buy and sell second-hand continental books and dictionaries.

Remember that, given sufficient notice, your local public library and perhaps even your school library, can obtain most books for you via the inter-library loan system. There may be a small fee, but it is a great deal cheaper than buying the books! It is, however, unreasonable to expect a local library to have German literary criticism in stock, given that it is a rather specialised interest.

●● Useful information sources ●●

Some students find it helpful to have a few notes about an author or a text before starting work on it. *The Oxford Companion to German Literature* is a good source of concise information (especially dates), although it does not usually give enough detail on any one text for A Level purposes. If you need a summary of a novel or play, these can be found in *Reclams Romanführer* and *Reclams Schauspielführer*. An alternative source of play summaries and analysis is the series *Friedrichs Dramatiker des Welttheaters* which has a volume on each of the more obvious playwrights.

READING NON-LITERARY TEXTS

If you are studying the **civilisation/background option**, or preparing a background option for your Speaking Test, you will need to study a *range of texts*. Many boards suggest or prescribe books in both English and German. If your answers are to be written in German in the exam, it is important to read at least some of your information in German so that you know the appropriate vocabulary, expressions and idioms and can include them in your writing.

●● Good notes are again important ●●

The reasons given above for reading literary texts in the original German apply equally here. And the quality of your notes needs to be especially clear at revision time, as re-locating all the material you have read may be impossible.

While your teacher will be the primary source of information about what to read, material and texts can be obtained via Grant and Cutler (whose Modern Languages catalogue has bibliographies for some topics), BH Blackwell Ltd, (see above for addresses) or via:

European Schoolbooks Ltd
The Runnings
Cheltenham
GL51 9PQ
Tel: 0242 245252

all of whom will supply by mail order or can supply your local bookshop. Again, your local or possibly your school library may help, given sufficient notice.

European Schoolbooks can also organise subscriptions to a range of German magazines covering a wide variety of interests, including magazines such as *Bravo* aimed at German teenagers.

The Goethe-Institut is also a good source of material, and may be contacted at

50 Prince's Gate
London
SW7 2PH (Also branches in Birmingham, Glasgow, Manchester and York)

⬤⬤ Other useful sources of materials ⬤⬤

Other available source materials include:

Authentik. A selection of articles from the German Press. Cassettes plus transcripts also available, 7 issues per annum. O'Reilly Institute, Trinity College, Dublin 2, Eire. UK promotion by CILT.

Thematisch Annual subscription service for 16–19 teachers: press articles, radio material, official documentation. Mary Glasgow Publications, Avenue House, 131–133 Holland Park Ave., London. W11 4UT.

Aktuell auf Deutsch Bi-monthly magazine designed for advanced level students of German. Mary Glasgow Publications Ltd, Avenue House, 131–133 Holland Park Ave, London. W11 4UT.

Aktuelles aus Radio and Presse (Macmillan 1989), C. Ekhard-Long. Topic-based listening and reading material with language exercises and follow-up creative tasks. Accompanying cassette available.

Deutschland heute: Politik – Wirtschaft – Gesellschaft. Ein landeskundliches Arbeitsbuch (Berg 1986), R. A. Beyer.

Tatsachen und Ansichten: Bundesrepublik Deutschland. Eine Materialsammlung für junge Ausländer (Eilers and Schünemann 1986).

Unsere Zeitung: für den Deutschen Sprachunterricht – ein Querschnitt durch die Deutsche Presse. Published by Eilers and Schünemann, Postfach 919, Bremen 1, FRG, UK. Distributor: European Schoolbooks, see above.

Deutsch 2000. An oral/aural course designed to help foreigners in German. Accompanying cassettes available. UK Distributor: European Schoolbooks.

Sprungbrett (Stanley Thornes 1990), D. Bonnyman, K. Oberheid. Designed as a bridging course for the first third of the A–Level course. Thematically based, with accompanying cassette.

Einsicht (Hodder and Stoughton 1989), P. Stocker, K. Saunders. Topic-based course, with accompanying cassettes.

Scala. Monthly illustrated magazine. Obtainable from the Embassy of the German Federal Republic, 23 Belgrave Square, London. SW1X 8PZ.

Scala Jugendmagazin: für Schüler im Ausland. Enquiries to the Press Attaché, Embassy of the German Federal Republic, 23 Belgrave Square, London, SW1X 8P2.

Sprach-Illustrierte. Quarterly, articles and vocabulary notes. Langenscheidt, Neusser Strasse 3, Munich 40, FRG UK Distributor; European Schoolbooks, see above

German Film Library, Unit B11. Parkhall Road Trading Estate, London. SE21 8EL.

Stern magazine has an archiving service.

Inter Nationes, 5300 Bonn-Bad-Godesberg. Supplies material on specific topics. Catagloue available from Inter Nationes, giving full details of written and recorded material available.

Informationen zur politischen Bildung. From Bundeszentrale für politische Bildung, Berliner Freiheit 7, D5300, Bonn 1.

Kultur Chronik. News and views from the Federal Republic. Available bi-monthly from *Inter Nationes.*

AMGS (Association for Modern German Studies) brings together teachers, lecturers and researchers interested in German language, literature and area studies. Newsletter, conferences, publication of conference papers in Modern German Studies. Information available from: Mr. P. Maudsley, 24A Upper Upper Richmond Road West, East Sheen, London, SW14 8AG.

Hatfield Polytechnic German Centre offers an extensive loan services of books, tapes and videos. Information on subscription from Hantfield Polytechnic German Centre, P.O. Box 109, Hatfield, Herts, AL10 9AB.

RLDU, Bishop Rd, Bishopston, Bristol, BS7 8LS, produces German A Level topic-based material.

German Life and Letters – A journal devoted to articles on all aspects of German culture – literature, drama, artistic movements, social history, and political life. Published quarterly by Basil Blackwell, 108 Cowley Road, Oxford, OX4 1JF.

German and the Germans (Penguin 1988), J. Ardagh.

West Germany Today (Blackwell 1989), Ed. K. Koch.

The USLEB (University of London) Modern Languages syllabus includes a comprehensive bibliography for the topics it prescribes for paper 3. The syllabus can be obtained from:

USLEB
Stewart House
32 Russell Square
London
WC1B 5DN

Similarly, the AEB syllabus is a mine of information, and can be obtained from:

AEB Publications Dept
Stag Hill House
Guildford
GU2 5XJ

Although it seems that there is a huge amount of material available, it is important to remember that no examiner expects you to have read every possible work on a topic. Be guided by your teacher. However, it *is* possible to find material for that 'extra reading' teachers often recommend for their A Level students.

One final quick source of information is the *Michelin Green Guide to Germany*, where the introduction has a very useful potted history of matters political, artistic, musical and literary, as well as giving a great deal of information about the major tourist destinations. It is available in English or German from bookshops.

SAMPLE QUESTIONS

Because there is such a range of books and topics set which varies from board to board and from year to year, it is not possible to give here examples of all the questions which will be useful to every student. What follows are examples of the *framework* of essay questions which are commonly set, together with suggestions of the type of essay structure which is most appropriate.

ESSAY QUESTIONS

(a) For and against

(i) X's plays are good theatre, but bad literature.
(ii) To what extent is it true to say that the theme of Y is the most important aspect of Z's work.
(iii) What makes Q a believable character in the novel P? (Remember that you are not obliged to agree with the question!)
(iv) Germany will deeply regret the costs of reunification. Discuss.

(b) Analysis of features

(i) What are the main features of T's drama?
(ii) Trace the historical inaccuracies in *Das Leben des Galilei*.
(iii) In what ways does Hauptmann chronicle *Bahnwärter Thiel*'s descent into insanity?
(iv) Describe the main features of the Federal German political system.

(c) Compare or contrast

(i) Compare any two works of literature dealing with the *Nazizeit*.
(ii) Compare the characters of X and Y in the play Q.
(iii) Of the poems by G you have read, compare the one you consider the most successful with the one you thought least good.
(iv) Compare the school system in the former GDR with that of the Federal Republic. What could the two systems have learned from each other?

(d) Development

(i) Trace the methods by which the National Socialists gained and held onto power between 1923 and 1945.
(ii) What are the stages in the Gods' search for *Der gute Mensch von Sezuan*?
(iii) From your reading of H's poetry, trace the development of his technique.
(iv) What led President Kennedy to say: '*Ich bin ein Berliner.*'

A very useful revision exercise is to question-spot, perhaps with the help of your teacher. Simply ask yourself what possible questions could be set about a particular topic or set book. Use the skeleton questions above to help you. And make sure you have prepared outline notes for them. That way, the phrasing of the questions in the actual examination will be less of an unpleasant surprise.

CONTEXT QUESTIONS

As well as essay questions, many exam boards also set **context questions** for both literary and background topics. As with essay titles, it is impossible to provide examples which cover the multitude of set books and topics which are set, and which are subject to change from time to time.
However, the following points are worthy of your attention.

(a) Literary passages with no sub-questions

Make sure you have:

- identified where the passage occurs in the book by stating what occurs immediately before and afterwards,
- commented on the features of the passage,
- commented on the significance of the passage to the work as a whole,
- identified any points of particular interest.

(b) Literary or non-literary passages with sub-questions

The main thing here is to answer the questions fully. It is a safe bet that a question worth 2 marks out of 25 will require two points to be made, whereas one worth, say, 6 marks will require a fuller answer. It is also worth making sure you have read all the questions so that you do not waste time giving the same information in answer to two part-questions. Finally, it is worth splitting your time in proportion to the number of marks available per part question.

STUDENTS ANSWER AND EXAMINER'S COMMENTS

The following answer was written under examination conditions, and represents a good performance at A Level. It refers to Friedrich Dürrenmatt's *Die Physiker*.

'Dürrenmatt cannot resist the urge to take hold of accepted conceptions and turn them upside down, thereby shocking his audience into serious reflection.' Do you agree?

'Die Physiker', classed as light hearted entertainment does have a very serious undertone. Many ideas in the play are in the realm of absurdity, i.e. when accepted conceptions are turned upside-down, yet perhaps the initial reaction of the audience is seeing the situation as somewhat humourous as opposed to shocking them into serious reflection. (1)

Paradox and symmetry play a large role in Dürrenmatt's work and are also very evident in 'Die Physiker'. Much of this however fails to shock the audience into reflection as in my opinion (2) it simply contributes more to the element of comedy. For example the ironic situation in which Inspektor Voß finds himself at the beginning of Act I (which is almost mirrored in the beginning of Act II). He is informed of the rules against smoking and drinking in the hospital yet soon after Newton, a patient is himself smoking and drinking.

The incident with Missionär Rose illustrates again Dürrenmatt's desired to turn accepted beliefs upside-down. (3) Despite being a religious man he marrys (4) a divorced woman. However, what the audience might reflect upon from this otherwise light relief, is the separation of Möbius from his family and the sacrifices he has had to make in his attempt to hide his discovery of the system of all possible inventions.

It is a general belief (6) that the owner and head doctor of an asylum is sane and we are led to believe this is the case with Matilda von Zahnd, until towards the end of the play, that is. After discovering she had photo-copied Möbius's manuscripts before he burnt them our original belief is negated. Doctor von Zahnd is made apparent (7) to be the only mad person in the asylum (despite her comment earlier, 'ich bin die letzte Normale meiner Familie'). Dürrenmatt's urge to take hold of accepted conceptions and beliefs and turn them upside down in this instance would shock the audience into serious reflection as after all Möbius's efforts, 'Die Welt ist in die Hände einer verrückten 'Irrenärztin gefallen' (Einstein). (8)

In spite of Möbius's (and finally the two rival physicists') imprisonment in the asylum there is also the irony (yet truth) in the sentence shared by each of them, 'Nur im Irrenhaus sind wir noch frei' implying the asylum is the only place they can be free from their responsibilities, and the irony of being voluntarily locked up.

There are less significant incidents also when Dürrenmatt's inclination towards paradox are apparent. On page 10 Newton comments on his failure to understand how someone can strangle another person, ignoring the fact we have just learnt of his performing this exact operation (he also says how he doesn't understand much about physics).

The three nurses murdered seemed unable to fight off weak scientists (9) with a lamp cord yet Dürrenmatt emphasizes how Dorothea Moser was a member of self defence and Irene Straub was the womens' national judo champion. Nurses who were there to help the patients ended up being murdered by them! Monika (the third victim) went to great lengths in order to get permission to marry Möbius (whom she loved and there are indications Möbius felt the same way) and again, paradoxically, because of this Möbius had to kill Monika.

'Verrückt aber weise
Gefangen aber frei
Physiker aber unschuldig'
is probably the most appropriate quotation in agreement with the statement (10) and paradox which

would almost definately (11) stimulate the audience into reflection. Cannot resist the urge..., (as in the title) suggests that Dürrenmatt was desperate to turn anything inside out or upside down and consequently not always achieving a good result. However, these three phrases are extremely clever and thought-provoking being as they are completely true and describe the predicament perfectly.

Another accepted belief is the power of the law in certain circumstances (?!). Nevertheless, Inspektor Voß seems to have very little authority and clearly fails to perform what his job requires.

"Ich habe drei Mörder gefunden, die ich mit gutem Gewissen nicht zu verhaften brauche".

Inspektor Voß is often seen as a character of comedy however at a closer glance an attack could be being made on the authority and power of the law and those who supposedly protect it.

The three physicists committed murder so they had greater freedom in the asylum but their actions actually restricted their freedom instead of increasing it (The male nurses were introduced, bars put on windows, the picture of General von Zahnd replacing the Geheimrat and liebe Kranke becoming the command of `Raus Kommen!)

Dürrenmatt also uses contrast which perhaps could be classed as a method of if not shocking his audience into serious reflection, then at least highlighting paradoxical situations. For example, the violence of the guards in contrast to the excellence of their carefully prepared food, the pretty yet muscular nurses and so on. These contrasts could well mean to provoke the thought that not all things are quite as they seem.

Possibly the largest paradox of the whole play is that although Möbius thought he had planned for every eventuality no-one can forsee the future. Möbius himself a scientist is nonetheless, caught by technology (as it hadn't occurred to him someone could photocopy his notes). Neither had he realized how evil Matilda von Zahnd was.

I agree (12) with the first phrase of the statement. Yet the paradox in 'Die Physiker' is not all in order to stimulate serious reflection. The play is first and foremost a comedy which the satire and irony, (13) repetitive dialogue and paradoxical remarks all contribute towards. It is only when the humour is looked further into (14) that the reality and message of the mechanical play are there to be discovered, the underlying debate of whether…

'Jeder Versuch eines Einzelnen für sich zu lösen, Was alle angeht, muß scheitern which 'Die Physiker' clearly professes.'

Examiner's Comments

1 Addresses the title.
2 Replace with impersonal it could be argued
3 Contrast Missionär Rose's puny physique with the fact that he is a father of six.
4 Spelling: marries.
5 Expression: 'a man of the cloth' would be preferable.
6 A little sloppy. Try: 'It is a reasonable assumption'.
7 Poor English: is made to appear to be the only mad person... .
8 Another apposite quotation here is *Nicht zugunsten der Welt, sondern zugunsten einer alten buckligen Jungfrau'*.
9 Make more of the incongruity of the super-fit nurses qualified in martial arts being easily overcome and strangled by the scientists.
10 Be more precise: with the statement in the title.
11 Spelling: definitely.
12 Impersonal usage is preferable: 'It therefore seems reasonable to agree...'.
13 There is paradox in the fact that the physicist who knows how everything works cannot foresee how relatively easily an evil personality can alter the course of events.
14 English style: 'is looked into further'.

PREPARING AND PRESENTING COURSEWORK

Much of what has been said about tackling examination essays applies to **coursework**. To re-cap, the extended essay should share the characteristics of a good essay, namely:

■ Answer the question.
■ Have a clear structure.
■ Have evidence proving each assertion made.
■ Consider other points of view.
■ Come to an obvious conclusion or makes it clear why not.
■ Be written in formal language avoiding errors of style.

Because coursework can be checked, however, it is expected to be more error-free than work written under examination conditions. Where coursework is written in German, it should be subjected to your very best checking procedures, as outlined in the Study Skills chapter on page 9. If you word-process it, you should try and find a program which has the Umlaut and ß available. Sometimes the ALT key plus certain codes can do the trick. Again, see the Study Skills chapter, page 9. You should be aware that no allowance is made for typing errors – they remain errors.

Examiners are concerned that candidates should:

- Give evidence of commitment and personal intellectual input.
- Write in accurate German.
- Base their work on material which originated in Germany.
- Be economical in quotation.
- Include a title sheet and bibliography.
- Write with plenty of space round their work.
- Stick fairly accurately to the word-count given.

STUDENT'S COURSEWORK WITH EXAMINER'S COMMENTS

Fleisch ist Mord, oder?

Einleitend möchte ich sagen, daß diese Frage mich sehr interessiert, denn ich bin Vegetarierin, und meine Familie (außer meinem Vater) essen auch kein Fleisch oder Fisch. In diesem Aufsatz wird ich diskutieren, warum so viele Leute Vegetarier sind, und die Probleme, die vom Vegetarismus verursacht werden.

In England heutzutage wird die Zahl der Leute, besonders Mädchen, die Vegetarier werden, täglich größer. Vor zehn Jahren, wenn man sagte, daß man vegetarisch war, wurde man als Spinner betrachtet. Jetzt, obwohl es vieler Fleischgerichten immer gibt (außer in einem vegetarischen Restaurant), kann mann in fast allen Gaststätten gutes Essen finden.

Die Wahl Fleisch und Fisch zu essen haben natürlich jeder, und ich würde nie sagen, daß alle Vegetarier werden sollen aber ich meine, daß alle die Argumente dafür und dagegen durchdenken sollen. Anders gesagt, glaube ich, daß man nicht unbedingt Fleisch zu essen als richtig sieht nur, weil man es macht.

Warum Vegetarier werden?

Zuerst will ich auf die verschiedenen Gründe eingehen, warum jemand Vegetarier werden sich entscheiden würde. Unter Leuten meiner Altersgruppe, glaube ich, daß es modisch ist, Vegetarier zu sein. Viele Mädchen kenne ich, die zwischen zwölf und zwanzig sind, die erstens auf das Fleisch verzichten, weil ihre Freund-

innen auch auf es verzichten. Sie kommen auf die Schliche Vivisektion und sich entscheiden, Vegetarier zu werden. Kein Fleisch essen sie während einiger Wochen aber, dann finden sie die Probleme, die diese Nahrung verursacht, und sie essen Fleisch wieder. Ein anderer Grund, weshalb Mädchen Vegetarierinnen werden, ist ihre ständige Sorgen um ihnen Aussehen. Die vegetarische Nahrung wird als sehr gesund betracht.

Natürlich gibt es viele Leute, die Fleisch einfach nicht mögen. Ich bin einer dieser Menschen. Vegetarierin wurde meine Mutter vor zehn Jahren, und vor fünf Jahren sagte sie, daß sie kein Fleisch mehr zubereiten würde. Um Fleisch zu essen, müßten wir es uns machen. Deshalb aßen wir nie Fleisch. Nach einigen Jahren kein Fleisch essen, will man nie es essen. Fleisch könnte ich nie jetzt essen, weil ich nicht die Substanz leiden könnte.

Einer der wichstigster Gründe, der viele Leute beeinflußt, ist wie die Tiere behandelt werden. Wenn die Tiere besser behandelt worden, wären nicht so viele Leute vegetarisch. Zum Beispiel, ohne Batteriehennen, würden Leute sich weniger sculdig fühlen, Hähnchen zu essen.

Die Weise, die man nützt, Tiere umzubringen, verursachen viele Leute auf Fleisch zu verzichten. Aber, wie mit Batteriehennen, wenn man wüßte, daß Tiere so schnell und mit so kleine Menge Schmerzes wie möglich getötet würden, würde man nichts dagegen haben.

Das Problem der Gesundheit

Wenn man vegetarisch werden will, muss man sorgfältig sein, gesund zu bleiben. Es ist möglich, eine ausgewogene Nahrung ohne Fleisch oder Fisch zu haben. Man muß sicherstellen, daß man alle der notwenige Nährstoffe ißt. Bitte sehen Sie das Schaubild und die Tabelle.

Viele Leute, die Vegetarier werden, glauben, daß man auch keine Molkereiprodukte oder Eier essen soll. Jemand, der keine dieser Produkte ißt, heißt auf Englisch »vegan«, aber auf Deutsch glaube ich, daß es kein Äquivalent gibt. Persönlich bin ich nicht »vegan«, weil ich glaube, daß es zu vielen Arbeit schaffen würde, um gesund zu sein. Ohne Tierprodukte essen, muß mann sehr sorgfältig sein, genug aller der Nährstoffe zu essen. Statt der Molkereiprodukte und Eier essen, soll man 20% getrockene Bohne, keimende Bohnen und Nüsse essen. Aber man müßte auch Nahrungszusätze nehmen.

Kein Leder oder Pelz tragen viele Leute, die »vegan« oder vegetarisch sind. Heutzutage in England sieht man fast nie Geschäfte, die nur Leder oder Pelz verkaufen, weil so viele Leute dagegen sind. (Die Pelzabteilung in Harrods, eines der berühmtsten exklusiven Kaufhäuser in London, wurde sogar zugemacht!) Es ist noch gar nicht lange her, da wurden diese Geschäfte von den Leuten, die dagegen sind, bombardierten. Natürlich haben diese Taten auf sich sehr viele Publicity gezogen. Deshalb hat die Zahl der Vegetarier und die Leute, die kein Leder oder Pelz tragen, schnell zugenommen.

Die Lage in Deutschland bleibt rund fünfundzwanzig Jahre hinten die in England. Tatsche, daß es kein Wort auf deutsch gibt, »vegan« zu sagen, erläutert meinen Punkt. Es wird auch vom Magazin »Stern« illustriert. Im März gab es einen Artikel, der »Nie wieder Fleisch« hieß. Wenn ein Artikel in einer englischen Zeitschrift Meat - Never Again? heißen würde, wäre es über Vegetarismus. Aber im »Stern« wurde ihn nur einmal erwähnt, und die Möglichkeit Vegetarismus, als Lösung »des Kampfes um Gesundheit und Genuß«, wurde nur als Witz gegeben.

Wie schon gesagt: ich bin persönlich Vegetarierin. Also bin ich natürlich dafür. Aber ich würde nie sagen, daß alle nie Fleisch essen sollen, denn, wenn alle Leute morgen vegetarisch würden, würden wir von Kälber überlaufen. Vegetarier essen Molkereiprodukte, also, weil die Kühe Milsch machen, müssen sie Kälber haben. Diese Kälber würden nicht gegessen. Es ist auch wahr, daß viele Bauer arbeitlos würden.

Obwohl die Änderung sehr allmählich sein müßte, würde ich endlich sehen, alle Vegetarier werden. Ich glaube, daß, weil man ohne Fleisch und Fisch leicht überleben kann, ist es grausam die Tiere zu züchten nur um sie zu essen. Ich glaube auch, daß man kein Recht hat, mit Natur zu stören.

Das Nahrungsmittel	Die Nährstoff, die besorgt werden
Getreide, Mehlarten, Nüsse und Samen	Eiweiß, Kohlenhydraten, Vitamine (besonders B), Minerale und Faser
Gemüse	Vitamine, Minerale und Faser
Meeresalgen	Eiweiß, Vitamine, Minerale (besonders Kalizium), Kalium, Jod und Eisen)
Obst (frisches und Dörrobst)	Minerale, Kohlenhydraten, Faser, Vitamine (besonders C in den Zitrusfruchten).
Molkereiprodukte und Eier	Vitamine (besonders B12 und B2), Eiweiß und Kalzium

Fig 6.1

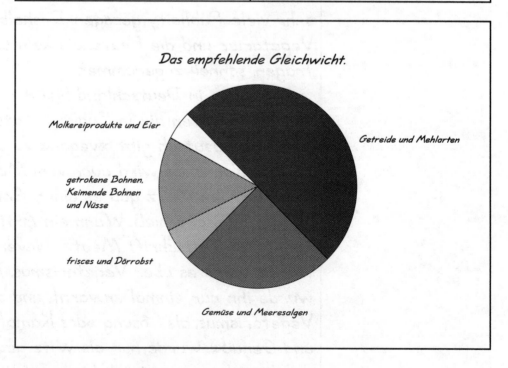

Das empfehlende Gleichwicht.

Molkereiprodukte und Eier

Getreide und Mehlarten

getrokene Bohnen, Keimende Bohnen und Nüsse

frisces und Dörrobst

Gemüse und Meeresalgen

Fig 6.2

Detailed bibliography:

Nie wieder Fleisch? Stern März 1991
VSUK Information Sheet: Guidelines on Nutrition

As a vegetarian what would be missing from your diet? The Vegetarian Society
The Neals Yard Bakery Wholefood Cookbook by Rachel Haigh (Dorling Kindersley London 1986)

Examiner's comments

This is a good attempt, though not faultless. The content is quite well thought out with a good range of treatment. There is a significant degree of personal involvement, and the content is interesting to read. The candidate draws conclusions from the material presented. It is well-structured with a clear ability to make logical links and develop ideas. The material has been organised to fit the sequence of thought chosen. If accuracy is disregarded, the language is fluent, with a good range of vocabulary and some complex sentences. There are some major errors of language, but not so serious as to mar the general impression.

When choosing a coursework topic, make sure you have chosen a topic – like the one above – which enables you to undertake personal research, present argument and show involvement. Avoid bland titles such as 'Meine Hobbys' or 'Deutsches Essen'.

BRIEF REVIEW OF GERMAN HISTORY

Many candidates have only hazy notions of **German history**, if any knowledge at all. Repeatedly, however, they will come across references to historical events in texts and will be short of a means of placing them in context.

The following 'potted' history is intended to provide a source of quick reference. Where appropriate, the German names for people, events and places are given in italics.

AD 9 Arminius, leader of the Germans, wins a major battle against the Romans in the *Teutoburger Wald*.
6th century Clovis, King of the Franks (*Franken*), converts to Christianity.
785 Charlemagne (*Karl der Große*) conquers the Saxons and the Bavarians and unites a Frankish Empire based on Aachen.
800 Charlemagne is crowned Emperor by the Pope.
814 Charlemage dies.
911 The eastern part of Charlemagne's Empire splits from the west (*Frankreich*) and chooses *Konrad I* as King.
1152–1190 *Friedrich Barbarossa* formally founds the Holy Roman Empire in which the Pope's influence is limited to religious matters.
1291 *Rudolf I* is the first Hapsburg on the throne.
1356 the Golden Bull (= edict from the Pope) establishes the election of the Kaiser by seven Electors (*Kürfürsten*) (George I of England was Elector of Hanover). Gradually the towns increased in importance and independence, and the Hanseatic League (*die Hanse*) of 200 such towns led by Lübeck was founded in 1358.
1386 Heidelberg University founded.
1450 Gutenberg invents printing.
1517 Martin Luther nails 95 *Thesen* to the doors of Wittenberg church condemning much of church practice. The Reformation has begun. He translates the Bible into modern German. By 1555 Protestantism is established as the faith of northern Germany.
1618–1648 The Thirty Years' War (*der dreißigjährige Krieg*) arises out of tension between Catholics and Protestants. Large areas of northern Germany are laid waste. The population is halved.
In the 17th and 18th century Prussia (*Preußen*) emerges as the best-organised state with a strong tradition of nobles (*Junker*) serving the state. Frederick the Great (*Friedrich der Große*) (1740–1786) enjoys a golden age as an 'enlightened despot'.
1789 French Revolution, followed after the execution of Louis XVIII by war. Prussia fares badly, the Holy Roman Empire worse.
1806 Napoleon enters Berlin, and the Austrian Emperor renounces the crown of the Holy Roman Empire, which is dissolved.

1813 Prussian troops harry the French retreating from their disastrous expedition to Moscow in 1812, and defeat them at the *Völkerschlacht* in Leipzig.

1815 The Congress of Vienna (*der Wiener Kongreß*) established the German Confederation (*der Deutsche Bund*) of 35 small states.

1834 Prussia suggests a customs union (*Zollverein*).

1848 A wave of ineffective revolutions sweeps across Europe.

1862 Bismarck becomes Prussian *Minister-President*.

1864 In alliance with Austria, Schleswig-Holstein is taken from Denmark.

1866 After seeking a quarrel with Austria, Bismarck's Prussia defeats Austria at Sadow and is undisputed leader of the northern German states.

1870 Bismarck provokes a war with France with a dubious telegram (*die Ems-Depesche*) and quickly defeats France at Sedan. France has to pay reparations and to cede Alsace and Lorraine (*Elaß-Lothringen*) to Germany.

1871 Wilhelm I is declared *Kaiser* in Versailles.

1888 Wilhelm II comes to the throne.

1890 Bismarck is dismissed. *Der Lotse geht von Bord.* Germany begins an arms race with France and Britain and seems threatening.

1914 *Erzherzog Ferdinand* is assassinated in Sarajevo. Six weeks later, Germany declares war on France and Russia. Following Germany's invasion of neutral Belgium, Britain joins in. Soon there is murderous stalemate on the Marne. Millions die.

1917 Russia pulls out following the Revolution; USA declares war on Germany after U-boat attacks.

1918 Defeated, the Kaiser abdicates on 9 November. Peace comes on 11th November, the first act of the Weimar Republic (*Weimarer Republik*).

1919 Treaty of Versailles imposes crippling reparations on Germany. Economic ruin follows, with inflation reaching several thousand percent per day by 1923. Anyone with savings loses them. The French invade the Rhineland to collect reparations, Hitler attempts a *Putsch* (coup d'état).

1929 The Wall Street Crash throws the fragile economy into fresh turmoil.

1932 The National Socialists (Nationalsozialisten = Nazis) win 38% of the votes.

1933 Hitler assumes the Chancellorship (*die Machtergreifung*) after a fire at the *Reichstag* building. He institutes a programme of public works and re-armament which improves the economy. But opponents are ruthlessly pursued; many liberals, Jews, communists, emigrate.

1936 German troops illegally enter the Rhineland which has been demilitarised under the Treaty of Versailles.

1938 Austria is joined to Germany (*Anschluß*) Hitler annexes the *Sudetenland* in Czechoslovakia.

1939 Hitler invades Poland; Britain declares war.

1942 The Final Solution (*Endlösung*) of the Jewish question means extermination camps for 6 million.

1944 Hitler escapes assassination in a plot led by Graf V Stauffenberg.

1945 Hitler's suicide is followed by peace on 8th May. Germany is in ruins, completely overrun by Russian, American British and French troops. Germany and Austria are each divided into four zones at the Potsdam Conference. Tension mounts between Britain, USA and France on the one hand, and Russia on the other. Millions of Germans are displaced as Poland is moved westwards and part of *Ostpreußen* is incorporated into the Soviet Union. The *Sudetenland* is cleared of Germans. The USA gives generous Marshall Aid.

1949 - 8th May The *Bundesrepublik Deutschland* is founded by the western allies. A liberal consitution, the *Grundgesetz* is imposed, and there is economic reform, Währungsreform. The Soviets blockade Berlin in an attempt to starve it out. The city is supplied by air by the Americans.

1949 - 7th October The Soviet zone becomes the *Deutsche Demokratische Republik*.

1953 Uprising in East Berlin put down by Russian troops.

1955 All allied troops withdraw from Austria, which becomes a neutral country.

1957 West Germany is a founder member of the Common Market. The West German *Wirtschaftswunder* means great prosperity. Throughout the 1950s millions fled west from the *DDR*. In **1961** this is finally stopped by the erection of the Berlin Wall.

1989 Protest movement led by the Protestant church in Leipzig results in the fall of the Berlin Wall.

1990 Reunification on 3rd October under Chancellor Helmut Kohl. Currency reforms in the East; Privatisation of state enterprises by the *Treuhand*. The extent of surveillance by the *DDR's Staatssicherheitsdienst (Stasi)* becomes apparent. Serious economic problems are the cost of unification, given the dilapidated state of *DDR* industry and infrastructure.

FURTHER READING

Rod Hares: *Gute Literaturnoten* (Hodder and Stoughton).
    A thoroughly sensible treatment of all the aspects of writing essays. Despite its title, it contains a useful chapter on background essays.
Stuart Sillars: *A-Level Revise Guide English* (Longman).
    A mine of useful information about how to get the best out of the study of literature, and how to tackle essays, context questions and coursework.

GRAMMAR: 1

GLOSSARY OF GRAMMATICAL TERMS

ADJECTIVES

ADVERBS

CASES

COMPARISONS

CONJUNCTIONS

NOUNS

NUMBERS

PREPOSITIONS

PRONOUNS

SPELLING

TIMES AND DATES

WORD ORDER

FURTHER READING

GETTING STARTED

Grammar is often seen as boring or irrelevant. It isn't, as it allows you to generate and understand sentences which you have not come across before, and helps your reading and listening comprehension. Find out how it works, and you have the key to much more German than you could ever hope to learn by heart.

There is much to be said for reading through a section at a time on a weekly basis. You will be surprised how often something which you half-knew will be fixed more firmly in that way. As always, make sure you do your grammar learning with a pen in your hand so that you are taking an active part in your learning. Try to find examples of the features you are reading about in the current work you are doing. And ask your teacher to clarify what doesn't seem clear at first glance.

ESSENTIAL PRINCIPLES

Not all students are taught using formal grammar in their English or German lessons nowadays. There is nothing to be frightened of in the use of **grammatical terms**. After all, a mechanic wouldn't attempt to describe what a spanner is every time he wanted to have one passed to him. He just uses the technical term, which is 'spanner'. These grammatical terms are the technical 'jargon' of language-learning, which give you access to the patterns of German and other languages to enable you to learn them quicker.

I have attempted to *define* them simply in this section of the chapter, and to give *examples*. There are further examples and explanations of these terms in the main body of this chapter.

Adjective

This is a word which describes a noun or pronoun. It gives information about such things as colour, type, disposition, etc.

Example: Er ist **krank**

Adverb

This is a word which describes a verb (adds to the verb). It gives information about how something is done.

Example: Er läuft **schnell**

Adverbs can also be used to add to adjectives or other adverbs.

Examples: Er ist **sehr** krank
Er läuft **besonders** schnell

Agreement

Adjectives in German which are immediately followed by a noun alter their spelling to *agree with*, or conform to, or 'match' the noun they describe, depending on the *article* (or *determiner*) which comes before them and the *case* of the noun.

Example: Es ist das **große** Haus mit dem **großen** Garten und zwei **großen** Bäumen.

Case

German has four **cases**, Nominative, Accusative, Genitive and Dative, which alter the article before the noun, the agreement of the adjective, and occasionally the spelling of the noun. They each are used in specific circumstances.

Clause

A **clause** is a part of a sentence which contains a subject and a verb which agrees with that subject. There are *main clauses* – which tell you most of the message of the sentence

Example: Er ist sehr krank

and *subordinate clauses* – which tell you something more about some other part of the sentence.

Example: Der Junge, **der sehr krank ist,** wohnt in Bonn.

Comparatives

A way of using adjectives and adverbs to *compare*, say, two people or things.

Examples: Ich bin **stärker** als du
Er läuft **schneller** als ich

Conjugation

The name given to the *pattern* that verbs follow. In German there are **weak verbs** which are regular, and **strong verbs**, which are irregular.

Imperatives

These are the command forms of verbs, and are used when telling people to do something. They include the 'Let's...' sort of command, which is a way of telling yourself and one or more other people to do something.

Examples: Hör zu!   Listen!
Hören Sie zu!   Listen!
Hören wir zu!   Let's listen!

Infinitive

The part of the verb you find when you look it up in a vocabulary list, and which means 'to....' It doesn't agree with a subject. Infinitives may be found in combination with other verbs.

Example: essen (to eat)

Interrogative Pronouns

These are question words. Their English equivalents mostly begin with '*wh*'.

Examples: Wer? (*who*) Was? (*what?*)

Irregular verbs

Verbs which *do not* follow one of the set patterns. The parts which indicate the vowel changes which these verbs undergo are written out for you in the verb table on page 197. They tend to be common verbs.

Present participle

This is part of a verb which is expressed by '..*ing*' in English.

Example: schlafend (while sleep*ing*)

Past Participle

This is part of the verb which is used with '*haben*' and '*sein*' to form the perfect and pluperfect tenses and with '*werden*' to form the passive. Irregular verbs have irregular past participles.

Examples: Ich habe **geschlafen.**   Sie haben sich **gewaschen.**
Wir sind **angekommen.**   Der Hund wurde **gesehen.**

Prepositions

These are words which are placed in front of nouns and pronouns to show position and other relationships.

Examples: Der Bus ist **neben** dem Lastwagen.
Maria ging **nach** Hause.

Pronouns

These are words which are used to avoid repeating a noun or proper name.

Examples: **Ich, sie, ihn, ihm,** etc.

Reflexive verbs

These are verbs where the person does the action to himself.

Example: **sich waschen – ich wasche mich**. (*I wash myself.*)

Relative pronouns

These introduce a *relative clause*, which is a clause which tells you something more about another part of the sentence. They can often be omitted in English, but never in German.

Examples:
(i) Hier ist der Mann, **den** ich suche.
(*There's the man I am looking for.*
There's the man that I am looking for.
There's the man who I am looking for.)
(ii) Sie ist eine Person, **die** sehr stark ist.
(*She's a person who is very strong.*)

Superlative

A way of using adjectives and adverbs to say who is the best, the fastest, etc.

(i) Ich bin die/der stärkste. (*I am the strongest.*)
(ii) Er läuft am schnellsten. (*He runs the fastest.*)

Tenses

These are the different forms of verbs which describe when something takes place, took place, will take place, etc. There are some differences in the use of **tenses** between German and English, but *future tenses* refer to the future, *present tenses* refer to now or to regular events which are still going on, and *past tenses* refer to events which have already taken place. The *conditonal* is used for conditions, while the *subjunctive* (*Konjunktiv*) has no direct equivalent in English. Look them up in Chapter 8.

ADJECTIVES

ADJECTIVES NOT FOLLOWED BY A NOUN

Adjectives which stand alone – usually after *sein, werden* and *scheinen* – do not have an adjective ending.

Example: Die Frau ist groß.   *The woman is tall.*

Point to watch: Students also learning French sometimes make adjectives standing alone agree, as they do in French. This is WRONG.

ADJECTIVES FOLLOWED BY A NOUN

Adjectives followed by a noun take an ending (= agree with the noun) which depends on four factors:

(i)   **the determiner (article) or lack of one in front of the adjective**
(ii) **the gender of the noun – masculine, feminine, or neuter**
(iii) **whether the noun is singular or plural**
(iv) **the case of the noun**

If there is more than one adjective before the noun, each one has the appropriate ending. Of course, once one ending has been worked out in these circumstances, all the others in front of the same noun will have the same ending.
    There are three sets of adjective endings, depending on which determiner is used:
(a) After *der/die/das*, etc; *dieser, jener, jeder, welcher, solcher, mancher* and *alle* (which is, of course, plural).

Masculine Singular		**Neuter Singular**	
Nominative:	der große Mann	Nominative:	das große Kind
Accusative:	den großen Mann	Accusative:	das große Kind
Genitive:	des großen Mannes	Genitive:	des großen Kindes
Dative:	dem großen Mann(e)	Dative:	dem großen Kind(e)
Feminine Singular		**Plural, all genders**	
Nominative:	die große Frau	Nominative:	die großen Leute
Accusative:	die große Frau	Accusative:	die großen Leute
Genitive:	der großen Frau	Genitive:	der großen Leute
Dative:	der großen Frau	Dative:	den großen Leuten

Points to watch:

■ Note that all Genitive and Dative Singular and all Plural endings are -*en*.

■ Note that -*es* or -s can be added to Masculine and Neuter nouns in the Genitive singular.

■ Note that -*e* can be added to single-syllable Masculine and Neuter nouns in the Dative Singular in formal writing.

■ Finally, remember to add -*n* to nouns which do not already have one in the Dative Plural of all genders (but *not* to those whose plural ends in -s). See NOUNS.

(b) After *ein/eine/ein*, etc, *kein, mein, dein, sein, ihr* (= her), *sein, unser, euer, Ihr* and *ihr* (= their) the adjective has the following endings:

Masculine Singular		**Neuter Singular**	
Nominative:	ein großer Mann	Nominative:	ein großes Kind
Accusative:	einen großen Mann	Accusative:	ein großes Kind
Genitive:	eines großen Mannes	Genitive:	eines großen Kindes
Dative:	einem großen Manne	Dative:	einem großen Kind
Feminine Singular		**Plural, all genders**	
Nominative:	eine große Frau	Nominative:	keine großen Leute
Accusative:	eine große Frau	Accusative:	keine großen Leute
Genitive:	einer großen Frau	Genitive:	keiner großen Leute
Dative:	einer großen Frau	Dative:	keiner großen Leuten

Point to watch: *Ein* itself, for reasons of logic, doesn't have a plural. If '*a*' is plural (i.e. 'some'), it follows the plural pattern for the third table, given below.

(c) Adjectives which are used alone before the noun have the following endings:

Masculine Singular		**Neuter Singular**	
Nominative:	kalter Kaffee	Nominative:	kaltes Wasser
Accusative:	kalten Kaffee	Accusative:	kaltes Wasser
Genitive:	kalten Kaffees	Genitive:	kalten Wassers
Dative:	kaltem Kaffee	Dative:	kaltem Wasser
Feminine Singular		**Plural, all genders** (also after *viele, mehrere* and *einige, ein paar* and numbers)	
Nominative:	kalte Milch	Nominative:	kalte Getränke
Accusative:	kalte Milch	Accusative:	kalte Getränke
Genitive:	kalter Milch	Genitive:	kalter Getränke
Dative:	kalter Milch	Dative:	kalten Getränken

Point to watch: In the Genitive singular for masculine and neuter, the ending is *-en*, which might just seem a little unexpected.

(d) Some adjectives do not take an ending:

(i) Those formed from town names, which always end in *-er*.
    Example: auf der Leipziger Messe   *at the Leipzig trade fair*
(ii) Those formed from numerals which always end in *-er*.
    Example: in den neunziger Jahren   *in the 90s*
(iii) Some colours and a few other words borrowed from other languages. These include: beige, lila, orange, rosa, sexy.

ADJECTIVES USED AS NOUNS

All adjectives and participles can be used *as nouns* in German. They are then written with a capital letter.

Example: der Deutsche/die Deutsche – *the German*

Adjective-type nouns take the same endings as they would if they were followed by a noun of the appropriate gender.

Example:

Masculine Singular	Feminine Singular	Plural
der Angestellte	die Angestellte	die Angestellten
den Angestellten	die Angestellte	die Angestellten
des Angestellten	der Angestellten	der Angestellten
dem Angestellten	der Angestellten	den Angestellten
Masculine Singular	**Feminine Singular**	**Plural**
ein Angestellter	eine Angestellte	Angestellte
einen Angestellten	eine Angestellte	Angestellte
eines Angestellten	einer Angestellten	Angestellter
einem Angestellten	einer Angestellten	Angestellten

ADJECTIVES WHICH TAKE THE DATIVE

A number of adjectives are followed by the *Dative* case. They usually follow the noun they govern.

Example: Es ist dem Schüler klar.   *It is clear to the student.*

The common ones are listed here:

ähnlich	*similar to*	günstig	*favourable to*
begreiflich	*comprehensible*	klar	*obvious*
behilflich	*helpful to*	möglich	*possible*
bekannt	*known to*	nötig	*necessary*
dankbar	*grateful to*	peinlich	*embarrassing*
fremd	*strange*	verständlich	*understandable*
nicht geheuer	*scary*	wichtig	*important*

Point to watch: Many of these can be translated with '*to me*' in English – much the same idea as the Dative.

ADJECTIVES WHICH TAKE THE GENITIVE

Der Terrorist ist immer eines Anschlags fähig.
The terrorist is always capable of an attack.

In English, this corresponds to *of*. The most frequent are:

bewußt	*conscious of*	voll	*full of*
fähig	*capable of*	wert	*worthy of*
schuldig	*guilty of*		

A large number of adjectives are linked to a noun by means of a preposition. *Auf* and *über* always take the Accusative in this circumstance.

Some common adjective + preposition combinations are:

abhängig von + Dat	*dependent on*	gewöhnt an + Acc	*accustomed to*
angewiesen auf + Acc	*to have to rely on*	gierig nach + Dat	*greedy for*
aufmerksam auf + Acc	*aware of*	hungrig nach + Dat	*hungry for*
begeistert von + Dat	*enthusiastic about*	interessiert an + Acc	*interested in*
bereit zu + Dat	*ready to*	neugierig auf + Acc	*curious about*
böse auf + Acc	*cross with*	stolz auf + Acc	*proud of*
böse mit + Dat	*cross with*	typisch für + Acc	*typical of*
dankbar für + Acc	*thankful for*	verheiratet mit + Dat	*married to*
einverstanden mit + Dat	*agreeable to*	verliebt in + Acc	*in love with*
empfindlich gegen + Acc	*sensitive to*	verschieden von + Dat	*different from*

There are many others. Make your own additions to this list as you come across them.

SOMETHING AND NOTHING

After *etwas* (something) and *nichts* (nothing) the adjective is written with a capital letter and has -*es* added.

Examples: etwas Gutes   *something good*
nichts Schlechtes   *nothing bad*
mit etwas kleinem in der Tasche   *with something small in the pocket*

Point to watch: Note the idiom: alles Gute!   *Best Wishes*

ADVERBS

Adverbs – which 'add information to a verb' – present relatively few problems in German.
    Most adjectives, present participles and past participles can be used as adverbs without any change.

Examples:

■ Er spielt Beethoven **sehr schön**.   *He plays Beethoven very nicely.*
■ Er ist **überraschend** früh hier angekommen.   *He arrived here surprisingly early.*
■ Er kam **gebückt** ins Zimmer.   *He came into the room stooped.*

There are different types of adverbs: of place, direction, manner and degree, as well as question-words.

(a) Adverbs of place

(i) *Hier, dort* and *da* all translate as 'here', 'there' and 'there'.

(ii) *Oben, unten* and *mitten* are usually followed by a preposition.
Examples:
- **Oben** auf dem Dach saß ein Vogel. *A bird sat up on the roof.*
- **Mitten** im Wald fand er seinen Hund. *He found his dog in the middle of the wood.*

(iii) *Innen and drinnen; außen and draußen*
Innen means 'on the inside'; *drinnen* means 'inside'.
Außen means 'on the outside'; *draußen* means 'outside'.

(iv) *Irgend-* and *nirgend-* can be tacked onto the front of words to convey the meaning 'or other' or 'at all'.
Examples:
- **Irgend**jemand hat meinen Kuli. *Someone or other has my pen.*
- **Nirgend**wo finden Sie einen besseren Stuhl. *You'll not find a better chair anywhere.*

(b) Adverbs of direction

Many adverbs and prepositions can have *hin-* or *her-* added onto the front of them. As a rule of thumb, the *hin-* prefix is used for motion *away from* the speaker, with the *her-* prefix being used for motion *towards* the speaker. *Hin* and *her* are also found used in the manner of a separable prefix to show movement.

Examples:
- Er ist aus Rußland hier**her** gekommen. *He came here from Russia.*
- Wo**hin** gehst du? *Where are you going (to)?*
- Gib das Buch **her**! *Hand over the book!*
- Vier weitere Schülerinnen sind **hin**zugekommen. *An additional four students arrived.*

(c) Adverbs of manner

(i) A good number of adverbs of *manner* do not occur as adjectives.

These include the following:

allerdings	*mind you*	leider	*unfortunately*
anscheinend	*apparently*	möglicherweise	*possibly*
beinahe	*almost*	sicherlich	*surely*
ebenfalls	*likewise, the same to you*	sonst	*otherwise*
einigermaßen	*to some extent*	umsonst	*in vain*
hoffentlich	*hopefully*	vielleicht	*perhaps*
immerhin	*all the same*	zweifellos	*doubtless*

(ii) A large number of adverbs can be formed by adding the suffix *-weise* to a noun

Examples:

ausnahms**weise**	*by way of exception*	stunden**weise**	*by the hour*
beispiels**weise**	*by way of example*	teil**weise**	*in part*

(iii) Adverbs can also be formed in large numbers by adding the suffix *-erweise* to adjectives or participles. They convey the additional implication that the speaker didn't expect matters to be as they were.

Examples:

erstaunlich**erweise**	*amazingly*	normal**erweise**	*normally*
glücklich**erweise**	*fortunately*	unerwartet**erweise**	*unexpectedly*
komisch**erweise**	*funnily*		

(d) Adverbs of degree

Many students seem to know only two or three of these, namely *sehr, etwas* and *ganz*. This is a shame, as very little effort is needed to make your writing seem much more sophisticated.

(i) adverbs of degree worth learning:

außerordentlich	*extraordinary*	mäßig	*moderately*
besonders	*especially*	relativ	*relatively*
fast	*almost*	völlig	*completely*
genug	*enough*	ziemlich	*fairly*
kaum	*hardly*	zu	*too*

(ii) Some adverbs of degree are usually found with a comparative.

Examples: Frankreich ist **bedeutend** größer als England. *France is significantly bigger than England.*

Others include:

entschieden	*decidedly*	weit(aus)	*considerably*
viel	*much*	wesentlich	*substantially*

(e) Question words include:

wann	*when*	woher	*where from*
bis wann	*until when, by when*	von wo	*where from*
seit wann	*how long for*	wie	*how*
wie lange	*how long*	warum	*why*
wie oft	*how often*	wieso	*why (colloquial)*
wo	*where*	weshalb	*why*
wohin	*where to*	wozu	*what . . . for*

As well as introducing direct questions, all of the above can introduce reported speech. See SUBJUNCTIVE in Chapter 8, GRAMMAR: 2.

CASES AND THEIR USE

The four **cases** in German are one of the principal areas of difficulty for English-speaking learners. But the rules for their use are relatively straightforward. Mastering them is a must for the serious A Level student.

(a) NOMINATIVE CASE

The Nominative case is used in the following situations.

(i) For the subject of a verb

Examples: **Ich** heiße Egon.   *My name is Egon.*
Heute schmeckte **der Fisch** ausgezeichnet.   *The fish was excellent today.*

(ii) After the verbs *sein, werden, bleiben, heißen* and *scheinen* and after the passive of *nennen*

Examples:

- Du bist und bleibst **mein Lieblingsvetter.**   *You are and remain my favourite cousin.*
- Er scheint **ein wunderbarer Fußballer.**   *He seems a wonderful footballer.*
- Karl I. wurde **Karl der Große** genannt.   *Charles I was called Charlemagne.*

(iii) In exclamations, when addressing people, and where there is no obvious reason for any other case

Examples:

- Ach **du liebe Zeit!**   *Hecky thump! / Bother!*
- Was hast du, **alter Freund?**   *What's the matter, my old friend?*
- Er saß im Auto, **der Hund** auf dem Schoß.   *He sat in the car, the dog on his lap.*

(b) THE ACCUSATIVE CASE

The accusative case is used in the following situations:

(i) For the direct object (the things that suffers the action of the verb) of active, transitive verbs

Example:

Ich habe **den Mann** gesehen.   *I saw the man.*

(ii) After certain prepositions. Some of them may take the Dative in certain circumstances. (See PREPOSITIONS below)

(iii) For expressions of definite time

Examples:

- **nächste Woche**   *next week*
- Es hat **den ganzen Monat** geregnet.   *It rained all month.*
- Donnerstag, **den 17. August 1995.**   *Thursday 17th August 1995.*

(iv) For measurements and distances

Examples:

- Diese schlampige Arbeit ist **keinen Pfennig** wert.   *This slapdash work isn't worth a pfennig.*
- Ich bin **den ganzen Weg** zu Fuß gegangen.   *I walked all the way.*

(v) For greetings and wishes

Examples:

- **Gute Besserung!**   *Get well soon!*
- **Herzlichen Glückwunsch!**   *Congratulations!*
- **Guten Abend!**   *Good evening!*

(c) THE GENITIVE CASE

(i) To denote 'of' or possession

Examples:

- Das Auto **meiner Eltern.**   *My parents' car.*
- Das Zwitschern **der Vögel.**   *The twittering of the birds.*
- Das Dach **des Hauses.**   *The roof of the house.*

(ii) With the names of people, towns or countries an alternative form similar to English usage is found (the Saxon Genitive)

Examples:

■ **Frau Krechels** Mercedes. *Frau Krechel's Mercedes.*
■ **Berlins** lebhafte Innenstadt. *Berlin's lively city centre.*

Point to watch: Note that there is NO apostrophe in German.

(iii) To show indefinite time

Examples:

■ **eines schönen Sommertages.** *One fine summer's day.*
■ **werktags.** *On working days.*

(iv) In some set phrases:

■ Ich bin **der Ansicht/ Auffassung/Meinung**, daß ... *I am of the opinion that ...*
■ Ich bin **schlechter Laune.** *I am in a bad mood.*
■ Ich bin **der festen Überzeugung**, daß... *I am firmly convinced that...*
■ **... letzten Endes** *... after all, in the final analysis*
■ **... meines Erachtens** *... in my view*
■ **... schweren Herzens** *... with a heavy heart*
■ Einmal **erster Klasse** nach Bonn, einfach, bitte. A single first-class ticket to Bonn, please.

(iv) After certain prepositions (see PREPOSTIONS)

(v) After certain adjectives (see ADJECTIVES)

(vi) *von* + Dative is used increasingly in preference to the Genitive, particularly to avoid a series of Genitives

Example:

■ Er guckte durch das Fenster **vom Hause** des Lehrers. *He looked through the window of the teacher's house.*

(d) THE DATIVE CASE

The Dative case is used in the following situations:

(i) For the indirect object of a verb

Example: Er gab **dem Mann** das Buch. *He gave the book to the man.*

Point to watch: Beware of missing the fact that the Dative is needed as it is not always immediately obvious from the English. The example above could be translated as: *He gave the man the book.*

(ii) After certain verbs which always take the Dative (see VERBS Chapter 8)

(iii) After certain adjectives. (see ADJECTIVES above)

(iv) To express advantage or disadvantage for someone

Examples:

■ Sie kaufte **ihm** eine Banane. *She bought a banana for him/She bought him a banana*
■ Man hat **mir** meinen Wagen gestohlen. *They stole my car from me.*
■ Das war **mir** ein Vergnügen. *It was a pleasure for me.*

(v) To show possession, especially with parts of the body or with clothing

Examples:

- Ich putzte **mir die Zähne.** *I cleaned my teeth.*
- Seine Mutter hat **ihm** den Kopf gewaschen. *His mother washed his hair. (Or: His mother gave him a real telling-off.)*
- Ich ziehe **mir** den grünen Pullover an. *I put on my green pullover.*

Note when it is NOT used:

- Ich putzte mein Zimmer. *I cleaned my room.*

Point to watch: Note that this case is not used for procedures which no-one else could possibly do for you, such as opening eyes.

(vi) In certain impersonal constructions expressing sensations

Examples:

- **Mir** ist warm. *I am hot.*
- **Ihm** wurde übel. *He felt sick.*

COMPARISONS

Adverbs and adjectives can be used in **comparative** (e.g. bigger, faster) and **superlative** (e.g. biggest, fastest) forms.
In German, the principle is much the same:

Examples:

- schnell* *fast*
- schnell**er** *faster*
- der/die/das schnellste* *the fastest*
- am schnellsten *in the fastest manner*

* takes the same endings as any other adjective

(a) COMMON EXCEPTIONS

(i) A number of common adjectives form comparatives in the usual way, but add an Umlaut

Examples:

- arm *poor*
- ärmer *poorer*
- der ärmste *the poorest*

These include:

alt	*old*	kurz	*short*
dumm	*stupid*	lang	*long*
groß	*large*	oft	*frequent*
hart	*hard*	scharf	*sharp*
jung	*young*	schwach	*weak*
kalt	*cold*	schwarz	*black*
klug	*clever*	stark	*strong*
krank	*ill*	warm	*warm*

(ii) Some adjectives and adverbs have very irregular comparative and superlative forms.

bald	eher	am ehesten	*soon*
gern	lieber	am liebsten	*willingly*
gut	besser	der beste	*good*
hoch	höher	der höchste	*high*
nah	näher	der nächste	*near*
oft	häufiger	am häufigsten	*frequently*
viel	mehr	der meiste	*much*

(c) Comparative sentence patterns

Note the ways of expressing positive and negative comparisons.

Examples:

- Ich bin aber intelligenter **als** du.   *But I am more intelligent than you.*
- Ich bin **nicht so** intelligent **wie** Albert Einstein.   *I am not as intelligent as Albert Einstein.*

(d) Superlative sentence patterns

Examples:

- Ich spiele am besten Tennis.   *I play tennis best of all.*
- Ich bin der beste (Tennisspieler).   *I am the best (tennis player).*
- Das wäre am besten.   *That would be best.*

CONJUNCTIONS

Conjunctions are words which join two clauses, such as *and, that, because*. In German conjunctions are divided into two categories, known as *co-ordinating* conjunctions and *sub-ordinating* conjunctions.

CO-ORDINATING CONJUNCTIONS

Co-ordinating conjunctions join two clauses which could otherwise stand as two German sentences in their own right without modification. It is worth committing the list of the *five most common ones* to memory. It is a fairly safe bet that, apart from the less common co-ordinating conjunctions, any conjunction other than the 'famous five' is a sub-ordinating conjunction.

Co-ordinating conjunctions have no effect on the word-order. They do NOT send the verb to the end of the clause, and they do NOT count in the '1-2-3' rule (see WORD ORDER below). Most of them can also link single words or phrases in lists.

(a) The 'famous five' co-ordinating conjunctions are:

und	*and*	sondern	*but not*
aber	*but*	denn	*for*
oder	*or*		

Example: Er kannte sie nicht lange **denn** er war erst seit ein paar Tagen in Berlin.   *He hadn't known her long for he had only been in Berlin a few days.*

(b) The less common co-ordinating conjunctions are:

allein	*but*	sowohl als (auch)	*and*
bald . . . bald	*now . . . now*	sowohl wie (auch)	*and*

beziehungsweise (bzw.)	*or*		teils . . . teils . . .	*partly . . . partly . . .*
doch	*but*		weder . . . noch . . .	*neither . . . nor*
entweder . . . oder . . .	*either . . . or . . .*		This one is only used in lists:	
nämlich	*as*		sowie	*and*

SUB-ORDINATING CONJUNCTIONS

Sub-ordinating conjunctions add a *sub-ordinate clause* (i.e. one which could not stand on its own as a German sentence without alteration) onto a main clause.

They send the verb to the end of the clause. If the verb is an auxiliary it usually comes after the past participle (but see MODAL VERBS in Chapter 8). A sub-ordinate clause always has a comma before the conjunction and after the verb, unless that position is the beginning or end of a sentence. The comma has nothing to do with taking breath, as in English, but merely marks the fact that it is a sub-ordinate clause.

Examples:

- Ich weiß genau, daß er heute kommt, ja, ganz genau.
- Daß er heute kommt, weiß ich ganz genau. *I am quite sure he is coming today.*

The subordinating conjunctions are listed below by category. In each list, the more common ones are given first.

(a) Conjunctions of time

(i) Common		**(ii) Less common**	
als	*when (single occasion in past)*	ehe	*before*
bevor	*before*	indem	*as*
bis	*until*	indessen	as
nachdem	*after (she had done that)*	kaum daß	*hardly, scarcely (had she . . .)*
seitdem	*since*	seit	*since*
sobald	*as soon as*	sowie	*as soon as*
während	*while, whilst*	solange	*as long as, while*
wenn	*when, whenever (repeated occasion), if*		
wie	*as*		

(b) Conjunctions of reason

(i) Common		**(ii) Less common**	
da	*as*	nun	*now that, seeing that*
weil	*because*	um so mehr als	*all the more because*
		zumal	*especially as*

(c) Conjunctions of purpose

(i) Common		**(ii) Less common**	
damit	*so that*	auf daß	*so that*
so daß	*in such a way that*		

(d) Conjunctions of result

(i) Common		**(ii) Less common**	
so daß	*so that, in such a way that*	derart daß	*so that, in such a way that*
als daß (only after	*in such a way that*		
zu, nicht genug and			
nicht so)			

(e) Conjunctions of concession

(i) Common		**(ii) Less common**	
obwohl	*although*	obgleich	*although*
zwar* . . . aber*	*although*	obschon	*although*
		wer . . . auch	*whoever*
		wann . . . auch	*whenever*
was . . . für + Acc	*what sort of*	wohin . . . auch	*wherever*
*(NB these are CO-ORDINATING		wo . . . auch	*wherever*
conjunctions)		wie . . . auch	*however*

(f) Conjunctions of manner and degree

(i) Common		**(ii) Less common**	
als	*than*	als wenn (+ subjunctive)	*as if*
als ob* (+ subjunctive)	*as if*	anstatt daß	*instead of*
dadurch daß	*by . . . ing*	statt daß	*instead of*
je . . . desto . . .	*the (more) the merrier)*	außer daß	*except that*
ohne daß	*without . . . ing*	außer wenn	*except when*
wie	*as, how*	insofern als	*in so far as*
		je nachdem ob	*depending on*
		nur daß	*only that*
* the ob may be omitted, in which case *als* is		sofern	*provided that*
immediately followed by the verb		soweit	*as far as*

(g) Conjunctions of condition

(i) Common		**(ii) Less Common**	
wenn	*if*	angenommen, daß	*assuming that*
		es sei denn, daß	*unless*
		im Falle, daß	*if*
		vorausgesetzt, daß	*provided that*

NOUNS

GENDER

All German nouns are grammatically masculine, feminine, or neuter. This presents a real problem for English learners in knowing which is which. The only real solution is to note the **gender** and the plural form when first encountering a word. However the following guidelines may help to reduce the labour.

(a) Masculine by meaning

(i) **male persons and animals** – der Lehrer, etc. – der Kater (*tomcat*), etc. See also (d) below.

(ii) **seasons, months and days of the week** – der Frühling – der Januar – der Montag

(iii) **points of the compass, winds, most sorts of weather** – der Norden – der Frost – der Wind

Exceptions: die Brise, das Eis, das Gewitter, das Wetter, die Witterung (*weather conditions*)

(iv) **rocks and minerals** – der Diamant – der Glimmerschiefer (*micaschist*) – der Granit – der Kalkstein (*limestone*) – der Sandstein – der Ton (*clay*)

Exceptions: das Erz (*ore*), die Kohle, die Kreide, die Lava, das Mineral

(v) **alcoholic drinks except das Bier** – der Wein – der Schnaps – der Wodka – etc

(vi) **makes of car** – der Audi – der BMW – der Ford – der Mercedes – der Porsche – der VW

(vii) **rivers outside Germany which do not end in -e or -a** – der Mississippi – der Kongo – der Severn

Exceptions: die Themse, die Wolga

(b) Feminine by meaning

(i) **female persons and animals** – die Frau – die Henne – die Katze. See also (d)

(ii) **aeroplanes, motorcycles and ships** – die Boeing – die BMW – die 'TS Hanseatic'

Exceptions: der Airbus, der Starfighter

(iii) **German rivers** – die Donau, die Elbe, die Ruhr, die Spree, die Weser

Exceptions: der Inn, der Lech, der Main, der Neckar, der Rhein

(iv) **names of numerals** – die Eins – die Million – die Milliarde

(c) Neuter by meaning

(i) **young persons and animals** – das Baby – das Kind – das Lamm. See also (d)

(ii) **metals and chemical elements** – das Aluminium – das Gold – das Kupfer – das Zinn (*pewter*)

(iii) **physical units** – das Atom – das Pfund

(iv) **letters of the alphabet** – das A und O – ein großes A

(v) **infinitives of verbs used as nouns** – das Essen – das Neinsagen

(vi) **colours and languages** – das Rot – das schwierige Deutsch

(vii) **English -ing forms** – das Meeting

(viii) **most countries, continents, provinces and towns** – das moderne Afrika – das alte Schottland – das neue Berlin

Exceptions: die Schweiz, die Pfalz, die Türkei, die Bretagne, die Normandie, der Irak, der Iran, der Kongo, der Libanon

(d) Unhelpful genders of names of human beings

die Geisel	*hostage*	das Mitgleid	*member*
das Genie	*genius*	die Person	*person*
das Individuum	*individual*	das Weib	*woman*

(e) Masculine by form

Nouns with the following endings are **masculine.**

-ant (en)	der Passant (*passer-by*)	*-ismus* (no pl)	der Kommunismus
-ig (e)	der Honig	*-us* (-en)	der Rhythmus
-or (en)	der Motor	*-ich* (e)	der Teppich
-ast (e)	der Kontrast	*-ling* (e)	der Liebling (*darling*)

(f) Feminine by form

Nouns with the following endings are **feminine.**

-a (-en)	die Villa	*-keit* (en)	die Freundlichkeit
-anz (no pl)	die Eleganz	*-schaft* (en)	die Freundschaft
-ei (en)	die Bücherei	*-sion* (en)	die Explosion
-enz (en)	die Tendenz	*-sis* (sen)	die Basis (die Basen)
-heit (en)	die Freiheit	*-tion* (en)	die Situation
-ie (n)	die Technologie	*-tät* (en)	die Aktivität
-ik (en)	die Musik	*-ung* (en)	die Landung
-in (nen)	die Lehrerin		

Exceptions: das Sofa, der Papagei (*parrot*), das Genie, der Atlantik, der Katholik, das Mosaik, der Pazifik

(g) Neuter by form

Nouns with the following endings are **neuter.**

-chen (-) das Mädchen		*-ment* (s)	das Apartement
-icht (e) das Dickicht (*thicket*)		*-tel*	das Zehntel
-il (e) das Krokodil		*-tum* (no pl) das Christentum	
-lein das Fräulein, das Büchleindy>			

(h) Compound words

These take the gender and the plurals of the last part.

Examples: der Stundenplan, die Straßenbahnhaltestelle, das Freibad

(i) Recent English loan words are predominantly masculine, with neuter being the next most common

Masculine: der Boom, der Compact Disc, der Computer, der Hit, der Jazz, der Job, der Sex, der Showdown, der Streß, der Trend

Neuter: das Baby, das Make-up, das Mountainbike, das Poster, das Puzzle (*jig-saw*)

Feminine: die Bar, die City, die Show, die Party, die Story

(j) Some nouns have two (or more) genders with different meanings

The more common ones are listed here.

- der Band (Ꞌe) *volume, book*   das Band (Ꞌer) *ribbon* – die Band (s) *pop group*
- der Gehalt (e) *content*   das Gehalt (Ꞌer) *salary*
- der Golf (e) *gulf*   das Golf (no pl) *golf*
- der Heide (n) *heathen*   die Heide (n) *heath*
- der Leiter (-) *leader*   die Leiter (n) *ladder*
- der Messer (-) *surveyor/gauge*   das Messer (-) *knife*
- der Pony (no pl) *fringe*   das Pony (s) *pony*
- der See (n) *lake*   die See (no pl) *sea*
- die Steuer (n) *tax*   das Steuer (-) *steering wheel*
- der Verdienst (no pl) *earnings*   das Verdienst (e) *merit*

PLURAL FORMS

Many attempts have been made to codify these **plural forms**, none of them totally satisfactory. I will confine my efforts to listing rules which always apply, and making some recommendations about what to do if you have to guess. Sadly, the only way to make real headway in learning plural forms is to note them with each new word. Examples have not been given here – the safest way is to check individual words.

(a) Masculine nouns

There are no hard-and-fast rules concerning the plurals of **masculine nouns**. The following guidelines might be helpful.

(i) The great majority of masculine nouns form their plural with *-e* or Ꞌe. The Umlaut is added in about half the cases.
(ii) The great majority of masculine nouns ending in *-el, -en* or Ꞌer form their plural with no change.
(iii) A small number of masculine nouns form their plural in *-er,* Ꞌer, -n and *-en*.

(b) Feminine nouns

(i) Over 90% of feminine nouns have the plural *-en* or *-n*.
(ii) Only *die Mutter* (Ꞌ) and *die Tochter* (Ꞌ) have the plural (Ꞌ).
(iii) No feminine nouns have plurals in (-) or (Ꞌer).

(c) Neuter nouns

(i) About 75% of neuter nouns have the plural (*-e*).
(ii) Most of the remainder have the plural (Ꞌer).

(d) Loan words from English or French

Most of these have plural in *-s*.

DECLENSION OF NOUNS

German nouns have slight *spelling changes* in the following cases:

(a) In the Genitive singular, masculine and neuter nouns add an *-s*, or, if single syllable words, often *-es*.
Examples: wegen des schlechten Wetter**s**
          trotz des Schnee**s**
(b) In the Dative plural, irrespective of gender, an *-n* is added if one is not already present, or unless the plural ends in *-s*.
Example: mit den Schüler**n**

WEAK NOUNS

These nouns are slightly irregular. All but one of them (*das Herz*) are masculine.

(a) The majority have *-en* throughout the plural and in all cases of the singular except the Nominative. They do not have an *-s* in the Genitive singular

Examples:

	Singular	Plural
Nominative	der Franzose	die Franzosen
Accusative	den Franzosen	die Franzosen
Genitive	des Franzosen	der Franzosen
Dative	dem Franzosen	den Franzosen
Nominative	der Mensch	die Menschen
Accusative	den Menschen	die Menschen
Genitive	des Menschen	der Menschen
Dative	dem Menschen	den Menschen

They include the following categories of nouns:

(i) **Those ending in -e in the Nominative singular (which is how they are listed in the dictionary).**
Examples: der Affe (*monkey*), der Bursche (*lad*), der Rabe (*raven*), der Schwabe (*Swabian*)
Exceptions: der Käse, and the eight nouns listed in (b)

(ii) **Some native nouns not ending in -e in the Nominative singular.**

These include:

der Bär	*bear*	der Herr	*gentleman*
der Bauer	*peasant*	der Hirt	*shepherd*
der Bayer	*Bavarian*	der Mensch	*human being*
der Fürst	*prince*	der Nachbar	*neighbour*
der Fotograf	*photographer*	der Narr	*fool*
der Held	*hero*	der Untertan	*subject*

(iii) **Foreign nouns ending in** -and, -ant, - aph, -arch, -at, -ent, -et, -ist, -krat, *-log, -nom, -on*
Examples: der Konfirmand, der Ministrant, der Seraph, der Monarch, der Automat, der Student, der Komet, der Organist, der Autokrat, der Astrolog, der Astronom, der Dämon

(iv) **Some other foreign words**
der Barbar, der Chirurg, der Kamarad, der Katholik, der Tyrann

(b) Eight masculine nouns behave like those in (a), except that they have *-ens* in the Genitive singular

Example:

	Singular	Plural
Nominative	der Name	die Namen
Accusative	den Namen	die Namen
Genitive	des Namens	der Namen
Dative	dem Namen	den Namen

The eight are:

der Buchstabe	*letter of the alphabet*	der Glaube	*belief*
der Friede	*peace*	der Name	*name*

| der Funke | *spark* | der Same | *seed* |
| der Gedanke | *thought* | der Wille | *will* |

(c) das Herz is declined like this:

	Singular	**Plural**
Nominative	das Herz	die Herzen
Accusative	das Herz	die Herzen
Genitive	des Herzens	der Herzen
Dative	dem Herzen	den Herzen

NUMBERS

CARDINAL NUMBERS

(a) These are as follows:

0	null	16	sechzehn *(NB spelling)*
1	eins	17	siebzehn *(NB spelling)*
2	zwei	18	achtzehn
3	drei	19	neunzehn
4	vier	20	zwanzig
5	fünf	21	einundzwanzig
6	sechs	22	zweiundzwanzig, etc
7	sieben	30	dreißig *(NB spelling)*
8	acht	40	vierzig
9	neun	50	fünfzig
10	zehn	60	sechzig *(NB spelling)*
11	elf	70	siebzig *(NB spelling)*
12	zwölf	80	achtzig
13	dreizehn	90	neunzig
14	vierzehn	100	hundert
15	fünfzehn		

101	hunderteins
102	hundertzwei
131	hunderteinunddreißig
200	zweihundert
999	neunhundertneunundneunzig
1000	tausend
1002	tausendzwei
1100	tausendeinhundert/elfhundert/eintausendeinhundert
654 321	sechshundertvierundfünfzigtausenddreihunderteinundzwanzig
1 000 000	eine Million *(NB spaces every 3 digits, no commas)*
56 500 200	sechsundfünzig Millionen fünfhunderttausendzweihundert *(NB new word after Millionen)*
1 000 000 000	eine Milliarde
2 000 000 000	zwei Milliarden

(b) Points of usage of cardinal numbers

(i) In practice, complex numbers are never written out in full: figures are used instead.

(ii) *Zwo* is used instead of *zwei* where there is any danger of confusion. It is common in public announcements, and on the telephone.

(iii) Longer numbers – such as telephone numbers after dialling codes – are written and read in pairs.

Example : 02264/54 65 07 is pronounced as: Null zwo zwo sechs vier, vierundfünfzig fünfundsechzig null sieben

(iv) Years are usually stated in hundreds:

Example: 1995 = neunzehnhundertfünfundneunzig

(v) Cardinal numbers can be used as nouns, particularly when discussing school grades.

Example: Ich habe eine Sechs in Mathe.   *I have a 6 in maths.*

(vi) 7 is usually written with a cross, to distinguish it from 1, eg 7

ORDINAL NUMBERS

(a) Virtually all ordinal numbers are formed as follows:

(i) 2nd, 4th, 6th and 8th - 19th add -te to the cardinal number

Examples: der vier**te**, der sechzehn**te**

Exceptions are:
1st   der erste
3rd   der dritte
7th   der siebte

(ii) 20th and upwards add -ste to the cardinal number

Examples: der zwanzigste, der dreiundzwanzigste, der hundertste, der tausendste, der millionste

However, if the number above 20 ends with part of the compound derived from a number less than 20, the endings in (i) apply.

Examples: der hunderterste, der tausenddritte, der zweihundertsechzehnte

(b) The use of ordinal numbers is straightforward

(i)   They are normally used as adjectives, and take the usual endings.
(ii) They can be compounded to give words like der *drittbeste*.
(iii) In writing, they are usually written as an abbreviation which must have a full stop.

Examples:

■   am 1.10. (pronounced: am ersten zehnten)   *on the first of the tenth*
■   der 324. Versuch   *the 324th attempt*

FRACTIONS

(a) Most fractions – except 'half' – are formed by adding -el to the ordinal

Examples: Ein Viertel(-), ein Zehntel(-), ein Drittel (-)   *a quarter, a tenth a third*

They can also function as adjectives which take no endings.

Example: mit einem Viertel Glas   *with a quarter of a glass*

(b) 'Half' can be either the noun *die Hälfte* or the adjective *halb*

(i) *Die Hälfte* is used as follows:

Examples:

- Ich habe nur die Hälfte gelesen *I have only read half of it.*
- Die Hälfte des Kuchens ist schon gegessen worden. *Half the cake has already been eaten.*

(ii) *halb* is used like this:

Examples:

- Ich aß eine halbe Banane. *I ate half a banana.*
- Ich bin nur halb fertig. *I am only half ready.*

(iii) One and a half is *anderthalb* or *eineinhalb.* The principle of eineinhalb continues with zweieinhalb, dreieinhalb, etc.

(c) Decimals are written with a comma and not a point in German

Example: Ich habe eine Durchschnittsnote von 2,3 (pronounced zwei Komma drei). *I have an average mark of 2.3.*

PREPOSITIONS

Prepositions express a relationship between one noun and another, often of position, hence the name.

In German prepositions are followed by different cases. For the majority of prepositions, it is merely a matter of knowing what they 'take' ('govern'). For example, *mit* takes the Dative. However, there is a group of common prepositions which take either Accusative or Dative according to their meaning.

Mastering the use of at least the common prepositions is one of the essential – but tricky – jobs of the A Level student. It really is worth committing the lists of the common prepositions and the case(s) they take to memory. I have listed the common and less common prepositions separately, for convenience.

(a) Prepositions which always take the Accusative

(i) Common		**(ii) Less common**	
bis	*as far as; until;*	à	*@ with prices*
durch	*through; throughout; by (see PASSIVE)*	betreffend** eingerechnet*	*regarding including*
für	*for*	per	*by*
gegen	*against; towards; in about; compared with*	pro wider	*per against*
ohne	*without*		
um	*round; about; at + clock times; concerning; by (degree of difference)*	* follows the noun ** may precede or follow the noun	

(b) Prepositions which always take the Dative

(i) Common	
aus	*out of; made of*
außer	*except for; out of (use)*
bei	*by; at; at the house of in view of; on the occasion of*
gegenüber**	*opposite; compared with; in relation to; towards*
mit	*with; (see also PASSIVE); by*
nach	*to; towards; after + time; according to*
seit	*since; for (uses a more recent tense than in English)*
** may precede or follow the noun	

| von | from; by (see PASSIVE); of |
| zu | to; sometimes at; for; as; towards; at + price |

Point to watch: aus and *zu* both look as though they might take the Accusative because they imply motion (see below). They NEVER take the Accusative.

(ii) Less common

ab	from
binnen	within (a given period)
dank	thanks to
entgegen**	contrary to
entsprechend	according to
laut	according to
zufolge	according to
mitsamt	together with
nahe	near to
nebst	in addition to
zuliebe*	for the sake of
zuwider*	contrary to

*follows the noun ** may precede or follow the noun

Point to watch: In the Dative plural, most nouns add an *-n* if they do not already have one. It's easy to forget it.

(c) Prepositions which take either Accusative or Dative

Ten common prepositions take either Accusative or Dative. Two basic rules apply to the majority of instances.

(i) If the preposition expresses position, then the Dative is used. If it expresses motion towards, the Accusative is used.

It may be helpful to memorise these mnemonic sentences:

D<u>a</u>tive is st<u>a</u>tion<u>a</u>ry or movement <u>at</u>. Acc<u>u</u>sative is m<u>o</u>vement t<u>o</u>.

Examples:

■ Ich gehe in die Stadt (*in* + Accusative – motion). *I go into town.*
■ Ich wohne in der Stadt (*in* + Dative – position). *I live in the town.*

This can lead to fine distinctions. The movement is relative to the noun.

Contrast:

■ Ich gehe ins Zimmer. *I walk into the room.* (I start outside the room and finish up inside it, so motion has occurred.)

with:

■ Ich gehe im Zimmer herum. *I walk around in the room.* (I start walking inside the room and finish walking inside the room, so no motion relative to the room has occurred.)

Verbs of arriving, appearing and disappearing are usually used in conjunction with a Dative.

Example: Ich bin am Bahnhof angekommen. *I arrived at the station.*

(ii) **If the preposition expresses a figurative sense, it often takes the Accusative.**

Example: Er weiß viel über die Stadt. *He knows a lot about the town.*

Although the above rules can apply to most of the Accusative/Dative prepositions, in practice the majority of them are most frequently found in the cases indicated in brackets. It is really *an, auf, in* and *über* which most often require careful thought.

an	*on (the side of); at; of*
auf	*on (top of); at; in;*
entlang* (usually + Acc)	*along*
hinter (usually + Dat)	*behind*
in	*in; inside*
neben (usually + Dat)	*next to*
über	*over; about; more than*
unter (usually + Dat)	*under; below; among*
vor (usually + Dat)	*in front of; before*
zwischen (usually + Dat)	*between*
*follows the noun	

(d) Prepositions which take the Genitive

(i) Common	
anstatt	*instead of*
statt	*instead of*
trotz	*despite, in spite of*
während	*during*
wegen	*because of*

(ii) less common

All of these eight may, alternatively, be followed by *von* + Dative, for example: unweit von der Schule *not far from the school*

They are listed as related groups, for ease of learning.

außerhalb	*outside (of)*
innerhalb	*within*
oberhalb	*above*
unterhalb	*below*
beiderseits	*on both sides of*
diesseits	*on this side of*
jenseits	*on the far side of*
unweit	*not far from*

(iii) least common

There are over 50 less common prepositions which take the Genitive, many of them mainly of commercial use. A selection is given below:

angesichts	*in view of*
anläßlich	*on the occasion of*
aufgrund	*on the strength of*
einschließlich	*including*
halber*	*for the sake of*
hinsichtlich	*with regard to*
seitlich	*at the side of*
um . . . Willen	*for the sake of*
vorbehaltlich	*subject to*
zugunsten	*in favour of, for the benefit of*
zwecks	*for the purpose of*

*follows the noun

Point to watch: Remember that singular masculine and neuter nouns add an *-s* in the Genitive.

PRONOUNS

Pronouns stand in the place of a noun, and are used to avoid repetition. The case is determined by the pronoun's function in the sentence.

PERSONAL PRONOUNS

Nominative		Accusative		Dative	
ich	*I*	mich	*me*	mir	*to me*
du	*you (singular, familiar)*	dich	*you*	dir	*to you*
Sie	*you (singular, formal)*	Sie	*you*	Ihnen	*to you*
er	*he or it*	ihn	*him or it*	ihm	*to him or it*
sie	*she or it*	sie	*her or it*	ihr	*to her or it*
es	*it*	es	*it*	ihm	*to it*
man	*one*	einen	*one*	einem	*to one*
wir	*we*	uns	*us*	uns	*to us*
ihr	*you (plural, familiar)*	euch	*you*	euch	*to you*
Sie	*you (plural, formal)*	Sie	*you*	Ihnen	*to you*
sie	*they*	sie	*them*	ihnen	*to them*

NB the Genitive is rarely found nowadays.

REFLEXIVE PRONOUNS

(a) **The Accusative reflexive pronouns** are as in the example below:	(b) **The Dative reflexive pronouns** are as follows:
ich wasche mich	ich wasche mir die Haare
du wäschst dich	du wäschst dir die Haare
Sie waschen sich	Sie waschen sich die Haare
er wäscht sich	er wäscht sich die Haare
sie wäscht sich	sie wäscht sich die Haare
es wäscht sich	es wäscht sich die Haare
man wäscht sich	man wäscht sich die Haare
wir waschen uns	wir waschen uns die Haare
ihr wascht euch	ihr wascht euch die Haare
Sie waschen sich	Sie waschen sich die Haare
sie waschen sich	sie waschen sich die Haare

Note that these are only distinctive after *ich* and *du*. See also CASES – DATIVE (above).

The **plural reflexive pronoun** can be used to express the idea of 'each other'.

Examples: Wir sehen uns morgen.   *We'll see each other tomorrow.*

DU AND SIE, IHR AND SIE

Germans are very concerned to use the correct form for 'you'. As time goes on the *du/ihr* forms are becoming used in a wider range of circumstances. However, amongst adults, it is safer to start with the *Sie* form. Often quite a little ceremony is made of the change to the use of '*du*'.
   The following are the main rules concerning choice of 'you'.

(a) *Du* is used:

- for speaking to God, oneself, a child (up to about age 15) and an animal,
- between children, students, relatives and close friends, blue-collar workmates, members of clubs and (left-wing) political parties.

(b) *Ihr* is used to address a group of people of which at least some would be addressed as '*du*'.

(c) *Sie* is used in all other cases, and particularly between adult strangers, and in most white-collar occupations.

ER, SIE AND ES

(a) It should be remembered that 'it' may refer to a masculine or feminine noun in German, and that *er* or *sie, ihn* or *sie, ihm* or *ihr* may be required. *Er* and *sie* do not refer solely to biological gender.

Examples:

- Hier ist die Banane. Ich habe sie gestern gekauft.   *Here is the banana. I bought it yesterday.*
- Hier ist der berühmte Wagen. Ich bin mit ihm zum Nordkapp gefahren.   *Here is the famous car. I drove it to North Cape.*

(b) There is occasional conflict between biological and grammatical gender, particularly with *das Mädchen* and *das Fräulein*. They can be referred to as either *es* or *sie*.

(c) After prepositions, special rules apply.

(i) *Es* is never used after a preposition. Instead the preposition has the prefix *da(r)* attached to give *darauf, danach*, etc.

Examples: Hier ist endlich das Schiff. Wir haben lang genug darauf gewartet   *Here is the ship at last. We've been waiting for it long enough.*

(ii) Where people are referred to in the singular, the normal forms of the pronouns are used after prepositions.

Example: Bist du mit ihr gekommen?   *Did you come with her?*

(d) *Es* is used in a variety of ways.

(i) Like the English 'it' with *sein* and *werden*. It also works in the plural.

Examples:

■ Es ist schön hier   *It is nice here.*
■ Es sind Eichhörnchen, die es gemacht haben. *It is squirrels that have done it.*

(ii) It can be used with impersonal constructions – see Chapter 8.

RELATIVE PRONOUNS

Relative pronouns correspond to 'who, whom, whose, which or that' in English. It is important to know the test for whether 'that' is in fact a relative pronoun, or best translated by *daß*. If 'who' or 'which' can be substituted for 'that' without changing the meaning, it is a relative pronoun. If the substitution cannot be made without generating nonsense, use *daß*.

Examples:

■ This is the house *that* Jack built.
  Substitute *which:*
  This is the house *which* Jack built.
  Therefore the original 'that' is a **relative pronoun**.
■ I think that you should go.
  Substitute *which*: I think *which* you should go.
  This is nonsense, and 'that' should be *daß*.

A further complication is that the relative pronoun is often missed out in English, in such sentences as: This is the book I am reading at the moment. This NEVER happens in German.

(a) The form of the relative pronoun

	Masculine	Feminine	Neuter	Plural	
Nominative	der	die	das	die	*who, which, that*
Accusative	den	die	das	die	*who(m), which, that*
Genitive	dessen	deren	dessen	deren	*whose, of which*
Dative	dem	der	dem	denen	*to whom, to which*

(b) Agreement

The relative pronoun agrees with the noun to which it refers in **number** (singular or plural) and **gender** (masculine, feminine or neuter), but NOT in **case**. The **case** of the relative pronoun is determined by its function in the relative clause.

(c) Case

If the suggested English translations of the relative pronoun are borne in mind, it is quite easy to sort out which case to choose.

Examples:

NOM
■ Ich bin eine Lehrerin, die oft nach Deutschland fährt. *I am a teacher who/that often travels to Germany.*
ACC
■ Ich bin ein Lehrer, den man oft in der Stadt sieht. *I am a teacher (that/who/whom) you can often see in town.*
GEN
■ Ich bin ein Mann, dessen Kinder artig sind. *I am a man whose children are well-behaved.*
DAT
■ Seefahrer sind Leute, mit denen ich nichts anfangen kann. *Seamen are people with whom I don't get on.*

(d) After *alles, nichts, etwas,* and the less frequent *einiges, folgendes, manches* and *vieles,* the relative pronoun is always *was.*

Example: Alles, was ich habe, ist meine Küchenschabe. *All I have left is my cockroach.*

(e) Note the idiomatic use of *das, was:*

Example: Ich habe nur das, was ich mitgebracht habe. *I only have what I have brought with me.*

(f) Other idiomatic uses of other relative pronouns include:

(i) *wo* as an alternative for in + relative.

Example: Das Dorf, wo ich wohne. *The village where I live.*

(ii) Where English uses 'when' as a relative pronoun, German will prefer a preposition + a relative pronoun:

Examples:

■ Der Tag, an dem wir heirateten, ist mir unvergeßlich. *The day when we got married is unforgettable for me.*
■ Die Zeit war eine, in der sich vieles ändern mußte. *The time was one when many things had to change.*

Point to watch: In German the punctuation rules require that relative pronouns have a comma in front of them. This is unlike many English relative clauses – beware!

INTERROGATIVE PRONOUNS

These are question words which change according to case. The case is determined by their function in the sentence.

(a) *wer*(who) declines as follows:

Nominative	wer	*who*
Accusative	wen	*who (m)*
Genitive	wessen	*whose*
Dative	wem	*to whom*

Examples:

■ Wessen Fahrrad ist das? *Whose bike is that?*
■ Wen hast du gesehen? *Who(m) did you see?*

(b) Where *what* is used as a question word in combination with a preposition, the preposition has *wo(r)-* added to the front of it. This has the advantage that you don't have to work out which case it should be!

Example: Womit habt ihr gespielt? *What did you play with?*

(c) Welcher (*which*) declines as follows:

	Masculine	Feminine	Neuter	Plural	
Nominative	welcher	welche	welches	welche	*which*
Accusative	welchen	welche	welches	welche	*which*
Genitive	welches	welcher	welches	welcher	*of which*
Dative	welchem	welcher	welchem	welchen	*to which*

(i) It agrees with the noun to which it refers.

Example: Welches Kind hat die Stinkbombe geworfen? *Which child threw the stinkbomb?*

(ii) It is also used as a slightly more formal alternative to the standard relative pronoun.

Example:

■ Der Vorsitzende des Kommittees, welcher seit Jahren dagegen gewesen ist, hat erstaunlicherweise zugestimmt. *The Chair of the committee, who had been against it for years, amazingly agreed to it.*

DEMONSTRATIVE PRONOUNS

(a) These agree with the noun to which they refer, and decline like this:

	Masculine	Feminine	Neuter	Plural
Nominative	dieser	diese	dieses	diese
Accusative	diesen	diese	dieses	diese
Genitive	dieses	dieser	dieses	dieser
Dative	diesem	dieser	diesem	diesen

Following this pattern are:

dieser *this*
jener *that*
solcher *such a*

(b) Some demonstratives have *der* + something, for example *derjenige*, and *derselbe*. Both parts of these compounds decline.

Example: Diejenigen, die in Hamburg wohnten, hatten keine Probleme. *Those who lived in Hamburg had no problems.*

SPELLING AND PUNCTUATION

SPELLING

(a) Similar sounds with different spellings

This presents few problems for the careful English-speaking learner – fewer in fact than for young Germans! The only ambiguity which causes serious problems English-speakers is between *e* and *ä*, although the sounds *are* actually different. It might be worth noting that there is no difference in sound between a -*d* and a -*t* at the end of a word, as in *das Rad* (bicycle) and *der Rat* (advice, council).

(b) The Umlaut

A more common mistake is 'Umlaut blindness', caused by English speakers assuming that they have no significance or are mere decoration. In fact they convey significant subtleties of meaning, as can be seen by checking out the sections on CONDITIONAL, SUBJUNCTIVE, PASSIVE, (see Chapter 8) and COMPARISONS, (see above). So an Umlaut mistake is a serious one. Work on eliminating them!

(c) ss or ß?

Although there is a move in some quarters to be rid of ß, it does not appear to be gaining ground. Therefore British learners would be best advised to learn how to use ß.

(i) ß is used:

■ before consonants, e.g. du läßt, er mußte, etc.,
■ at the end of a word or part of a compound, e.g. der Fuß, die Fußgängerzone,
■ between two vowels if the first vowel is long, e.g. die Füße, viele Grüße.

(ii) **ss** is used

- between two vowels if the first vowel is short, e.g. die Flüsse, lassen, müssen

(d) triple consonants

(i) Occasionally a triple consonant will be found in German when a compound word is formed, and the triple consonant is followed by a further consonant.

Example: Fett + Tropfen = Fetttropfen

(ii) However, if the multiple consonant is followed by a vowel, one of the three consonants is dropped.

Example: Schiff + Fahrt = Schiffahrt

PUNCTUATION

Punctuation in German has a more grammatical rationale than in English, where sense and breathing play a role.

(i) Capital letters are used:

- at the start of sentences,
- for all nouns, wherever they occur,
- for the 'polite' personal pronouns except *sich,* and their related possessives (*Sie, Ihnen Ihr.*),
- in letters, for the 'familiar' personal pronouns and their related possessives (*Du, Dir, Dein, Ihr, Euch, Euer*),
- in titles of books, films, etc.

They are not used for nationalities which are adjectives or adverbs.

Example: Ein britisches Schiff hatte eine Aufschrift auf deutsch. *A British ship had some lettering in German.*

(ii) Commas are used:

- in lists, but not before the *und*

Example: Er hatte zwei Hunde, eine Katze und einen Hamster. *He had two dogs, a cat, and a hamster.*

- where there are two main clauses linked by a co-ordinating conjunction

Example: Mein Vater wohnt in Hamburg, und meine Mutter wohnt in Berlin. *My father lives in Hamburg and my mother lives in Berlin.*

- where there is a subordinate clause

Examples:

- Ich wohnte in Flensburg, als ich zweiundzwanzig war. *I lived in Flensburg when I was twenty-two.*
- Als ich zweiundzwanzig war, wohnte ich in Flensburg. *When I was twenty-two I lived in Flensburg.*

Point to watch: The second example shows the word order sequence verb – comma – verb which is very common.

(iii) No comma is used if the subordinate clause is simply a 2-word clause consisting of zu + an infinitive

Example: Ich beschloß zu gehen. *I decided to go.*

(iv) Exclamation marks are used:

■ after commands (even whispered ones!)

Example: Setzen Sie sich! *Sit down.*

■ after interjections

Examples: Ach! Verdammt! *Oh! Bother!*

■ Often after the opening of a letter

Example: Lieber Herr Braun!   *Dear Mr Brown,*
         Wie geht es Ihnen?   *How are you?*

This usage is rapidly being replaced by the following punctuation

    Lieber Herr Braun,
       wie geht es Ihnen?

Point to watch: Note the lower case *w* on *wie*.

(v) Direct Speech is written as follows:

Ich sagte: „Wie heißt du?"

(vii) The semi-colon

The semi-colon is a rarity in German and is best avoided by English learners. If translating, break a lengthy English sentence with semi-colons into two sentences.

TIMES AND DATES

TIMES OF THE CLOCK

There are two ways of telling the time, the everyday way and using the 24-hour clock.

(a) The everyday way

(i) The basics

1.00	Es ist ein Uhr
3.00	Es ist drei Uhr
4.05	Es ist fünf (Minuten) nach vier
4.15	Es ist Viertel nach vier
4.30	Es ist halb fünf (*beware!!*)
4.45	Es ist Viertel vor fünf
4.55	Es ist fünf (Minuten) vor fünf
12.00	Es ist Mittag/Mitternacht

(ii) More complicated ways of doing it

4.15	Es ist Viertel fünf
4.25	Es ist fünf vor halb fünf
4.35	Es ist fünf nach halb fünf
4.45	Es ist dreiviertel fünf

(b) The 24-hour clock

1.00	Es ist ein Uhr
3.00	Es ist drei Uhr
14.05	Es ist vierzehn Uhr fünf
14.15	Es ist vierzehn Uhr fünfzehn
14.30	Es ist vierzehn Uhr dreißig
14.145	Es ist vierzehn Uhr fünfundvierzig
14.55	Es ist vierzehn Uhr fünfundfünfzig

| 12.00 | Es ist zwölf Uhr |
| 00.01 | Es ist null Uhr eins |

DAYS

All of these are *masculine*.

Montag	*Monday*	Freitag	*Friday*
Dienstag	*Tuesday*	Samstag	*Saturday*
Mittwoch	*Wednesday*	Sonnabend	*Saturday*
Donnerstag	*Thursday*	Sonntag	*Sunday*

Note the usage Am Sonntag   *on Sunday*

Point to watch: Be wary of missing the correct meaning of *Sonnabend.*

MONTHS

All of these are *masculine*.

Januar	*January*	Juli	*July*
Februar	*February*	August	*August*
März	*March*	September	*September*
April	*April*	Oktober	*October*
Mai	*May*	November	*November*
Juni	*June*	Dezember	*December*

Note the following usages:

(i) im März   *in March*
(ii) Juni and Juli are often pronounced Juno and Julei on the telephone to reduce confusion.

DATES

(a) The major public holidays are:

Neujahr	*New Year's Day*
Rosenmontag	*Carnival Monday, before Pancake Day*
Aschermittwoch	*Ash Wednesday*
Karfreitag	*Good Friday*
zu Ostern	*at Easter*
Ostersonntag	*Easter Sunday*
Ostermontag	*Easter Monday*
Fronleichnam	*Corpus Christi*
der erste Mai	*May Day*
Pfingsten	*Whitsun (NB usually the week after the British Spring Bank Holiday)*
Christi Himmelfahrt	*Ascension Day*
Mariä Himmelfahrt	*Feast of the Assumption (15.8.)*
der Tag der deutschen Einheit	*German Unification Day (3.10)*
Allerheiligen	*All Saints' (1.11)*
der 1. Advent	*First Sunday in Advent*
Buß- und Bettag	*Day of penitence & prayer*
der Heilige Abend	*Christmas Eve*
der erste Weihnachtstag	*Christmas Day*
der zweite Weihnachtstag	*Boxing Day*
Silvester	*New Year's Eve*

(b) Asking about and giving the date

(i) The following patterns are used in speech:

■ Der wievielte ist heute? Heute ist der 1. September 1995. *What is the date today? It's the 1st September 1995.*
■ Am wievielten beginnt das Schuljahr? Am 8. September. *When does the school year begin? On the 8th September.*

(ii) In letters, the date is written thus: at the top right hand side of a letter.

Hamburg, den 1.5.95

(c) The year is given as follows:

Either: 1995
Or: im Jahre 1995

Point to watch: beware of using the English structure of 'in 1995' in German – it's WRONG!

DEFINITE AND INDEFINITE TIME

(a) Definite time (which could if necessary be identified using a calendar) is shown by using the Accusative case:

(i) To show duration.

Example: Ich war den ganzen Tag unterwegs. *I was on the road all day.*

(ii) To show a specific time.

Examples:

■ letzte Woche *last week*
■ nächsten Monat *next month*

(b) Indefinite time (which would be impossible to find exactly on a calendar) is shown by using the Genitive case

Example:

■ eines Morgens *one morning*
■ eines schönen Sommertages *one fine summer's day*

NB eines Nachts *one night* (even though Nacht is feminine)

Some times are expressed by adverbs, generally ending in -s.

Examples

■ morgens *in the mornings*
■ werktags *on working days*

WORD ORDER

Word order in German, or more exactly the order of certain groups of words, follows a number of rules.

VERBS

(a) The verb is the second idea in a simple sentence. It may come after the subject, after another element, or after a subordinate clause. In compound tenses, the auxiliary occupies the position of second idea in the sentence, while the remainder of the sentence is sandwiched between the auxiliary and the past participle or infinitive. It may be helpful to think of this rule as the '1 - 2 - 3 rule'.

Examples:
Ich kaufe immer Kleidung mit meiner Mutter. *I always buy clothing with my mother.*
Mit meiner Mutter kaufe ich immer Kleidung.
Immer kaufe ich Keidung mit meiner Mutter.

Als ich jung war, habe ich in London gewohnt. *When I was young I lived in London.*

Starting a sentence with an element other than the subject does not change the fundamental meaning. However, an element other than the subject at the beginning of the sentence is usually being emphasised.

(b) Where two sentences are joined by a co-ordinating conjunction (e.g. *und, aber, oder*) the conjunction does not count in the word order and has no effect on it.

Example: Mein Vater spielt Karten aber meine Mutter spielt Klavier. *My father is playing cards but my mother is playing the piano.*

(c) Where a clause is joined by a subordinating conjunction, the verb or the auxiliary goes to the end of that clause.

Examples: Es regnete, als er in Berlin ankam. *It was raining when he arrived in Berlin*
Man kann sehen, was in zwei Jahren passieren wird. *You can see what will happen in a couple of years.*

(d) In modern German, it is usual to avoid putting one clause inside another one (*Ineinanderschachteln*).

Example: Ich mußte meiner Mutter mitteilen, daß wir heiraten wollten.
is preferable to:
Ich mußte meiner Mutter, daß wir heiraten wollten, mitteilen *I had to tell my mother that we wanted to get married.*

(e) See also SUBJUNCTIVE in Chapter 8 for the 'avalanche rule'.

TIME, MANNER, PLACE

In German, time usually comes as early as possible in a sentence, more or less the opposite of the English habit.

(a) The order of adverbs or adverbial phrases which are next to each other is usually **Time** before **Manner** (how) before **Place**

TIME   MANNER   PLACE
  ↓   ↓   ↓

Example: Karin kommt am Montag sehr gern zur Schule. *Karin likes coming to school on Mondays very much.*

(b) If there is more than one expression of a particular type, the more general one comes first.

TIME   TIME   PLACE
(general) (more specific)

  ↓   ↓   ↓

Example: Sie kommt jeden Tag um 8 Uhr in der Schule an. *She arrives at school every day at 8.*

Dative and Accusative

The order of Dative and Accusative objects in German is fixed.

(a) If both Dative and Accusative are nouns, the Dative comes first.

DATIVE   ACCUSATIVE
↓   ↓

Example: Ich gebe dem Hund einen Ball.   *I give the dog a ball.*

(b) If both Dative and Accusative are pronouns, the Accusative comes first.

ACC DAT
↓   ↓

Example: Ich gebe es ihm.   *I give it him.*

(a) and (b) can be remembered by the mnemonics

DAN (Dative and Accusative for Nouns) and PAD (Pronouns – Accusative then Dative)

Some learners prefer PADAN as a memory aid (Pronoun before Noun)

(c) If one is a pronoun and the other is a noun, no matter which way round this is, the pronoun comes first.

ACC   DAT
↓   ↓

Examples: Ich gebe es dem Hund.   *I give it to the dog.*

DAT ACC
↓   ↓

Ich gebe ihm den Ball.   *I give him the ball.*

This can be remembered as GROLPEO (Get rid of little pronouns early on)

<table>
<tr><td>**FURTHER READING**</td><td>Rogers and Long: *Alles Klar* (Nelson Harrap)
A book of Grammar exercises with cartoons, aimed at the beginning of Lower Sixth. A very practical proposition as a self-help book, and quite fun.</td></tr>
</table>

Practice in German Grammar (Stanley Thornes/MGP)
A recent course in grammar intended for Lower Sixth. It has clear explanations, some good exercises, and is based around contemporary texts.

Martin Durrell: *Hammer's German Grammar and Usage (2nd Edition)* (Edward Arnold)
This is the modern standard work on German grammar, and has all the lists of exceptions, as well as a really good range of up-to-date examples. If you are intending to study German beyond A Level it would be very useful. Some students may find it too full of detail for A Level.

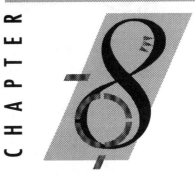

GRAMMAR: 2

GETTING STARTED

Verbs are often seen as tricky. Yet German verbs are relatively straightforward. (Ask anyone who has grappled with French!) Mastering them is the key to releasing all the subtleties of meaning which they convey. As ever, careful checking and continuous analysis of your own performance will pay dividends.

VERBS

PRESENT TENSE

FUTURE TENSE

PERFECT TENSE

IMPERFECT TENSE

PLUPERFECT TENSE

FUTURE PERFECT

PASSIVE

SUBJUNCTIVE

COMMAND FORMS

MODAL VERBS

INFINITIVES

PARTICIPLES

OTHER VERB USAGE

COMMON REGULAR VERBS

IRREGULAR VERB TABLE

ESSENTIAL PRINCIPLES

VERBS

A **verb** is a 'doing word'. It conveys information about what is done, who or what does it, and when the action took place, takes place, or will take place.

PERSONS

The form of all verbs in German is determined in part by the 'subject'. This is generally the person or thing which performs the action of the verb. (But see PASSIVE, below)
 The subject can be one of three possible 'persons'.
  The **first** person is used when the speaker performs the action of the verb, e.g. ich, wir.
  The **second** person is used when the person being spoken to performs the action of the verb, e.g. du, Sie, ihr.
  The **third** person is used when neither the speaker nor the person being spoken to is performing the action of the verb, i.e., the action is being performed by someone else, e.g. er, sie (=she), es, man, sie (=they), Fritz, die Kinder.

TENSES

The verb also indicates by its form when the action described occurs, has occurred or will occur. The main tenses and their uses are:

Present

e.g. Ich spiele Tennis, ich fahre nach Hause.
 It is used to denote actions which are happening now actions which habitually happen actions which will happen in the future.
 So ich spiele Tennis can mean: *I am playing tennis* (implied: now); *I play tennis* (implied: regularly); *I am playing tennis* (implied: at some point in the future).
 Note that the addition of 'nicht' creates an additional set of meanings in English. So ich spiele nicht Tennis can mean: *I do not play tennis*, as well as: *I am not playing tennis*.

Future:

e.g. Ich werde Tennis spielen, ich werde nach Hause fahren.
 It is used to denote actions which will happen in the future, often some time from now.
 So ich werde Tennis spielen can mean: *I shall (will) play tennis; I shall (will) be playing tennis*.

Perfect

e.g. Ich habe Tennis gespielt, ich bin nach Hause gefahren
 The Perfect is the most frequent past tense in speech and informal writing such as letters, to talk about actions which are over. It translates a variety of English past tenses.
 So ich habe Tennis gespielt can mean: *I played tennis; I was playing tennis; I have played tennis; I have been playing tennis*.

Imperfect (also known as Simple Past)

e.g. Ich spielte Tennis, ich fuhr nach Hause.
 The Imperfect is the most frequent past tense in formal writing such as books and newspapers. Some common ones are also found in speech and informal writing mixed freely with perfect tenses. Like the Perfect, it translates a variety of English past tenses.
 So ich spielte Tennis can mean: *I played tennis; I was playing tennis; I used to play tennis; I would play tennis (on Sundays)*.

Pluperfect

e.g. Ich hatte Tennis gespielt, ich war nach Hause gefahren.

The Pluperfect is used in combination with either the perfect or the imperfect to denote actions in the past which happened before other actions in the past. This is similar to English usage.

So ich hatte Tennis gespielt can mean: *I had played tennis*; *I had been playing tennis*.

Future Perfect

e.g. Ich werde Tennis gespielt haben, ich werde nach Hause gefahren sein.

The Future Perfect denotes actions which will have been completed by some time in the future. It is rare in German, but its use is similar to English usage.

So ich werde Tennis gespielt haben can mean: *I shall (will) have played tennis*; *I shall (will) have been playing tennis*.

Conditional

e.g. Ich würde Tennis spielen, ich würde nach Hause fahren.

The conditional tense denotes actions which would happen, usually if some other condition is met, as in English.

So ich würde Tennis spielen can mean: *I would play tennis (if ....)*; *I would be playing tennis (if .....)*

Conditional Perfect

e.g. Ich hätte Tennis gespielt, ich wäre nach Hause gefahren.

The conditional perfect denotes actions which would have happened had something else not prevented them.

So ich hätte Tennis gespielt can mean: *I would have played tennis (if only....)*; *I would have been playing tennis (if only ...)*

MOODS

As well as all the different tenses, verbs come in two **moods**, *indicative* and *subjunctive*. There is a complete set of tenses in each mood. There is no precise 'meaning' for the subjunctive, as it is virtually non-existent in English. But virtually all the verbs learnt for GCSE are in the indicative, which can be regarded as the 'normal' mood. The subjunctive is used in set circumstances, and it is probably best to learn what 'triggers it off'.

ACTIVE and PASSIVE

For each tense, the majority of verbs can be '**active**' or '**passive**' in voice. Verbs are 'active' when the subject of the sentence (e.g. ich, du, Herr Braun, die Männer) performs the action of the verb. For example, in the sentence: Ich esse die Banane, the eating is done by 'ich', so it is an active sentence and the verb is active. This may be regarded as the 'normal' voice.

In a sentence with a passive verb, the subject of the sentence suffers the action of the verb. So the previous example becomes: Die Banane wird (von mir) gegessen. It would be quite in order to omit the 'von mir', thus leaving the identity of who performed the action open to speculation.

The passive is found rather more frequently in German than in English, and needs to be known at A Level and AS.

WEAK, STRONG and MIXED VERBS

In German there are two sorts of verbs, regular (i.e. those which follow a rule) and irregular (i.e. those which do not always follow a rule and which therefore have to be learnt). Regular verbs are often referred to as 'weak' verbs in German, perhaps because they do not have a 'mind of their own'.

Irregular German verbs are often referred to as 'strong' verbs, perhaps because they are 'strong-minded'.

In any dictionary there is an overwhelming majority of weak verbs. However, in any lengthy piece of German there is probably a majority of strong verbs, which often express common actions.

Some dictionaries and grammars refer to 'mixed verbs'. These are verbs which are irregular, but share some of the characteristics of weak verbs. Be that as it may, they are still irregular, and need to be specially mastered.

FORMS OF GERMAN VERBS

When a verb is listed in a dictionary, it is given in the *Infinitive*, e.g. spielen, *to play* fahren, *to travel*.

In describing the formation of tenses, the infinitive will normally be the starting point.

PRESENT TENSE

(a) Weak verbs

Remove -en from the infinitive
add the following endings:

1st person:	ich	-e	wir	-en
2nd person:	du	-st	ihr	-t
			Sie	-en
3rd person:	er/sie/es/man	-t	sie	-en

Example:

ich spie**le**	wir spiel**en**
du spiel**st**	ihr spiel**t**
	Sie spiel**en**
er/sie/es/man spiel**t**	sie spiel**en**

(b) Strong verbs

Check the verb table. If there is no vowel change listed under '3rd person present', then the verb behaves in the same way as weak verbs. If there is a vowel change, it affects the du and er/sie/es/man forms only. The endings are the same as for weak verbs.

Example with a vowel change:

ich fahr**e**	wir fahr**en**
du f**ä**hr**st**	ihr fahr**t**
	Sie fahr**en**
er/sie/es/man f**ä**hr**t**	sie fahr**en**

Example without a vowel change:

ich geh**e**	wir geh**en**
du geh**st**	ihr geh**t**
	Sie geh**en**
er/sie/es/man geh**t**	sie geh**en**

Verbs (strong or weak) whose infinitives end in -den, -ten, -chnen, -cknen, -dnen, -fnen, -gnen, or -tnen take the endings -**est** and -**et** in the second and third person singular in order to make pronunciation easier.

Examples: du arbeitest, er öffnet, du trocknest.

Points to watch:
(a) Remember that the present tense renders not only '*I go*' but also '*I am going*' and '*I do (not) go*'. Resist the temptation to translate the separate parts of '*I am going*' into German – it's WRONG!
(b) The present tense is quite often used to give a future meaning:
Ich fahre morgen nach München. = *I am going to Munich tomorrow.*

FUTURE TENSE

This is formed in the same way for both weak and strong verbs.
The verb is in two parts, the present tense of 'werden' and, at the end of the clause or sentence, the infinitive of the verb in question.

Example:

(a) Weak verbs

spielen:

ich werde ..... spielen	wir werden ..... spielen
du wirst ..... spielen	ihr werdet ..... spielen
	Sie werden ..... spielen
er/sie/es/man wird ..... spielen	sie werden ..... spielen

(b) Strong verbs

fahren:

ich werde ..... fahren	wir werden ..... fahren
du wirst ..... fahren	ihr werdet ..... fahren
	Sie werden ..... fahren
er/sie/es/man wird ..... fahren	sie werden ..... fahren

Point to watch: 'werden' itself follows the same pattern, although it is sometimes used without the infinitive in such sentences as: 'Ich werde Lehrer.'

PERFECT TENSE

This tense is formed in two parts, with the present tense of 'haben' or 'sein' and, at the end of the clause or sentence, the past participle of the verb in question. The present tense of 'haben' or 'sein' are referred to as the 'auxiliary' verbs. Perhaps the German term *'Hilfsverben'* is clearer!

(a) Weak verbs

The vast majority of weak verbs, including reflexives, form the perfect tense using 'haben' as the auxiliary. See below: 'haben' or 'sein'?

The past participle is usually formed by adding **ge-** to the infinitive, removing the **-en** and replacing it with **-t**, as in: **ge**spielt.

If the infinitive ends in -den, -ten, -chnen, -cknen, -dnen, -fnen, -gnen, or -tnen (see present tense), then an extra **-e** is added before the final **-t** to make the whole thing pronounceable, as in: gearbeit**et**.

However, if the infinitive ends in -ieren (because it is a loan word from Italian), then no ge- is added, as in: repariert, studiert.

The same applies if the verb starts with a prefix which does not separate. These prefixes are: be-, ent-, emp-, er-, ge-, miß-, ver- and zer-. Example: erzählt, mißhandelt.

If the verb has a prefix which *does* separate, it is tacked onto the past participle ahead of the ge-, as in: **ab**geholt.

Once the past participle has been formed, the only change in the verb is to the auxiliary.

Example:

ich habe ..... gespielt	wir haben ..... gespielt
du hast ..... gespielt	ihr habt ..... gespielt
	Sie haben ..... gespielt
er/sie/es/man hat ..... gespielt	sie haben ..... gespielt

(b) Strong and 'mixed'

While many of these verbs form the perfect tense with 'haben' as the auxiliary, a good number of them use 'sein' as the auxiliary. See 'haben or sein?' below.

Because these verbs are irregular, the only safe way to discover the past participle is to look the verb up in a verb table. If the verb you are looking for does not appear to be in the table, consider the possibility that it is a compound of another verb, with one of the prefixes mentioned above on the front. Compounds like befahren and abfahren behave just the same as fahren, for example.

Some dictionaries and glossaries list only the vowel changes. So fahren would appear as fahren (ä,u,a). The final vowel in the list is the past participle vowel, the other two being the third person singular present and the imperfect (see below).

Strong verbs proper have a past participle which ends in -en, and may or may not have a different main vowel from the infinitive, as in essen - gegessen or gewinnen - gewonnen. Much the same, incidentally, is true of irregular English verbs such as to win and to eat.

'Mixed' verbs are verbs which follow the pattern of weak verbs BUT have a vowel change. The past participle of these verbs ends in -t, as in: bringen – gebracht, wissen – gewußt.

The same rules about prefixes which do or do not separate apply as for weak verbs, see above.

Examples:

essen

ich habe ..... gegessen	wir haben ..... gegessen
du hast ..... gegessen	ihr habt ..... gegessen
	Sie haben ..... gegessen
er/sie/es/man hat ..... gegessen	sie haben ..... gegessen

kommen

ich bin ..... gekommen	wir sind ..... gekommen
du bist ..... gekommen	ihr seid ..... gekommen
	Sie sind ..... gekommen
er/sie/es/man ist ..... gekommen	sie sind ..... gekommen

wissen

ich habe ..... gewußt	wir haben ..... gewußt
du hast ..... gewußt	ihr habt ..... gewußt
	Sie haben ..... gewußt
er/sie/es/man hat ..... gewußt	sie haben ..... gewußt

(c) 'haben' or 'sein'?

The choice of 'haben' or 'sein' as auxiliary can cause some difficulty, as there is no equivalent distinction in English. At GCSE it is often approached as either a matter of learning which verbs take 'sein' (in many verb tables, those verbs which require 'sein' are marked with *), or of applying a simple rule of thumb which is:

Verbs of motion, plus bleiben, sein and werden require 'sein' as an auxiliary.

A more sophisticated version of the same rule of thumb includes a mention of a 'change of state' e.g. einschlafen, explodieren, schmelzen.

For many purposes the above rule will do. However, the ambitious A Level student will want to be absolutely accurate.

So the following rules will need to be added to the 'rule of thumb':

—most verbs meaning 'happen', 'succeed', or 'fail' plus 'begegnen' take 'sein' as an auxiliary.

These include:

begegnen	*meet (by chance)*
fehlschlagen	*fail*
gelingen	*succeed*
geschehen	*happen*
glücken	*succeed*
mißglücken	*fail*
mißlingen	*fail*
passieren	*happen*
vorgehen	*happen*
vorkommen	*occur*
zustoßen	*happen to*

—verbs which do not have an accusative object and are therefore intransitive. This category actually includes all the others mentioned.

Point to watch: Some verbs, depending on their meaning, take 'sein' or (less frequently) 'haben'. Fahren, while usually taking 'sein', as in: Ich bin nach Hause gefahren, can take 'haben' if there is an accusative object, as in:

Ich habe meinen Sohn nach Hause gefahren.

Other verbs which may commonly be found with this characteristic include:

brechen	*break*
dringen	*enter, insist on*
folgen	*obey, follow*
irren	*roam about, be wrong*
stoßen	*push, bump into*

And for perfectionists: some verbs of motion take 'sein' when they involve movement from one place to another, but take 'haben' when they refer to the activity per se without any mention of destination:

Ich bin nach Calais geschwommen.	*I swam to Calais.*
Ich habe in Calais geschwommen.	*I swam in Calais.*

Other verbs which may commonly be found with this characteristic include:

reiten	*ride*
rudern	*row*
segeln	*sail*
tanzen	*dance*
treten	*step*

IMPERFECT TENSE

(a) Weak verbs

Remove -en from the infinitive add the following endings:

1st person:	ich	-te	wir	-ten
2nd person:	du	-test	ihr	-tet
			Sie	-ten
3rd person:	er/sie/es/man	-te	sie	-ten

Example:

ich spiel**te**	wir spiel**ten**
du spiel**test**	ihr spiel**tet**
	Sie spiel**ten**
er/sie/es/man spiel**te**	sie spiel**ten**

(b) Strong verbs

Because these verbs are irregular, the only safe way to discover the imperfect tense is to look the verb up in a verb table. If the verb you are looking for does not appear to be in the table, consider the possibility that it is a compound of another verb, with one of the prefixes mentioned above on the front. Compounds like befahren and abfahren behave just the same as fahren, for example.

Some dictionaries and glossaries list only the vowel changes. So fahren would appear as fahren (ä,u,a). The last vowel but one in the list is the imperfect vowel, the other two being the third person singular present and the past participle.

The form you have looked up is the 3rd (and 1st) person singular. To that, add the following endings:

1st person:	ich	NONE	wir	-en
2nd person:	du	-st	ihr	-t
			Sie	-en
3rd person:	er/sie/es/man	NONE	sie	-en

Example:
fahren – entry in verb table: fuhr

ich fuhr	wir fuhr**en**
du fuhr**st**	ihr fuhr**t**
	Sie fuhr**en**
er/sie/es/man fuhr	sie fuhr**en**

Point to watch: in practice, because the Imperfect Tense is mainly used in books and newspapers, it is much more common in the 3rd person singular and plural than in its other forms. Nevertheless, you need to be sure of recognising it in the other persons if it crops up in a text, so be aware of them!

PLUPERFECT TENSE

This tense uses the imperfect tense of 'haben' or 'sein' as auxiliaries (*Hilfsverben*) and the past participle at the end of the clause or sentence.

The choice of 'haben' or 'sein' as auxiliary is governed by the same rules as for the perfect tense.

The past participle is formed in the same way as for the perfect tense. So it has to be looked up for strong and mixed verbs, but can be worked out for weak verbs.

Example:

(a) Weak verb

ich hatte ..... gespielt	wir hatten ..... gespielt
du hattest ..... gespielt	ihr hattet ..... gespielt
	Sie hatten ..... gespielt
er/sie/es/man hatte ..... gespielt	sie hatten ..... gespielt

(b) Strong verbs

essen
ich hatte ..... gegessen	wir hatten ..... gegessen
du hattest ..... gegessen	ihr hattet ..... gegessen
	Sie hatten ..... gegessen
er/sie/es/man hatte ..... gegessen	sie hatten ..... gegessen

kommen
ich war ..... gekommen	wir waren ..... gekommen
du warst..... gekommen	ihr wart ..... gekommen
	Sie waren ..... gekommen
er/sie/es/man war ..... gekommen	sie waren ..... gekommen

wissen
ich hatte ..... gewußt	wir hatten ..... gewußt
du hattest ..... gewußt	ihr hattet ..... gewußt
	Sie hatten ..... gewußt
er/sie/es/man hatte ..... gewußt	sie hatten ..... gewußt

FUTURE PERFECT

This is formed for both strong and weak verbs by using the present tense of 'werden' as an auxiliary, and, at the end of the clause or sentence, a 'past infinitive'. The past infinitive is formed by following the past participle (see: Perfect tense) with the infinitive of 'sein' of 'haben', as appropriate.

Examples:

(a) Weak verbs

ich werde ..... gespielt haben
du wirst ..... gespielt haben
er/sie/es/man wird ..... gespielt haben

wir werden .... gespielt haben
ihr werdet ..... gespielt haben
Sie werden ..... gespielt haben
sie werden ..... gespielt haben

(b) Strong verbs

ich werde ..... gegessen haben
du wirst ..... gegessen haben
er/sie/es/man wird ..... gegessen haben

wir werden .... gegessen haben
ihr werdet ..... gegessen haben
Sie werden ..... gegessen haben
sie werden ..... gegessen haben

ich werde ..... gekommen sein
du wirst ..... gekommen sein
er/sie/es/man wird ..... gekommen sein

wir werden .... gekommen sein
ihr werdet ..... gekommen sein
Sie werden ..... gekommen sein
sie werden ..... gekommen sein

ich werde ..... gewußt haben
du wirst ..... gewußt haben
er/sie/es/man wird ..... gewußt haben

wir werden .... gewußt haben
ihr werdet ..... gewußt haben
Sie werden ..... gewußt haben
sie werden ..... gewußt haben

PASSIVE

There are two sorts of passive in German, the 'werden-passive' and the 'sein-passive'.

(a) The werden-passive is the more common, and expresses a process

It is found in all the same tenses as the Active verbs, and in indicative and subjunctive moods. However, the future perfect form is very rare, and the future very often has the present substituted for it.

It is also found in idiomatic impersonal forms, such as:

Es wurde getanzt.   *There was dancing going on.*

All verbs form their passive in the same way, regardles of whether they are strong or weak. The principle is that the appropriate tense of "werden" is used in conjunction with the past participle of the verb in question. The past participle is found at the end of the clause or sentence as usual.

Examples: hören (weak) sehen (strong)

Present

ich werde gehört	*I am (being) heard*
du wirst gehört	*you are (being) heard*
er/sie/es/man wird gehört	*he is (being) heard*

wir werden gehört	*we are (being) heard*
ihr werdet gehört	*you are (being) heard*
Sie werden gehört	*you are (being) heard*
sie werden gehört	*they are (being) heard*

ich werde gesehen	*I am (being) seen*
du wirst gesehen	*you are (being) seen*
er/sie/es/man wird gesehen	*he/she/it/one is (being) seen*

wir werden gesehen	*we are (being) seen*
ihr werdet gesehen	*you are (being) seen*
Sie werden gesehen	*you are (being) seen*
sie werden gesehen	*they are (being) seen*

Imperfect

ich wurde gehört	*I was (being) heard*
du wurdest gehört	*you were (being) heard*
er/sie/es/man wurde gehört	*he was (being) heard*
wir wurden gehört	*we were (being) heard*
ihr wurdet gehört	*you were (being) heard*
Sie wurden gehört	*you were (being) heard*
sie wurden gehört	*they were (being) heard*

ich wurde gesehen	*I was (being) seen*
du wurdest gesehen	*you were (being) seen*
er/sie/es/man wurde gesehen	*he/she/it/one was (being) seen*

wir wurden gesehen	*we were (being) seen*
ihr wurdet gesehen	*you were (being) seen*
Sie wurden gesehen	*you were (being) seen*
sie wurden gesehen	*they were (being) seen*

Point to watch: Note that there is NO UMLAUT on the auxiliary in this tense. The pronunciation is fairly crucial to avoiding confusion.

Perfect

For the perfect and pluperfect passive (and for the rare future perfect passive) a special form of the past participle of 'werden' (which is normally 'geworden') is used, namely 'worden'. This is because a second ge- would sound cumbersome.

Ich bin... gehört worden	*I have been/was heard*
du bist... gehört worden	*you have been/were heard*
er/sie/es/man ist... gehört worden	*he/she/it/one has been/was heard*

wir sind... gehört worden	*we have been/were heard*
ihr seid... gehört worden	*you have been/were heard*
Sie sind... gehört worden	*you have been/were heard*
sie sind... gehört worden	*they have been/were heard*

Ich bin... gesehen worden	*I have been/was seen*
du bist... gesehen worden	*you have been/were seen*
er/sie/es/man ist... gesehen worden	*he/she/it/one has been/was seen*

wir sind... gesehen worden	*we have been/were seen*
ihr seid... gesehen worden	*you have been/were seen*
Sie sind... gesehen worden	*you have been/were seen*
sie sind... gesehen worden	*they have been/were seen*

Pluperfect

The principle is exactly as for the perfect, except that the auxiliary is the pluperfect of 'werden'.

Ich war... gehört worden	*I had been (being) heard*
du warst... gehört worden	*you had been (being) heard*
er/sie/es/man war... gehört worden	*he/she/it/one had been (being) heard*

wir waren... gehört worden	*we had been (being) heard*
ihr wart... gehört worden	*you had been (being) heard*
Sie waren... gehört worden	*you had been (being) heard*
sie waren... gehört worden	*they had been (being) heard*

Ich war... gesehen worden	*I had been (being) seen*
du warst... gesehen worden	*you had been (being) seen*
er/sie/es/man war... gesehen worden	*he/she/it/one had been (being) seen*

wir waren... gesehen worden	*we had been (being) seen*
ihr wart... gesehen worden	*you had been (being) seen*
Sie waren... gesehen worden	*you had been (being) seen*
sie waren... gesehen worden	*they had been (being) seen*

(b) The sein-passive expresses a state

The sein-passive is used to show the **state** the subject of the verb is in as a result of some previous action. It may be helpful to look upon the past participle as an adjective.

It is formed for both weak and strong verbs by using the appropriate tense of the verb 'sein' and the past participle of the verb in question. It is most commonly found in present and imperfect tenses.

Examples:

Present tense

ich bin verletzt	*I am injured*
du bist verletzt	*you are injured*
er/sie/es/man ist verletzt	*he/she/it/one is injured*

wir sind verletzt	*we are injured*
ihr seid verletzt	*you are injured*
Sie sind verletzt	*you are injured*
sie sind verletzt	*they are injured*

Imperfect tense

ich war verletzt	*I was injured*
du warst verletzt	*you were injured*
er/sie/es/man war verletzt	*he/she/it/one was injured*

wir waren verletzt	*we were injured*
ihr wart verletzt	*you were injured*
Sie waren verletzt	*you were injured*
sie waren verletzt	*they were injured*

Points to watch:

(a) Deciding whether to use the 'werden-passive' or the 'sein-passive' requires you to determine whether an action (therefore werden-passive) or a state (therefore sein-passive) is being described. The following pairs of examples may help:

Der Tisch wird abgeräumt.	*The table is being cleared.*
	(Someone is even now clearing the table.)
Der Tisch ist abgeräumt.	*The table is cleared.*
	(because someone has already done it)
Dresden wurde 1945 zerstört.	*Dresden was destroyed in 1945.*
	(the action took place that year)
Dresden war 1946 zerstört.	*Dresden was destroyed in 1946.*
	(the action had taken place at some time beforehand)

If you really cannot decide between the two sorts of passive, the 'werden-passive' is about four times as common as the 'sein-passive'.

(b) Native English speakers need to be aware of the possibility of misleading interference from the English 'is/was/were' auxiliary where the German requires the 'werden-passive'.

THE AGENT IN THE PASSIVE – WHODUNNIT?

The passive is often used without specifying who performed the action. However, it may be necessary to express who or what performed the action, translating the English 'by'.

There are three possibilities:

(a) **von** + Dative – agent, human or inanimate
Der Ball wurde von dem Mädchen geschlagen. (*The ball was hit by the girl.*)
Das Haus wurde vom Sturm beschädigt. (*The house was damaged by the storm.*)
(b) **durch** + Accusative - means
Er wurde durch lautes Singen geweckt. (*He was woken by means of loud singing.*)
(c) **mit** + Dative - instrument
Der Stuhl wurde mit einem Schraubenzieher montiert. (*The chair was assembled with a screwdriver.*)

A test for (c) is to see if 'Hilfe' could be inserted after 'mit' without changing the meaning.

ALTERNATIVES TO THE PASSIVE

There are various ways of expressing the same or similar meanings to the passive.

(a) Use of 'man'

This is often used if there is no clue as to the identity of the subject.
In den Sommerferien hat man mein Klassenzimmer angestrichen. (*Person or persons unknown painted my classroom in the holidays/They painted ....*)

(b) Use of a reflexive

Die Tür öffnete sich. (*The door opened (itself).*)

(c) The infinitive with zu after 'sein' has a passive meaning, similar to 'is to be' in English:

Die Briefe sind im Büro abzuholen. (*The letters can be fetched from the office.*)

SUBJUNCTIVE

As well as all the different tenses, verbs come in two moods, indicative and subjunctive. There is a complete set of tenses in each mood. There is no precise 'meaning' for the subjunctive, as it is virtually non-existent in English. But virtually all the verbs learnt for GCSE are in the indicative, which can be regarded as the 'normal' mood. The subjunctive is used in set circumstances, and it is probably best to learn what 'triggers it off'.

The **subjunctive forms** are most conveniently divided into two groups, Konjunktiv I and Konjunktiv II.

Konjunktiv I includes:

Active	Passive
present subjunctive - er sehe	er werde gesehen
perfect subjunctive - er habe gesehen	er sei gesehen worden
future subjunctive - er werde sehen	er werde gesehen werden

Konjunktiv II includes:

Active	Passive
past (or imperfect) subjunctive - er sähe	NONE
pluperfect subjunctive - er hätte gesehen	er wäre gesehen worden
conditional - er würde sehen	er würde gesehen werden

FORMS OF THE SUBJUNCTIVE

Konjunktiv I

(a) Present subjunctive

This is regular for all verbs except 'sein':
Remove the -en from the infinitve and add the following endings:

ich	-e	wir	-en
du	-est	ihr	-et
er/sie/es/man	-e	Sie	-en
		sie	-en

Examples:

ich	singe	wir	singen
du	singest	ihr	singet
er/sie/es/man	singe	Sie	singen
		sie	singen

ich	spiele	wir	spielen
du	spielest	ihr	spielet
er/sie/es/man	spiele	Sie	spielen
		sie	spielen

'sein' is irregular

ich	sei	wir	seien
du	seist (seiest)	ihr	seiet
er/sie/es/man	sei	Sie	seien
		sie	seien

Note that the subjunctive is the same as the indicative for many weak verbs, except in the 3rd person singular. The forms -est and -et are felt to be stilted and are generally avoided.

(b) Compound tenses of Konjunktiv I

The subjunctive form of the auxiliary verb is used. Nothing else changes. As elsewhere, the subjunctive is most distinctive in the 3rd person singular.

Examples:

Perfect: Er habe gespielt; Er sei gegangen
Future: Er werde spielen

Konjunktiv II

This has two alternative forms. There is no difference in meaning between the simple and compound forms of Konjunktiv II. See also uses of the subjunctive, below.

(a) The simple form (the imperfect subjunctive, the past subjunctive)

(i) weak verbs

For all weak verbs, it is identical to the imperfect tense, eg ich spielte.

(ii) strong verbs

For most verbs, take the imperfect form (look it up in the strong verb table), add an Umlaut if possible, plus the same subjunctive endings as for the present subjunctive:

ich	-e	wir	-en
du	-est	ihr	-et
er/sie/es/man	-e	Sie	-en
		sie	-en

Examples:

Fahren:

ich	führe	wir	führen
du	führest	ihr	führet
er/sie/es/man	führe	Sie	führen
		sie	führen

Sehen:

ich	sähe	wir	sähen
du	sähest	ihr	sähet
er/sie/es/man	sähe	Sie	sähen
		sie	sähen

Bleiben:

ich	bliebe	wir	blieben
du	bliebest	ihr	bliebet
er/sie/es/man	bliebe	Sie	blieben
		sie	blieben

Some common strong verbs have irregular stems for the imperfect subjunctive. They include:

sein	er wäre
haben	er hätte
werden	er würde

dürfen	er dürfte
müssen	er müßte
können	er könnte
mögen	er möchte
brauchen	er bräuchte
brennen	er brennte
bringen	er brächte
denken	er dächte
helfen	er hülfe
kennen	er kennte
stehen	er stünde
sterben	er stürbe
wissen	er wüßte

If in doubt, check the verb table!

(b) The compound form (the 'conditional')

This is formed for both strong and weak verbs with the Konjunktiv II of werden and the infinitive of the verb in question.

Examples:

kaufen:

ich	würde kaufen	wir	würden kaufen
du	würdest kaufen	ihr	würdet kaufen
er/sie/es/man	würde kaufen	Sie	würden kaufen
		sie	würden kaufen

gehen:

ich	würde gehen	wir	würden gehen
du	würdest gehen	ihr	würdet gehen
er/sie/es/man	würde gehen	Sie	würden gehen
		sie	würden gehen

USES OF THE SUBJUNCTIVE

The subjunctive is used:

(a) to express reported speech,
(b) to express conditions,
(c) after als (ob), wie wenn,
(d) to soften the tone of a statement or request,
(e) in wishes and instructions.

(a) Reported speech

This is quite a tricky area for many native speakers of English. Many Germans find some aspects of it hard, too. There are two distinct sorts of usage, one in formal written language, and one colloquial. Not all Germans are very aware of the rules which apply to the formal written language, and may attempt to persuade you to use the colloquial version if asked for help. Indeed, only the best-educated really do the formal version well! A Level Examiners are amongst this well-educated elite, and you will therefore have to master both kinds of usage.

(i) Formal written language

The Konjunktiv I should be used to show indirect speech *wherever the form is distinct from the indicative*. This will normally be in the 3rd person singular, except for 'sein'. The tense of the Konjunktiv I chosen will reflect what the original speaker *actually said*. So a necessary process is establishing clearly what the original speaker (probably) said.

The table below should help:

What the speaker originally said	Formal written reported speech, Konjunktiv I
present:	**present subjunctive:**
Ich esse eine Banane. *I am eating a banana.*	Sie sagte, sie esse eine Banane. *She said she was eating a banana.*
future:	**future subjunctive:**
Ich werde eine Banane essen. *I shall eat a banana.*	Sie sagte, sie werde eine Banane essen. *She said she would eat a banana.*

simple past/imperfect	**perfect subjunctive**
Ich aß eine Banane.	Sie sagte, sie habe eine Banane gegessen.
I ate a banana.	*She said she had eaten a banana.*
perfect	**perfect subjunctive**
Ich habe eine Banane gegessen.	Sie sagte, sie habe eine Banane gegessen.
I have eaten a banana.	*She said she had eaten a banana.*
pluperfect	**perfect subjunctive**
Ich hatte eine Banane gegessen.	Sie sagte, sie habe eine Banane gegessen.
I had eaten a banana.	*She said she had eaten a banana.*

Although the examples given here are of a strong verb, weak verbs behave in exactly the same way.

Note that reported speech of originals in the simple past, perfect and pluperfect is identical.

However, if the Konjunktiv I form is NOT distinctive from the indicative, then Konjunktiv II should be used.

Examples:

(i) With a strong verb:

What the speaker originally said	**Formal written reported speech, Konjunktiv II**
present:	**imperfect (past) subjunctive:**
Wir essen eine Banane.	Sie sagten, sie äßen eine Banane.
We are eating a banana.	*They said they were eating a banana.*
future:	**future subjunctive:**
Wir werden eine Banane essen.	Sie sagten, sie würden eine Banane essen.
We shall eat a banana.	*They said they would eat a banana.*
simple past/imperfect	**pluperfect subjunctive**
Wir aßen eine Banane.	Sie sagten, sie hätten eine Banane gegessen.
We ate a banana.	*They said they had eaten a banana.*
perfect	**pluperfect subjunctive**
Wir haben eine Banane gegessen.	Sie sagten, sie hätten eine Banane gegessen.
We have eaten a banana.	*They said they had eaten a banana.*
pluperfect	**pluperfect subjunctive**
Wir hatten eine Banane gegessen.	Sie sagten, sie hätten eine Banane gegessen.
We had eaten a banana.	*They said they had eaten a banana.*

(ii) With a weak verb:

What the speaker originally said	Formal written reported speech, Konjunktiv II
present:	**imperfect (past) subjunctive:**
Wir spielen Fußball. *We are playing football.*	Sie sagten, sie spielten Fußball. *They said they were playing football.*
future:	**future subjunctive:**
Wir werden Fußball spielen. *We shall play football.*	Sie sagten, sie würden Fußball spielen. *They said they would play football.*
simple past/imperfect	**pluperfect subjunctive**
Wir spielten Fußball. *We played football.*	Sie sagten, sie hätten Fußball gespielt. *They said they had played football.*
perfect	**pluperfect subjunctive**
Wir haben Fußball gespielt. *We have played football.*	Sie sagten, sie hätten Fußball gespielt. *They said they had played football.*
pluperfect	**pluperfect subjunctive**
Wir hatten Fußball gespielt. *We had played football.*	Sie sagten, sie hätten Fußball gespielt. *They said they had played football.*

For all these examples, the Konjunktiv I form would have been the same as the indicative. Therefore the Konjunktiv II is required in order to be 'distinctively subjunctive'.

Points to watch: The Konjunktiv I may be used to distance the writer from the views expressed, or to at least remain neutral about them. This is most common in journalism, where it is used either to seem objective, or to stay on the right side of the libel laws.

The appearance of the Konjunktiv is sufficient to announce that a sentence is reported speech. It may be that there is no equivalent of the 'Sie sagte' found in the examples above.

The word *daß* is often omitted, as in the examples. There is much to be gained by doing so, as reported speech is difficult enough without the additional complication of having to send the verb to the end of the clause.

When translating from English, beware of being misled by the tense of English reported speech. ALWAYS write down what you think the original speaker said and work from that.

(ii) Colloquial usage

In everyday spoken German, reported speech is rendered by the indicative where formal written usage would require Konjunktiv I, and by Konjunktiv II. Konjunktiv II is often preferred in past contexts, and where there is a longer report.

Modal verbs and haben, sein and werden usually appear in Konjunktiv II in the imperfect (past) subjunctive – er könnte, müßte, sollte, wollte, dürfte, möchte, wäre, hätte, würde. The same can be said of kommen, tun and wissen (käme, täte and wüßte). Virtually all other verbs will be used in the würde (conditional) form in the Konjunktiv II in speech.

What the speaker originally said	Colloquial reported speech:
present:	**present or conditional**
Ich esse eine Banane.	Sie hat gesagt, sie ißt eine Banane./ Sie hat gesagt, sie würde eine Banane essen.
I am eating a banana.	*She said she was eating a banana.*
future:	**future or conditional:**
Ich werde eine Banane essen.	Sie hat gesagt, sie wird eine Banane essen./ Sie hat gesagt, sie würde eine Banane essen.
I shall eat a banana.	*She said she would eat a banana.*
perfect	**pluperfect or perfect subjunctive**
Ich habe eine Banane gegessen.	Sie hat gesagt, sie hätte eine Banane gegessen. Sie hat gesagt, sie hat eine Banane gegessen.
I have eaten a banana.	*She said she had eaten a banana.*
pluperfect	**pluperfect subjunctive or pluperfect**
Ich hatte eine Banane gegessen.	Sie hat gesagt, sie hätte eine Banane gegessen. Sie hat gesagt, sie hatte eine Banane gegessen.
I had eaten a banana.	*She said she had eaten a banana.*

Note that the subjunctive tenses of colloquial reported speech are very similar to those used in English.

Although the examples given here are of a strong verb, weak verbs behave in exactly the same way.

(b) Expressing conditions

The subjunctive is used in expressing certain conditions.

There are three sorts of conditions in German. Each sort has a 'wenn-clause' and a 'consequence clause'.

(i) Open conditions

The first sort, the open condition, does not use conditional or subjunctive forms, because it is really a statement of fact.

The wenn-clause has the present tense, the consequence clause has the future or present tense.

Example:

Wenn du auf der Autobahn einschläfst, wirst du sterben.
If you go to sleep on the motorway you will die.

(ii) Possibilities

The second sort of condition expresses things which might – or might not – happen. It is sometimes called the 'impossible' or 'unreal' condition.

The wenn-clause has the Konjunktiv II (imperfect subjunctive), the consequence clause has Konjuntiv II, often in the würde-form (conditional).

Examples:

Wenn das Wetter schön wäre, könnten wir nach Bonn fahren.
If the weather was fine we could go to Bonn./
If the weather were fine we could go to Bonn.

Die Kinder wären froh, wenn die Schule ausfallen würde
The children would be delighted if school were (was) cancelled.

Wir würden es verstehen, wenn es keine Gehaltserhöhung gäbe
We would understand if there were (was) no pay rise.

The modal verbs can be used in their conditional form.

Example:

Ich könnte nach Berlin kommen, wenn ich Zeit hätte.
I could come to Berlin if I had time.

See also Modal Verbs.

Point to watch: It is considered better style to avoid using two würde-forms in the same sentence where possible.

(iii) Regrets

The pluperfect subjunctive form of Konjunktiv II is used to express regrets – things which could have happened in the past, but didn't.
   Both the wenn-clause and the consequence clause are in the pluperfect subjunctive of Konjunktiv II.

Examples:

Ich hätte es verstanden, wenn es keine Gehaltserhöhung gegeben hätte.
We would have understood if there had been no pay rise.

Wir wären nach Neuschwanstein gefahren, wenn das Wetter schön gewesen wäre.
We would have gone to Neuschwanstein if the weather had been good.

Modal verbs can be combined with Konjunktiv II as follows:

Examples:

Wir hätten kommen können, wenn wir nicht etwas anderes hätten machen müssen.
We could have come if we had not had to do something else.

Points to watch: It is of no importance whether the wenn-clause or the consequence clause comes first in a sentence, although, of course, the word-order rules must be obeyed.
   The conjunction 'wenn' may be omitted. If it is omitted, quite often 'so' is inserted.

Example:

Hätte ich viel Geld, so würde ich nicht mehr arbeiten gehen.
If I had lots of money I would not go out to work.

(c) After *als ob* and *wie wenn*

'Als ob' and 'wie wenn' act as 'triggers' for the Konjunktiv II.

(i) If the action after the als ob/wie wenn clause takes place at the same time as the action in the main clause of the sentence, the Imperfect Subjunctive is used.

Example:

Er tat, als ob er Bond nicht sähe.
He acted as if he didn't see Bond.

(ii) If the action in the als ob/wie wenn clause took place before the action in the main clause of the sentence, the pluperfect subjunctive is used.

Example:

Er tat, als ob er Bond nicht gesehen hätte.
He acted as if he hadn't seen Bond.

(iii) If the action in the als ob/wie wenn clause will take place after the action in the main clause of the sentence, the würde-form is used.

Examples:
Er tat, als ob er Bond nicht sehen würde.
He acted as if he wouldn't see Bond.

Es sieht aus, als ob es schneien würde.
It looks as though it will snow.

(iv) The ob in als ob can be omitted. Note the effect on the word order.

Example:

Er tat, als sähe er Bond nicht.
He acted as if he didn't see Bond.

(d) To soften the tone of a statement or request

The Konjunktiv II is often used, especially colloquially, to moderate the tone of a statement or request.

Examples:

Ich hätte eine Frage noch.
I have another question.

Das wär's.
That's all.

Könnten Sie mir bitte sagen, wo ich ein Taxi finden werde?
Could you please tell me where I can find a taxi?

(e) In wishes and instructions

(i) A number of set phrases use what is in fact Konjunktiv I to express (often pious) wishes.

Examples:

Gott sei Dank!
Thank God.

Es lebe die Königin!
Long live the Queen.

Gelobt sei Jesus Christus!
May Jesus Christ be praised.

(ii) A wenn-clause with Konjunktiv II can be used to express a wish, often with bloß, nur or doch inserted.

Examples:

Wenn ich bloß mein Abitur hinter mir hätte.
If only I had my A Levels behind me.

Wenn deine Mutter dich doch nur in Ruhe gelassen hätte.
If only your mother had left you in peace.

As in other conditional sentences, the wenn may sometimes be omitted.

Example:

Hätte deine Mutter dich doch nur in Ruhe gelassen.
If only your mother had left you in peace.

(iii) Sometimes instructions are given in Konjunktiv I.

Example: Man finde einen Schraubenzieher.
          Find a screwdriver.

COMMAND FORMS (Imperatives)

Every verb has four **command forms**, based on the present tense. Which form is used depends on who you are talking to. (See Grammar: 1.)

(a) For those you would normally address as Du

For both weak and strong verbs, remove the -st from the du-form of the present tense, and add an exclamation mark! If there is an Umlaut on the vowel of a strong verb, remove it.

Examples: Kauf!
            Komm!
            Fahr schneller!
            Nimm deine Windjacke mit!

Sometimes an -e is added after a -d , -h or -t

Examples: Finde dein Heft!
            Schreite schneller!
            Siehe da!

(b) For those you would normally address as ihr

For both weak and strong verbs, the ihr form of the present tense is used, but without ihr.

Examples: Findet eure Hefte!
            Schreitet schneller!
            Kommt!
            Nehmt eure Windjacken mit!

(c) For those you would normally address as Sie

For both weak and strong verbs, use the Sie form of the present tense, as in the examples:

Examples: Finden Sie Ihre Hefte!
            Schreiten Sie schneller!
            Kommen Sie!
            Nehmen Sie Ihre Windjacken mit!

(d) To express 'let's', use the wir form as in the examples below. This applies to both weak and strong verbs.

Examples: Finden wir unsere Hefte.
Let's find our notebooks.
Schreiten wir schneller.
Let's walk quicker.
Gehen wir.
Let's go.
Nehmen wir unsere Windjacken mit.
Let's take our jackets with us.

It is also possible to use lassen + uns. Again, this applies to both strong and weak verbs.

Examples: Laß uns schneller gehen.
Let's walk quicker.

MODAL VERBS

There is a group of verbs in German which control the infinitive of another verb (dependent infinitive). These are known as **modal verbs,** and will be familiar to anyone who has learnt: *Ich kann Tennis spielen etc.* in the first weeks of learning German. They can be used to express a whole variety of subtle meanings.

The modal verbs are:

> dürfen
> können
> mögen
> müssen
> sollen
> wollen

lassen can behave in much the same way as a modal verb when it means 'to have something done' (as opposed to doing it yourself).

(a) The following general points can be made about modal verbs:

(i) In a simple sentence, the modal verb occupies the 'verb' position in the word order, and the dependent infinitive is at the end of the clause.

Example: Ich will Tennis spielen, aber ich muß meine Hausaufgaben machen.
I want to play tennis but I have to do my homework.

In subordinate clauses, the same principle applies:

Example: Ich war nicht da, weil ich nicht ausgehen durfte.
I wasn't there because I wasn't allowed out.

(ii) The dependent infinitive can be a more complex one:

Example: Sie muß es gemacht haben.
She must have done it.

(iii) In tenses other than the present, only the tense of the modal verb changes. The dependent infinitive remains the same.

Examples: Sie wird es machen müssen.
She will have to do it.
Sie konnte es nicht vermeiden.
She couldn't avoid it.

(iv) There is an alternative form of the past participle which is used when the modal verb has a dependent infinitive. The alternative form is actually the same as the infinitive of the modal verb. If there is no dependent infinitive, the ge- past participle is used.

Examples: Ich habe nicht kommen können.
            I wasn't able to come.
            Ich hätte ihm nicht zuhören sollen.
            I shouldn't have listened to him.
            Wir haben einfach gemußt.
            We just had to.

(v) If a modal verb is used with a compound tense in a subordinate clause there will be three verbs at the end of the clause. In that case the 'avalanche' rule applies and the auxiliary moves to the head of the queue of verbs.

Example: Er ist nicht hier, weil er nicht hat kommen können.
            He isn't here because he hasn't been able to come.
            Sie weiß jetzt, daß sie es nicht hätte machen sollen.
            She knows now that she shouldn't have done it.

Native speakers will often try to avoid the need for this construction, particularly in speech, as it can sound clumsy.

(vi) Sometimes the dependent infinitive is omitted after modal verbs if it is clear from the context what it would have been. This is usually a verb of motion or tun.

Examples: Ich will nach Leipzig.
            I want to go to Leipzig.
            Wir könnten morgen vielleicht ins Kino.
            We could go to the cinema tomorrow.
            Das kann ich nicht.
            I can't do that.

There are also a few common idiomatic phrases which work on the same principle.

Examples: Ich kann nicht mehr.
            I can't go on.
            Was soll das?
            What's the meaning of this?
            Du kannst mich mal (offensive)
            Why don't you take a running jump?

(b) The meanings of modal verbs are very subtle. In addition, their meaning sometimes changes when they are negative. The following examples for each modal verb should provide sufficient guidance.

(i) dürfen

(a) It most often means 'to be allowed to'.

Example: Ich darf nicht kommen.
            I am not allowed to come, I may not come.

(b) In the negative, it means 'must not'. See also müssen.

Example: Hier darf man nicht rauchen.
            You must not smoke here.

NB the idiom: Das darf doch nicht wahr sein.
            That can't be true.

(c) It is frequently used as a substitute for können when politeness is intended:

Examples: Was darf es sein?
            What can I get you?
            Darf ich um das Vergnügnen bitten?
            Would you like to dance?

Wir freuen uns, Sie hier in Iburg begrüßen zu dürfen.
We are pleased to be able to welcome you here in Iburg.

(d) It can express (strongish) probability.

Example: Er dürfte eigentlich schon in Köln sein.
He ought to be in Cologne by now.

(ii) können

(a) It most often means 'to be able to'.

Examples: Ich kann Fußball spielen.
I can/am able to play football.
Ich habe leider nicht pünktlich kommen können.
I am afraid I wasn't able to arrive on time.

(b) It can express possibility, like the English 'may, could, might'.

Examples: Das kann sein.
That may be so.
Er könnte vielleicht krank sein.
He might perhaps be ill.

(c) It can mean to know how to do something.

Example: Sie kann Deutsch.
She can speak German.
Ich kann 'Für Elise'.
I know (and can play) 'Für Elise'.

(d) It is often substituted for dürfen colloquially.

Example: Kannst du ausgehen?
Are you allowed out?

(e) German is very precise in differentiating between the two meanings of 'could have done' or 'might have done'. Note the contrast between the pair of examples:

Examples: Er hätte den Telefonanruf nicht machen können.
He couldn't have made the phone call.
(It might have been made by someone else.)
Er könnte den Telefonanruf nicht gemacht haben.
He couldn't have made the phone call.
(It wasn't physically possible for him to have made it.)

(iii) mögen

(a) It most often means 'to like'.

Example: Ich mag schwimmen.
I like swimming.
Ich möchte eine Banane.
I'd like a banana.
Er mochte seine Tante nicht
He didn't like his aunt.
Ich möchte länger mit ihm gesprochen haben
I should have liked to talk with him at greater length.

(b) It is used to express possibility, often implying some element of concession.

Examples: Das mag wohl sein, aber...
That may well be so, but ...
Der Durchschnittsmensch mag das nicht glauben, aber...
The average person may not believe this, but...
Er mochte über siebzig Jahre alt sein.
He would be over 70.

(iv) müssen

(a) It most often means 'to have to'.

Examples: Ich muß jetzt gehen.
I have to go now.
Das muß man gesehen haben.
You have to have seen it!
Muß das sein?
Is that really necessary?

(b) In the negative, it corresponds to 'needn't' or 'don't have to'.

Example: Wir müssen das Buch nicht jetzt lesen.
We don't have to/needn't read that book now.

NB – 'mustn't' is usually expressed by 'darf nicht'.
– Germans often use 'nicht brauchen' in preference to the negative of müssen.

(c) It can express logical deduction.

Examples: A plus B gleicht C, also muß 2mal A plus 2mal B 2mal C gleichen
A + B = C, so 2A + 2B must equal 2C
Etwas muß vorgekommen sein.
Something must have happened.

(d) If the deduction is a more complex one, or there is greater diffidence, then Konjunktiv II is used.

Examples: Soviel Geld wie Paul Getty müßte man haben.
I wish I had as much money as Paul Getty.
Das müßte genug davon sein.
That ought to be enough of that.

(e) German is very precise in differentiating between the two meanings of 'might well have done' or 'ought to have done'. Note the contrast between the pair of examples:

Examples: Er hätte den Telefonanruf machen müssen.
He should have made the phone call (he needed to, but didn't).
Er müßte den Telefonanruf gemacht haben.
He must have made the phone call.
(it seems in the light of the evidence that he made it).

(v) sollen

(a) It most often means 'to be obliged to, to have to' There is often an 'external' obligation.

Examples: Um wieviel Uhr sollen wir bei dir sein?
When should we be at your place?
Du solltest Maria doch vom Bahnhof abholen, oder?
Shouldn't you have picked Maria up from the station?

(b) It can often be the equivalent of a command.

Examples: Er soll auf mich warten.
He is to wait for me.
Du sollst nicht töten.
Thou shalt not kill.
Sagen Sie ihm, er solle morgen zurückkommen.
Tell him to come back tomorrow.

(c) It may express an intention, with the meaning 'are to', is supposed to', etc.:

Examples: Hier soll die neue Umgehungsstraße gebaut werden.
This is where the new by-pass is to be built.
Was soll das bedeuten?
What's that supposed to mean?
Wann sollen wir uns treffen?
When shall we meet?

(d) It may express sarcasm.

Examples: Soll das ein Stuhl sein?
Do you call that a chair?
Sollte er wirklich jetzt Lehrer werden wollen?
Is he really wanting to be a teacher now?

(e) It may express rumour.

Example: Er soll andere Freundinnen gehabt haben.
He is said to have had other girl-friends.

(f) The Konjunktiv II is often used to express 'should (have)', or 'ought to (have)'.

Examples: Warum sollte ich kein Motorrad fahren?
Why shouldn't I drive a motorbike?
Das hättest du mir aber eher sagen sollen.
You should have told me that earlier.

(g) German is very precise in differentiating between the two meanings of 'should have done'. Note the contrast between the pair of examples:

Examples: Er hätte den Telefonanruf machen sollen.
*He should have made the phone call
(but for some reason, didn't).*
Er sollte den Telefonanruf gemacht haben.
*He should have made the phone call
(it is a fair bet that he has done it by now).*

(vi) wollen

(a) It most often means 'to want to, to wish to'.

Examples: Ich wollte eher ankommen.
I wanted to arrive earlier.
Ich will meinem Sohn helfen.
I want to help my son.
Ich will nur das Beste für dich.
I only want the best for you.
Machen Sie, was Sie wollen.
Do what you like.
Ich wollt'* ich wär'* ein Huhn, da hätt'* ich nichts zu tun
I wish I were a hen, I'd have nothing to do.

NB *The final -e can be omitted in verse and dialect.

(b) It can express willingness.

Examples: Willst du mich in die Stadt fahren?
Will you drive me to town?
Er will den Diebstahl nicht zugeben.
He won't admit the theft.

(c) It can express intention.

Examples: Wir wollen nächstes Jahr anbauen.
We're hoping to extend our house next year.
Er wollte gerade gehen, als das Telefon klingelte.
He was just about to go when the phone rang.

(d) Some idioms use wollen.

Examples: Die Tasche wollte sich nicht schließen lassen.
The bag wouldn't close.
Keiner will es gewesen sein.
No-one will admit to it.

INFINITIVES

Forms of the infinitive

(a) The infinitive is the part of the verb listed in a dictionary, and means 'to ....'

Examples: kaufen   *to buy*
essen   *to eat*
sein   *to be*

There are also other infinitives for most verbs:

(b) The perfect infinitive, which is the past participle of the verb with 'haben' or 'sein'.

Examples: gekauft haben   *to have bought*
gegessen haben   *to have eaten*
gewesen sein   *to have been*

(c) The passive infinitive, which is the past participle of the verb with 'werden' or 'sein' (see also: passive).

Examples: gekauft werden   *to be bought*
gegessen werden *to be eaten*
verletzt sein   *to be injured*

(d) The perfect passive infinitive, which is the participle of the verb plus 'worden sein'.

Example: verletzt worden sein   *to have been injured*

The infinitive without 'zu'

It is found at the end of the clause – see also word order.
The infinitive is used without zu:

(a) In conjunction with the modal verbs dürfen, können, mägen, müssen, sollen and wollen.

Example: Sie will Tennis spielen.
She wants to play tennis.
Er muß schnell gefahren sein.
He must have driven quickly.

Much fuller details are given under MODALS.

(b) After some verbs of perception: fühlen, hören, sehen, spüren.

Examples: Ich hörte ihn ankommen.
I heard him arrive.
Er fühlte seine Wangen erröten.
He felt his cheeks go red.

(c) After lassen, meaning to have someone do something for you.

Example: Ich ließ meine Uhr reparieren. Ich konnte das selbst nicht machen.
I had my watch repaired. I couldn't do it myself.

(d) After certain verbs of motion – fahren, gehen, kommen, schicken. The verb in the infinitive gives the reason for going.

Examples: Ich gehe jetzt schlafen.
I am going to bed.
Er geht samstags immer eislaufen.
He always goes skating on Saturday.

(e) After bleiben, finden and haben followed by a verb of place.

Example: Er blieb plötzlich stehen.
He suddenly halted.
Sie fand die Zeitung auf dem Tisch liegen.
She found the newspaper lying on the table.

(f) In a few idioms.

Examples: Das nennst du singen!
Do you call that singing?
Sie lehrte mich jodeln.
She taught me how to yodel.
Der Opa legte sich schlafen.
Grandpa went to bed.

(g) As an alternative past participle where a modal verb, lassen, sehen or hören governs a dependent infinitive.

Examples: Ich habe nicht kommen können.
I wasn't able to come.
Er hat sein Auto reparieren lassen.
He had his car mended.
M hat Bond nicht hineinkommen sehen/hören.
M didn't see/hear Bond come in.

The infinitive with 'zu'

It is found at the end of the clause. For separable verbs, the zu is inserted between the separable prefix and the verb and written as a single word. In complex infinitives the zu comes between the past participle and the auxiliary, the three words being written separately.

Examples: Es ist schön, hier zu sein.
It is nice to be here.
Er hat vor, in der Stadt einzukaufen.
He intends to go shopping in town.

The infinitive with zu is used:

(a) After certain prepositions.

(i) um ...... zu – *in order to*

Examples: Sie schickte ihm DM 1000, um einen alten Wagen zu kaufen.
            She sent him DM 1000 to buy an old car.
            Er ist zu jung, um die Politik zu verstehen.
            He is too young to understand politics.

(ii) ohne ..... zu – *without*

Example: Er fuhr nach Dover, ohne tanken zu müssen.
            He drove to Dover without refuelling.

(iii) statt .... zu / anstatt .... zu – *instead of*

Example: Er spielte Tennis, anstatt seine Hausaufgaben zu machen.
            He played tennis instead of doing his homework.

(iv) außer ... zu – *except /besides*

Example: Was blieb ihnen übrig, außer zu arbeiten?
            What else could they do but work?

(b) After the following verbs:

(i) bekommen – *to get*

Example: Wenn dein Vater dich zu fassen bekommt...
            When your father gets his hands on you ...

(ii) bleiben – *to remain*

Example: Das bleibt noch zu sehen.
            That remains to be seen.

(iii) brauchen – *to need*

Example: Das brauchst du nicht zu machen.
            You needn't do that.

(iv) drohen – *to threaten*

Example: Das Haus droht einzustürzen.
            The house is threatening to collapse.

(v) geben – *to give*

It is most frequent with verstehen.

Example: Er gab mir zu verstehen, daß er mich liebe.
            He gave me to understand that he loved me.

(vi) haben zu – *to have to*

Example: Ich habe viel zu erledigen.
            I have a lot to do.

(vii) scheinen – *to seem*

Example: Das Oper schien ihm nicht zu gefallen.
            He didn't seem to like the opera.

(viii) sein – *to be*

The dependent infinitive after the zu has a passive meaning

Examples: Dort ist das Fleisch nicht zu haben.
            Meat is not to be had there.
            Der Direktor ist nicht zu sprechen.
            The Director is not available (to be spoken to).

(ix) versprechen – *to promise*

Example: Das Wetter verspricht heiß zu werden.
            The weather promises to be hot.

(x) wissen – *to know how to*

Example: Sie weiß mit den Schülern fertig zu werden.
            She knows how to deal with the students.

(c) After the adjectives einfach, interessant, leicht, schwer, schwierig.

Example: Dieses Problem ist schwer zu lösen.
            This problem is hard to solve.

(d) In comparative phrases.

Example: Man sollte sich lieber auf etwas freuen, als über Probleme nachzudenken.
            It is better to look forward to something than to worry about problems.

(e) In exclamations.

Example: Ach, wieder zu Hause zu sein!
            Oh, to be at home!

(f) In small ads.

Example: VW-Käfer zu verkaufen.
            VW Beetle for sale.

The infinitive used as a noun

(a) (i) The infinitive of almost any German verb can be used as a noun. They are all neuter, don't normally appear in the plural, and have a capital letter. The 'sich' from reflexive verbs is usually omitted.

Example: Das Wandern ist schön.
            Hiking is lovely.

(ii) Infinitive nouns are often compounded with another element to make a longer word.

Examples: Das Schlafengehen ist was Schönes.
            Going to bed is a lovely thing.
            Das Untereinanderreden der Schüler war unerträglich.
            The chattering of the students among themselves was unbearable.

(b) Infinitive nouns are used with prepositions.

(i) beim + infinitive

Examples: Beim Radfahren hat er einen Schuh verloren.
While cycling he lost a shoe.

(ii) zum + infinitive

Examples: Zum Tennisspielen ist er viel zu alt.
He's far too old to play tennis.
Der Tee war zu kalt zum Trinken.
The tea was too cold to drink.
Ich verwende das zum Schreiben.
I use it for writing.
Das ist zum Lachen.
That's laughable.

(iii) ins + infinitive

Example: Der Wagen geriet ins Schleudern.
The car went into a skid.

<table><tr><td>PARTICIPLES</td><td>There are two participles in German, the past participle (familiar from forming the perfect tense) and the present participle.</td></tr></table>

PAST PARTICIPLE

For its formation, see PERFECT TENSE.

(a) As well as being used as a part of a verb, it can be used as an adjective, taking an adjective ending like any other adjective.

Examples: das gewünschte Kind   *the longed-for child*
mein geschnittener Finger   *my cut finger*

(b) They can often be compounded.

Example: ein hartgekochtes Ei   *a hard-boiled egg*

(c) Like other adjectives, they may be used as adverbs.

Example: Nervlich zerstört verließ er den Prüfungsraum.
He left the examination room with his nerves in tatters.

(d) Like other adjectives, they may be used as nouns.

Example: der/die Vorsitzende   *the chairperson*

(e) It may be used in extended constructions where more information is added before the participle. In effect, the 'adjective' is extended by additional information. In English a relative clause would be needed. This usage is confined to written German, but is common in newspapers.

Examples: Ich habe das von meiner Mutter neulich geschickte Paket erhalten.
I received the packet which my mother sent recently.

(f) A few idioms use past participle constructions

offen gesagt   *to be frank*
nebenbei bemerkt   *incidentally*
gesetzt den Fall, daß... *asssuming that...*

wohl gemerkt	*mind you,*
strenggenommen	*strictly speaking*
MWSt und Bedienung inbegriffen	*VAT and service inclusive*
verdammt!	*damn!*
wie ausgemacht	*as arranged*
wie gesagt	*as I said*
wie erwartet	*as expected*
wie vorausgesehen	*as foreseen*

(g) A clause using the past participle can be introduced with obwohl.

Example: Obwohl vom Publikum heiß geliebt, wurde der Fußballer von der
Direktion wegen Diebstahl entlassen.
*Although very popular with the public the footballer was sacked by the
management for dishonesty.*

(h) Some past participles are used as prepositions.

(i) ausgenommen   *except*
    eingeschlossen*   *including*

These, chameleon-like, take on the case of the noun they accompany.
*Eingeschlossen follows the noun.

Examples: Allen dankten sie, ausgenommen dem fiesen Deutschlehrer.
They thanked all of them except the vindictive German teacher.
Alle kamen, mein Vetter eingeschlossen.
They all came, including my cousin.

(ii) eingerechnet* + Acc   *including (in the sum)*

It follows the noun.

(i) Vorausgesetzt(, daß) is used as a conjunction.

Example: Wir wollen schwimmen gehen, vorausgesetzt, daß das Schwimmbad
heute auf hat.
We want to go swimming provided that the swimming pool is open today.

PRESENT PARTICIPLE

This is formed for both weak and strong verbs by adding a -d to the infinitive.

Example: singend   *singing*

Point to watch: it should NOT be used as part of an attempt to translate the English
continuous forms such as 'I was singing'. For translations of the English -ing, see
below.

(a) As well as being used as a part of a verb, it can be used as an adjective, taking an
adjective ending like any other adjective.

Examples: das singende Pferd   *the singing horse*
Der Fliegende Holländer   *The Flying Dutchman*

(b) They can often be compounded.

Example: eine Regierung von atemberaubender Unfähigkeit
a breath-takingly incompetent government

(c) Like other adjectives, they may be used as adverbs.

Example: Er lief überraschend schnell.
He ran surprisingly quickly.

(d) Like other adjectives, they may be used as nouns.

Example: der/die Sterbende   *the dying person*

(e) The present participle may also be used as an adjective or adjectival noun with zu.

Examples: ein nicht zu übersehender Fehler
a mistake which cannot be overlooked
der/die Auszubildende
the trainee

(f) It may be used in extended constructions where more information is added before the participle. In effect, the 'adjective' is extended by additional information. This usage is confined to written German, but is common in newspapers.

Examples: Der Elefant auf den Hinterbeinen stehend tanzte zur Musik der Kapelle.
The elephant, standing on its hind legs, danced to the music of the band.

(g) Some present participles are used as prepositions.

betreffend + Acc *   *concerning*
entsprechend + Dat*   *accordance with*

*Both of these follow the noun they qualify.

Translation of the English present participle (-ing)

The present participle is much less frequently used in German than in English. German prefers the following alternatives.

(a) An infinitive used as a noun.

Examples: Ich habe keine Lust zum Schrieben.
I don't feel like writing.
Beim Aussteigen hat sie ihren Schuh verloren.
She lost her shoe while getting out.

(b) An infinitive + zu.

Examples: Er verließ das Haus, ohne ein Wort zu sagen.
He left the house without saying a word.
Anstatt seine Hausaufgaben zu machen, hörte er Musik.
Instead of doing his homework he listened to music.

(c) An infinitive after verbs of perception.

Examples: Wir hörten ihn kommen.
We heard him coming.
Wir sahen sie abfahren.
We saw them leaving.

(d) A relative clause.

Example: Der Hund, der unter dem Tisch sitzt, gehört meiner Mutter.
The dog sitting under the table belongs to my mother.

(e) A clause introduced by daß, indem, ehe, nachdem, ohne daß, anstatt daß, etc.

Examples: Er ging an ihr vorbei, ohne daß sie ihn sah.
He went past her without her seeing him.
Er hat mir sehr geholfen, indem er mir das Auto.
geliehen hat, nachdem er gemerkt hatte, daß ich in der Klemme war
He helped me a great deal by lending me the car after noticing that I was in a jam.

(f) Using 'wie' after verbs of hearing or seeing.

Examples: Ich hörte, wie er die Treppe hinaufkam.
I heard him coming upstairs

(g) Using a second main clause after 'und'.

Examples: Sie saß zu Hause und las.
She was sitting at home reading.

Point to watch: English has -ing as part of the continuous form of most tenses, e.g. I was washing. This CANNOT be rendered in German using a present participle. Doing so is a really bad mistake.

VERBS FOLLOWED BY THE NOMINATIVE

The following verbs are followed by the Nominative case, or by an adjective standing alone:

bleiben	*to remain*
heißen	*to be called*
scheinen	*to seem*
sein	*to be*
werden	*to become*

Examples: Du bist mein Freund.
You are my friend.
Sie wurde rot.
She blushed.
Er scheint auch ein solcher.
He seems to be a person like that, too.
Er heißt Herr Braun.
He is called Herr Braun.

VERBS FOLLOWED BY THE DATIVE

The following verbs are followed by the Dative case. English-speaking learners of German find this a bit strange, and the only known cure is to learn which they are!

(i) Common verbs taking the Dative include:

antworten	*to answer*
begegnen	*to meet (by chance/for the first time)*
danken	*to thank*
folgen	*to follow*
gehören	*to belong to*
helfen	*to help*
passen	*to suit*
trauen	*to trust*
wehtun	*to hurt*

Examples: Er hat mir nicht geantwortet.
He didn't answer me.
Ich habe meiner Mutter im Garten geholfen.
I helped my mother in the garden.
Er hat sich am Arm wehgetan.
He hurt his arm.

(ii) There are some less common ones including:

ähneln	*to resemble*
ausweichen	*to avoid*
dienen	*to serve*
drohen	*to threaten*
einfallen	*to occur*
sich ergeben	*to surrender*
gehorchen	*to obey*
gleichen	*to resemble*
gratulieren	*to congratulate*
imponieren	*to impress*
kündigen	*to sack, give notice*
sich nähern	*to approach*
nutzen (nützen)	*to be of use*
raten	*to advise*
schaden	*to harm*
schmeicheln	*to flatter*
trotzen	*to defy*
vorbeugen	*to prevent*

Examples: Es nutzt mir nichts.
It is no use to me.
Wein auf Bier, das rate ich dir;
Bier auf Wein, das laß sein.
I advise wine after beer, not the other way round.

(iii) Verbs meaning to 'happen to someone' are used with a Dative.

Examples: So etwas ist mir noch nie passiert.
Nothing like that has ever happened to me.
Was kann mir denn in der Disko passieren?
What can happen to me in the disco, then?

(iv) Verbs beginnning with bei-, ent-, entgegen-, nach- , wider- and zu- usually take the Dative.

Examples:

beitreten	*to join a party*
entsprechen	*to correspond to*
entgegenkommen	*to come towards*
nacheilen	*to hurry after*
widersprechen	*to contradict*
zuhören	*to listen to*

IMPERSONAL VERBS

A good number of verbs are used with the subject es. These are known as impersonal verbs. They include the following:

(a) Weather verbs.

Examples: Es regnet.
It is raining.
Es schneit.
It is snowing.

(b) Verbs referring to other natural occurrences.

Examples: Es zieht.
There is a draught.
Es riecht stark nach Stinktier.
There is a strong odour of skunk.

(c) Verbs referring to noises.

Examples: Es klingelt.
The bell is ringing.
Es zischte.
There was a hissing noise.

(d) With sein and werden.

Examples: Es ist zu spät.
It is too late.
Es wurde hell.
It got light.

(e) Various idioms

Es fehlte mir an Geld.	*I lacked the money.*
Es gefällt mir hier.	*I like it here.*
Wie geht es dir?	*How are you?*
Es geht um Leben und Tod.	*It's a matter of life and death.*
Es handelt sich um Liebe.	*It's a matter of love.*
Es heißt, daß er noch lebt.	*It is said that he is still alive.*
Es kommt darauf an.	*It depends.*
Es macht nichts.	*It doesn't matter.*
Es kam zu einem Zusammenstoß.	*A clash occurred.*
Es lebt sich gut in Berlin.	*It's good living in Berlin.*
Es wurde darßber gesprochen.	*It was talked about.*

Es ist mir kalt.	*I am cold.*
Es fällt mir schwer.	*I find it hard.*
Es gefällt mir.	*I like it.*
Es gelingt mir.	*I succeed.*
Es tut mir leid.	*I am sorry.*
Das reicht mir.	*That's enough for me.*
Es schmeckt mir sehr gut.	*It tastes lovely.*

ES gibt and es ist

Although both of these are rendered by 'there is/there are' in English, they are not interchangeable in German, but have distinct uses.

(a) Es gibt (and less commonly, es geben) points to existence as such, without reference to a particular place:

(i) in broad, general statements

Examples: Es gibt viele Gründe dafür.
There are many reasons for it.
So etwas gibt es nicht mehr.
There aren't any of those any more.

(ii) to point to permanent existence in a large areas such as a country or a city

Examples: In Köln gibt es ja das Römisch-Germanische-Museum.
In Cologne there is the German-Roman Museum.
Es gibt eine Drachenhöhle auf dem Drachenfels.
There is a dragon's cave on the Drachenfels.

(iii) to record the likely or actual consequences of an event

Examples: Wenn ich zu spät nach Hause komme, gibt es Krach.
If I get home too late there'll be a row.
Bei einem Verkehrsunfall heute auf der B3 soll es drei Tote gegeben haben.
In an accident on the B3 it is reported that three people were killed.

(b) **Es ist/es sind** shows the presence of something at a particular time and place. If it is not used at the beginning of a clause, the 'es' often disappears.

Compare: Es war ein Löwe im Garten
Ein Löwe war im Garten

Es ist/sind is used.

(i) to refer to a temporary presence in a large area

Example: Es waren Wolken im Himmel.
There were clouds in the sky.

(ii) to refer to a permanent or temporary presence in a restricted area

Examples: Es war ein verrostetes Fahrrad in der Garage.
There was a rusty bicycle in the garage.
Es ist jemand an der Tür.
There is someone at the door.

(iii) to talk about the weather

Example: Es war schön gestern.
The weather was nice yesterday.

NB es gibt would also do

Example: Gestern gab es Schnee.
There was snow yesterday.

(iv) to talk about events

Example: Letzte Woche war in Berlin eine Demonstration.
There was a demonstration in Berlin last week.

NB es gibt would also do

CLAUSES ANTICIPATED BY ES

In some cases, where a verb is followed by a subordinate clause (daß, wenn ...) or an infinitive phrase, an 'es' is inserted.

Examples: Ich würde es an deiner Stelle vergessen, daß du es je gewußt hast.
If I were you I would forget that I had ever known it.
Ich kann es mir leisten, erster Klasse zu fahren.
I can afford to travel first class.

The most common verbs involved include:

*auf*geben	*to give up*
*aus*halten	*to stand it*
begrüßen	*to welcome*
erleben	*to experience*
*fertig*bringen	*to manage it, achieve*
genießen	*to enjoy*
hassen	*to hate*
leisten	*to afford*
lieben	*to love*
schaffen	*to manage it, achieve*
schätzen	*to value*
überlegen	*to consider*
vergessen	*to forget*
zeigen	*to show*

TRANSITIVE AND INTRANSITIVE VERB PAIRS

In English, numbers of verbs can be transitive or intransitive according to circumstances. In German there are often distinct – if related – verbs which echo this usage.

(i) German verbs which can be transitive or intransitive will take sein in the perfect when intransitive and haben when transitive.

Examples: Ich bin nach Berlin gefahren (intransitive).
I drove to Berlin.
Ich habe meinen Wagen nach Berlin gefahren (transitive).
I drove my car to Berlin.

(ii) Some verbs which have the same meaning in English are quite different in German.

Examples: Er baut Weizen an.
He grows wheat.
Der Weizen wächst gut.
The wheat grows well.
Mutti verließ das Haus um acht Uhr.
Mum left the house at eight.
Ich ließ das Geschirr ungespült.
I left the crockery unwashed.
Der Zug ist pünktlich abgefahren.
The train left on time.
Anne machte die Tür auf.
Anne opened the door.
Die Tür ging auf.
The door opened.

(iii) Some transitive/intransitive verbs in English use related verbs in German.

Examples: Sie beantwortete die Frage.
She answered the question.
Sie antwortete nicht.
She didn't answer.
Die Flugzeuge versenkten das Schiff.
The aircraft sank the ship.
Das Schiff sank.
The ship sank.

(iv) Some verbs which need to be followed by an Accusative use a reflexive pronoun if there is no obvious object.

Examples: Das hat sich geändert.
That has changed.
Sie fühlte sich krank.
She felt ill.
Die Tür öffnete sich.
The door opened.
Die Räder drehten sich.
The wheels turned.

REFLEXIVE VERBS

There are three sorts of **reflexive verb** in German.

(i) Those which have an accusative reflexive pronoun and cannot be used without it. These include:

sich bedanken	*to thank*
sich beeilen	*to hurry*
sich befinden	*to be situated*
sich benehmen	*to behave*
sich eignen	*to be suited*
sich erkälten	*to catch a cold*
sich verabschieden	*to say goodbye*

For reference, the present tense of 'sich beeilen' is given below.

ich beeile mich
du beeilst dich
er/sie/es/man beeilt sich
wir beeilen uns
ihr beeilt euch
Sie beeilen sich
sie beeilen sich

(ii) Those transitive verbs which are being used reflexively.

Examples:		
	sich fragen	*to wonder*
	sich waschen	*to wash oneself*
	sich kämmen	*to comb oneself*

(iii) Those where the reflexive pronoun is Dative and is additional to an Accusative object. For reference, an example is written out below.

ich habe mir die Haare gewaschen
du hast dir die Haare gewaschen
er/sie/es/man hat sich die Haare gewaschen
wir haben uns die Haare gewaschen
ihr habt euch die Haare gewaschen
Sie haben sich die Haare gewaschen
sie haben sich die Haare gewaschen

Point to watch: Sometimes these expressions are given as 'sich die Haare waschen' in vocabularies. Beware! the 'sich' is Dative, not Accusative!

VERBS FOLLOWED BY A PREPOSITION

Many verbs are followed by a particular preposition. The prepositions are listed here alphabetically.

(i) an + Dative

arbeiten an	*to work at*
erkennen an	*to recognise by*

erkranken an	*to fall ill with*
sich freuen an	*to take pleasure in something*
gewinnen an	*to gain in (e.g. importance)*
hängen an	*to cling to, be fond of*
mitwirken an	*to play a part in*
sich orientieren an	*to get one's bearings by,* *to take a lead from*
riechen an	*to sniff*
teilnehmen an	*to take part in*
verlieren an	*to lose (some)*
Es fehlt mir an	*I lack*

(ii) an + Accusative

denken an	*to think of*
erinnern an	*to remind*
sich erinnern an	*to remember*
sich gewöhnen an	*to get used to*
glauben an	*to believe in*

(iii) auf + Accusative

achten auf	*to pay attention to*
aufpassen auf	*to look after (children)*
sich beziehen auf	*to refer to*
drängen auf	*to press (for payment)*
sich erstrecken auf	*to extend to*
folgen auf	*to follow on from*
sich freuen auf	*to look forward to*
sich gründen auf	*to be based on*
hinweisen auf	*to point out to*
hoffen auf	*to hope for*
sich konzentrieren auf	*to concentrate on*
reagieren auf	*to react to*
schimpfen auf	*to curse about*
sich spezialisieren auf	*to specialise in*
sich verlassen auf	*to rely on*
verzichten auf	*to do without*
warten auf	*to wait for*
zählen auf	*to count on*
zurückkommen auf	*to come back to*

(iv) auf + Dative

basieren auf	*to be based on*
bestehen auf	*to insist on*
beruhen auf	*to be based on*

(v) aus + Dative

bestehen aus	*consist of*
entnehmen aus	*to infer from*
sich ergeben aus	*to result from*
folgern aus	*to conclude from*
schließen aus	*to conclude from*

(vi) für + Accusative

sich (bei jemandem) bedanken für	*to thank (someone) for*
sich begeistern für	*to be enthusiastic about*
danken für	*to thank for*
sich entscheiden für	*to decide on*

halten für	*to consider (that)*
sich interessieren für	*to be interested in*
sorgen für	*to take care of/look after*

(vii) in + Accusative

sich mischen in	*to meddle in*
sich verlieben in	*to fall in love with*
sich vertiefen in	*to become engrossed in*

(viii) in + Dative (very rare!)

sich täuschen in	*to be mistaken in one's judgement of*

(ix) mit + Dative

anfangen mit	*to make a start on*
aufhören mit	*to stop doing something*
sich abfinden mit	*to put up with, be content with*
sich befassen mit	*to deal with*
sich beschäftigen mit	*to occupy oneself by*
drohen mit	*to threaten with*
rechnen mit	*to count on*
sprechen mit	*to speak to*
telefonieren mit	*to speak on the phone with*
übereinstimmen mit	*to agree with*
sich unterhalten mit	*to converse with*
vergleichen mit	*to compare with*
sich verheiraten mit	*to marry (as one of the happy couple, not as the priest)*
sich verloben mit	*to get engaged to*
versehen mit	*to provide with (often ironic)*
zusammenstoßen mit	*to collide with*

(x) nach + Dative

sich erkundigen nach	*to enquire after*
fragen nach	*to ask after*
greifen nach	*to make a grab for*
hungern nach	*to hunger after*
riechen nach	*to smell of*
rufen nach	*to call after, to call for*
schreien nach	*to yell for*
schmecken nach	*to taste of (usually something bad)*
streben nach	*to strive for*
suchen nach	*to search for*
telefonieren nach	*to phone for (a doctor)*
verlangen nach	*to ask for, long for, crave*

(xi) über + Accusative

sich ärgern über	*to be annoyed about*
sich (bei jemandem) beklagen über	*to complain about (to someone)*
denken über	*to think about*
sich freuen über	*to be pleased about*
informieren über	*to inform about*
nachdenken über	*to think over*
schreiben über	*to write about*
sprechen über	*to discuss*
sich streiten über	*to argue over*
urteilen über	*to make a judgement about*
verfügen über	*to have at one's disposal*

wissen über	*to know about*
sich wundern über	*to be surprised at*

(xii) um + Accusative

sich bemühen um	*to take trouble over*
sich handeln um	*to be a question of, to be a matter of*
kämpfen um	*to fight for*
konkurrieren um	*to compete for*
ums Leben kommen	*to die*
um Geld spielen	*to play for money*
streiken um	*to strike over*

(xiii) von + Dative

abhalten von	*to keep from*
abhängen von	*to depend on*
befreien von	*to liberate from*
sich distanzieren von	*to dissociate oneself from*
sich erholen von	*to recover from*
erzählen von	*to tell of/about*
hören von	*to hear of*
lesen von	*to read about*
träumen von	*to dream of*

(xiv) vor + Dative

bewahren vor	*to protect from*
sich drücken vor	*to dodge, skive*
sich ekeln vor	*to be disgusted by*
fliehen vor	*to flee from*
sich fürchten vor	*to be frightened of*
Angst haben vor	*to be frightened of*
sich hüten vor	*to beware of*
retten vor	*to save from*
sich schämen vor	*to be ashamed of something in front of someone*
sich scheuen vor	*to shrink from*
sich verbergen vor	*to hide from*
warnen vor	*to warn about*

(xv) zu + Dative

autorisieren zu	*to authorise to*
berechtigen zu	*to give the right to*
einladen zu	*to invite to*
führen zu	*to lead to*
herausfordern zu	*to challenge*
neigen zu	*to tend towards*
provozieren zu	*to provoke to*
veranlassen zu	*to cause to*
verführen zu	*to seduce*
es zu etwas bringen	*to attain something*

A LIST OF THE MORE COMMON REGULAR VERBS

The verbs below all follow the same pattern.

abholen (*sep*)	*to pick up, fetch*	antworten	*to answer*
abräumen (*sep*)	*to clear away*	arbeiten	*to work*
abspülen (*sep*)	*to clear away*	aufhören (*sep*)	*to stop*
anmachen (*sep*)	*to switch on*	aufmachen (*sep*)	*to open*

aufpassen (sep)	to pay attention	prüfen	to test
aufräumen (sep)	to tidy up	rauchen	to smoke
aufwachen (sep)*	to wake up	regnen	to rain
ausmachen (sep)	to switch off	reichen	to reach, to pass
auspacken (sep)	to unpack	reisen*	to travel
sich beeilen	to hurry	reparieren	to repair
begrüßen	to greet	sagen	to say
besichtigen	to visit	sammeln	to collect
bestellen	to order	schauen	to look
besuchen	to visit	schicken	to send
bezahlen	to pay	schmecken	to taste
brauchen	to need	schneien	to snow
buchen	to book	segeln	to sail
danken (+D)	to thank	sparen	to save
decken	to cover, set table	spielen	to play
drücken	to press, push	starten	to start
einkaufen (sep)	to shop	stecken	to put
einpacken (sep)	to pack	stellen	to put
fehlen	to be missing	eine Frage stellen	to ask a question
fragen	to ask	stimmen	to be right
sich freuen	to be pleased	suchen	to look for
gestatten	to allow	tanken	to fill up with petrol
glauben	to think	tanzen	to dance
gucken	to look	teilen	to share
heiraten	to marry	telefonieren	to telephone
sich hinsetzen (sep)	to sit down	träumen	to dream
hoffen	to hope	turnen	to do gymnastics
hören	to hear	üben	to practise
kapieren	to understand	überraschen	to surprise
kaufen	to buy	verdienen	to earn
klingeln	to ring	verkaufen	to sell
klopfen	to knock	vermieten	to rent out
kriegen	to get	versuchen	to try
lachen	to laugh	vborbereiten (sep)	to prepare
landen	to land	sich vorstellen (sep)	to introduce oneself
legen	to put	wählen	to choose
lernen	to learn	warten	to wait
machen	to make, to do	sich waschen	to wash oneself
meinen	to think	wechseln	to change money
melden	to announce, register	wiederholen	to repeat
mieten	to rent	wohnen	to live
nähen	to sew	wünschen	to wish
öffnen	to open	zahlen	to pay
organisieren	to organise	zeichnen	to draw
parken	to park	zeigen	to show
planen	to plan	zuhören (sep)	to listen to

IRREGULAR (STRONG) VERB TABLE

Infinitive	3rd person sing. present	3rd person sing. imperfect	Past participle	Konjunktiv II	Meaning
anbieten	bietet an	bot an	hat angeboten	böte an	to offer
anerkennen	erkennt an	erkannte an	hat anerkannt	erkennte an	to recognize
anfangen	fängt an	fing an	hat angefangen	finge un	to begin
anhalten	hält an	hielt an	hat angehalten	hielte un	to stop
annehmen	nimmt an	nahm an	hat angenommen	nähme an	to accept
anrufen	ruft an	rief an	hat angerufen	riefe an	to call (out to)
aufstehen	steht auf	stand auf	ist aufgestanden	stünde auf	to get up
aussehen	sieht aus	sah aus	hat ausgesehen	sähe aus	to look
backen	bäckt	buk/backte	hat gebacken	büke	to bake
befehlen	befiehlt	befahl	hat befohlen	beföhle/beföhle	to command
beginnen	beginnt	begann	hat begonnen	begänne/begönne	to begin

Infinitive	3rd person sing. present	3rd person sing. imperfect	Past participle	Konjunktiv II	Meaning
behalten	behält	behielt	hat behalten	behielte	to keep
beißen	beißt	biß bisse	hat gebissen	bisse	to bite
bekommen	bekommt	bekam	hat bekommen	bekame	to get
sich benehmen	benimmt sich	benahm sich	hat sich benommen	benähme sich	to behave
beschließen	beschließt	beschloß	hat beschlossen	beschlösse	to decide on
beschreiben	beschreibt	beschrieb	hat beschrieben	beschriebe	to describe
besitzen	besitzt	besaß	hat besessen	besäße	to possess
bestehlen	bestiehlt	bestahl	hat bestohlen	bestähle	to rob
sich bewerben	bewirbt sich	bewarb sich	hat sich beworben	bewürbe	to apply
biegen	biegt	bog	hat/ist gebogen	böge	to bend, turn
bieten	bietet	bot	hat begoten	böte	to offer
binden	bindet	band	hat gebunden	bände	to bind
bitten	bittet	bat	hat gebeten	bäte	to ask
bleiben	bleibt	blieb	ist geblieben	bleibe	to stay
braten	brät	briet	hat gebraten	briete	to roast
brechen	bricht	brach	hat gebrochen	bröche	to break
brennen burn	brennt	brannte	hat gebrannt	brennte	to burn
bringen	bringt	brachte	hat gebracht	brächte	to bring
denken	denkt	dachte	hat gedacht	dächte	to think
dringen	dringt	drang	ist/hat gedrungen	dränge	to penetrate
dürfen	darf	durfte	hat gedurft	dürfte	to be allowed
einfallen	fällt ein	fiel ein	ist eingefallen	fiele ein	to fall
einladen	lädt ein	lud ein	hat eingeladen	lüde ein	to invite
einschlafen	schläft ein	schlief ein	ist eingeschlafen	schliefe ein	to go to sleep
einsehen	sieht ein	sah ein	hat eingesehen	sähe ein	to realize
einsteigen	steigt ein	stieg ein	ist eingestiegen	stiege ein	to get in
eintreten	tritt ein	trat ein	ist eingetreten	tröte ein	to occur
empfangen	empfängt	empfing	hat empfangen	empfinge	to reserve
empfehlen	empfiehlt	empfahl	hat empfohlen	empföhle	to recommend
entscheiden	entscheidet	entschied	hat entschieden	entschiede	to decide
sich entschließen	entschließt sich	entschloß sich	hat sich entschlossen	entschlösse sich	to decide
entstehen	entsteht	entstand	ist entstanden	entsünde	to arise
erfahren	erfährt	erfuhr	hat erfahren	erführe	to learn
erhalten	erhält	erhielt	hat erhalten	erhielte	to receive, maintain
erkennen	erkennt	erkannte	hat erkannt	erkennte	to recognize
erklingen	erklingt	erklang	hat erklungen	erklänge	to resound
erscheinen	erscheint	erschien	ist erschienen	erschiene	to appear
erschrecken	erschrickt	erschrak	ist erschrocken	erschräke	to be startled

NB The transitive verb erschrecken *'frighten'* is weak, i.e. erschreckte, erschreckt.

essen	ißt	aß	hat gegessen	äße	to eat
fahren	fährt	führ	ist/hat gefahren	führe	to drive
fallen	fällt	fiel	ist gefallen	fiele	to fall
fangen	fängt fängt	fing	hat gefangen	finge finge	to catch
fernsehen	sieht fern	sah fern	hat ferngesehen	sähe fern	to watch television
fertigbringen	bringt fertig	brachte fertig	hat fertiggebracht	brächte fertig	to manage
finden	findet	fand	hat gefunden	fände	to find
fliehen	flicht	floh	ist geflohen	flähe	to flee
fliegen	fliegt	flog	ist/hat geflogen	fläge	to fly
fließen	fließt	floß	ist geflossen	flösse	to flow
freibekommen	bekommt frei	bekam frei	hat freibekommen	bekäme frei	to get (off)
fressen	frißt	fraß	hat gefressen	fräße	to eat
frieren	friert	fror	hat/ist gefroren	fröre	freeze
geben	gibt	gab	hat gegeben	gäbe	to grab
gefallen	gefällt	gefiel	hat gefallen	gefiele	to like, please
gehen	geht	ging	ist gegangen	ginge	to go
gelingen	gelingt	gelang	es ist gelungen	gelange	to receive
gelten	gilt	galt	hat gegolten	gälte/gölte	to be worth
genießen	genießt	genoß	hat genossen	genosse	to enjoy
geschehen	geschieht	geschah	ist geschehen	geschähe	to happen
gewinnen	gewinnt	gewann	hat gewonnen	gewänne/gewönne	to win

Infinitive	3rd person sing. present	3rd person sing. imperfect	Past participle	Konjunktiv II	Meaning
gießen	gießt	goß	hat gegossen	gösse	*to pour*
gleiten	gleitet	glitt	ist geglitten	glitte	*to glide, slide*
begleiten *'accompany'* is weak, i.e. begleitete, begleitet.					
greifen	greift	griff	hat gegriffen	griffe	*to seize, grip*
haben	hat	hatte	hat gehabt	hätte	*to have*
halten	hält	hielt	hat gehalten	hielte	*to keep*
heben	hebt	hob	hat gehoben	höte	*to lift*
heißen	heißt	hieß	hat geheißen	hieße	*to be called*
helfen	hilft	half	hat geholfen	hülfe/hälfe	*to help*
kennen	kennt	kannte	hat gekannt	kennte	*to know*
klingen	klingt	klang	hat geklungen	klänge	*to sound*
kommen	kommt	kam	ist gekommen	käme	*to come*
können	kann	konnte	hat gekonnt	könnte	*to be able to*
kriechen	kriecht	kroch	ist gekrochen	kröche	*to be able to*
laden	lädt	lud	hat geladen	lüde	*to load, invite*
lassen	läßt	ließ	hat gelassen	ließe	*to leave; let*
laufen	läuft	lief	ist gelaufen	liefe	*to run*
leiden	leidet	litt	hat gelitten	litte	
leihen,	leiht	lieh	hat geliehen	liehe	*to lend, borrow*
lesen	liest	las	hat gelesen	läse	*to suffer*
liegen	liegt	lag	hat gelegen	läge	*to lie*
liegenlassen	läßt liegen	ließ liegen	hat liegengelassen	ließe liegen	*to leave behind*
losfahren	fährt los	fuhr los	ist losgefahren	führe los	*to leave*
loswerden	wird los	wurde los	ist losgeworden	würde las	*to get rid of*
lügen	lügt	log	hat gelogen	löge	*to lie (tell lies)*
meiden	meidet	mied	hat gemieden	miede	*to avoid*
mögen	mag	mochte	hat gemocht	mächte	*to like*
müssen	muß	hat gemußt	müßte	müsse	*to have to*
nehmen	nimmt	nahm	hat genommen	nähme	*to take*
nennen	nennt	nannte	hat genannt	nennte	*to name*
raten	rät	riet	hat geraten	riete	*to advise*
reißen	reißt	riß	hat gerissen	risse	*to tear*
reiten	reitet	ritt	ist/hat geritten	ritte	*to ride*
rennen	rennt	rannte	hat/ist gerannt	rennte	*to run*
riechen	riecht	roch	hat gerochen	röche	*to smell*
rufen	ruft	rief	hat gerufen	riefe	*to call*
schaffen	schafft	schuf	hat geschaffen	schüfe	*to create*
scheinen	scheint	schien	hat geschienen	schiene	*to seem*
schiefgehen	geht schief	ging schief	ist schiefgegangen	ginge schief	*to go wrong*
schießen	schießt	schoß	hat geschossen	schösse	*to shoot*
schlafen	schläft	schlief	hat geschlafen	schliefe	*to sleep*
schlagen	schlägt	schlug	hat geschlagen	schlüge	*to hit*
schließen	shließt	schloß	hat geschlossen	schlösse	*to shut*
schneiden	schneidet	schnitt	hat geschnitten	schrutle	*to cut*
schreiben	schreibt	schrieb	hat geschrieben	shriebe	*to write*
schreien	schreit	schrie	hat geschrie(e)n	shriee	*to scream, shout*
schweigen	schweigt	schwieg	hat geschwiegen	schwiege	*to be silent*
schwimmen	schwimmt	schwamm	ist/hat geschwom-men	schwömme	*to swim*
sehen	sieht	sah	hat gesehen	sähe	*to see*
sein	ist	war	ist gewesen	wäre	*to be*
singen	singt	sang	hat gesungen	sänge	*to sing*
sinken	sinkt	sank	ist gesunken	sünke/sänke	*to sink*
sitzen	sitzt	saß	hat gesessen	säße	*to sit*
spazierengehen	geht spazieren	ging spazieren	ist spazierengegangen	ginge spazieren	*to go for a walk*
sprechen	spricht	sprach	hat gesprochen	spräche	*to speak*
springen	springt	sprang	ist gesprungen	spränge	*to jump*
stattfinden	findet statt	fand statt	hat stattgefunden	fände statt	*to take place*
stehen	steht	stand	hat gestanden	stünde	*to stand*
stehlen	stiehlt	stahl	hat gestohlen	stähle	*to steal*
es stiehlt					
steigen	steigt	stieg	ist gestiegen	stiege	*to climb*

Infinitive	3rd person sing. present	3rd person sing. imperfect	Past participle	Konjunktiv II	Meaning
sterben	stirbt	starb	ist gestorben	stürbe	to die
streichen	streicht	strich	ist/hat gestrichen	striche	to stroke
streiten	streitet	stritt	hat gestritten	stritte	to argue
teilnehmen	nimmt teil	nahm teil	hat teilgenommen	nähme teil	to take part
tragen	trägt	trug	hat getragen	trüge	to carry; wear
treffen	trifft	traf	hat getroffen	träfe	to strike; meet
treiben	treibt	trieb	ist/hat getrieben	triebe	to drive; drift
treten	tritt	trat	ist getreten	träte	to step
trinken	trinkt	trank	hat getrunken	tränke	to dring
tun	tut	tat	hat getan	tate	to do
übernehmen	übernimmt	übernahm	hat übernommen	übernähme	to accept, take on
umsteigen	steigt um	stieg um	ist umgestiegen	stiege um	to change (trains)
unterbringen	bringt unter	brachte unter	hat untergebracht	brachte unter	to accommodate
sich unterhalten	unterhält sich	unterhielt sich	hat sich unterhalten	unterhielte	to entertain
verbringen	verbringt	verbrachte	hat verbracht	verbrächte	to spend
verderben	verdirbt	verdarb	hat/ist verdorben	verdürbe	to spoil, ruin
vergessen	vergißt	vergaß	hat vergessen	vergäße	to forget
vergleichen	vergleicht	verglich	hat verglichen	vergliche	to compare
verlassen	verläßt	verließ	hat verlassen	verließe	to leave
verlieren	verliert	verlor	hat verloren	verlöre	to lose
verschwinden	verschwindet	verschwand	ist verschwunden	verschwande	to disappear
versprechen	verspricht	versprach	hat versprochen	verspräche	to promise
verstehen	versteht	verstand	hat verstanden	verstünde	to understand
verzeihen	verzeiht	verzieh	hat verziehen	verziehe	to forgive
vorbeifahren	fährt vorbei	fuhr vorbei	ist vorbeigefahren	führe vorbei	to drive past
vorkommen	kommt vor	kam vor	ist vorgekommen	kame vor	to come forward, occur
vorlesen	liest vor	las vor	hat vorgelesen	läse vor	to read (out)
vorschlagen	schlägt vor	schlug vor	hat vorgeschlagen	schlüge vor	to suggest
wachsen	wächst	wuchs	ist gewachsen	wüchse	to grow
waschen	wäscht	wusch	hat gewaschen	wüsche	to wash
wenden	wendet	wandte/ wendete	hat gewandt/ gewendet	wendete	to turn
werden	wird	wurde	ist geworden	würde	to become
werfen	wirft	warf	hat geworfen	würfe	to throw
wissen	weiß	wußte	hat gewußt	wüßte	to know
ziehen	zieht	zog	hat/ist gezogen	zöge	to pull; move
zwingen	zwingt	zwang	hat gezwungen	zwänge	to force

GETTING STARTED

Learning **vocabulary** is perhaps the least attractive part of studying a foreign language, but it is most important in order to improve. It is best to learn vocabulary *regularly* in short sessions, trying to memorise not more than twenty words at a time. It is necessary to go over what was learned so it can become really firmly rooted in ones memory. A good way to learn new words is by actually **using them**. So before writing an essay or preparing a discussion on a particular topic, look at the relevant vocabulary and then think of sentences in which to use it.

Some people find it useful to write out the words they want to learn. Thus they remember the sequence of the letters better and get a feeling for the spelling. Others speak the words onto a tape with short pauses after each word followed by the English meaning. The tape can then be listened to at various times and opportunities.

Some students copy out all their vocabulary onto small file cards (the German word or phrase on one side, the English equivalent on the other) which can be kept in pocket size boxes. At odd intervals they will review the cards and then put them into one of three sections: a) know very well, b) not quite sure, c) not really learned yet.

Others find it useful to create memory aids or funny sentences for new words, e.g.: die Gabel – it's what you gobble your food with, i.e. a fork.

It is worth trying various methods (or mixing them) in order to find a personal way of learning new words.

This chapter is the work of Alex Reich, a native speaker who is Head of German at Upper Chine School, Sandown, Isle of Wight.

HOW TO USE THIS VOCABULARY GUIDE

PHRASES

YOU AND YOURS

LEISURE

SOCIAL ISSUES

CURRENT AFFAIRS

TECHNOLOGY

CULTURE AND GEOGRAPHY

ESSENTIAL PRINCIPLES

This guide consists of seven parts, each of which is divided into a number of sections. At the beginning of the sections there are some phrases or sentences which give some key ideas and can be learned as units for inclusion into essays, etc. They are followed by nouns, verbs and adjectives, all in alphabetical order.

Nouns are given with their plural forms, or they are marked 'no plural' or 'plural only', except for the lists of virtues and vices (Tugenden und Laster) which by logic do not have plurals. The '(-)' means the noun does not change in the plural.

Irregular verbs are given in the infinitive, third person singular present, imperfect and past participle. Verbs taking 'sein' in the perfect are marked with an *. Seperable verbs have their prefix in italics, e.g.: *an*fangen (fängt an, fing an, angefangen).

CONTENTS

I. PHRASES

1) **Meinungen**	204
2) **Zustimmen**	204
3) **Ablehnen**	204
4) **Gegenargumente**	204
5) **Vorschläge**	204–5
6) **Erklären**	205
7) **Zugeständnisse machen**	205
8) **Andere herausfordern**	205
9) **Abwägen**	205
10) **Zusammenfassen**	205
11) **Einleiten**	206
12) **Zeitenfolge**	206
13) **Begründen**	206
14) **Vergleichen**	206

II. YOU AND YOURS

1) **Ausbildung**	206–10
a) Die Schule	207
b) Der Schüler/ die Schülerin	207–8
c) Die Lehrer	208
d) Die Prüfungen	208
e) Die Ausbildung	209
f) Die Universität	209
g) Die Bildungspolitik	209–10
2) **Jugend**	210–11
a) Allgemeines	210
b) Der Konflikt	210–11
c) Die Eltern	211
3) **Ehe und Familie**	211–13
a) Ehe und Partnerschaft	211–12
b) Die Familie	212–13
4) **Frauenfragen - Männerfragen**	213–14
5) **Gesundheit**	214–17
a) Der Körper	214–15
b) Krankheit und Heilung	215
c) Die ärztliche Behandlung	215–16
d) Rauchen, Drogen, Alkohol, Aids	216–17
6) **Das Alter**	217–18

7) **Die Religion**	217–18
a) Das Christentum	218
b) Andere Religionen	218
8) **Die Psychologie**	218–19
9) **Person und Personenbeschreibung**	219–20
a) Der Körper	219
b) Das Aussehen	219
c) Die Sinne	219
d) Gute Eigenschaften, Tugenden	219–20
e) Schlechte Eigenschaften, Laster	220

III. LEISURE

1) **Freizeit**	221
2) **Mode**	221–2
a) Die Kleidung	221–2
b) Die Modeindustrie	222
3) **Sport**	222–3
4) **Fernsehen, Radio und Kino**	223–5
a) Fernsehen und Radio	223–4
b) Gefahren des Fernsehens	224
c) Das Kino	224
5) **Reisen**	225

IV. SOCIAL ISSUES

1) **Statistik und Gesellschaftskunde**	225–6
2) **Arbeit und Arbeitslosigkeit**	226–8
3) **Umwelt**	228–31
a) Umweltprobleme	228–9
b) Luft- und Wasserverschmutzung	229
c) Umweltschutz	230
d) Die Energie	230–1
4) **Stadt und Land**	231–3
a) Gebäude in der Stadt	231–2
b) Stadtprobleme	232
c) Das Landleben	232
d) Die Landschaft	232–3

5) Verbrechen und Kriminalität 233

6) Recht und Gesetz 233–5
 a) Redewendungen 233–4
 b) Die Organe des
  Rechtsstaats 234
 c) Das Privatrecht 234
 d) Das öffentliche Recht 234–5

V. CURRENT AFFAIRS

1) Zeitungen, Journalismus 235–6

2) Das Wetter 236–7

3) Politik 237–9
 a) Der Abgeordnete 238
 b) Das Parlament 238
 c) Die Parteien 238–9
 d) Politischer Alltag 239

4) Handel und Wirtschaft 239–42
 a) Der Großhandel 239–40
 b) Finanzwesen 240–1
 c) Der Kleinhandel 241
 d) Die Wirtschaftspolitik 241
 e) Europa 241–2
 f) Die persönlichen Finanzen 242

5) Die Wiedervereinigung 242–3
 a) Die ehemalige DDR 242–3
 b) Die Bürgerbewegung 243
 c) Die Wiedervereinigung
  und ihre Probleme 243

6) Ausländer 244–5
 a) Die Einwanderungspolitik 244–5
 b) Rassismus 245

7) Die Dritte Welt 245–6

8) Krieg und Frieden 246–8
 a) Das Militär 246–7
 b) Der Konfliktfall 246–8
 c) Der Frieden 248

VI. TECHNOLOGY

1) Technology und
  Gesellschaft 248–9
 a) Im Büro 248–9
 b) In der Industrie 249

2) Die neue Technologie/
  Informatik 249–50

3) Medizin und Forschung 250–1
 a) Forschung allgemein 250
 b) Medizinische Forschung 250–1

4) Der Verkehr 251–4
 a) Die Eisenbahn 251
 b) Der Flugverkehr 251–2
 c) Die Schiffahrt 252
 d) Straßen 252–3
 e) Fahrzeuge 253
 f) Der Straßenverkehr 253–4

5) Verbindungen 254

6) Die Raumfahrt 254–5

VII. CULTURE AND GEOGRAPHY

1) Die deutschsprachigen
  Länder 255
 a) Die Schweiz 255
 b) Österreich 255
 c) Liechtenstein 255

2) Geographie 255–7
 a) Flüsse 255
 b) Das Gebirge 255
 c) Die Meere 256
 d) Allgemeine Begriffe 256
 e) Ländernamen 256
 f) Geographische
  Bezeichnungen 256
 g) Städtenamen/
  Ländernamen 256–7

3) Essen und Trinken 257–8
 a) Die Ernährung 257
 b) Die Getränke 257–8

4) Literatur und Theater 258–60
 a) Literatur allgemein 258–9
 b) Literaturkritik 259
 c) Das Theater 259–60

5) Kunst und Musik 260–1
 a) Die Musik 260
 b) Die Kunst 260–1

PHRASES

1) Meinungen

Ich bin der Meinung, daß ...   *I am of the opinion that ...*
Ich bin der Ansicht, daß ...   *I am of the opinion that ...*
Ich glaube, daß ...   *I think/believe that ...*
Ich meine, daß ...   *I think that ...*
Ich denke, daß ...   *I think that ...*
Ich finde, daß ...   *I find that ...*
Für micht ist wichtig, daß ...   *For me it is important that ...*
Für meine Begriffe ist ...nötig   *In my opinion ... is necessary*
Wichtig wäre für mich, daß   ... *It would be important to me that ...*
Wie ich das sehe, ...   *As I see it*
Man darf ... nicht vergessen   *One must not forget*
Man muß auch ... bedenken   *One must also consider ...*
Meiner Meinung nach braucht man...   *In my opinion one needs ...*
Es geht uns alle an, daß ...   *It is a matter of concern for all of us*
In großem Maße wird ... nicht beachtet   *To a great extent ... is ignored*
Im allgemeinen   *in general*
Es ist aber auch eine Frage von   *it is also a question of*
Ich würde aber raten, daß ...   *I would advise*
Soweit das mich angeht   *as far as I am concerned*
Dagegen ist einfach nichts zu sagen: *One cannot say anything against it:*
Ich finde das Problem ist auf ... zurückzuführen   *I think the problem can be traced back to ...*

2) Zustimmen

Da gebe ich dir recht   *I agree with you*
Du hast recht   *You are right*
Das stimmt   *That's correct*
Da stimme ich zu   *I agree to this*
Ich bin ganz Ihrer Meinung   *I agree with you completely*
Ohne Zweifel   *Without doubt*
Ganz bestimmt   *definitely*
Ich bin damit einverstanden   *I agree to that*
Das finde ich auch   *I think that, too*

3) Ablehnen

Ich muß Ihnen aber widersprechen   *I must contradict you*
Leider kann ich nicht zustimmen   *Unfortunately, I cannot agree*

Ich bin ganz anderer Meinung   *I have a quite different opinion*
Andererseits muß man auch sagen, daß ...   *On the other hand one must also say that ...*
Ich bin nicht damit einverstanden   *I do not agree with that.*
Das kann ich nicht akzeptieren   *I cannot accept that.*
Das mag sein, aber ...   *That may be, but ...*
Trotzdem wäre es möglich, daß ...   *Nevertheless, it would be possible that ...*
Aber gleich wichtig für mich wäre ...   *Equally important for me would be*
Zweifellos stimmt es oft, daß ... aber ...   *Undoubtedly it is often true that ... but ...*
(Das) Stimmt gar nicht, ganz im Gegenteil.   *That is not true, quite the opposite*
Es hat doch keinen Sinn ...   *There is no point in ...*
Nein, das sehe ich nicht ein, daß   *No, I do not see why ...*
Ich finde, das liegt eher daran   *I think it is rather caused by ...*
Das finde ich nicht von Bedeutung.   *I do not consider it of importance.*

4) Gegenargumente

Das kann man aber nicht beweisen   *One cannot prove that*
Das ist aber nicht bewiesen   *It is not proven*
Das ist schon möglich, aber ...   *That may be possible, but*
Ist es wirklich so, daß ...   *Is it really true that*
Ich frage mich, ob ...   *I ask myself whether/if ...*
Das würden die meisten Leute nicht gern akzeptieren   *Most people would not willingly accept this*
Du darfst nicht hinnehmen, daß ...   *You must not tolerate the fact that*
Das Schwierige an so einem Plan könnte sein, daß ...   *The difficulty with such a plan could be that*
Du darfst nicht vergessen, daß ...   *You must not forget that ...*
(noun) .... ist nicht zu leugnen, aber ...   *.... cannot be denied, but ...*

5) Vorschläge

Ich schlage vor, daß wir ...   *I suggest that we ...*

Ich würde vorschlagen, daß ...   *I would suggest that ...*
Mein Vorschlag wäre, ... zu machen   *My suggestion would be to ...*
Ich möchte dazu sagen, daß ...   *I would like to add that ...*
Meiner Meinung nach sollte man zuerst ...   *In my opinion one should first..*

6) Erklären

Sehen Sie nicht ein, daß ...   *Don't you see that ...*
Aber verstehen Sie nicht, daß ...   *Don't you understand that ...*
Wie erklärt man diesen Trend?   *How does one explain this trend?*
Ob es daran liegt, daß ...   *Is it because of ...*
Ob es möglich ist zu sagen, ...   *Whether it is possible to say ...*
Vor allem finde ich, liegt es an ...   *Most of all I think it is caused by ...*
Ohne ... wäre die Situation nicht so schlimm/hoffungslos   *Without ... the situation would not be so bad/ hopeless*
Den Einfluß von ... darf man nicht vergessen/außer Acht lassen   *One must not forget the influence of ....*
Wenn Leute ein Bedürfnis nach haben, ist es vielleicht auf ... zurückzuführen.   *If people have a need for ... , it is perhaps to be traced back to ...*

7) Zugeständnisse machen

Ich wollte das nicht ganz glauben   *I did not really want to believe this*
Ich war einfach anderer Meinung, aber ...   *I was just of another opinion, but ....*
Das stimmt genau.   *That's exactly right*

8) Andere herausfordern

Findest du nicht, daß ...   *Don't you think that ...*
Was sagst du dazu?   *What do you say about it?*
im Gegensatz zu ...   *in contradistinction to*
Im Gegenteil!   *On the contrary*

9) Abwägen

Einerseits ... andererseits ...   *on the one hand ... on the other hand*
Auf der einen Seite, auf der anderen Seite   *on the one hand ....on the other hand*

Wenn man ... richtig bedenkt, muß man sich fragen,...   *if one really considers ... , one must ask oneself*
Die Vorteile davon sind ..., die Nachteile aber ...   *the advantages of it are ... , the disadvantages however ...*
Für die meisten Leute aber ist es keine Frage von ...   *for most people it is not a question of ...*
jedoch   *however*
trotzdem   *despite*
immerhin/nichtsdestoweniger   *nevertheless*
Man darf nicht vergessen, daß ...   *one should not forget that...*
Man muß bedenken/beachten, daß ...   *one ought to consider that ...*
Dabei ist zubedenken, daß ...   *one needs to think about ...*
Wir sollten auch ... in Erwägung ziehen   *one also needs to take ... into account*
im Grunde genommen/grundsätzlich   *basically*
in erster Linie/vor allem   *mainly*
sowohl ... als auch ...   *not only .... but also ....*
... sowie auch...   *..... as well as ....*
statt ... zu ..., ...   *instead of ...., to ...*
Statt immer nur zu klagen, kann man auch etwas Konstruktives tun.   *instead of only complaining, one can do also something constructive*
anstatt, daß ...   *instead of ....,*
im übrigen/noch dazu   *over and above that*
außerdem/darüber hinaus   *anyway/ in addition*

10) Zusammenfassen

Im Endeffekt   *in the end*
Letzten Endes   *in the end*
Entscheidend für mich ist, daß ...   *It is decisive for me that ...*
Nicht zu zweifeln, daß ...   *It is not to be doubted that ...*
Es ist nicht zu leugnen, daß ...   *It cannot be denied that ....*
Es läßt sich nicht widerlegen ...   *It cannot be refuted*
Es liegt auf der Hand, daß ...   *It is obvious that ...*
Offensichtlich   *apparently*
Selbstverständlich   *of course*
Auffallend ist dabei, daß ...   *It is striking that ...*
Aus diesem Grund ist zu schließen, daß ...   *For this reason one must conclude that ...*

Daher/daraus ist zu schließen   *From this it is to be concluded* Schließlich/zum Schluß   *finally*

Letzten Endes/Alles in allem   *finally/all in all*

Um alle Punkte zusammenzufassen   *in order to sum up all points*

Um nach ... zu beurteilen   *in order to judge according to ...*

11) Einleiten

Es geht um ...   *We are concerned with ...*

Es handelt sich um ...   *It is a matter of ...*

Es handelt von ...   *It deals with ...*

Es ist eine Frage von ...   *It is a question of ...*

Es betrifft uns alle, ...   *It concerns us all ...*

Es geht uns alle an, daß ...   *It concerns us all that ...*

Es ist Geschmacksache, ob ...   *It is a matter of taste whether ...*

Es ist eine umstrittene Frage   *It is a matter of controversy whether ...*

Es besteht die Möglichkeit, daß ...   *There is the possibility that ...*

Eine entscheidende Rolle spielt hier ...   *A decisive part is played by*

Von Bedeutung ist hier auch ...   *It is of importance here ...*

Viele weisen auf die Wichtigkeit von ... hin   *Many point to the importance of*

12) Zeitenfolge

im Laufe der nächsten Jahre   *in the course of the next few years*

in den letzten Jahren   *in recent years*

in letzter Zeit   *recently*

in nächster Zeit   *in the near future*

gegenwätig   *at present*

fortan/von jetzt an   *from now on*

über viele Jahre hinaus   *over many years*

13) Begründen

aufgrund dessen   *because of which*

unter diesen Umständen   *under these circumstances*

der Grund besteht darin, daß   *the reason for it is that ...*

Anlaß dazu gibt ...   *the reason for it is*

Was dazu geführt hat, ist, daß ...   *What has led to it is ...*

Ausgangspunkt von ... war ...   *the origin of this was ...*

Das ist oft auf ... zurückzuführen   *this can often be traced back to ...*

Das liegt darin, daß...   *it is caused by*

Entscheidend ist, ob/daß ...   *the crux of the matter is whether/that ...*

Es nützt nichts, daß jetzt alle protestieren   *it is of no use that everyone is protesting now*

Das hat als Folge, daß ...   *The consequence of it is that*

... Folge davon ist, daß ...   *the upshot of it is*

Daraus ergibt sich, daß ...   *it follows that*

Das Ergebnis davon kann nur ... sein   *the result of it can only be ...*

Die Situation spitzt sich zu.   *The situation is becoming more acute.*

Hat sich die Lage verbessert?   *Has the situation improved?*

Ich will nicht bestreiten, daß ... aber was hilft es, wenn ...   *I do not want to question that, but what good is it, if ...*

14) Vergleichen

einigermaßen   *to some extent*

es sei denn   *unless*

in großen Maße   *on a large scale*

nicht im geringsten   *not in the slightest*

lange nicht/keineswegs   *not at all/really*

in dieser Hinsicht   *in this respect*

in vieler/aller Hinsicht   *in all/many respects*

im Vergleich mit   *compared to*

im Verhältnis zu   *in relation to*

mit Ausnahme von   *with the exception of*

von ... abgesehen   *apart from*

---

1. Die Ausbildung

Peter wird ins nächste Schuljahr versetzt   *Peter is allowed to move up a year*

Sie muß sitzenbleiben   *She has to repeat a year*

Gabi hat ihre Prüfung in Englisch bestanden   *Gabi has passed her exams in English*

Er ist zum zweiten Mal im Abitur durchgefallen   *He has failed his A-levels for the second time*

Diese Worte wollen mir nicht in den Kopf   *I can't get these words into my head.*

Wir sollen das Gedicht auswendig lernen   *We are to learn the poem by heart*

Ich zerbreche mir noch den Kopf   *I am racking my brains*

Herr Meier geht stur nach dem Buch vor   *Mr. Meier follows the text-book slavishly*

a) Die Schule

die Aufnahmeprüfung (-en)   *entrance exam*

das Abitur (no plural)   *A-levels*

die Einschulung (-en)   *starting school*

der Elternabend (-e)   *parents' evening*

der Elternsprechtag (-e)   *parents' day*

die Förderstufe (-n)   *first two years of secondary schooling*

die Gesamtschule (-n)   *comprehensive school*

der Grundkurs (-e)   *subsidiary subject for Abitur*

die Grundschule (-n)   *primary school*

das Gymnasium (-ien)   *grammar school*

das Hauptfach/Kernfach (-er)   *main subject*

die Hauptschule (-n)   *secondary school*

der Kindergarten (-en)   *kindergarten*

das Lehrbuch (-er)   *text book*

der Leistungskurs (-e)   *main subject for Abitur*

die Nachhilfestunde (-n)   *extra lesson*

das Nebenfach (-er)   *subsidary subject*

die Oberstufe (-en)   *sixth form*

der Pennäler (-) (*coll.*)   *schoolboy*

die Penne (-n) (*coll.*)   *school*

das Pflichtfach (-er)   *compulsory subject*

die Realschule (-n)   *secondary school*

die mittlere Reife (-en)   *Realschule leaving qualification*

die Schülervertretung (-en) (die SMV)   *school council*

die Schulpflicht (no plural)   *compulsory schooling*

der Schulsprecher/in   *head pupil* (plural: Schulsprecher/innen)

die Sonderschule (-en)   *special school*

der Vertrauenslehrer/in   *student council liason teacher*

das Wahlfach (-er)   *optional subject*

das Wissen (no plural)   *knowledge*

die Schule besuchen   *to attend school*

in die Schule gehen   *to go to school* (geht, ging, gegangen*)

lernen   *to learn*

das Abitur machen   *to take A-levels*

pauken, büffeln (*coll.*)   *to learn, swot*

sitzenbleiben (bleibt sitzen, blieb sitzen, sitzengeblieben)   *to repeat a year*

studieren   *to study*

am Unterricht teilnehmen (nimmt teil, nahm teil, teilgenommen)   *to attend lessons*

unterrichten   *to teach*

versetzt werden (wird, wurde, worden*)   *to move into the next year*

b) Der Schüler/die Schülerin

Was Hänschen nicht lernt, lernt Hans nicht mehr   *What Hans doesn't learn when little he won't learn as a big boy.* (German proverb)

Meinem Bruder fällt das Lernen schwer (fällt schwer, fiel schwer, schwergefallen*)   *My brother finds learning hard*

Er würde am liebsten die Bücher in die Ecke schmeißen (schmeißt, schmiß, geschmissen)   *He would rather throw his books away*

Sie ist den anderen in der Klasse haushoch überlegen   *She is way above the others in class*

die Anstrengung (-en)   *effort*

das Arbeitstier (-e)   *workaholic*

die Aufmerksamkeit (-en)   *attention*

das Betragen   *behaviour*

der Gammler (-)   *a slow, idle pupil*

die Gedächtnisstütze (-n)   *memory aid*

der Fleiß   *industry, effort*

die Konzentrationsschwäche (-n)   *problems with concentration*

der Legastheniker (-)   *dyslexic pupil*

die Legasthenie (no plural)   *dyslexia*

die Ordnung (no plural)   *tidiness*

der Streber (-)   *a swot*

der Wissensdurst (no plural)   *thirst for knowledge*

ablenken   *to distract*

abschreiben (schreibt ab, schrieb ab, abgeschrieben)   *to copy*

begreifen (begreift, begriff, hat begriffen)   *to understand*

das Wesentliche beherrschen   *to know the basics*

sich bemühen   *to make an effort*

sich durchwursteln (*coll.*)   *to muddle through*

dem Unterricht folgen   *to follow the lesson*

Wissenslücken füllen   *to fill gaps in knowledge*

etwas auswendig lernen   *to learn by heart*

sich konzentrieren   *to concentrate*

es kostet große Mühe   *it costs a great effort*

unter Druck lernen   *to learn under presure*

Fortschritte machen   *to make progress*

sich den Stoff reinziehen (*coll.*) (zieht rein, zog rein, reingezogen)   *to learn, revise*

schwänzen   *to play truant*

sein Bestes tun (tut, tat, getan)   *to do one's best*

es will mir nicht in den Kopf   *I can't understand it*

sich den Kopf zerbrechen (zerbricht, zerbrach, zerbrochen)   *to rack one's brain*

begabt   *gifted*

faul   *lazy*

konzentrationsfähig   *able to concentrate*

ordentlich   *tidy*

pünktlich   *punctually*

überfordert   *overtaxed, out of one's depth*

c) Die Lehrer

die Disziplin (no plural)   *discipline*

der Kollege/in

(plural: Kollegen/innen)   *colleague*

das Kollegium (-ien)   *the staff*

die Lehrerkonferenz (-en)   *staff meeting*

der Lehrplan (-̈e)   *curriculum*

der Lehrstoff   *teaching material*

ein trockener Pauker (-) (*coll.*)   *a boring teacher*

die Rahmenrichtlinien (pl.)   *curriculum*

der Schulleiter/ der Direktor   *head teacher*

der Studienrat/in (-̈e/-innen)   *fully qualified, permanently employed teacher*

der Studienreferendar/in (-e/innen)   *teacher on probation*

der Versuch (-e)   *experiment*

die Zeugniskonferenz (-en)   *staff meeting to discuss school reports*

beaufsichtigen   *to supervise*

sich *durch*setzen   *to be assertive*

sich in die Schüler *ein*fühlen   *to empathize with the pupils*

erklären   *to explain*

ermahnen   *to warn*

eine Strafarbeit geben (gibt, gab, gegeben)   *to give extra work*

Verständnis haben für + Acc.   *to have understanding for*

korrigieren   *to mark*

labern (*coll.*)   *to waffle*

loben   *to praise*

motivieren   *to motivate*

nachsitzen (sitzt nach, saß nach, nachgesessen)   *to be in detention*

einen Schüler *nach*sitzen lassen   *to put a pupil in detention*

schwafeln (*coll.*)   *to waffle*

hohe Ansprüche stellen   *to make high demands*

zur Diskussion stellen   *to put for discussion*

tadeln   *to scold*

abwechslungsreich   *varied*

autoritär   *authoritarian*

gerecht/fair   *just*

kameradschaftlich   *friendly*

konsequent   *consistent*

lasch   *lax*

locker   *laid back*

streng   *strict*

unnahbar   *unapproachable*

unterhaltsam   *entertaining*

unberechenbar   *unpredictable*

d) Die Prüfungen

das Abschlußzeugnis (-se)   *final school report*

der Aufsatz (-̈e)   *essay*

die Hausarbeit/Facharbeit (-en)   *coursework*

die Klassenarbeit (-en)   *continuous assessment test*

die Klausur (-en)   *A-level exam*

der Konkurrenzkampf (-̈e)   *competition*

der Leistungsdruck (no plural)   *pressure to achieve results*

die Lernkontrolle (-n)   *test*

die Note (-n)   *mark, grade*

der Notendurchschnitt (-e)   *average grade/mark*

der Punkt (-e)   *points (at Abitur)*

die mündliche/schriftliche Prüfung (-en)   *oral/written exam*

das Referat (-e)   *talk given by a pupil*

der Test (-s)   *test*

die Zensur (-en)   *mark*

das Zeugnis (-se)   *school report*

eine Prüfung bestehen (besteht, bestand, bestanden)   *to pass an exam*

es zu etwas bringen (bringt, brachte, gebracht)   *to achieve something*

durchfallen in (fällt durch, fiel durch, durchgefallen*)   *to fail*

durchkommen (kommt durch, kam durch, durchgekommen*)   *to get through*

kapieren (*coll.*)   *to understand*

eine Arbeit (-en) schreiben (schreibt, schrieb, geschrieben)   *to do a continuous assessment test*

verstehen (versteht, verstand, verstanden)   *to understand*

sich vorbereiten auf + Acc.   *to prepare oneself for*

wiederholen   *to repeat*

ausreichend   *sufficient*
befriedigend   *satisfactory*
leistungsorientiert   *to be orientated towards results*
mangelhaft   *insufficient*
unangekündigt   *unannounced, without warning*
unter Examensbedingungen   *under exam conditions*

e) Die Ausbildung

eine technische Ausbildung   *a technical apprenticeship*
der Ausbildungsplatz (-e)   *training place*
der/die Auszubildende (-n)   *apprentice*
der Azubi (-s) (short form)   *apprentice*
die Berufsschule (-n)   *technical college*
der Bewerber (-)   *applicant*
der zweite Bildungsweg   *reaching Abitur as a mature student*
die Gesellenprüfung (-en)   *exam at the end of apprenticeship*
die Lehre (-n)   *apprenticeship*
das Lehrjahr (-e)   *year in training*
der Lehrling (-e)   *apprentice*
die Lehrstelle (-n)   *training place*
das Lehrstellenangebot (-e)   *offer of training places*
der Meister (-)   *trainer, master craftsman*
die Volkshochschule (-n)   *adult education centre*
die Weiterbildung/Fortbildung (no plural)   *further education*
die Lehre abbrechen (bricht ab, brach ab, abgebrochen)   *to give up an apprenticeship*
den Realschulabschluß nachholen   *to do one's Realschule leaving certificate later in life*
ein Versager sein   *to be a failure*
abgewiesen werden   *to be turned down*

f) Die Universität

das (zinslose) Darlehen (-)   *(interest free) loan*
der Dozent (-en)   *lecturer*
die Fachhochschule (-n)   *tertiary technical college*
der akademische Grad   *academic degree*
die Geisteswissenschaften (plural only)   *the arts*
der Härtefall (-e)   *case of hardship*
die technische Hochschule (-n)   *technial university*
der Hochschulabschluß (-sse)   *university degree*
der Hörsaal (-e)   *lecture theatre*
die Mensa (-s or -en)   *canteen*

die Naturwissenschaften (plural)   *the sciences*
der Numerus Clausus (NC)   *restriction of entry into university*
das Semester (-)   *term (two per year)*
das Staatsexamen   *final exam set by the ministry of education*
der Studienplatz (-e)   *place at university*
die Universität (-en)   *university*
das Universitätsgelände (no plural)   *university campus*
die Vorlesung (-en)   *lecture*
die Wohnungsnot (-e)   *lack of accomodation*
die Zentralstelle zur Vergabe von Studienplätzen (ZVS)   *like UCAS*

BAFÖG bekommen (bekommt, bekam bekommen)   *to get a grant*
Forschung betreiben (betreibt, betrieb betrieben)   *to do research*
dozieren   *to lecture*
forschen   *to research*
promovieren   *to do a doctorate*
studieren   *to study*
vorlesen (liest vor, las vor, vorgelesen)   *to lecture*
zur Untermiete wohnen   *to live as a lodger*

überfüllt   *overcrowded*
überlaufen   *overcrowded*

g) Die Bildungspolitik

die Bildungsdebatte (-n)   *debate on education*
die Bildungspolitik (no plural)   *education policy*
die Chancengleichheit (no plural)   *equality of opportunity*
der Etat (-s) für Schulen   *budget for schools*
der geburtenstarke/-schwache Jahrgang (-e)   *year with a high/low birthrate*
der Kultusminister   *secretary of state for education*
das Kultusministerium (-en)   *department of education*
die Lernmittelfreiheit (no plural)   *right to have a free education*

gründliche Untersuchungen anstellen   *to make a detailed investigation*
für die Zukunft ausbilden   *to educate for the future*
Einfluß ausüben auf (+ Acc)   *to exercise an influence on*
sich ein Urteil bilden über (+ Acc)   *to form a judgement on*

Reformen durchführen *to carry out reforms*
die Erwartungen der Eltern erfüllen *to fullfill parental expectations*
das Niveau erhöhen *to raise standards*
zur Selbständigkeit erziehen (erzieht, erzog, erzogen) *to educate towards independence*
die Rahmenrichtlinien revidieren *to revise the curriculum*
einen ausgewogenen Lehrplan schaffen *to create a balanced curriculum*
die Klassenstärke senken *to reduce class sizes*
sich Problemkindern widmen *to devote oneself to problem children*
er hat kein Verständnis für Kunst *he has no understanding for art*

gut ausgestattet *well equipped*

2. Jugend

a) Allgemeines

ein gutes/schlechtes Verhältnis haben mit *to have a good/bad relationship with*
Claudia kommt schwer mit ihrer Schwester zurecht. *Claudia finds it hard to cope with*
Probleme durchsprechen (spricht durch, sprach durch, durchgesprochen) *to talk problems over*
Meine Eltern nerven mich *my parents get on my nerves*
Sie können sich gut in meine Lage versetzen *They can put themselves in my position*
Es besteht eine Kluft zwischen mir und meinen Eltern *There is a rift between me and my parents*
Er kann mit seinen Eltern über nichts reden *He can't talk to his parents about anything.*
Ich komme gut mit meinem Bruder aus (kommt aus, kam aus, ausgekommen*) *I get on well with my brother*
Er hat immer Krach mit seiner Oma *He always has arguments with his gran*
Meine Eltern sind schwer in Ordnung. *My parents are o.k.*
Sie versteht sich gut mit ihrem Vater (versteht, verstand, verstanden) *She gets on well with her Dad.*
die Beziehung (-en) *relationship*
das Einzelkind (-er) *only child*
der Halbstarke (-n) *rowdy*
der Jugendliche (-n) *youngster*

der Jugendrichter (-) *judge in a juvenile court*
das Jugendschutzgesetz (-e) *law for the protection of young people*
Rechte und Pflichten *rights and obligations*
die Spannung (-en) *tension*
das Stiefkind (-er) *stepchild*
der Stiefvater/Stiefmutter *step-father/ mother*
das Streitgespräch (-e) *argument*
der Streitpunkt (-e) *area of conflict*
der Teenager (-) *teenager*
das Verhältnis (-se) *relationship*

Kinder aufziehen (zieht auf, zog auf, aufgezogen) *to bring up children*
mit jemandem auskommen *to get on with someone*
sich ausmalen *to imagine*
was mich belastet *what bothers me*
diskutieren *to discuss*
erziehen (erzieht, erzog, erzogen) *to educate*
Entscheidungen fällen *to make decisions*
kritisieren *to criticize*
respektieren *to respect*
über alles sprechen (spricht, sprach, gesprochen) *to talk about everything*
sich streiten *to argue*
was mir wirklich wichtig ist *what is really important to me*

angesehen *respected*
autoritär/antiautoritär *authoritarian/ anti-authoritarian*
fein *fine*
gebildet *educated*
höflich *polite*
kultiviert *sophisticated*
minderjährig *under-age*
schwer in Ordnung sein *to be o.k.*
selbständig *independent*
tolerant *tolerant*
toll *great*
verständnisvoll *understanding*
volljährig *of full age, over 18*
zivilisiert *civilized*
von einem Extrem zum anderen *from one extreme to the other*

b) Der Konflikt

Frau Meier ist auf ihre Tochter böse. *Mrs. Meier is angry with her daughter*

der Ausgang (no plural) *time one is allowed to go out (until)*
bis in die frühen Morgenstunden *until the early hours*

die Autorität (-en) *authority*
das Benehmen/ die Manieren *manners*
die Clique (-n) *group of friends*
Ferien mit dem Freund/der Freundin
     holidays with boyfriend/girlfriend
der Freund/die Freundin *boyfriend/*
     girlfriend
die Klamotten (*coll.*) *clothes*
die Kleidung (no plural) *clothes*
die Mode *fashion*
die Schulnoten (pl) *grades at school*
der Umgang (no plural) *company*
kleinliche Vorschriften (plural) *petty*
     rules

beleidigen *to insult*
sich benehmen (benimmt sich, benahm
     sich, sich benommen) *to behave*
beschimpfen *to call names*
*weg*bleiben dürfen *to be allowed to stay*
     out
fluchen *to swear*
hinterfragen *to question*
meckern *to moan*
nörgeln *to pick on*
in Frage stellen *to question*
die Beherrschung verlieren (verliert
     verlor, verloren) *to lose control*
böse *angry, naughty*
ungezogen *bad mannered, naughty*
wütend *furious*

c) Die Eltern

Eltern haften für ihre Kinder *parents*
     are responsible for their children
Sie gehen in die Luft *they blow up*
Petra und ihre Eltern vertragen *Petra*
     and her parents get on again
  sich wieder (vertragen,
     verträgt, vertrug, vertragen)
Seine Mutter wurde böse mit ihm *His*
     mother got angry with him

das offene Gespräch *frank discussion*
ein Gespräch unter vier Augen *one-to-*
     one confidential talk

bestehen auf (+ Acc.) *to insist on*
sich kümmern um (+ Acc) *to look after*
reizen *to provoke*
schimpfen mit (+ Dat) *to tell off*
sorgen für (+ Acc) *to take care of*
strafen *to punish*
*über*einstimmen mit (+ Dat) *to agree*
     with
sich versöhnen mit (+ Dat) *to make up*
     after an argument
sich wieder vertragen *to get on again*
böse werden mit (+ Dat) *to get angry with*
anständig *decent*

aufgeschlossen *open minded*
engstirnig *narrow minded*
kompromißbereit *willing to compromise*
spießig (*coll*) *middle class*
verkalkt (*coll*) *senile*
voreingenommen *prejudiced*
vorwurfsvoll *reproachful*
wohlmeinend *well-meaning*

3. Ehe und Familie

a) Ehe und Partnerschaft

bis der Tod euch scheidet *until death*
     parts you
gemeinsame Interessen haben *to have*
     common interests
das gegenseitige Verständnis *mutual*
     understanding
die Ehe ist zerrüttet *the marriage has*
     broken down
er macht ihr einen Heiratsantrag *he*
     makes a proposal of marriage
die Ehescheidung wird zu einfach
     gemacht *divorce is being made too*
     easy
er klagt auf Scheidung *he is suing for*
     divorce
gute Freunde bleiben *to remain good*
     friends
die Ehe geht in die Brüche *the marriage*
     is breaking down
er ist geschieden *he is divorced*
einen Sohn/eine Tochter aus erster Ehe
     haben *to have a son/daughter from*
     the first marriage
sie reden nicht mehr miteinander *they*
     don't talk to each other any more
er will ungebunden sein *he wants to be*
     free
wegen unvereinbarem Charakter
     geschieden *to be divorced on*
     grounds of incompatability

die Affaire (-n) *affair*
der letzte Ausweg (-e) *last resort*
die Braut (-e) *bride*
der Bräutigam (-e) *bridegroom*
das Brautpaar (-e) *bride and bridegroom*
der Bund für's Leben *marriage*
die Ehe (-n) *marriage*
die kinderlose Ehe *childless marriage*
die wilde Ehe *common law marriage*
der Ehebruch (no plural) *adultery*
die Ehefrau (-n)/Gattin (-nen) *wife*
der Ehemann (-er)/Gatte (-n) *husband*
das Ehevermittlungsinstitut (-e) *dating*
     agency
die Eifersucht (no plural) *jealousy*
der Familienrichter (-) *judge sitting in a*
     family court

die Flitterwochen (plural only)
honeymoon
die emanzipierte Frau (-en)
emancipated woman
der feste Freund/die feste Freundin   *a*
steady boy friend/girl friend
die Freundschaft (-en)   *friendship*
der Geschlechtsverkehr (no plural)
sexual intercourse
die Hochzeit (-en)   *wedding*
der Lebenspartner (-)   *partner for life*
die Leidenschaft (-en)   *passion*
die Liebe (no plural)   *love*
der Mädchename (-n)   *maiden name*
die Mitgift (-en)   *dowry*
das Paar (-e) ohne Trauschein
unmarried couple
der Partnertausch (no plural)   *swapping*
of partners
der Polterabend (-e)   *party on the night*
before the wedding
die Scheidung (-en)   *divorce*
die hohe Scheidungsrate   *the high*
divorce rate
die Sehnsucht (-e)   *longing*
der Seitensprung (-e)   *affair*
das elterliche Sorgerecht (no
plural)   *custody (of children)*
die kirchliche Trauung (-en)   *church*
wedding
die standesamtliche Trauung (-en)
registry office wedding
der Trauzeuge (-n)   *best man*
die Treue/Untreue (no plural)
faithfulness/unfaithfulness
die Umarmung (-en)   *embrace*
die Unabhängigkeit (-en)   *independence*
das böswillige Verlassen (no plural)
desertion
der/die Verlobte (-n)   *fiance*
der Verlobungsring (-e)   *engagement ring*
die Zärtlichkeit (-en)   *tenderness*
die Zuneigung (-en)   *sympathy*

sich *anschweigen*   *to live in hostile*
silence
seinen Willen *durch*setzen   *to get one's*
way
einen Partner finden (findet, fand,
gefunden)   *to find a partner*
einen gemeinsamen Haushalt führen   *to*
live together
miteinander gehen (geht, ging,
gegangen)   *to go out with someone*
sich das Ja-Wort geben (gibt, gab,
gegeben)   *to say 'Yes' in the*
marriage ceremony
fremdgehen (geht fremd, ging
fremdgegangen)   *to have an affair*
heiraten   *to marry*
sich *kennen*lernen   *to get to know*

sich scheiden lassen (läßt, ließ, gelassen)
to get divorced
sich auseinander leben   *to grow apart*
die Verlobung lösen   *to break off an*
engagement
poltern   *to have a pre-wedding party*
mit jemanden schlafen (schläft, schlief,
geschlafen)   *to have sex with*
someone
verliebt sein in + Acc   *to be in love with*
sich verloben mit + Dat   *to become*
engaged to
(versteht, verstand, verstanden) sich
verstehen + Dat   *to get on*
aneinander *vorbei*leben   *to live separate*
lives
häufig den Partner wechseln   *to live*
promiscuously
sich wieder verheiraten   *to re-marry*
zusammen leben   *to live together*

bösartig   *nasty*
getrennt lebend   *seperated*
geschieden   *divorced*
eifersüchtig   *jealuous*
ledig   *single*
verheiratet   *married*
verlobt   *engaged*
verwitwet   *widowed*

b) Die Familie

Familie und Beruf unter einen Hut
bringen   *to manage family and*
career
mehr Männer als früher helfen im
Haushalt   *more men than before*
help in the house
das liegt in der Familie   *it runs in the*
family
der Apfel fällt nicht weit vom Stamm   *the*
apple does not fall far from the tree
das gehört zu den
Kindheitserinnerungen   *that is part*
of childhood memories
wichtige Entscheidungen gemeinsam
treffen   *to make important decisions*
together
sich die Hausarbeit teilen   *to share the*
housework

die Abstammung (-en)   *ancestry*
die Abtreibung (-en)   *abortion*
die Beerdigung (-en)   *funeral*
die Empfängnisverhütung (-en)
contraception
der Enkel/die Einkelin (plural: Enkel/
innen)   *grandson, granddaughter*
der Erbe (-n)   *heir*
die Erbschaft (-en)   *inheritance*
der Erziehungsurlaub (no plural)   *leave*
to bring up a small child

die Familienplanung (-en) *family planning*

die Großfamilie/Kleinfamilie (-n) *large/small family*

der Kinderhort (-e) *day-care centre for children, creche*

die Kinderkrankheit (-en) *childhood illness*

die Kindertagesstätte (-n) *day-care centre for children*

im Kindesalter *during the time of being a child*

von Kindesbeinen an *from childhood on*

die Kindesmißhandlung (-en) *child abuse*

das Kleinkind (-er) *toddler*

das Kondom (-s) *condom*

die Konfirmation (-en) *confirmation*

der Kusin (-s)/der Vetter (-) *boy-cousin*

die Kusine (-n)/die Base (-n) *cousin*

die Mutter-Kind-Beziehung (-en) *mother-child relationship*

der Mutterschaftsurlaub (no plural) *maternity leave*

der Pate/Patin (die Paten) *god parent(s)*

die Pille (-n) *the pill*

das Retortenbaby (-s) *test-tube baby*

der Schwager (-) *brother-in-law*

die Schwägerin (-nen) *sister-in-law*

die Schwangerschaft (-en) *pregnancy*

der Schwangerschaftsabbruch (-e) *abortion*

die Schwiegereltern (plural only) *parents-in-law*

die Schwiegermutter (-e) *mother-in-law*

der Schwiegervater (-e) *father-in-law*

die Tagesmutter (-e) *childminder*

das Testament (-e) *will*

der Todesfall (-e) *death*

die Trauer *mourning*

ganz wie der Vater/die Mutter *just like his/her father/mother*

das Vorbild (-er) *example, role-model*

der Vormund (-er) *guardian*

die Windel (-n) *nappies*

der Witwer/die Witwe (-n) *widower/widow*

die Zwillinge *twins*

abstammen *to descend from*

sich binden an (bindet, band, gebunden) *to attach oneself to*

empfangen (empfängt, empfing, empfangen) *to conceive*

entbinden (entbindet, entband, entbunden) *to give birth*

erben *to inherit*

sich von den Eltern lösen *to detach oneself from the parents*

nachahmen *to imitate*

Wäsche waschen (wäscht, wusch, gewaschen) *to wash clothes*

schwanger werden *to become pregnant*

trauern um *to mourn for*

entfernt verwandt *distantly related*

geborgen sein *to feel secure*

kindgemäß *suitable for a child*

mütterlicherseits *on the mothers side*

streng *strict*

verstorben *deceased*

4. Frauenfragen - Männerfragen

Männer und Frauen sind gleichberechtigt *men and women are equal*

in beruflichen Führungspositionen sind Frauen noch relativ selten, weil ... *women are rare in leading positions, because ...*

Frauen entscheiden sich für eine Kombination von Familie und Beruf *women choose a combination of family and career*

gleicher Lohn für gleiche Arbeit *equal pay for equal work*

leitende Angestellte *executives*

die Auseinandersetzung (-en) *argument*

die Beratung (-en) *advice*

die Berufstätigkeit (-en) *carreer*

das Bewußtsein (no plural) *consciousness*

eine partnerschaftliche Beziehung (-en) *a relationship between equal partners*

die Chancengleichheit (-en) *equal opportunities*

das Fortkommen (no plural) *getting on in life*

die emanzipierte Frau (-en) *emancipated woman*

die erwerbstätige Frau (-en) *working woman*

Frauen in der Lebensmitte *middle-aged women*

die Frauenbewegung (-en) *women's movement*

das Frauenhaus (-er) *refuge for women*

die Frauenministerin (-nen) *secretary of state for women*

die Frauenrechtlerin (-nen) *fighter for woman's rights*

die Genußfrau (-en) *hedonist*

die Gesetzgebung (-en) *law-making*

die Gleichberechtigung (no plural) *equality*

der Hausmann (-er) *house-husband*

das Heimchen am Herde *the homely woman (derogative)*

die Karrierefrau (-en) *career woman*

das Kindergeld (no plural) *family allowance*

die Kinderkrippe, Kindertagesstätte (-n)
creche, nursery
der Konkurrenzkampf (⁓e) *rivalry*
die Lebensanschauung (-en) *philosophy of life*
die Lösung (-en) *solution*
der traditionelle Männerberuf (-e) *a job traditionally done by men*
die Mißhandlung (-en) *abuse*
die Rolle (-en) *role*
der Rollentausch (-e) *swapping of roles*
die Schuldzuweisung (-en)
recrimination
die Stärke (-n) *strong point*
aus freien Stücken *of one's own free will*
die Vergewaltigung (-en) *rape*
die Vorkämpferin (-nen) *pioneer,*
die Wertorientierung (-en) *values*
der Wiedereinstieg in den Beruf *re-entry into working life*
die Zufluchtstätte (-n) *refuge*
die Zwangsjacke (-n) *straitjacket*

abbauen *to break down*
abschrecken *to deter*
anstreben *to aim for*
ausmachen *to identify*
benachteiligen *to discriminate against*
sich *durch*setzen *to assert oneself*
sich *ein*setzen *to do what one can*
fordern *to demand*
gleichziehen (zieht gleich, zog gleich, gleichgezogen) *to catch up*
darüber hinwegtäuschen *to hide the fact*
kämpfen für + Acc *to fight for*
Sticheleien *los*lassen *to have a dig at s.o.*
mißhandeln *to abuse*
streiten für + Acc *to fight for*
sich selbst im Wege stehen (steht, stand, gestanden) *to be one's own worst enemy*
Zuflucht suchen *to take refuge*
in Kraft treten (tritt, trat, getreten) *to come into force*
überwiegen (überwiegt, überwog, überwogen) *to predominate*
unterordnen *to subordinate*
unterstützen *to support sich*
unterwerfen (unterwirft, unterwarf, unterworfen) *to submit to*
verdrängen *to repress*
vergewaltigen *to rape*
vorankommen (kommt voran, kam voran, vorangekommen*) *to make good headway*
sich *weiter*bilden *to continue one's education*
sich in den Schmollwinkel zurückziehen (zieht zurück, zog zurück, zurückgezogen) *to sulk*
sich *zu*trauen *to have confidence*

alleinstehend *single*
außerhäuslich *outside the house*
ausgeprägt *marked*
berufstätig *working*
gemeinnützig *charitable*
gleichberechtigt *equal*
leistungsorientiert *goal-oriented*
körperbewußt *aware of one's body*
militant *militant*
partnerschaftlich *on a partnership basis*

5. Gesundheit

das Herz schlägt *the heart beats*
der Schweiß rann mir von der Stirne *the sweat was running down my forehead*
Kopf hoch! *chin up*
Warum lassen Sie den Kopf so hängen? *Why are you so down in the mouth?*
mein Fuß ist ganz wund *my foot is raw*
Er hat sich den Fuß verstaucht *He sprained his ankle*
das geht über meine Kräfte *that's too much for me*
ich muß eine strenge Diät einhalten *I have to keep to a strict diet*
die Krankheit ist ansteckend *the disease is contagious*
sich einer Operation unterziehen *to undergo an operation*
ans Bett gefesselt sein *to be confined to bed*
seine Gesundheit wiederherstellen *to restore one's health*
einen Zahn plombieren *to fill a tooth*
auf seine Gesundheit achten *to mind one's health*
es geht um Leben und Tod *it is a matter of life and death*

a) Der Körper

der Augapfel (⁚) *eye-ball*
die Augenbraue (-n) *eye-brow*
der Bauch (-e) *stomach*
der Blinddarm (⁓e) *appendix*
der Blutkreislauf (⁓e) *circulation*
der Daumen (-) *thumb*
die Eingeweide (-n) *bowels*
die Handfläche (-n) *palm*
die Hüfte (-n) *hip*
die Fingerspitze (-n) *finger-tip*
der Fußknöchel (-) *ankle*
die Gallenblase (-n) *gall-bladder*
der Gaumen (-) *palate*
das Gehirn (-e) *brain*
das Gehör (no plural) *hearing*
das Herz (-en) *heart*
der Knöchel (-) *knuckle*
die Luftröhre (-n) *windpipe*
die Lunge (-n) *lungs*

die Mandeln (plural only)   *tonsils*
das Mark (no plural)   *marrow*
der Nabel (-)   *navel*
die Narbe (-n)   *scar*
die Nasenspitze/Zungenspitze (-n)   *tip of nose, tip of tongue*
das Nervensystem (-e)   *nervous system*
die Niere (-n)   *kidney*
der Oberarm/Unterarm (-e)   *upper arm, forearm*
die Oberlippe/Unterlippe (-n)   *upper/lower lip*
der Oberschenkel/Unterschenkel (-)   *thigh, shank*
der Puls (-e)   *puls*
die Pupille (-n)   *pupil*
das Rückgrat/die Wirbelsäule (-n)   *spine*
der Schädel (-)   *skull*
das Schienbein (-e)   *shin*
die Schläfe (-n)   *temple*
die Sehne (-n)   *sinew*
das Skelett (-e)   *skeleton*
die Sohle (-n)   *sole of foot*
die Stimmbänder (plural only)   *vocal cords*
die Taille (-n)   *waist*
der Unterleib (-e)   *abdomen*
das Zahnfleisch (no plural)   *gums*

b) Krankheit und Heilung

die Ansteckung (-en)   *infection, contagion*
die Besserung (no plural)   *recovery*
der Blutverlust (no plural)   *loss of blood*
die Blutübertragung (-en)   *blood transfusion*
das Dragee (-s)   *capsule*
die Erschöpfung (no plural)   *exhaustion*
das Geschwulst (ˆe)   *swelling*
das Geschwür (-e)   *ulcer*
die Grippe   *influenza*
das Heilmittel (-), die Arznei (-en)   *remedy*
die Heiserkeit (no plural)   *hoarseness*
der Keuchhusten (no plural)   *whooping-cough*
die Kinderlähmung (-en)   *polio*
der Knochenbruch (ˆe)   *fracture*
die Krankheit (-en)   *illness*
der Krebs (no plural)   *cancer*
die Lungenentzündung (-en)   *pneumonia*
die Masern (plural only)   *measles*
das Naturheilmittel (-)   *natural remedy*
das Rezept (-e)   *prescription*
der Rückfall (ˆe)   *relapse*
die Salbe (-n)   *ointment*
der Scharlach (no plural)   *scarlet fever*
der Schlaganfall (ˆe)   *stroke*
die Schmerzen (plural)   *pain*

der Schnupfen (no plural)   *a cold*
die Spritze (-n)   *injection*
der Sonnenstich (-e)   *sunstroke*
die Tablette (-n)   *pill*
der Verband (ˆe), das Pflaster (-)   *dressing/plaster*
die Verletzung (-en)   *injury*
die Watte (no plural)   *cotton wool*
der Zusammenbruch (ˆe)   *breakdown, collapse*

*an*schwellen (schwillt an, schwoll an, angeschwollen)   *to swell up*
bluten   *to bleed*
desinfizieren   *to disinfect*
sich erholen von   *to recover from*
heilen   *to heal*
hinken   *to limp*
impfen   *to vaccinate*
schmerzen   *to ache*
zu Rate ziehen (zieht, zog, gezogen)   *to consult*

angeboren   *congenital*
bewußtlos   *unconscious*
bösartig   *malignant*
erblich   *hereditary*
erschöpft   *exhausted*
kräftig   *vigorous, strong*
kränklich   *sickly*
schläfrig   *drowsy*
schwindelig   *dizzy*
stumm   *dumb*
taub   *deaf*
verkrüppelt   *cippled*
widerstandsfähig   *robust*

c) Die ärztliche Behandlung   *medical treatment*

der Arzt (ˆe), die Ärztin (-innen)   *doctor*
die Bestrahlung (-en)   *radiotherapy*
die örtliche Betäubung   *local anaesthetic*
die Blutübertragung (-en)   *blood transfusion*
der Chirug (-en)   *surgeon*
der Hausarzt/in (plural: Hausärzte/innen)   *GP*
die Hebamme (-n)   *midwife*
der Heilpraktiker/in (plural: Heilpraktiker/innen)   *practioner of alternative medicine*
die Intensivstation (-en)   *intensive care unit*
der Oberarzt (ˆe)   *consultant*
die Operation (-en)   *operation*
der Operationssaal (ˆe)   *operating theatre*
das Röntgenbild (-er)   *X-ray picture*
die Schutzimpfung (-en)   *vaccination*
die Vollnarkose (-n)   *general anaesthetic*
die Vorbeugung (-en)   *prevention*

jemanden beatmen   *to give s.o. artificial respiration*

behandeln   *to treat*

jemanden künstlich am Leben erhalten (erhält, erhielt erhalten)   *to keep s.o. alive artificially*

den Hirntod feststellen   *to establish that s.o. is brain dead*

um das Leben kämpfen   *to fight for life*

Schmerzen lindern   *to relieve pain*

operieren   *to operate*

untersuchen   *to examine*

das Leiden unnötig verlängern   *to prolong suffering unnecessarily*

die Zigarre (-n)   *cigar*

der Zug (-̈e)   *here: drag (on cigarette)*

sich eine Zigarette drehen   *to roll a cigarette*

inhalieren   *to inhale*

auf Lunge rauchen (*coll*)   *to inhale*

Beim Thema Rauchen scheiden sich die Geister   *With regard to smoking opinions differ*

sich verstümmeln   *to mutilate oneself*

schlicht und einfach   *quite simply*

unbestritten   *unarguably*

d) Rauchen, Drogen, Alkohol, Aids

Rauchen

Man raucht,...   *People smoke....*

... weil es die Freunde tun   *....because friends do it*

... weil es einen lässigen Eindruck macht   *... because it looks cool*

... weil es Spaß macht   *... because it is fun*

... weil es beruhigt   *... because it calms*

... wegen der Reklame in der Zeitung und im Kino   *... because of the advertisements in the newspaper and cinema*

Man raucht nicht, ...   *People don't smoke*

... weil es stinkt   *... because it smells*

... weil es so viel kostet   *... because it costs so much*

... weil es ungesund ist   *... because it is not healthy*

... weil ich viel Sport treibe   *... because I do a lot of sport*

... wegen der Krebsgefahr ...   *because of the danger of cancer*

... weil es asozial ist   *... because it is antisocial*

... weil es in der Schule verboten ist   *... because it is forbidden in school*

Er hat sich vor drei Monaten das Rauchen abgewöhnt.   *He gave up smoking three months ago*

die Belästigung (-en)   *annoyance*

aus Geck   *for effect/for image*

der Lungenzug (-̈e)   *inhalation into the lungs*

das Passivrauchen   *passive smoking*

die Pfeife (-n)   *pipe*

das Rauchverbot am Arbeitsplatz   *smoking ban at work*

der Tabak (no plural)   *tobacco*

die Tabaksteuer (-n)   *tax on tobacco*

das Vorbild (-er)   *example, role-model*

die Zigarette (-n)   *cigarette*

Drogen

der Abhängige (-n)   *addicted person*

der Dealer (-)   *dealer*

die Droge (-n) (usually plural)   *drug(s)*

die Drogenberatung (-en)   *advice centre for drug addicts*

die Drogenfahndung (-en)   *police effort to fight drugs*

der Drogenmißbrauch (no plural)   *drug abuse*

die Einstiegsdroge (-n)   *a drug which leads to further drug abuse*

die Entziehungskur (-en)   *withdrawal therapy*

die Entzugserscheinung (-en)   *withdrawal symptoms*

das Heroin   *heroin*

aus Neugierde (no plural)   *out of curiosity*

der Rausch (no plural)   *a high*

das Rauschgift (-e)   *narcotic drugs*

der Rauschgifthandel (no plural)   *drug trafficking*

die Rehabilitation (no plural)   *rehabilitation*

die Wiedereingliederung (-en)   *rehabilitation*

aufgeben (gibt auf, gab auf, aufgegeben)   *to give up*

beschlagnahmen   *to confiscate*

sich *einspritzen*   *to inject*

legalisieren   *legalize*

sich kaputt machen   *to destroy oneself*

nur der Dealer macht Kasse   *only the dealer gains (financially)*

auf harte Drogen umsteigen (steigt um, stieg um, umgestiegen)   *to move on to hard drugs*

heroinsüchtig werden   *to become addicted to heroin*

rückfällig werden   *to slide back (into taking drugs)*

stumpfsinnig   *moronic*

Alkohol

der Alkoholiker (-) *alcoholic*
die Aufklärung (-en) *education campaign*
der Blutalkoholspiegel (no plural) *bloodalcohol level*
der Kater (-) *hangover*
die Promillegrenze (-n) *the legal alcohol limit*
die Trunkenheit am Steuer *drink-driving*
die Trunksucht (no plural) *alcoholism*
sich betrinken (betrinkt, betrank, betrunken) *to get drunk*
betrunken *drunk*
blau sein (coll.) *to be drunk*
voll sein *to be full (of alcohol)*

Aids

das menschliche Abwehrsystem (-e) *human immune system*
der Befund (-e) *diagnosis*
der Geschlechtsverkehr (no plural) *sexual intercourse*
der/die Homosexuelle (-n) *homosexual, lesbian*
das Kondom (-e) *condom*
der Virus (plural: Viren) *virus*

an AIDS erkrankt sein *to be infected with AIDS*
die Krankheit verläuft tödlich *the illness leads to death*
sich verbreiten *to spread*
zusammenbrechen *to break down*

6. Das Alter

mit 60 Jahren in Rente gehen *to retire at 60*
die Sinne lassen nach *the senses are getting weaker*
Er ist auf einem Ohr taub *He is deaf in one ear*
rund um die Uhr betreuen *to give 24-hour care*
Peters alter Onkel ist ganz auf fremde Hilfe angewiesen *Peter's old uncle is completely dependent on help from outsiders*
Sie ist nach langem Leiden aus dem Leben geschieden *After long suffering she has passed away*
die Alten (plural) *old people*
das Altersheim (-e) *old people's home*
der Enkel/die Enkelin (-nen) *grandchild*
das Essen auf Rädern *meals on wheels*
der Greis (-e)/die Greisin (-nen) *old person*
die Herzkrankheit (-en) *heart disease*
der Infarkt (-e) *heart attack*

die Alzheimersche Krankheit *Alzheimer's disease*
nachlassende Kräfte (plural) *diminishing strength*
der Krebs (no plural) *cancer*
der Lebensabend (no plural) *retirement*
die Lebenserwartung (-en) *life expectancy*
das Pflegeheim (-e) *nursing home*
die Rente (-n)/die Pension (-en) *pension*
die Rentenversicherung (-en) *pension scheme*
das Rheuma *rheumatism*
das Ruhegeld (-er) *pension*
der Ruhestand (no plural) *retirement*
der Schlaganfall (-̈e) *stroke*
im Schoße der Familie *within the family group*
die Sterbehilfe (-n) *euthanasia*
im Vollbesitz seiner geistigen Kräfte *in full possession of one's faculties*
die Wohlfahrt (-en) *charity, welfare*
Beiträge bezahlen *to pay contributions*
gestalten *to form*
sich kümmern um (+ Acc) *to look after*
pflegen *to take care of someone, to nurse*
herzkrank sein *to suffer from heart disease*
sterben (stirbt, starb, gestorben*) *to die*
an Krebs sterben *to die of cancer*
alt werden (wird, wurde, geworden*) *to get older*

aktiv *active*
blind *blind*
pflegebedürftig *in need of care*
senil *senile*
unheilbar *incurable*

7. Die Religion

Meine Familie ist Mitglied einer Kirche *My family are church members*
Wir nehmen regelmäßig am Gottesdienst teil *We attend church services regularly*
Er spürt die Gegenwart Gottes *He feels the presence of God*
Führe uns nicht in Versuchung *Do not lead us into temptation*
Jesus Christus ist von den Toten auferstanden (auferstehen, aufersteht, auferstand, auferstanden) *Jesus Christ rose from the dead*
Jeder soll auf seine Art seelig werden *Everyone should become saved in his own way.*
Sie ringt um ein tieferes Verständnis des Lebens (ringen, ringt, rang, gerungen) *She is searching for a deeper understanding of life*

Religion ist Privatsache *religion is a private matter*

a) Das Christentum

das Abendmahl (no plural) *mass, Holy Communion, last supper*
der Aberglaube (no plural) *superstition*
der Altar (-e) *altar*
die Beichte (-n) *confession*
die Bergpredigt (no plural) *sermon on the mount*
die Bibel *the Bible*
die Buße (no plural) *repentence*
der Dom (-e) *cathedral*
das Evangelium *gospel*
die Freikirche (-n) *free church*
das Gebet (-e) *prayer*
das Gebetbuch (-er) *prayer book*
die zehn Gebote *ten commandments*
das Gesangbuch (-er) *hymn-book*
der (persönliche) Glaube (no plural) *(personal) faith*
der Gottesdienst (-e) *church service*
der Heide (-n) *heathen*
die Kanzel (-n) *pulpit*
die Kapelle (-n) *chapel*
die Kirche (-n) *church*
die evangelische Kirche *Protestant Church*
die römisch-katholische Kirche *Roman-Catholic church*
die Konfirmation (-en) *confirmation*
die Lebensphilosophie (-n) *philosophy of life*
Ostern *Easter*
der Papst (-e) *pope*
der Pfarrer/der Pastor *minister of religion (Protestant)*
Pfingsten *Whitsun/Pentecost*
die Predigt (-en) *sermon*
der Priester *priest (Catholic)*
die Religionsfreiheit (no plural) *religious freedom*
die Religionsgemeinschaft (-en) *religious group*
die heilige Schrift (-en) *Holy Scripture*
die anglikanische Staatskirche *Church of England*
der Sünder (-) *sinner*
der jüngste Tag *the day of judgement*
die Taufe (-n) *baptism*
das Vaterunser *The Lord's Prayer*
Weihnachten (pl) *Christmas*

b) Andere Religionen

die Frage nach dem Woher und Wohin *the question of origin and destiny*
keiner Religion angehören *to belong to no religious group*
der Agnostiker (-) *agnostic*
die Almosen (plural only) *alms*

der Gebetsteppich (-e) *prayer mat*
der Islam *Islam*
die fünf Säulen des Islam *the five pillars of Islam*
der Jude (-n)/die Jüdin (-nen) *jew*
das Judentum *Judaism*
der Koran *Koran*
das Laubhüttenfest *feast of tabernacles*
die Moschee (-n) *mosque*
das Paradies *paradise*
das Passa-Mahl *passover-meal*
der Rabbiner (-) *rabbi*
der Sabbat *sabbath*
das Schicksal (-e) *fate, destiny*
die Sekte (-n) *sect*
der Sinn des Lebens *the meaning of life*
die Synagoge (-n) *synagogue*
das alte Testament *the Old Testament*
die Toleranz (no plural) *tolerance*
die Unterwerfung *submission*
das Versöhnungsfest *Day of Atonement*
das erwählte Volk Gottes *God's chosen people*
die Wahrheit (-en) *truth*
die Wallfahrt (-en) *pilgrimage*

anbeten *to adore*
beten *to pray*
bekehren *to convert*
bekennen *to confess*
bereuen *to repent*
erlösen *to redeem*
feiern *to celebrate*
glauben an (+ Acc) *to believe in*
offenbaren *to reveal*
prophezeien *to prophecy*
taufen *to baptize*
verdammen *to damn*
vergeben (vergibt, vergab, vergeben) *to forgive*

abergläubig *superstitious*
christlich *christian*
fromm *pious*
geistlich *spiritual*
göttlich *divine*
heidnisch *pagan*
kirchlich *belonging to the church*
religiös *religious*
reumütig *remorseful, repentant*
unsterblich *immortal*

8. Die Psychologie

die Analyse (-n) *analysis*
die Depression (-en) *depression*
die Einbildung (-en) *delusion*
das psychiatrische Krankenhaus *psychiatric hospital*
die Magersucht (no plural) *anorexia*
die Nervenklinik (-en) *mental hospital*

der Nervenzusammenbruch (no plural)
  nervous breakdown
der Psychiater (-) *psychiatrist*
der Psychologe (-n) *psycholigist*
die Seele (-n) *soul*
das Seelenleben *spiritual life.*
der Stress *stress*
die Telefonseelsorge *(like the)*
  Samaritans
die Therapie (-n) *therapy*
das Unbewußte (no plural)
  unconsciousness
das Unterbewußte (no plural)
  subconsciousness
die Wahnvorstellung (-en) *delusion*
leiden an (+ Acc) *to suffer from*
mit den Nerven am Ende sein *to be at*
  breaking point, to be at the end of
  one's tether
unter Streß stehen (steht, stand,
  gestanden) *to be under stress*
Rat suchen *to seek advice*
die Nerven verlieren (verliert, verlor,
  verloren) *to lose one's nerves*

deprimierend *depressing*
deprimiert *depressed*
geistesgestört *mentally disturbed*
geisteskrank *mentally ill*
niedergeschlagen *depressed*
verzweifelt *desperate*

9. Person und Personenbeschreibung

a) Der Körper *the body*

for list of parts of the body see page .000

blinzeln *to blink*
gähnen *to yawn*
kauen *to chew*
keuchen *to pant, gasp*
niesen *to sneeze*
schluchzen *to sob*
Schluckauf haben *to have hiccoughs*
schwitzen *to sweat, perspire*
weinen *to weep, to cry*
kurzsichtig *short-sighted*
weitsichtig *far-sighted*

b) Das Aussehen *appearance*

allem Anschein nach *to all appearances*
sie machte ein saures Gesicht *she made*
  a sour face
sie lacht über das ganze Gesicht *she is*
  all smiles
Er kann sehr gut Gesichter
  schneiden *He is good at making*
  faces
er zuckte die Achseln *he shrugged his*
  shoulders

die körperliche Beschaffenheit *physique*
die Gangart (-en) *gait*
die Gesichtsfarbe (-n) *complexion*
der Gesichtsausdruck (-e) *facial*
  expression
die Miene (n) *facial expression*
die Schwäche (n) *weakness*

bäumeln *to dangle*
erblassen *to pale*
schwächen *to weaken*
sich verhalten *to conduct oneself*
sich ruhig verhalten *to keep calm*

anmutig *graceful*
anziehend *attractive*
auffallend *striking*
beleibt *corpulent, fat*
kräftig *strong*
mager *skinny*
glatt rasiert *clean shaven*
schlank *slim*
schmächtig *slight*
ungeschickt *awkward*
vollschlank *plump*
wackelig *wobbly*

c) Die Sinne *the senses*

der flüchtige Blick (-e) *glance*
der Duft (-e) *smell*
das Gehör (no plural) *hearing*
die Helligkeit (-en) *brightness*
der ohrenbetäubende Lärm *deafening*
  noise
der Tastsinn *touch*

anstarren *to stare*
bemerken *to notice*
betrachten *to examine*
wahrnehmen (nimmt wahr, nahm wahr,
  wahrgenommen) *to perceive*

betäubend *numbing*
durchbohrend *piercing*
einförmig *monotonous*
köstlich *delicious*
lärmend *noisy*
schlüpfrig *slippery*
unangenehm *unpleasant*
verstohlen *furtive*

d) Gute Eigenschaften, Tugenden *good qualities, virtues*

die Ausdauer *perserverance*
die Begeisterung *enthusiasm*
die Bescheidenheit *modesty*
die Dankbarkeit *thankfulness*
die Demut *humility*

die Duldsamkeit *tolerance*
die Ehrlichkeit *honesty*
die Entschlossenheit *determination*
die Freigebigkeit *generosity*
die Frömmigkeit *piety*
die Mäßigung *moderation*
das Mitleid *compassion*
die Nächstenliebe *love of one's neighbour*
das Pflichtgefühl *sense of duty*
das Selbstvertrauen *self-confidence*
die Weisheit *wisdom*

sich *an*strengen *to make an effort*
sich bemühen *to make an effort*
Opfer bringen für (+ Acc)(bringt, brachte, gebracht) *to make sacrifices for*
*nach*ahmen *to imitate*
Rücksicht nehmen auf (+Acc) (nimmt, nahm, genommen) *to take care of*
sich verlassen auf (+Acc) *to rely on*

barmherzig *charitable*
ehrwürdig *worthy of respect/venerable*
fleißig *industrious*
gesellig *sociable*
gesprächig *talkative*
gewissenhaft *conscientious*
gütig *gracious*
gutmütig *good-natured*
herzlich *cordial*
mutig *brave*
selbstlos *unselfish*
sparsam *thrifty*
unerschrocken *fearless*
vorsichtig *careful*
zurückhaltend *reserved*

e) Schlechte Eigenschaften, Laster *bad qualities, vices*

die Abneigung (gegen +Acc) *dislike*
die Anmaßung/Arroganz *arrogance*
die Befangenheit *self-consciousness*
die Drohung (-en) *threat*
der Ehrgeiz *ambition*
der Eigensinn *stubborness*
die Einbildung *presumption*
die Eitelkeit *vanity*
die Engstirnigkeit *narrow-mindedness*
die Feigheit *cowardice*
die Feindseligkeit (-en) *impudence*
die Gewalttätigkeit (-en) *violence*
die Gier *greed*
der Haß *hatred*
das Heimweh *home-sickness*
der Kummer *grief*
das Leiden (-) *suffering*
das Mißtrauen *distrust*
der Neid *jealousy*
die Rache *revenge*
die Schande *shame*
die Ungeduld *impatience*

die Ungerechtigkeit (-en) *injustice*
die Unruhe *uneasiness*
der Vorwurf *reproach*
die Verachtung *scorn*

Er beneidet seinen Bruder um seine gute Stimme *He is jealous of his brother's good voice*
Nichts kann sie aus der Fassung bringen (bringt, brachte, gebracht) *Nothing can distress her*
Sie können langweilige Leute nicht leiden *They can't stand boring people*
ärgern *to annoy*
sich *auf*regen *to get excited*
belästigen (+Acc) *to bother*
beschimpfen, beleidigen *to insult*
bestürzt sein *to be aghast*
mißbrauchen *to abuse*
mißbilligen *to disapprove*
murren *to moan*
quälen *to torture*
schaudern über (+Acc) *to shudder*
schmeicheln *to flatter*
entsetzt sein *to be horrified*
stöhnen *to sigh*
verabscheuen *to loath*
verachten *to despise*
verspotten *to tease*

abscheulich *horrible*
anmaßend/arrogant *arrogant*
befangen *self-conscious*
boshaft *malicious*
ehrgeizig *ambitious*
eigennützig *selfish*
ekelhaft *disgusting*
empörend *shocking*
empört *indignant*
entsetzlich *horrid*
feige *cowardly*
furchtsam *timid*
garstig *nasty, mean*
gereizt *irritable*
geringschätzig *disdainful*
gleichgültig *indifferent*
hochmütig *haughty*
langweilig *boring*
mißtrauisch *distrustful*
neidisch *jealous*
peinlich *embarrassing*
trübsinnig *gloomy*
ungeduldig *impatient*
ungerecht *unjust*
unverschämt *impudent*
unzufrieden *discontent*
verblüfft *startled*
verdächtig *suspicious*
verschwenderisch *wasteful*
widerwillig *reluctant*
wütend *angry*

LEISURE

1. Freizeit

eine sinnvolle Art, Freizeit zu
  verbringen *a sensible way of
  spending free*
die Freizeit gestalten *to use free time*
Noch vor einhundert Jahren war Freizeit
  ein absolutes Fremdwort. *A
  hundred years ago, free-time
  was an unknown concept.*
in gemütlicher Runde beieinandersitzen
  to sit together in a comfortable group
Innere Leere und Langeweile sind die
  Kehrseite von zuviel Freizeit *Inner
  emptiness and boredom are a
  disadvantage of too much free time*
Ohne Arbeit ist Freizeit nichts wert.
  Without work, free time has no value

der Ausgleich (-e) *balancing out*
die Belastung (-en) *stress*
die sportliche Betätigung (-en) *physical
  exercise*
nach Dienstschluß *after work*
die Entspannung (-en) *relaxation*
die Erholung *relaxation*
der Feierabend (-e) *time after work in
  the evening*
die Freizeit *free time*
die Freizeitbeschäftigung (-en) *free time
  activities*
die Freizeitgesellschaft (-en) *leisure
  society*
die Freizeitgestaltung (-en) *shaping
  leisure time*
das Freizeitangebot (-e) *offer of things to
  do in one's free time*
nach dem Gefühl *guided by feelings*
der Gestaltungswunsch *desire to shape,
  plan*
die Geselligkeit (-en) *social gathering*
die Langeweile (no plural) *boredom*
die Leidenschaft (-en) *passion*
der Nervenkitzel *thrill*
die Selbstverwirklichung (-en)
  development of one's personality
der Spaß (-sse) *fun*
die Vielfalt *variety*
der Verein (-e) *club*
das Vergnügen *enjoyment*
das Verhalten *attitude, behaviour*
die Verkürzung der Arbeitszeit *shorter
  working hours*
die frei verfügbare Zeit *time at one's
  disposal*
aktiv *active*

sich *aus*ruhen *to rest*
*aus*weichen *to avoid*
belästigen *to bother*
sich *ent*schließen *to decide*
sich *ent*spannen *to relax*

sich erholen *to relax*
es mangelt an (+Acc) *there is a lack of*
es ist sinnvoll *it makes sense*
unterschätzen *to underestimate*

anstrengend *exhausting*
äußerst *extremely*
überwiegend *largely*
eigenständig *independent*
gelegentlich *occasionally*
gering *low, minor*
gezielt *with a purpose*
leidenschaftlich *passionately*
nützlich *useful*
regelmäßig *regularly*
rücksichtslos *inconsiderate*
ständig *steadily*
seltsamerweise *unexpectedly*
ungebunden *free, without ties*
vorzugsweise *preferably*

2. Mode

Kleider machen Leute *clothes make the
  man*
sich nach der Mode richten mit der Mode
  gehen *to follow fashion*
jeden Trend mitmachen *to follow each
  trend*
von sich reden machen *to get talked
  about*
eine eigene Handschrift entwickeln *to
  develop one's own style*
Furore machen *to cause a stir*

a) Die Kleidung

der Absatz (-̈e) *heel*
der Arbeitsanzug (-e) *overall*
der Ärmel *sleeve*
der Aufschlag (-̈e) *lapel*
der Faltenrock (-e) *pleated skirt*
der Filzhut (-e) *felt-hat*
das Futter *lining*
der Gürtel *belt*
der Hosenträger *braces*
die Kapuze (-n) *hood*
das Knopfloch (-er) *buttonhole*
das Konfektionskleid (-er) *off-the-peg
  dress*
das Kostüm (-e) *lady's suit*
der Pelzmantel (-) *fur coat*
der Reißverschluß (-sse) *zip-fastener*
die Schnalle (-n) *buckle*
der Schnürsenkel *shoelace*
der Seidenstrumpf (-̈e) *silk stocking*
die Spitze (-n) *lace*
die Volkstracht (-en) *traditional
  costume*
der Zylinder *top hat*

ablegen *to take off*
aussuchen *to select*

bügeln *to iron*
aus dem Katalog bestellen *to order from a catalogue*
einen Knopf annähen *to sew on a button*
falten *to fold*
nähen *to sew*
passen *to fit/ suit*
stopfen *to darn*
tragen *to wear*
waschen *to wash*
zusammenlegen *to fold*

abgetragen *worn out*
bügelfrei *non-iron*
gemustert *patterned*
plissiert *pleated*
schäbig *shabby*
schick *smart*
schlampig *slovenly*
wasserdicht *waterproof*

b) Die Modeindustrie

im Stil der 70iger Jahre *in the style of the 70s*

das Atelier (-s) *work-shop*
die Boutique (-n) *boutique*
der Designer *designer*
der Entwurf (-e) *designs*
die Idee (-n) *idea*
der Konfektionär (-e) *merchant of fashion*
die Kreativität *creatitvity*
der Kürschner *furrier*
der Laufsteg (-e) *cat walk*
das Modell (-e) *model*
der Modemacher *designer*
der Modeschöpfer *designer of fashion*
die Modeschau (-en) *fashion show*
das Manequin (-s) *model*
die Nadel (-n) *needle*
die Näherin (-nen) *seamstress*
die Nähmaschine (-n) *sewing machine*
die Phantasie (-en) *imagination*
der Schneider/in *taylor*
das Schnittmuster *paper pattern*
der Stil *style*

entwerfen *to design*
hauteng *close to the skin*
herstellen *to produce*
kreieren *to create*
phantasievoll *full of imagination*
praktisch *practical*
provozierend *provoking*
schaffen *to create*
schrill *loud*
spleenig *crazy*
sportlich *sporty*
verkäuflich *for sale, salable*

3. Sport

Jeder dritte Bundesbürger treibt Sport *every third citizen of the Federal Republic practices a sport*
Der Freizeitsport wird großgeschrieben *Sport as leisure activity is very important*
Fußball ist die mit Abstand beliebteste Sportart *Football is by far the most popular sport*
die Grenzen der Leistungsfähigkeit *the limits of what can be achieved*
Sport treiben *to practice sport*
Mitglied in einem Verein sein *to be member in a club*
der Amateur (-e) *amateur*
der Behindertensport *sport for the disabled*
der Beifall *applause*
das Bootsrennen *boat-race*
der Boxkampf (e) *boxing-match*
der Breitensport *sport for everyone*
ehrenamtlich *honorary*
das Endspiel (-e) *final*
das Ergebnis (-se) *score*
der Gegner *opponent*
das Gewichtheben *wieght-lifting*
der Gewinn (-e) *win*
der Hochleistungssport *sport with the highest achievements*
der Hochsprung (-e) *high jump*
die Hürde (-n) *hurdle*
die Konkurrenz *opposition*
die Kraftmaschine (-n) *exercise machine*
das Kugelstoßen *shot put*
der Kurzstreckenlauf (-e) *short distance run*
der Langstreckenlauf (-e) *long distrance run der Leistungssport *sport for those who want to achieve*
die Mannschaft (-en) *team*
der Masseur (-e) *masseur*
die Medaille (-n) *medals*
die Niederlage (-n) *defeat*
das Pferderennen *horse-race*
der Profi (-s) *professionals*
der Punktsieger *winner on points*
die Regeln *rules*
der Rekord (-e) *record*
die Rennbahn (-en) *race-course*
der Schiedsrichter *referee*
das Schlittschuhlaufen *skating (on ice)*
der Sieg (-e) *victory*
das Speerwerfen *throwing the javelin*
der Sieger *winner*
die olympischen Spiele *Olympic games*
der Spitzensport *top level sport*
die Sportart (-en) *type of sport*
die Sportgeräte *sport equipment*
der Sportler/in *sportman/woman*
die Sportmedizin *medical support of sport*

der Sportplatz (-e) *sportsground*
die Sportveranstaltung (-en) *sports-meeting, event*
der Sportverein (-e) *sports-club*
der Stabhochsprung *pole-vaulting*
der Staffellauf *relay-race*
Trimm dich! *keep fit*
der Trainer *trainer*
die Tribüne (-n) *grandstand*
die Trimm-Aktion (-en) *keep fit campaign*
der Turner *gymnast*
das Turnfest (-e) *meeting of gymnasts*
die Turnhalle (-n) *gymnasium*
die Übung (-en) *practice*
der Verlust (-e) *loss*
der Weitsprung (-e) *long jump*
die Weltmeisterschaft (-en) *world championships*
der Wettkampf (-e) *contest*
der Zuschauer *spectator*

*auf*schlagen *to serve (in tennis)*
auspfeifen *to boo, whistle at*
fechten *to fence*
*heraus*fordern *to challenge*
hurra rufen *to cheer*
konkurrieren *to compete*
ringen *to wrestle*
rodeln, schlittenfahren *to toboggan*
*tei*lnehmen an (+Acc) *to take part in*
üben *to practice*
wetten *to bet*
zurückschlagen *to repulse, to repel*

biegsam, geschmeidig *supple, flexible*
körperlich *physical*
siegreich *victorious*
sportlich *sportsmanlike*
ungleich/ nicht gewachsen *unequal*

4. Fernsehen Radio und Kino

im Fernsehen übertragen *to transmit by television*
Ich habe das heute morgen im Radio gehört *I heard that this morning on the radio*
Haben Sie das Bootrennen im Fernsehen gesehen? *Did you see the boatrace on TV?*
im Rundfunk sprechen *to talk over the radio*
das Programmangebot erweitern *to extend the choice of TV-channels*
vor dem Bildschirm sitzen *to sit in front of the TV-set*
in die Röhre gucken (*coll.*) *to watch TV*

a) Fernsehen und Radio
der/die Ansager/in *announcer*
die Aufnahme (-en) *recording*
der Bildschirm (-e) *TV-screen*

der Dokumentarfilm (-e) *documentary*
die Fernsteuerung (-en) *remote control*
der Fernsehsessel *TV-armchair*
die Feuilleton-Sendung (-en) *magzine programme*
die Glotze (-n) (*coll.*) *TV-set*
das Hörspiel (-e) *radio play*
der Intendant (-en) *manager, director of a TV or radio station*
das Kabelfernsehen *cable TV*
der Kriminalfilm (-e) *detective film*
das Mikrophon (-e) *microphone*
die ernste Musik *serious music*
der/die Nachrichtensprecher/in *news-reader*
die Nachrichtensendung (-en) *news*
das Programm (-e) *channel*
die Reklame (-n) *advert*
die Regionalsendung (-en) *regional programme*
die Röhre (-n) (*coll.*) *TV-set*
der Rundfunk *radio and TV*
der private Rundfunk *private radio/TV*
das Rundfunkgerät (-e) *radio sets*
die öffentlich-rechtliche Rundfunkanstalt (-en) *the state funded, but independent radio/TV station*
das Satellitenfernsehen *satellite TV*
der Schulfunk *school TV or radio*
der Sender *the transmitter, channel*
der Senderaum (-e) *studio*
die Sendung (-en) *programmes*
die politische Sendung (-en) *programme about politics/current affairs*
der Spielfilm (-e) *thriller*
die Seifenoper (-n) *soap-opera*
die Serie (-n) *serial*
die Unterhaltungsmusik *light music*
die Unterhaltungssendung (-en) *entertainment programme*
mit Untertiteln *with subtitles*
der Verkehrshinweis (-e) *traffic news*
die Viefalt *variety*
der Video-Film (-e) *video*
der Videorekorder *video recorder*
die Wellenlänge *wave-length*
die Wiederholung (-en) *repeat*
die Werbung *advertising*
das Wunschkonzert (-e) *request programme*
der Zuschauer *viewer*
der Zuhörer *listener*
der Zeichentrickfilm (-e) *cartoon*

*auf*wenden *to use*
glotzen (*coll.*) *to watch TV*
im Fernsehen übertragen *to televise*
informieren *to inform*
manipulieren *to manipulate*
einen Sender stören *to jam a radio station*

senden, übertragen   *to transmit*
sich unterhalten lassen   *to be entertained*
sich berieseln lassen   *to let it wash over you*
teilhaben   *to take part in*
verschieben   *to postpone*
vorschreiben   *to stipulate*
vorspielen   *to perform*

b) Gefahren des Fernsehens

eine heile Welt vorspielen   *to present a good world*
die Reklame weckt immer neue Wünsche   *advertising creates more and more wishes*
die Auswirkung auf das Verhalten   *the effect on one's behaviour*
sie können nichts mehr mit sich anfangen   *they don't know what to do with themselves*
zu viel Zeit für das Fernsehen aufwenden   *to spend too much time in front of the TV*
die Gewalt verherrlichen   *to glorify violence*

eine Alternative bieten   *to offer an alternative*
die Brandstiftung (-en)   *arson* die Schießerei (-en)   *shooting*
die Entführung (-en)   *abduction* die Schlägerei (-en)   *fist-fight*
am Fernseher kleben   *to be glued to the TV* der Krieg (-e)   *war*
die Gewaltdarstellung (-en)   *depiction of violence* der Raub   *theft*
die Phantasie verlieren   *to lose imagination*
die Scheinwelt (-en)   *bogus world*
die unkritische Haltung   *uncritical attitude*
die Verharmlosung (-en)   *harmlessness*
die Verherrlichung   *glorification*

c) Das Kino

einen Film drehen   *to shoot a film*
einen Film herstellen   *to produce a film*
die Szene spielt in   *the scene is in*
er hat nur eine kleine Rolle in diesem Film   *he only plays a small part in this film*
sich auf der Leinwand die Ehre geben   *to grace the screen*
es geht um Alltagsleben   *it is about everyday life*
es geht ihnen der Ruf voraus   *their reputation has already been established*

die Albernheit (-en)   *silliness*
die Besetzung   *cast*

das Drehbuch (-er)   *script*
der Durchhänger   *scene which fails to be funy*
der Gegenwartsfilm (-e)   *film dealing with current issues*
die Heimatschnulze (-n)   *a schmaltzy, nostalgic film*
die Klamotte (-n)   *awful old film*
die Probe (-en)   *rehearsal*
der Regisseur (-e)   *manager, director of film*
der/die Schauspieler/in   *actor, actress*
der Sittenfilm (-e)   *film about morals*
die Verleihfirma (-en)   *film distributor*

abweichen   *to differ*
anknüpfen   *to take up*
anlaufen   *to be released*
aufnehmen   *to shoot (a film)*
auf etwas eingehen   *to give one's time and attention to* Aufschluß geben   *to give information*
auf etwas abfahren   *to be mad about something*
beeinflussen   *to influence*
Bilanz ziehen   *to take stock*
einrahmen   *to frame*
Furore machen   *to cause a sensation*
zur Geltung kommen   *to show to advantage*
die Hauptrolle spielen   *to play the main part*
jemanden mit etwas abspeisen   *to fob someone off with something*
auf seine Kosten kommen   *to get ones money's worth*
pleite sein (*coll.*)   *to be broke*
umsetzen   *to render*
verfilmen   *to screen*
vorbestellen   *to book in advance*
weglassen   *to leave out*

allerdings   *mind you*
aufschlußreich   *informative*
derb   *coarse, uncooth*
einschlägig   *appropriate*
gebildet   *educated*
geschickt   *skillful*
herkömmlich   *conventional*
hochgebauscht   *hyped up*
schleppend   *dragging, slow-moving*
überwiegend   *mainly, predominantly*
unmittelbar   *direct*
unter die Haut gehend   *hard-hitting*
unterlegen   *inferior*
unwahrscheinlich   *unlikely*
verhältnismäßig   *reasonably*
verheerend   *devastating*
vollendet   *accomplished*
wesentlich   *essential*
wohlwollend   *benevolent*
zusammengewürfelt   *like a jigsaw*

5. Reisen

Vorurteile haben den Reiseländern ein
Image verschafft *Prejudice has
given the holiday countries an image*
Urlaub als Gegenbild zur Arbeitswelt
*Holiday as an opposite to the world
of work*
eine bezaubernde Landschaft
enchanting landscape
ein Gebiet außergewöhnlicher Schönheit
an area of exceptional beauty
Tourismus als Wirtschaftszweig
tourism as a part of the economy
ins Ausland fahren *to travel abroad*

das Abenteuer *adventure*
der Aktivurlaub *activity holiday*
der Alltag *every day life*
die Anziehungskraft (-e) *attraction*
der Berg (-e) *mountain*
der Bildungsurlaub *educational holiday*
die Bucht (-en) *bay*
die Erfahrung (-en) *experience*
die Erholungsreise (-n) *relaxation
holiday*
das Erlebnis (-se) *adventure*
die Fahrt (-en) *journey*
der Ferienort (-e) *holiday resort*
die Ferien (pl.) *holidays*
die Gastfreundlichkeit (-en) *hospitality*
das Gebiet (-e) *area*
die Hochzeitsreise (-n) *honey-moon*
die Kultur (-en) *culture*
die Küste (-n) *coast*
die Landschaft (-en) *landscape*

das Naherholungsgebiet (-e) *resort near
a big city*
der Naturschutzpark (-s) *nature reserve*
die Pauschalreise (-n) *package tour*
die Pension (-en) *guesthouse*
die Reise (-n) *journey, travel*
das Reiseland (-er) *holiday countries*
der Reiz (-e) *attraction*
Ruhe und Erholung *calm and relaxation*
die Sehenswürdigkeit (-en) *sight*
der Strandurlaub *beach holiday*
das Tal (-er) *valley*
der Tourismus *tourism*
die Unterkunft (-e) *accomodation*
die Unterhaltungsmöglichkeiten
entertainments
der Urlaub *holiday*
der Urlaub auf dem Bauernhof *farm
holiday*
das Vorurteil (-e) *prejudice*
die Wanderung (-en) *hike*

gelten als (gilt, galt, gegolten) *to be seen
as*
*kennen*lernen *to get to know*
verstärken *to reinforce*
wegfahren *to go away*

anspruchslos *without having many
demands*
erholsam *relaxing*
gepflegt *tidy*
malerisch *picturesque*
mittelalterlich *medieval*
romantisch *romantic*
reizvoll *attractive*

SOCIAL ISSUES

1. Statistik und Gesellschaftskunde

das Alter (no plural) *age*
der Altersaufbau (no plural)
demographic structure
das Altersgeld (-er) *pension*
die Anpassung (-en) *adaptation*
der Ansatz (-e) *starting point*
im Augenblick *at the moment*
der Ausländer (-) *foreigner*
der Auswanderer (-) *emigrant*
der Beitrag (-e) *contributions*

die Bevölkerung (-en) *population*
die Breite (-n) *breadth*
die Dauer (no plural) *duration*
die Einkommenssteuer (-n) *income tax*
der Einwohner (-) *inhabitant*
der Emigrant (-en) *emigrant*
der Erwerbstätige (-n) *working person*
die Ewigkeit (-en) *eternity*
das Fassungsvermögen (-) *capacity*
das Flächenmaß (-e) *measure of area*
der Geburtenrückgang (-e) *drop in the
birthrate*

die Gegenwart (no plural) *present*
das Gehalt (-er) *salary*
der Generationen-Vertrag (-e) *contract
between generations*
der Grenzwert (-e) *limit*
die Häufigkeit (-en) *frequency*
das Hohlmaß (-e) *liquid measure*
der Immigrant (-en) *immigrant*
der Inhalt (-e) *contents*
der Jahresverdienst (-e) *annual
earnings*
der Jahrgang (-e) *age group*
das Jahrzehnt (-e) *decade*
die Lebenserwartung (-en) *life
expectancy*
die Kindheit (no plural) *childhood*
die Kleinigkeit (-en) *trifle*
der Kubikmeter (-) *cubic metre*
das Längenmaß (-e) *measure of length*
die Lücke (-n) *gap*
die Meinungsforschung (no plural)
science of conducting opinion polls
die Meinungsumfrage (-n) *opinion poll*
die Mischung (-en) *mixture*

die Nachwelt (no plural) *posterity*
der Pillenknick *drop in the birthrate due to the contraceptive pill*
das Prozent (-e) *per cent*
der Quadratmeter (-) *square metre*
das Raummaß (-e) *cubic measure*
die Rente (-n) *pension*
die Rentenversicherung (-en) *pension companies*
der Rentner (-) *pensioner*
das Schaltjahr (-e) *leap-year*
die Sozialabgabe (-n) *contribution to social security*
das Sparbuch (-̈er) *savings book*
der Sparvertrag (-̈e) *savings scheme*
die Steuer (-n) *tax*
der Steuerzahler (-) *tax payer*
die Umfrage (-n) *survey*
das Verhältnis (-se) *proportion*
die Vorväter (plural only) *ancestors*
der Zeitabschnitt (-e) *period*
der Zeitpunkt (-e) *point in time*
der Zeitraum (-̈e) *period*
der Zinssatz (-̈e) *interest rate*
die Zukunft (no plural) *future*

ab-,verkürzen *to shorten*
abziehen (zieht ab, zog ab, abgezogen) *to subtract*
aufbrauchen *to consume*
aufhäufen *to heap up*
aufhören *to stop*
befragen *to question*
beisteuern, beitragen zu (+ Dat) (trägt bei, trug bei, beigetragen) *to contribute to*
berechnen *to calculate*
jemandem etwas entziehen *to deprive someone of something*
Man entzieht ihm die Sozialhilfe (entzieht, entzog, entzogen) *They deprive him of social benefit*
erweitern *to widen*
sich hinziehen (zieht sich hin, (zog sich hin, hingezogen) *to linger*
multiplizieren *to multiply*
senken *to lower*
vergehen (vergeht, verging, vergangen*) *to elapse*
vergrößern *to enlarge*
verkleinern *to lessen*
vermindern *to diminish*
vertiefen *to deepen*
wieder aufnehmen (nimmt auf, (nahm auf, aufgenommen) *to resume*
zusammenrechnen/ -zählen *to total up*

augenblicklich *instantaneous*
äußerst *extremely*
ausreichend *sufficient*
(un)bestimmt *(in)definite*
dauerhaft *durable*
ewig *eternal*

schwerwiegend *grave*
sofort *instantly*
ständig *constant*
unzählig *innumerable*
vollkommen *completely*
vorher *previously*
zahlreich *numerous, countless*

2. Arbeit und Arbeitslosigkeit

sie ist gerade bei der Arbeit *she's at work at the moment*
einen Beruf einschlagen *to take up a career*
Er gibt seinen früheren Chef als Referenz an *He names his former boss as referee*
Sein Lohn liegt unter dem Existenzminimum *He is not earning a living wage*
Die Firma macht viele Arbeitsplätze in der Produktion überflüssig *The firm makes many production jobs superfluous*
Manche Arbeiter kommen mit dem technischen Wandel nicht zurecht *Some workers dont cope with technological change*
der Schlichtungsversuch scheiterte *the attempt at arbitration failed*
Sie möchte einen Beruf in Richtung Krankenpflege ergreifen *She'd like to enter into a career that has something to do with nursing*
in den Anzeigenteil der Zeitung sehen *to look in the advertisements section of the newspaper*
Wie sehen die Aufstiegsmöglichkeiten aus? *What are the career prospects?*
Man hat ihm wieder eine Absage erteilt *They have given him a rejection again*
Sie verdient ihr Brot mit Musikunterricht. *She earns her living by giving music lessons*
Er bezieht Arbeitslosenunterstützung *he is on the dole*
er geht stempeln *he is on the dole*
Sie hat gute Kenntnisse in Englisch und Französisch *She has a good knowledge of English and French*

der Abteilungsleiter (-) *head of department*
die Annonce (-n) *advertisement*
der/die Angestellte (-n) *white-collar worker*
der/die leitende Angestellte (-n) *middle manager*
der Arbeiter (-) *blue-collar worker*
der Arbeitgeber (-) *employer*
der Arbeitnehmer (-) *employee*

das Arbeitsamt (-er)   *job centre*
die Arbeitsbedingung (-en)   *working condition*
die Arbeitsbeschaffung   *creation of jobs*
die Arbeitsgenehmigung (-en)   *work permit*
die ungelernte Arbeitskraft (-e)   *unskilled worker*
der/die Arbeitslose (-n)   *unemployed person*
das Arbeitslosengeld (-er)   *unemployment benefit*
die Arbeitslosenrate   *rate of unemployment*
die Arbeitslosigkeit (no plural)   *unemployment*
der gesicherte Arbeitsplatz (-e)   *secure job*
der Arbeitsvertrag (-e)   *job contract*
die Arbeitszeit (-en)   *working hours*
die gleitende Arbeitszeit (-en)   *flexi-time*
die Arbeitszeitverkürzung (-en)   *reduction in working time*
der Aufsichtsrat (-e)   *the board of directors*
der Aufsichtsratsvorsitzende (-n)   *chairman of the board of directors*
die Aussperrung (-en)   *lock-out*
das Bankwesen (no plural)   *banking*
das Baugewerbe (no plural)   *construction industry*
die Beförderung (-en)   *promotion*
die Belegschaft (-en)   *staff*
der Beruf (-e)   *vocation*
der Berufsberater (-)   *careers advisor*
die Berufswahl (no plural)   *choice of career*
der Betriebsleiter (-)   *works manager*
der Bewerber (-)   *applicant*
der Chef (-s), die Chefin/-nen   *boss*
die persönlichen Daten (plural)   *personal details*
die Dauerarbeitslosen (plural)   *long-term unemployed*
der Dienst (-e)   *duty*
im Dienst   *on duty*
der öffentliche Dienst   *public service*
die Dienstleistungen (plural only)   *service industries*
der Direktor (-en)   *director*
die Dunkelziffer (-n)   *number of unreported cases*
die Eigeninitiative (-n)   *own initiative*
das Einkommen (no plural)   *income*
der Erwerbstätige (-n)   *worker*
der Feierabend (no plural)   *end of work (for the day)*
die Filiale (-n)   *branch*
die Forderung (-en) nach (+Dat)   *demand for*
die Fotokopie (-n)   *photocopy*
die Ganztagsstelle (-n)   *full-time job*

die Gegenmaßnahme (-n)   *counter-measure*
das Gehalt (-er)   *salary*
die Gelegenheitsarbeit (no plural)   *casual work*
das Gewerbe (no plural)   *trade*
die Gewerkschaft (-en)   *trade union*
der Gewerkschaftler (-)   *trade unionist*
die Gleitzeit (no plural)   *flexi-time*
die Halbtagsstelle (-n)   *part-time job*
die Hauptstelle (-n)   *head office*
die Hauptverkehrszeit (-en)   *rush-hour*
der Hilfsarbeiter (-)   *unskilled worker*
das Hotelgewerbe (no plural)   *hotel trade*
das Krankengeld (-er)   *sick pay*
die Kündigung (-en)   *notice of dismissal*
die Laufbahn (-en)   *career*
der Lebenslauf (-e)   *c.v.*
der Lebensstandard (no plural)   *standard of living*
der Lebensunterhalt (no plural)   *livelihood*
der Lohn (-e)   *wage*
die Lohnerhöhung (-en)   *pay increase*
die Lohn- und Gehaltsempfänger (plural only)   *salaried and wage earning people*
der Lohnstop (no plural)   *pay freeze*
die Lohntüte (-n)   *pay envelope*
der Lohnzettel (-)   *pay slip*
der Mangel an Arbeitskräften   *shortage of workers*
der Mindestlohn (-e)   *minimum wage*
die Mitbestimmung (no plural)   *worker participation in management*
der Mutterschaftsurlaub (no plural)   *maternity leave*
der Mutterschutzurlaub (no plural)   *maternity leave*
der Pendler (-)   *commuter*
das Personal (no plural)   *personnel, staff*
der Personalleiter (-)   *personnel manager*
ein begehrter Posten (-)   *a sought-after job*
die Qualifikation (-en)   *qualification*
der Rationalisierungsschub (-e)   *drive to rationalise*
die Schichtarbeit (no plural)   *shift work*
der Schlichter (-)   *arbitrator*
die Schlichtungsverhandlung (-en)   *strike settlement negotiations*
die Sozialversicherung (-en)   *social security*
der (Staats)beamte (-n)   *civil or public servant*
die Stelle (-n)   *post*
die freie Stelle (-n)   *vacancy*
das Stellenangebot (-e)   *job offer*
der Streik (-s)   *strike*
der Tarif (-e)   *tarif, rate of pay*
die Tarifverhandlung (-en)   *pay negotiation*

der Tarifvertrag (-̈e) *pay settlement*
die Überstunde (-n) *overtime*
die Umschulung (-en) *re-training*
die Unterlage (-n) *document*
das Vorstellungsgespräch (-e) *job interview*
der Verkaufsleiter (-) *sales manager*
der Vertrauensmann (-̈er) *shop steward*
der Vorarbeiter (-) *foreman*
die Wirtschaft (no plural) *economy*
der Zahltag (-e) *pay day*

sich *an*passen *to adapt*
*an*stellen *to incite*
Streikposten *auf*stellen *to set up pickets*
sich *aus*kennen in *to have knowledge about*
beschäftigen *to employ*
betroffen sind vor allem *the most affected are*
sich *be*werben um (+ Acc) (bewirbt sich, bewarb sich, sich beworben) *to apply*
*ein*sparen *to cut back, to save*
entlassen (entläßt, entließ, entlassen) *to dismiss, sack*
fristlos entlassen *to dismiss on the spot*
höhere Löhne fordern *to demand higher wages*
um Rat fragen *to ask for advice*
konkurrieren *to compete with*
kündigen *to dismiss, sack*
pendeln *to commute*
schuften (*coll*) *to work hard*
streiken *to strike*
in den Streik treten *to go on strike*
in Apathie umschlagen *to descend into apathy*
verhandeln *to negotiate*
befördert werden *to be promoted*

arbeitslos *unemployed*
betriebsam *industrious*
ehrgeizig *ambitious*
fleißig *industrious*
industriell *industrial*
leistungsfähig/tüchtig *efficient*
unbedingt notwendig *imperative*
unentbehrlich *indispensible*
unter-/überqualifiziert *under-/over-qualified*

3. Umwelt

a) Umweltprobleme

Wind und Strömung sorgten für eine langsame Verteilung des Ölteppichs *wind and currents caused the slow enlargement of the oil slick*

der Müllberg wächst *the mountain of rubbish grows*
der fahrlässige Umgang mit der Natur *the careless treatment of nature*
dem Ausrotten gefährdeter Tiere ein Ende bereiten *to bring the extinction of endangered aimals to an end*
... vor radioaktiver Bestrahlung schützen *to protect from radioactive rays*
die Zerstörung der Landschaft in Grenzen halten *to limit the destruction of the landscape*
dem Risiko eines nuklearen Unfalls zuvorkommen *to prevent the risk of a nuclear accident*
das Problem der vergifteten Flüsse lösen *to solve the problem of the poisoned rivers*
Probleme bei der Entsorgung radioaktiver Abfallprodukte reduzieren *to reduce problems with the disposal of radioactive waste*
Alle Hersteller werden bald dem Verbot von FCKW unterworfen *All manufacturers will soon have to abide by the ban on CFCs*
Diese Maßnahmen werden Zorn entfachen *These measures will incur wrath*
Er steht in Verdacht, Chemikalien ins Abwasser geschüttet zu haben. *He is suspected of having poured chemicals into the drains*
es lohnt sich *it is worth it*

der Abfall (-̈e) *rubbish*
die Abgase (plural only) *exhaust fumes*
das Abwasser (-̈) *sewage*
der Atommüll (no plural) *radioactive waste*
die Atomwaffe (-n) *nuclear weapon*
der Auspuff (-e) *car exhaust*
die Belastung (-en) *harm, level of pollution*
die Bestrahlung (-en) *radiation*
der Brand (-̈e) *fire*
die Chemikalie (-n) *chemical*
die Dreckschleuder (-n) (*coll*) *pollutant*
das Erdbeben (-) *earthquake*
der Erdrutsch (no plural) *landslide*
die Geröllmassen (plural only) *piles of rubble*
das Gift (-e) *poison*
die Katastrophe (-n) *catastrophy*
die Kernenergie (-n) *nuclear power*
die Lärmbelästrigung (-en) *noise pollution*
die Luftverschmutzung (-en) *air pollution*

der Meßwert (-e) *measured value/level of pollution*
der Müll (no plural) *waste*
die Nichteinhaltung (-en) *failure to comply with*
der Ölteppich (-e) *oil slick*
die Ozonschicht (-en) *ozone layer*
das Risiko (-en) *risk*
der Schadstoff (-e) *harmful substance*
der Tanker (-) *oil tanker*
die Überschwemmung (-en) *flood*
der Umweltschutz (no plural) *protection of the environment*
der Umweltschützer (-) *environmentalist*
der Umweltsünder (-) *polluter*
die Umweltverschmutzung (no plural) *pollution*
die Unachtsamkeit (-en) *carelessness*
das Unglück (-e) *disaster*
der Unkrautvertilger (-) *weed killer*
das Unkrautvernichtungsmittel (-) *weed killer*
der Verkehrslärm (no plural) *traffic noise*
die Verseuchung (-en) *contamination*
der Waldschaden (-̈e) *damage to forests*
das Waldsterben (no plural) *the dying of forests*
das Waschmittel (-) *detergent*
die Wegwerfgesellschaft (-en) *throw-away society*

ausfallen (fällt aus, fiel aus ausgefallen) *to fail, stop working*
bergen *to save, rescue*
nachrüsten *to instal afterwards, retro-fit*
sperren *to close off*
vergiften *to poison*
vermuten *to assume*
verschmutzen *to pollute*
verseuchen *to contaminate*
verunreinigen *to contaminate*
verunsichern *to put into a state of uncertainty*

atomar *nuclear*
ausführlich *in great detail*
erheblich *considerable*
günstig *favourable*
krebserzeugend, krebserregend *cancer-causing*
lauernd *lurking*
leibhaftig *real*
überlastet *overloaded*
überschüßig *surplus*
unerhört *outrageous*
unfallträchtig *likely to cause an accident*
verseucht *contaminated*
zusätzlich *in addition*

b) Luft- und Wasserverschmutzung *air and water pollution*

Diese Firma läßt noch immer Chemikalien ins Gewässer ab *This firm still releases chemicals into rivers*
Das Öl sickert ins Grundwasser *The oil seeps into the water-table*

das Abschmelzen der Polkappen *melting of ice-caps*
der Anstieg des Meeresspiegels *rise in the sea-level*
das Auspuffrohr (-e) *exhaust pipe*
die Autoabgase (plural only) *car exhaust fumes*
in Bodennähe *near the ground*
die Emission (-en) *emission*
die Erwärmung der Erdatmosphäre *global warming*
das Fischsterben (no plural) *the dying of fish*
die Fluorchlorkohlenwasserstoffe *chlorofluorocarbons*
die FCKW (plural only) *CFCs*
der Hautkrebs (no plural) *skin-cancer*
das Grundwasser (-) *water table*
die Klimaveränderung (-en) *changes in the climate*
das Kohlendioxid (-e) *carbon dioxide, CO_2*
das Kohlenmonoxid (-e) *carbon monoxide, CO*
der Kohlenstoff (-e) *carbon*
das Kühlmittel (-) *coolant*
der Nadelwald (-̈er) *pine forest*
das Ozonloch (-̈er) *hole in the ozone layer*
die Ozonschicht (-en) *ozon layer*
der saure Regen (no plural) *acid rain*
der Sauerstoff *oxygen*
das Schwefeldioxid *sulphur dioxide, SO_2*
die Spitzen der Bäume (plural) *tips of the trees*
die Sprühdose (-n) *aerosol spray*
der Stausee (-n) *reservoir*
der Stickstoff (-e) *nitrogen*
ultraviolette Strahlen (plural) *ultraviolet rays*
das Treibgas (-e) *propellant (in aerosol)*
der Treibhauseffekt (-e) *greenhouse effect*
die Überflutung der Küstengebiete (plural only) *flooding of coastal regions*
das Waldsterben (no plural) *forests dying because of acid rain*
der Wasserspiegel (no plural) *water level*
der Wasserstoff *hydrogen*
die Wasserverschmutzung (-en) *water pollution*
die Wasservorräte (plural only) *water reserves*

c) Umweltschutz

Müll weitmöglichst wiederverwenden *to re-use waste as much as possible*

umweltfreundlichere formen des Verkehrs finden *to find more environmentally friendly types of transport*

mehr Bürgerinitiativen organisieren *to organize more pressure groups*

Gesetze gegen Umweltverschmutzung *laws against pollution*

weniger gefährliche Energiequellen erschließen *to use less dangerous sources of energy*

Umwelt schützen – Rad benützen *Protect the environment – use your cycle*

Kernkraft – Nein Danke *Nuclear power – no thanks*

auf weiteren Konsum verzichten *to abstain from further consumption*

die Schadstoffbelastung (-en) mindern *to reduce damage by pollutants*

das Überleben der Menschheit sichern *to secure the survival of humanity*

Die Verursacher sollten entstandene Schäden beseitigen *The people responsible should repair existing damage*

Gegenmaßnahmen *einleiten* *to introduce counter-measures*

Man muß auf die Umwelt Rücksicht nehmen (nimmt, nahm, genommen) *One must show consideration for the environment*

Man muß mit den Rohstoffen sparsamer umgehen *one must use the raw-materials more economically*

der Altglaskontainer (-) *bottle bank*

die Altpapiersammlung (-en) *collection of paper for recycling*

der Brandschutz (no plural) *fire prevention*

die Einschränkung (-en) *restriction*

das Gesundheitsamt (-er) *public health department*

die Grünen (plural only) *Green Party*

der Katalysator (-en) *catalytic converter*

die Kläranlage (-n) *water treatment works*

die Mehrwegflasche (-n) *re-usable bottle*

das Naturschutzgebiet (-e) *protected landscape*

das umweltfreundliche Produkt (-e) *environmentally friendly product*

die Rettungswacht (no plural) *rescue team*

frei von Schadstoffen (plural) *free from harmful substances*

das Umweltbewußtsein (no plural) *environmental awareness*

das Umweltbundesamt (no plural) *Federal Office for the environment*

die Umwelterziehung (-en) *environmental education*

die Wiederaufbereitungsanlage (-n) *recycling plant*

abbauen *to decompose*
begrenzen *to limit*
beseitigen *to eliminate*
es besteht die Hoffnung *there is the hope*
durchführen *to carry out*
einschränken *to reduce*
entschärfen *to defuse (a situation)*
reduzieren *to reduce*
reinigen *to clean*
sammeln *to collect*
säubern *to clean*
schonen *to protect*
schützen *to protect*
sparen *to save*
sich verpflichten zu *to commit oneself to*
verringern *to reduce*
das Gesetz verschärfen *to tighten the law*
verzichten auf (+ Acc) *to do without*
vorbeugen *to prevent*
wiederverwenden *to use again*

biologisch *abbaubar* *bio-degradable*
ehrenamtlich *honorary*
umweltschonend *protecting the environment*
umfassend *comprehensive*
vorbeugend *preventive*

d) Die Energie

den Verbrauch auf das Nötigste einschränken *to limit/reduce the usage to the absolute necessity*

sie können nicht kontinuierlich Energie liefern *they can't produce energy continually*

Arabien *Arabia*

der Atomstrom (no plural) *electricity made from nuclear power*

der Bergarbeiter (-) *miner*

die radioaktive Bestrahlung (-en) *radioactive radiation*

der Brennstoff (-e) *fuel*

die Doppelfenster (-) *double glazing*

die Elektrizität (no plural) *electricity*

die Endlagerung radioaktiver Abfälle *the storage of radioactive waste*

der Energiebedarf (no plural) *energy requirement*

der Energieverbrauch (no plural) *energy consumption*

das Erdgas (no plural) *gas*

der Erdölexport (-e) *oil export*

die erdölexportierenden Länder *oil-exporting countries*

die Gezeitenenergie (-n) *tidal power*

die Isolierung (-en) *insulation*

das Kernkraftwerk (-e) *nuclear power station*

der Kernschmelz (-en) *meltdown*

die Kohle (-n) *coal*

das Kohlebergwerk (-e) *coal mine*

der Naheosten *middle east*

das Öl *oil*

der Öltanker (-) *oil tanker*

die technische Panne (-n) *technical break-down*

der Reaktor (-en) *reactor*

das Rohöl (no plural) *crude oil*

die Rohrleitung (-en) *pipe-line*

die Sonnenenergie (-n) *solar energy*

die Wasserkraft (-̈e) *hydro-electric power*

die Wellenenergie (-n) *wave power*

die Windenergie (-n) *wind energy*

*auseinander*brechen (bricht auseinander, brach auseinander, auseinandergebrochen) *to break up*

alternative Energiequellen entwickeln *to develop alternative energy resources*

isolieren *to insulate*

das Dach isolieren *to insulate the roof*

auf Grund laufen *to run aground*

das Öe läuft aus *the oil leaks*

in Betrieb nehmen (nimmt, nahm, genommen) *to start, to commission*

Energie sparen *to save energy*

*still*legen *to close down*

4. Stadt und Land

a) Gebäude in der Stadt, Einwohner

die Allee (-n) *avenue*

die Altbauwohnung (-en) *older housing*

die Ausstellungshalle (-n) *exhibition hall*

das Ballungsgebiet (-e) *conurbation*

die Baustelle (-n) *building site*

die Behörde (-n) *administration, authority*

die Börse (-n) *stock exchange*

die Botschaft (-en) *embassy*

der Bürger (-) *citizen*

der Bürgermeister (-) *mayor*

der Bürgersteig (-e) *pavement*

das Denkmal (-̈er) *monument*

die Durchgangsstraße (-n) *main through road*

die Eigentumswohnung (-en) *owner-occupied flat*

die Einbahnstraße (-n) *one-way street*

der Einwohner (-) *inhabitant*

das Fachwerkhaus (-̈er) *half-timbered house*

die Gasse (-n) *alley*

das Gebäude (-) *building*

das Geschäftshaus (-̈er) *commercial building*

das Gewerbegebiet (-e) *light industrial estate*

die Großstadt (-̈e) *big town, city*

das Grundstück (-e) *building plot*

das Halteverbot (-e) *clearway*

das Hochhaus (-̈er) *sky-scraper*

die Hypothekenzinsen (plural only) *mortgage rates*

das Industriegebiet (-e) *industrial estate*

die Kleinstadt (-̈e) *small town*

das Konsulat (-e) *consulate*

das Lagerhaus (-̈er) *warehouse*

das kulturelle Leben *cultural life*

die städtische Lebensweise *city way of life*

die Litfaßsäule (-n) *advertising column*

das Messezentrum (-en) *trade fair/exhibition centre*

das Nachtlokal (-e) *night club*

die Nebenstraße (-n) *side street*

der Oberbürgermeister (-) *Lord Mayor of a big town*

das Parkverbot (-e) *no parking area*

die Sackgasse (-n) *cul-de-sac*

die Schlafstadt (-̈e) *commuter town*

die Sozialwohnung (-en) *flat at low rent*

der Stadtbus (-se) *local bus*

der/die Stadtplaner/in *town planning officer*

die Stadtplanung (-en) *town planning*

die Straßenlampe (-n) *street light*

das Straßenschild (-er) *street sign*

die Umgehungsstraße (-n) *by-pass*

der Verkehr (no plural) *traffic*

die öffentlichen Verkehrsmittel (plural only) *public transport*

das Verkehrsschild (-er) *traffic sign*

die Verwaltung (-en) *administration*

die Wohnsiedlung (-en) *housing estate*

der Wohnungsbau *the building of flats*

das Wohnungsbauprogramm (-e) *housing programme*

das Wohnviertel *residential area*

der Wolkenkratzer *sky-scraper*

abreißen (reißt ab, riß ab, abgerissen) *to pull down*

besetzen *to occupy*

instandsetzen   *to repair*
leerstehen (steht leer, stand leer,
    leergestanden)   *to stand empty*
modernisieren   *to modernize*
sanieren   *to clean up, modernise*
vernachlässigen   *to neglect*
verschönern   *to make pretty*
zentral gelegen   *situated in the centre*

b) Stadtprobleme

die Grundstückspreise schnellen in die
    Höhe   *in land prices are going
    through roof*
alte Menschen getrauen sich nicht aus
    dem Haus   *old people daren't leave
    their house*
Schafft Spielplätze statt Parkplätzen
create playgrounds instead of carparks
der Trend zu Einpersonenhaushalten
        tendency to one person households
im Freien übernachten   *to sleep rough*

die Anonymität (no plural)   *anonymity*
der Berufsverkehr (no plural)
        commuter traffic
die Betonwüste (-n)   *concrete jungle*
die Bodenspekulation (-en)   *speculation
    on property*
die Brandstiftung (-en)   *arson attack*
die Demonstration (-en)   *protest march*
die Einsamkeit (no plural)   *loneliness*
das Elendsviertel (-)   *slum*
die Feuerwehr (-en)   *fire-service*
die Hausbesetzer (-)   *squatters*
die Hausbesetzung (-en)   *squats*
die Luftverschmutzung (no plural)   *air-
    pollution*
der Polizeieinsatz (-e)   *police action*
der Raub (no plural)   *robbery*
die Stadtflucht (no plural)   *exodus from
    towns and cities*
der Straßenraub (no plural)   *mugging
    (the crime)*
der Überfall (-e)   *mugging (the incident)*
der Slum (-s)   *slum*
der Verkehrslärm   *traffic noise*
die Wohnungsnot   *shortage of housing*

betteln   *to beg*
vernachlässigen   *to neglect*

baufällig   *delapidated*
heimatlos   *homeless*
obdachlos   *homeless*

c) Das Landleben

der Anbau von (+ Dat) *the cultivation of ...*
das Bauernhaus (-er)   *farmhouse*
das Feld (-er)   *field*
die Forstwirtschaft (no plural)   *forestry*
die Genossenschaft (-en)   *co-operative*

die Gerste (no plural)   *barley*
der Hafer (no plural)   *oats*
die Herde (-n)   *herd*
das Heu (no plural)   *hay*
der Kleinbauer (-n)   *small-holder*
der Kunstdünger (-)   *artificial fertilizer*
das Landgut (-er)   *estate*
der Landwirt (-e), der Bauer (-n)   *farmer*
die Landwirtschaft (no plural)   *farming,
    agriculture*
der Mähdrescher (-)   *combine harvester*
die Milchviehhaltung (-en)   *dairy
    farming*
der Mist (no plural)   *dung*
die Pflanzung (-en)   *cultivation*
der Roggen (no plural)   *rye*
die Scheune (-n)   *barn*
der Stall (-e)   *shed/stable*
die Überproduktion (-en) von (+Dat)
    over-production of
die Viehzucht (no plural)   *cattle breeding*
das Weideland (-er)   *pasture*
der Weinbauer (-n)   *wine-grower, vintner*
der Weinberg (-e)   *vinyard*
die Weinlese (-n)   *grape harvest*
der Weizen (no plural)   *corn*
der Winzer (-)   *wine-grower, vintner*

düngen   *to spread fertilizer*
entwässern,   *to drain*
die unberührte Natur erleben   *to
    experience unspoiled countryside*
aufforsten   *to reafforest*
ernten   *to reap*
grasen   *graze*
brach *liegen*lassen   *to set aside (from
    agricultural use)*
pachten,   *to rent*
pflügen   *to plough*
reifen   *to ripen*
säen   *to sow*
streicheln, tätscheln   *to pat*
trocken legen   *to drain*
verpachten   *to lease out*
züchten   *to breed*

abgelegen   *far away from another town*
ländlich   *rural*
unfruchtbar   *barren*
wild   *fierce*

d) Die Landschaft   *landscape*

wo sich Fuchs und Hase Gute Nacht
    sagen   *to live far out in the sticks
    (idiom)*
am Arsch der Welt (*coll.*)   *in the middle
    of nowhere*

die Anhöhe (-n)   *hill*
die Aussicht (-en)   *view*
im Freien   *in the open air*
die Fußgängerbrücke (-n)   *footbridge*

das Gestrüpp (no plural) *undergrowth*
der Graben (-) *ditch*
das Gut (-̈er) *estate*
der Hain (-̈e) *copse*
der Hang (-̈e) *slope*
das Häuschen (-) *cottage*
die Hecke (-n) *hedge*
die Heide *heath, moore*
das Kliff (-s)/die Klippe (-n) *cliff*
die Lichtung (-en) *clearing*
das Moor (-e) *fen*
der Pfad (-e) *path*
der Steg (-e) *small footbridge*
das Strohdach (-̈er) *thatched roof*
der Tau (no plural) *dew*
der Teich (-e) *pond*
der Wald (-̈er) *forest*
der Weg (-e) *way, path*
der Steinbruch (-e) *quarry*

bewaldet *wooded*
einsam *lonely*
gesperrt *no through way*
verlassen *deserted*

5. Verbrechen und Kriminalität

(For more words and phrases see also
6. Recht und Gesetz)
er ist des Mordes angeklagt *he is
    accused of murder*
bei ihm wurde eine Hausdurchsuchung
    vorgenommen *his house was
    searched*
einen Meineid leisten *to commit perjury*
einen Urteilsspruch fällen *to pass
    judgement*

der Angeklagte (-n) *defendant*
die Anklage (-n) *accusation*
das Bereicherungsdelikt (-e) *crime of
    gain*
die Bestechung (-en) *bribe*
der Betrüger (-) *swindler*
die Bewährung (-en) *probation*
der Bewährungshelfer (-) *probation
    officer*
der Beweis (-e) *evidence*
der Diebstahl (-̈e) *theft*
der Eid (-e) *oath*
der Einbrecher (-) *burglar*
der Einbruch (-̈e) *burglary*
der Ganove (-n) *rogue, scoundrel*
das Gefängnis (-se) *prison*
das Gericht (-e) *court of law*
die Geschworenen (plural only) *jury*
der/die Geschworene (no plural)
    member of jury
das Gesetz (-e) *law*
das Geständnis (-se) *confession*
die Gewaltkriminalität (no plural)
    crimes of violence
die Haft (no plural) *imprisonment*

der Haftbefehl (-e) *warrant*
die Jugendkriminalität (no plural) *youth
    crime*
die Jugendstrafe (-n) *youth punishment*
der Krawall (-e) *riot*
der Ladendieb (-e) *shop-lifter*
der Laienrichter/Friedensrichter (-)
    magistrate
die verbrecherische Laufbahn *criminal
    career*
der Mord (-e) *murder*
der Mörder (-) *murderer*
der Raub (no plural) *robbery*
die Raubkriminalität (no plural) *robbery*
die Raubquote (-n) *number of robberies*
der Rechsanwalt (-e) *lawyer*
der Richter (-) *judge*
der Schaufenstereinbruch (-̈e) *smash-
    and-grab raid*
die Schlägerei (-en) *fist fight*
der Schwarzhandel (no plural) *black
    market*
der Staatsanwalt (-e) *public prosecutor*
der Sträfling (-e) *prisoner*
der Taschendieb (-e) *pick-pocket*
der Totschlag (no plural) *manslaughter*
die Überführung (-en) *conviction*
die Untersuchung (-en) *investigation*
das Urteil (-e) *verdict*
das Verbrechen (-) *crime*
der Verbrecher (-) *criminal*
der Verfahrensabschluß (-sse) *verdict,
    end of case*
die Verhandlung (-en) *court case*
die Verurteilung (-en) *condemnation*
der Zeuge (-n) *witness*

bestechen (besticht, bestach, bestochen)
    to bribe
einbrechen (bricht ein, brach ein,
    eingebrochen) *to burgle*
erpressen *to extort from*
morden *to murder*
rauben *to rob*
schwarzarbeiten *to work in the black
    economy*
schwarzfahren (fährt schwarz, fuhr
    schwarz, schwarzgefahren) *to
    travel without a valid ticket
    or: to drive without a licence*
töten *to kill*
vollziehen (vollzieht, vollzog,
    vollzogen) *to carry out a sentence*

gesetzwidrig *illegal*

6) Recht und Gesetz

a) Redewendungen

Recht sprechen *to administer justice*
Zwei Junge Männer sitzen auf der
    Anklagebank *Two young men are
    sitting in the dock*

Die Klage wurde abgewiesen   *The complaint was dismissed*

Er ist des Mordes angeklagt   *He is accused of murder*

Bei ihm wurde eine Hausdurchsuchung vorgenommen   *His house was searched*

Mein Nachbar hat gegen mich einen Prozeß angestrengt   *My neighbour has brought an action against me*

Er wurde als Rechtsanwalt zugelassen   *He was called to the bar.*

einen Meineid leisten   *to commit perjury*

einen Urteilsspruch fällen   *to pass a sentence*

Das Urteil wird morgen verkündet.   *Sentence will be pronounced tomorrow*

Der Angeklagte beteuert seine Unschuld   *The accused protests his innocence (pleads not guilty)*

Berufung einlegen   *to make an appeal*

ein Verbrechen begehen   *to commit a crime*

ins Gefängnis schicken   *to put into prison*

Können Sie dafür den Beweis erbringen?   *Can you furnish proof?*

Wir müssen jetzt doch noch den Rechtsweg beschreiten   *In the end, we have to take legal action.*

Er ist schuld daran   *It is his fault*

Viele Leute fordern heutzutage härtere Strafen zur Abschreckung   *Many people nowadays demand more severe punishments as a deterrent.*

Bekennen Sie sich schuldig?   *Do you plead guilty?*

eine Berufung verwerfen   *to dismiss an appeal*

Der Richter setzte sie auf freien Fuß   *The judge set them free*

Peter sagte gegen seinen besten Freund aus   *Peter gave evidence against his best friend*

Er handelte in Notwehr.   *He acted in self-defence*

Sie wurde zu drei Monaten Gefängnis verurteilt.   *She was sentenced to three months imprisonment.*

unter Eid   *on oath*

b) Die Organe des Rechtsstaates

das Arbeitsrecht (no plural)   *labour law*

der Friedensrichter (-)   *justice of the peace*

die Gerechtigkeit (no plural)   *justice*

das Gericht (-e)   *court of law*

das Gerichtsverfahren (-)   *legal proceedings*

die Geschworenen (plural only)   *jury*

das Gesetz (-e)   *law, statute*

das Gewohnheitsrecht (no plural)   *common law*

der Jurist (-en)   *lawyer*

die Menschenrechte (plural only)   *human rights*

der Prozeß (-sse)   *trial*

das Recht (no plural)   *justice, legal system*

das Recht (-e)   *right*

der Rechtsanwalt (-̈e)   *lawyer, barister*

die Rechtssprechung (no plural)   *jurisdiction*

der Rechtsstaat (-en)   *state based on the rule of law*

der Richter (-)   *judge*

das Schöffengericht (-e)   *trial by jury*

der Staatsanwalt/-in (plural: Staatsanwälte/innen)   *public prosecutor*

das Strafgesetzbuch (-̈er)   *penal (legal) code*

das Strafrecht (no plural)   *penal law*

die Verordnung (-en)   *bye-law*

die Urkunde (-n)   *charter*

das Völkerrecht (no plural)   *international law*

c) Das Privatrecht

die Alimente (plural only)   *maintenance payments*

die Beleidigung (-en)   *libel, slander*

das bürgerliche Gesetzbuch (BGB)   *civil code of law*

das Privatrecht (no plural)   *civil law*

der Schadensersatz (no plural)   *compensation*

die Scheidung (-en)   *divorce*

der Unterhalt (-e)   *maintenance*

die Verleumdung (-en)   *slander*

vor Gericht bringen (bringen, bringt, brachte, gebracht)   *to take to court*

einen Prozeß führen   *to take legal action*

jemanden verklagen   *to take someone to court*

d) Das öffentliche Recht

der Angeklagte (-n)   *defendant*

die Anklage (-n)   *accusation*

die Anklagevertretung (no plural)   *counsel for the prosecution*

der Augenzeuge/in (-en/innen)   *eye-witness*

die Aussage (-n)   *statement*

die Bandenkriminalität (no plural)   *organized crime*

die Beschuldigung (-en)   *accusation*

die Bestechlichkeit (-en)   *corruption*

die Bestechung (-en) *bribery*
der Betrug (-e) *fraud*
der Betrüger (-) *swindler*
die Bewährung (-en) *probation*
der Bewährungshelfer (-) *probation officer*
das Beweismaterial (-ien) *evidence*
der Dieb (-e) *thief*
der Einbrecher (-) *burglar*
der Einbruch (-e) *burglary*
der Eid (-e) *oath*
die Erpressung (-en) *blackmail*
das Gefängnis (-sse) *prison*
die Gesetzesbertretung (-en) *violation of law*
die lebenslängliche Freiheitsstrafe (-n) *life sentence*
die Haft (no plural) *imprisonment*
der Haftbefehl (-e) *warrant*
die Hinrichtung (-en) *execution*
die Körperverletzung (-en) *grievous bodily harm*
der Meineid (-e) *perjury*
der Mittäter (-) *accomplice*
der Mörder (-) *murderer*
das Opfer (-) *victim*
der Räuber (-) *robber*
das öffentliche Recht (no plural) *criminal law*
der (gute) Ruf (-e) *(good) reputation*
die Sachbeschädigung (-en) *damage to property*
die Steuerhinterziehung (-en) *tax evasion*
die Strafe (-n) *penalty*
das Strafgesetzbuch (StgB) *criminal code of law*
die Straftat (-en) *crime, criminal offence*
der Taschendieb (-e) *pick-pocket*
die Überführung (-en) *conviction*
die Unterschlagung (-en) *embezzlement*
das Urteil (-e) *sentence*
der Verdacht (no plural) *suspicion*
die Vergewaltigung (-en) *rape*
die Verhaftung (-en) *arrest*
das Verkehrsdelikt (-e) *traffic offence*
die Verteidigung (-en) *counsel for the defence*
der Vorbestrafte (-n) *person with a criminal record*
die Warnung (-en) *caution*

die Wiedereingliederung von Strafgefangenen *the rehabilitation of prisoners*
die Zelle (-n) *cell*

ableugnen *to deny*
anklagen *to accuse*
aussagen *to testify*
begnadigen *to pardon*
behaupten *to assert*
belasten *to incriminate*
mutwillig beschädigen *to damage in vandalism*
beschuldigen *to accuse of*
beschlagnahmen *to confiscate*
entlasten *to exonerate*
erpressen *to extort*
*frei*lassen (läßt frei, ließ frei, freigelassen) *to release*
freisprechen (spricht frei, sprach frei, freigesprochen) *to discharge, to acquit*
kriminell leben *to lead a criminal life*
kriminell werden *to become a criminal*
mißbrauchen *to misuse*
plädieren *to plead*
überführen *to convict*
untersuchen *to investigate*
verdächtigen *to suspect*
verhaften *to arrest*
eine Strafe verhängen verhängt, verhing, verhangen) *to impose a sentence*
verhören *to interrogate*
verleumden *to slander*
verurteilen *to condemn*
zu einer Geldstrafe verurteilen *to fine*
vollziehen (vollzieht, vollzog, vollzogen) *to carry out (a sentence)*
vorladen (lädt vor, lud vor, vorgeladen) *to summon*

erschwerend *aggravating*
gesetzlich, rechtmäßig *legal*
hart *severe*
mildernd *extenuating*
milde *lenient*
offenbar *evident*
rechtmäßig *legitimate*
ungerecht *unjust*
ungesetzlich *illegal*
unschuldig *innocent*
verdächtig *suspicious*

CURRENT AFFAIRS

1. Zeitungen, Journalismus

sie verfügt über ein ausgedehntes Korrespondentennetz *it has an extensive network of correspondents*
sie greifen in die Privatsphäre ein *they invade people's privacy*

Ein bekannter Politiker verklagt eine Zeitung auf Schadenersatz *A well known politician is suing a newspaper for damages*
Es besteht die Gefahr, daß Pressekonzerne ihre Macht mißbrauchen *There is the danger that press companies abuse their power*

Nur schlechte Zeitungen entwerfen ein Zerrbild (entwerfen, entwirft, entwarf, entworfen) *Only bad newspapers give a distorted picture*

Boulevardzeitungen wollen durch ihre Aufmachung Aufmerksamkeit erregen *Tabloid newspapers want to attract attention with their lay-out*

das Abonnement (-s) *subscription*
die Annonce (-n) *small advertisement*
die Anzeige (-n) *large advertisement*
die Auflage (-n) *circulation*
die Aufmachung (-en) *presentation, layout*
der Augenzeuge (-n) *eye witness*
die Ausgabe (-n) *edition*
die Balkenüberschrift (-en) *banner headline*
der Bericht (-e) *report*
die Bildunterschrift (-en) *caption*
die Blockschrift (no plural) *block letters*
die Boulevardzeitung (-en) *tabloid*
die Enthüllung (-en) *revelation*
aktuelle Ereignisse (plural only) *current affairs*
das Farbmagazin (-e) *colour supplement*
die Fernsehzeitschrift (-en) *TV-times*
das Feuilleton (-s) *feature pages*
die Illustrierte (-n) *magazine*
das Inserat (-e) *small advertisement*
der Journalist (-en) *journalist*
das Käseblatt (-er) *small local paper*
die Klatschspalte (-n) *gossip column*
der Knüller (-) *scoop*
der Kommentar (-e) *comment, analysis*
die Kritik (-en) *critique, review*
der Kummerkasten (-) *problem page*
der Leitartikel (-) *editorial*
die Leserschaft (no plural) *readership*
die Lokalzeitung (-en) *local newspaper*
die Meinungsvielfalt (no plural) *variety of opinions*
die Meldung (-en) *news item*
die Nachricht (-en) *news item*
der Nachrichtendienst (-e) *press/news service*
der Nachruf (-e) *obituary*
die Presseagentur (-en) *press agency*
die Pressefreiheit (no plural) *freedom of the press*
die Pressekonzentration (-en) *ownership of various papers by one person/company*
der Pressephotograf (-en) *press photographer*
die Problemseite (-n) *problem page*
der Redakteur (-e) *editor*
die Redaktion (-en) *editor's office*
die Regenbogenpresse (no plural) *rainbow press, tabloid magazine*
die Regionalzeitung (-en) *regional newspaper*

die Reportage (-n) *in depth report*
der Reporter (-) *reporter*
die Schlagzeile (-n) *headline*
der Sensationsbericht (-e) *sensational report*
der Skandal (-e) *scandal*
die Sonntagszeitung (-en) *Sunday newspaper*
die Spalte (-n) *column*
die Tageszeitung (-en) *daily newspaper*
der Verlag (-e) *publishing house*
der Verleger (-) *publisher*
die Verleumdung (-en) *libel*
das Wochenblatt (-er) *weekly paper*
die seriöse Zeitung (-en) *quality paper*
die Zensur (-en) *censorship*
das Zerrbild (-er) *distorted picture*

abonnieren *to subscribe*
sich *ab*spielen *to take place*
berichten *to report*
*durch*blättern *to flick through*
von vorne bis hinten durchlesen (liest durch, las durch, durchgelesen) *to read through from beginning to end*
sich ereignen *to take place*
erscheinen *to be published*
geschehen (geschieht, geschah, geschehen) *to take place*
sich auf dem laufenden halten *to keep oneself informed/ up to date*
eine Zeitung herausgeben (gibt heraus, gab heraus, herausgegeben) *to publish a newspaper*
melden *to report*
schildern *to report*
vorgehen (geht vor, ging vor, vorgegangen) *to take place*

auflagenstark *with a big circulation*
ausführlich *detailed*
monatlich *monthly*
objektiv *objective*
reißerisch *sensational*
richtunggebend *influential*
sachlich *objective, factual*
täglich *daily*
unsachlich, subjektiv *subjective*
voreingenommen *biased*
wöchentlich *weekly*

2. Das Wetter

Auf der Rückseite eines nach Osteuropa ziehenden Tiefs fließt ziemlich kalte Meeresluft nach Mitteleuropa. Nach nur kurzem, wenig wetterwirksamen Zwischenhocheinfluß folgen weitere Tiefausläufer nach. *Behind a low pressure front which is moving to Eastern Europe cold sea-air is coming to Central Europe. After a short,* ineffective temporary high pressure front further areas of low pressure will follow.

Nach Durchzug einer Warmfront Temperaturrückgang, von Westen auffrischender Wind *After warm air has passed through, temperatures will drop; increasing wind from the west*

der Bodenfrost (no plural) *ground frost*
die Brise (-n) *breeze*
die Dürre (-n) *drought*
die Eintrübung (-en) *clouding over*
die Feuchtigkeit (no plural) *humidity*
das Gewitter (-) *thunderstorm*
der Hagel (no plural) *hail*
das Hagelkorn (-er) *hailstone*
die Hitzewelle (-n) *heat-wave*
das Hoch (no plural) *high*
der Höchstwert (-e) *maximum temperature*
die Hochzelle (-n) *small area of high pressure*
die Kaltfront (-en) *cold-front*
das Klima (no plural) *climate*
der Luftdruck (no plural) *atmospheric pressure*
die Meeresluft (no plural) *sea-air*
der Niederschlag (-e) *precipitation (rain or snow)*
das Regengebiet (-e) *band of rain*
der Rauhreif (no plural) *hoar-frost*
der Regenbogen (-) *rainbow*
der Regenguß (-sse) *heavy shower*
der Regentropfen (-) *rain-drop*
die Schneewehe (-n) *snowdrift*
der Sprühregen (no plural) *drizzle*
der Sturmwind (-e) *gale*
der Tageswert (-e) *day-time temperature*
der Tau (no plural) *dew*
das Tauwetter (no plural) *thaw*
das Tief (no plural) *low*
der Tiefausläufer (-) *area of low pressure*
der Tiefstwert (-e) *minimum temperaure*
ein umfangreicher Tiefdruckkomplex (-e) *a large area of low pressure*
die Trockenheit (-en) *drought*
das Unwetter (-) *bad weather*
die Wetterlage (-en) *overall situation of the weather*
die Wettervorhersage (-n) *weather forecast*
die Windstille (-n) *calm*
die Wolkenauflockerung (-en) *breaks in the clouds*
der Wolkenbruch (-e) *cloudburst*
das Zwischenhoch (no plural) *temporary high pressure*

durchnässen *to soak*
frösteln *to shiver*

hageln *to hail*
heulen *to howl*
in Strömen regnen *to pour down*
rieseln *to drizzle*
tauen *to thaw*
tröpfeln *to trickle, drip*
überschwemmen *to flood, submerge*
wüten *to rage*

bedeckt *overcast*
dunstig *hazy*
drohend *threatening*
feucht *moist, damp*
frostig *chilly, frosty*
nebelig *foggy, close*
schwül *sultry*
stellenweise *in places*
unbeständig *changeable*
verhangen *overcast*
vorübergehend *temporary, passing*
wetterwirksam *affecting the weather*

3. Politik

aus politischen Gründen *for political reasons*
einen Vertrag unterzeichnen *to sign a treaty*
an einer Versammlung *teil*nehmen *to attend a meeting*
der Beschluß ist noch nicht gefaßt *the decision has not been reached yet*
eine Resolution verabschieden *to pass a resolution*
das Kabinett ist zurückgetreten *the cabinet has resigned*
an die Macht kommen *to come to power*
eine vernichtende Niederlage *a crushing defeat*
der Antrag wurde abgelehnt *the motion was defeated*
die Vertrauensfrage stellen *to ask for a vote of confidence*
die Gesetzesvorlage wurde mit großer Mehrheit angenommen *the bill was passed by a large majority*
Der neue Kanzler verspricht, die Reform zu einem Eckpfeiler seiner Politik zu machen *The new Prime Minister promises to make reform a cornerstone of his policy*
zum Handeln anspornen *to incite to action*
es besteht kein Wahlzwang *one is not forced to vote*
Die Opposition gewann bei der letzten Wahl an Boden *The opposition gained ground at the last election*
Dr. Meier stellt sich für den Bundestag zur Wahl *Dr. Meier is standing for election as M.P.*

(a) Der Abgeordnete(-n)   *member of parliament*

die Beliebtheit (no plural)   *popularity*
die Briefwahl (-en)   *postal vote*
die Bundestagswahl (-en)   *elections for the federal parliament*
die Hochrechnung (-en)   *election-result forecast based on a sample*
der Kandidat (-en)   *candidate*
die Kommunalwahl (-en)   *local election*
die Landtagswahl (-en)   *elections for the state parliament*
die Mehrheit (-en)   *majority*
eine geringe/absolute Mehrheit   *a small/absolute majority*
das Mehrheitswahlrecht (no plural)   *first-past-the-post voting system*
die Meinungsumfrage (-n)   *opinion poll*
die Nachwahl (-en)   *by-election*
das Plakat (-e)   *poster*
die Podiumsdiskussion (-en)   *panel debate*
die 5 Prozent-Klausel   *the 5 % clause (a party needs at least 5 % of the vote to be represented in the German parliament)*
der überwältigende Sieg (-e)   *landslide victory*
die Stimme (-n)   *the vote*
das Verhältniswahlrecht (no plural)   *proportional representation*
die Wahlbeteiligung (-en)   *the turnout (of voters)*
die Wahl (-en)   *election*
der Wähler (-)   *voter*
der Wahlhelfer (-)   *person helping with carrying out an election*
der Wahlkampf (-e)   *election campaign*
der Wahlkreis (-e)   *constituency*
die Wahlniederlage (-n)   *electoral defeat*
das Wahlrecht (no plural)   *right to vote*
die Wahlrede (-n)   *election campaign speech*
die Wahlurne (-n)   *ballot-box*
die Wahlversammlung (-en)   *(party) campaign meeting*
der Wahlzettel/Stimmzettel (-)   *ballot paper*

die Stimme abgeben (gibt ab, gab ab, abgegeben)   *to vote*
zur Urne gehen (geht, ging, gegangen*)   *to cast ones vote*
Stimmen verlieren (verliert, verlor, verloren)   *to lose votes*
wählen   *to vote, elect*

geheim   *secret*
stimmberechtigt   *those allowed to vote*
unmittelbar   *direct*
wahlberechtigt   *allowed to vote*

b) Das Parlament *parliament*

der Amstvorgänger (-)   *predecessor in office*
der Außenminister (-)   *Foreign Secretary*
der Beschluß (-sse)   *resolution*
der Bundeskanzler   *Chancellor (office like Prime Minister)*
der Bundespräsident   *president of the Federal Republic*
die/der Delegierte (-n)   *delegate*
der Finanzminister (-)   *Chancellor of the Exchequer*
die Gesetzgebung (no plural)   *legislation*
der Innenminister (-)   *Home Secretary*
das Kabinett (-e)   *cabinet*
der Kultusminister (-)   *Education Secretary*
die Opposition (no plural)   *opposition*
der Parlamentsbeschluß (-sse)   *act of parliament*
der Parteichef (-s)   *party leader*
der Politiker (-)   *politician*
die Regierung (-en)   *the government*
ein Sitz im Parlament   *a seat in parliament*
die Sitzung (-en)   *sitting*
das Staatsoberhaupt (-e)   *Head of State*
die Verfassung (no plural)   *constitution*
der Verteidigungsminister (-)   *Defence Secretary*
über einen Antrag abstimmen   *to vote on a proposal*
ein Gesetz aufheben (hebt auf, hob auf, aufgehoben)   *to repeal an act*
ein Gesetz einbringen (bringt ein, brachte ein, eingebracht)   *to introduce a bill*
ein Gesetz entwerfen (entwirft, entwarf, entworfen)   *to draw up a bill*
auf der Tagesordnung stehen (steht, stand, gestanden)   *to be on the agenda*
ein Gesetz verabschieden   *to pass a bill*
ein Gesetz verwerfen (verwirft, verwarf, verworfen)   *to reject a bill*
rechtskräftig werden (wird, wurde, geworden)   *to become law*
zurücktreten (tritt zurück, trat zurück, zurückgetreten*)   *to resign*

c) Die Partei (-en) *the party*

Die großen Parteien sprechen ungefähr zweidrittel der Wähler an   *the large parties appeal to about two thirds of the voters*
zum linken Flügel der Partei gehören   *to belong to the left wing of a party*
Diese Partei ist aus der Arbeiterbewegung hervorgegangen   *This party evolved from the workers' movement*

die Christlich Demonkratische Union
(CDU) *Christian Democratic Union*
die Fraktion (-en) *coalition party*
die Freie Demokratische Partei (FDP) *Free Democratic Party*
die Grünen *the Green Party*
die Koalition (-en) *coalition*
die Kommunistische Partei Deutschlands (KPD) *The Communist Party of Germany*
die Linke (no plural) *the left (politically)*
der Listenplatz (-e) *place on the party list*
die Partei (-en) *party*
die Parteiführung (-en) *party leadership*
das Parteimitglied (-er) *party member*
die Parteispende (-n) *donation to a party*
der Parteitag (-e) *party conference*
die Rechte (no plural) *the right (politically)*
die Sozialdemokratische Partei Deutschlands (SPD) *Social Democratic Party*
die Sozialdemokraten *Social Democrats*
die Sozialistische Einheitspartei Deutschlands (SED) *The Socialist Party of Germany (ruled in former East Germany as the only party until Nov. 1989)*

ansprechen (spricht an, sprach an, angesprochen) *to appeal to*
befürworten *to support*
fortsetzen *to continue*
gründen *to found*
vertreten sein *to be represented*

konservativ *conservative*
liberal *liberal*
reaktionär *reactionary*
sozialdemokratisch *social democrat*

d) Politischer Alltag *everyday politics*

die Auseinandersetzung (-en) *disagreements*
weitreichende Bedeutung (-en) *far-reaching importance*
die Bindung (-en) *commitment*
die Bürgerinitiative (-n) *ciizen's initiative*
die Entscheidung (-en) *decision*
die straffe Führung (-en) *strong leadership*
die Gefahr (-en) *danger*
die Kehrtwendung (-en) *U-turn*
eine schwere Krise *a deep crisis*
das Machtkartell (-e) *monopoly of power*
radikale Maßnahme (-n) *radical measures*
eine aufrührerische Rede (-n) *an inflammatory speech*

eine durchgreifende Reform (-en) *a complete reform*
der Skandal (-e) *scandal*
die Unterschriftensammlung (-en) *petition*
der Widerstand (-e) *resistance*
ein klares Ziel (-e) *a clear aim*

mit einem Problem fertig werden *to tackle a problem successfully*

düster *bad*
eindeutig *unmistakeably*
gestutzt *cut short*
geschrumpft *shrunk*
langandauernd *long-lasting*

4. Handel und Wirtschaft

a) der Großhandel *wholesale/foreign trade*

einen Absatzmarkt finden für (+Acc) *to find an outlet for*
nicht im Handel sein *to be off the market*
unser Handel ist zurückgegangen *our trade has decreased*
es besteht ein großer Bedarf nach (+Dat) *there is a great demand for*
seinen Zahlungsverpflichtungen nachkommen *to meet one's liabilities*
das Geschäft wirft jetzt Gewinn ab *the company is now showing a profit*
sie gehen wie warme Semmeln *they are selling like hot cakes*
den Markt überschwemmen *to flood the market*
sie verkaufen es mit Verlust *they are selling it at a loss*
es herrscht starke Nachfrage nach (+ Dat) *there is a great demand for ...*
ein Markt mit starker Konkurrenz *a highly competitive market*
die Produktion drosseln *to cut back production*
einen Betrieb stilllegen *to close down a factory*
in finanzielle Schwierigkeiten geraten *to get into financial difficulties*
wie der Preis, so die Ware *you get what you pay for*

die Absendung (-en) *dispatch*
die Abfertigung (-en) *dispatch*
die Aktiengesellschaft (-en) *company quoted on the stock market*
das Angebot (-e) *goods on offer*
der Auftrag (-e) *order*
die Ausfuhr (-en) *export*
die Beförderung (-en) *delivery, transport*
die Belegschaft (-en) *work force*

die Bestellung (-en)   *order*

der Betrieb (-e)   *firm*

das Brutto-/Nettogewicht (-e)   *gross/net weight*

der Dienstleistungsbetrieb (-e)   *service industry*

die Einfuhr (-en) *import*

der Einzelhandel (no plural) *retail trade*

der Export (-e) *export*

die Fabrik (-en) *factory*

die Firma (-en)   *firm*

das Geschäft (-e)   *business*

der Gewinn (-e)   *profit*

die GmbH (Gesellschaft mit beschränkter Haftung)   *limited company*

der Großhandel (no plural)   *wholesale trade*

die Haftung (-en)   *liability*

die Hochkonjunktur (-en)   *boom, up turn*

der Import (-e)   *import*

die Industrie- und Handelskammer   *chamber of commerce*

der Jahresumsatz (-e)   *annual turnover*

der Katalog (-e) *catalogue*

der Kauf (-e) *purchase*

die Konjunktur (-en)   *economic situation*

der Konkurrent (-en)   *competitor*

der multinationale Konzern (-e)   *multinational company*

das Lagerhaus (-er) *warehouse*

der Leiter/der Chef (-s) *boss*

die Lieferung (-en)   *delivery*

die Marktschwankung (-en)   *market fluctuation*

die freie Marktwirtschaft (-en)   *free market economy*

das Muster (-)   *sample, pattern*

das Modell (-e)   *pattern*

die Probe (-n)   *sample*

die Produktivität pro Kopf   *productivity per head*

die Quittung (-en)   *receipt*

die Rechnung (-en)   *invoice, bill*

die Rezession (no plural)   *recession*

das Risiko (plural: Risiken)   *risk*

die Schiffsladung (-en)   *cargo*

die Schutzmarke (-n)   *trade-mark*

der Teilhaber (-)   *partner*

der Überschuß (-sse)   *surplus*

das Unternehmen (-)   *business*

der Verlust (-e)   *loss*

das Verzeichnis (-se)   *catalogue*

die Ware (-n)   *merchandise*

die Wirtschaft (-en)   *economy*

die Wohlstandsgesellschaft (-en)   *affluent society*

die Zahlungsbilanz (-en)   *balance of payments*

der Zolltarif (-e)   *customs duty*

schnell erledigen   *to dispatch*

konkurrieren mit (+ Dat)   *to compete with*

vollziehen (vollzieht, vollzog, vollzogen)   *to execute*

flau, schlaff, lose   *slack*

vertraulich   *confidential*

b) Finanzwesen

die Bilanz aufstellen   *to strike a balance*

Geld auf der Bank haben   *to have money in the bank*

Geld von der Bank abheben   *to withdraw money from the bank*

Die Firma hat mir 500,– DM gutgeschrieben   *The firm put 500.– DM to my credit*

die Siemens-Aktie steht hoch im Kurs   *the Siemens share has a high value*

die Aktie (-en)   *share*

der Aktionär (-e)   *shareholder*

das Bankkonto (-en)   *bank account*

das Bargeld (no plural)   *cash*

die Börse (-n)   *stock-exchange*

der Börsenmarkler (-)   *stock-broker*

der Börsensturz (-e)   *collapse of share prices*

die Bürgschaft (-en)   *security*

die Devisen (plural only)   *foreign currency*

die Fusion (-en)   *merger*

die Geldanlage (-n)   *investment*

der Geldautomat (-en)   *cash-dispenser*

der Kapitalanleger (-)   *investor*

die Kontoüberziehung (-en)   *overdraft*

der Kredit (-e)   *loan*

der Kurs (-e)   *exchange rate/value of shares*

die Marktschwankung (-en)   *market fluctuations*

die Münze (-n)   *coin*

der Scheck (-s)   *cheque*

der Schein (-e)   *note*

der Schuldner (-)   *debtor*

Soll und Haben   *debit and credit*

der Spekulant (-en)   *speculator*

die Übernahme (-n)   *takeover*

das Übernahmeangebot (-e)   *takeover bid*

die Übertragung (-en)   *transfer*

der Umrechnungskurs (-e)   *exchange rate*

der Vorschuß (-sse)   *advance*

die Währung (-en)   *currency*

das Wertpapier (-e)   *share*

der Wucher (no plural)   *loans at extortionate rates of interest*

der Zins (-en)   *interest*

berechnen   *to calculate*

das Geschäft blüht   *business is booming*

bargeldlos *einkaufen*   *to shop without cash/with plastic*
einzahlen, *hinter*legen   *to deposit*
ein Konto führen   *to have an account*
handeln mit (+ Dat)   *to deal in*
Geld (ver)leihen   *to lend money*
sparen für (+ Acc.)   *to save for*
an der Börse spekulieren   *to speculate on the stock exchange*
eine Schuld tilgen   *to pay off a debt*
übertragen (überträgt, übertrug, übertragen)   *to transfer*

gewinnbringend   *advantageous*
reichlich   *ample*
verschuldet   *in debt*

c) Der Kleinhandel   *retail trade*

eine Rechnung bezahlen   *to settle an account*
bankrott machen   *to go bankrupt*
einen Preis erzielen   *to fetch a price*
die Preise steigen/fallen   *prices are going up/down*
preisgünstig verkaufen   *to sell at a good price*

der Besitzer (-)   *owner*
der Eigentümer (-)   *proprietor*
der Laden (-)   *shop*
der Ladenschluß (no plural)   *closing time*
der Ladentisch (-e)   *counter*
der Nutzen (no plural)   *benefit*
der Pächter (-)   *someone who rents a shop*
der äußerste Preis   *lowest price*
zum Preis von (+ Dat)   *at the price of*
der Räumungsverkauf (-e)   *clearance sale*
der lange Samstag (-e)   *Saturday when German shops stay open until the evening*
das Schaufenster   *shop window*
der Tante-Emma-Laden (coll.)   *corner shop*
der Umsatz (-e)   *turnover*
der Verbrauch (no plural)   *consumption*
der Verbraucher (-)   *consumer*
der Vorteil (-e)   *benefit*
das Warenhaus (-er)   *store, department store*
die Werbung/die Reklame   *publicity*
der Winter-/Sommerschlußverkauf   *winter/summer sales*

versteigern   *to sell by auction*

d) die Wirtschaftspolitik   *economic policy*

um seine Spitzenposition zu behaupten   *in order to maintain its leading position*
die BRD nimmt hinter den USA die zweite Stelle ein   *Germany is in second place behind the USA*
den Anschluß verpassen   *to miss the boat*
Man muß die Wirtschaft eines Landes auf eine solide Grundlage stellen   *One has to put the economy of a country onto a firm footing*
die Voraussetzung für die Lösung aller wirtschaftlichen Probleme   *the precondition for solving all economic problems*
das Handelsvolumen hat sich rasch vergrößert   *the trade has increased rapidly in volume*
die Schuldenkrise der Entwicklungsländer   *the debt crisis of third world countries*

die Abwertung (-en)   *devaluation*
das Außenhandelsdefizit (-e)   *trade gap/deficit*
das Bruttosozialprodukt (-e)   *gross national product*
der Etat (-s)   *the (government's) budget*
das Finanzamt (-er)   *Inland Revenue*
die Handelsbilanz (-en)   *balance of trade*
der Haushaltsplan (-e)   *budget*
die Mehrwertsteuer (no plural)   *V.A.T.*
die Steuer (-n)   *tax*
die Steuereinnahme (-n)   *revenue from taxes*
die Subvention (-en)   *subsidy*
eine stabile Währung (-en)   *a stable currency*
die Wirtschaftslage (-n)   *economic situation*
das Wirtschaftsministerium (plural: Wirtschaftsministerien)   *Department of Trade and Industry*
die Zahlungsbilanz (-en)   *balance of payments*
der Zinsanstieg (-e)   *rise in interest rates*

e) Europa   *Europe*
Grenzen-überschreitend zusammenarbeiten   *to work together across borders*
gemeinsam die Probleme der Zukunft lösen   *to solve the problems of the future together*
Der ECU wird als Kunstwährung eingeführt   *The ECU is being introduced as an artificial currency*
Man einigt sich (nicht) auf die Schaffung der Währungsunion.   *The creation of monetary union is (not) agreed upon*
Es war die Politik der kleinen Schritte   *It was a policy of small steps*
die Abhängigkeit der Landwirtschaft von Subventionen abbauen   *to reduce the depency of the agricultural industry on subsidies*

die Weiterentwicklung der Politischen
Union mit den Zielen einer
gemeinsamenAußen- und
Sicherheitspolitik *the further
development of the political union with
the aims of a common foreign and
defence policy*

die Abschaffung der Grenzformalitäten
the abolition of the border controls

die Agrarpolitik (-en) *agricultural policy*

die Ausdehnung der Gemeinschaft *the
enlargement of the European
community*

der Binnenmarkt (-̈e) *the single market*

die Entscheidungskraft *the power to
make decisions*

das grenzenlose Europa *Europe without
frontiers*

der/die Europa-Abgeordnete (-n)
*Member of the European
parliament*

die europäische Einigung *European
union*

die europäische Union *European Union*

das Gipfeltreffen (-) *the summit meeting*

der Maastricht-Vertrag *the Maastricht
treaty*

die Mitgliedsländer der EU *the member
countries of the EU*

das Referendum (plural: Referenden)
referendum

die föderative Struktur (-en) *federal
structure*

die Überschüsse (plural) *over-
production*

eine politisch handlungsfähige Union *a
community capable of taking political
action*

der Welthandel (no plural) *world trade*

f) Die persönlichen Finanzen *personal finances*

Peter ist immer knapp bei Kasse *Peter
is always short of money*

Wir leben von der Hand in den Mund
We live from hand to mouth

Diese Firma steckt noch immerin den
roten Zahlen *This firm is still in the
red*

Sie können sich kein Auto leisten *They
are not able to afford a car*

Du lebst über deine Verhältnisse *You
are living beyond your means*

Die Reichen leben wie Gott in
Frankreich *The rich live in luxury*

der Abzug (-̈e) *deduction (for tax, ect)*

die Ausgaben (plural only) *outgoings*

die Begüterten (plural only) *the wealthy*

das Darlehen (-) *loan*

das Einkommen (-) *income*

die Einkommensschwachen (plural)
people with a low income

die Geldsorgen (plural only) *money
problems*

die Hypothek (-en) *mortgage*

die Hypothekenzinsen (plural only)
mortgage interest rates

das Jahreseinkommen (-) *annual
income*

die Kaufkraft (no plural) *purchasing
power*

die Krankenversicherung (-en) *health
insurance*

die Kreditkarte (-en) *credit card*

die Lebenshaltungskosten (plural) *cost
of living*

der Lebensstandard (-s) *standard of
living*

die Miete (-n) *rent*

die Raten (plural only) *hire-purchase
payments*

die Steuergruppe (-n) *tax bracket*

die Steuervergünstigung (-en) *tax
allowance*

brutto/netto *gross/net*

5. Die Wiedervereinigung

a) die ehemalige DDR *the former GDR*

der Ausreiseantrag (-̈e) *application for
emmigration*

die Bespitzelung (-en) *spying on people*

der volkseigene Betrieb (-e) *factory run
by the state*

die komunisitische Diktaur *communist
dictatorship*

der Eiserne Vorhang *the Iron Curtain*

die Freizügigkeit (-en) *freedom of
movement*

die Jugendweihe *festivity to celebrate a
young person entering adolescence*

der Informant (-en) *informer*

das Kombinat (-e) *union of businesses
which produced similar items in
socialist countries*

die Mauer, die Berliner Mauer *the wall,
the Berlin wall*

der Mauerschütze (-n) *armed border
guard (at the Berlin wall)*

die Meinungsfreiheit (no plural)
freedom of speech

das Ministerium für Staatssicherheit
minstry for state security

der Ostblock (no plural) *eastern block*

der Passierschein (-e) *border pass*

die Planwirtschaft (-en) *planned
economy*

die Pressefreiheit (no plural) *freedom of
the press*

die Selbstschußanlage (-n) *automatic shooting system*
der Sozialismus (no plural) *socialism*
die Sozialistische Einheitspartei Deutschlands (SED) *Socialist party of the GDR*
der Spitzel (-) *informer*
der Stacheldraht (∸e) *barbed wire*
die Subvention (-en) *subsidy*
die Überwachung (-en) *surveillance*
die Versorgungsschwierigkeit (-en) *difficulties with supply*
die Verweigerung der Grundrechte *denial of basic human rights*
das Visum *visa*
die Volkspolizei *people's police*

inhaftieren *to imprison*
sozialistisch *socialist*
volkseigen *belonging to the people*

b) Die Bürgerbewegung (-en) *people's movement*

der Bürgerrechtler (-) *person campaigning for civil rights*
die Demokratisierung (-en) *democratisation*
der Demokratisierungsprozeß *process of democratisation*
die Demonstration (-en) *protest march*
das Ereignis (-se) *event*
die kirchlichen Gruppen (plural) *church groups*
die Volksvertretung (-en) *representation of the people*
die freien Wahlen *free elections*

Verhandlungen *auf*nehmen (nimmt auf, nahm auf, aufgenommen) *to start negotiations*
demonstrieren *to protest*
fordern *to demand*
*zurück*treten (tritt zurück, trat zurück, zurückgetreten*) *to resign*

c) Die Wiedervereinigung und ihre Probleme

die Herstellung gleicher Lebensverhältnisse *the creation of equal living conditions*
die Bewältigung *coping with*
Hüben und Drüben *this side and that side, West and East Germany*
das kurze Hochgefühl *the short lived euphoria*
Truppen *abziehen* *to withdraw troops*
die Grenzkontrollen beseitigen *to abolish boarder controls*
einen Vertrag billigen *to ratify a treaty*
der soziale Abstieg (no plural) *loss of social status*

die Arbeitsbeschaffungsmaßnahme (-n), ABM *job creation scheme*
das Anliegen (-) *concern*
der Aufschwung (no plural) *upturn*
das Begrüßungsgeld (-er) *money paid to East Germans as they came to West Germany*
der Einigungsvertrag (no plural) *treaty of unification*
der Grenzübergang (∸e) *border crossing point*
die Kosten der Einheit (plural only) *costs of unity*
die freie Marktwirtschaft (-en) *free market economy*
der Ossi (-s) *East German*
die Preisfreigabe (-n) *lifting of price controls*
die Staatsfürsorge (no plural) *state welfare*
der Strukturwandel (no plural) *structural changes*
die Treuhand *organization formed to transfer the former state-owned industries to private ownership*
die Übergangsfrist (-en) *transitional period*
der Umbruch (∸e) *upheaval, radical change*
der Umsiedler (-) *person moving from East to West Germany*
die Verdrossenheit (no plural) *displeasure*
die Verteilung des Wohlstandes *distribution of the wealth*
illusionäre Vorstellung (-en) *illusionary idea*
das Vorwärtskommen (no plural) *getting ahead*
die Währungsunion (no plural) *monetary union*
die Wende (no plural) *turnround, fall of the Communist Regime*
der Wessi (-s) *West German*
die Wettbewerbswirtschaft (-en) *economy based on competition*
die Wohnungsknappheit (no plural) *shortage of accomodation*
der zweite Jahrestag der deutschen Vereinigung *the second anniversary of German unification*
die Zuversicht (no plural) *confidence*

öffnen *to open*
in Kraft treten (tritt, trat, getreten*) *to come into being*
unterzeichnen *to sign*

konkurrenzfähig *competitive*
übereilt *rushed*

6. Ausländer

a) Die Einwanderungspolitik *immigration policy*

Gastarbeiter sind ein notwendiger Faktor der Wirtschaft *guestworkers are a necessary part of the economy*

nicht wenige Deutsche wollen die Gastarbeiter in ihre eigenen Länder abschieben *quite a few Germans want to repatriate foreign workers to their own countries*

Unfreundlichkeit seitens vieler Deutscher *unfriendliness from many Germans*

der völlig andersartige Kulturkreis *the completely different culture*

zweisprachige Analphabeten, die weder die deutsche noch die eigene Sprache beherrschen *bi-lingually illiterate, without proper knowledge of German or their own language*

das Recht auf Einbürgerung in die BRD *right to citizenship in the FRG*

kommunales Wahlrecht für Ausländer *the right of foreigners to vote in local elections*

die Familienzusammenführung *re-unification of families*

finanzielle Anreize zur Rückkehr in die Heimat *financial incentives to return home*

nur gebrochen Deutsch sprechen *to speak only broken German*

Man darf die Ausländerfeindlichkeit nicht wuchern lassen *Hostility towards foreigners must not be allowed to get out of hand*

der Andersartige (-n) *person who is different*

der Angriff (-e) *attack*

die Arbeitserlaubnis (-se) *work permit* (rarely in plural)

unqualifizierte Arbeit *unskilled work*

die Aufenthaltserlaubnis (-se) rarely in plural) *residence permit*

das Aufenthaltsrecht (no plural) *right of residence*

das Aufnahmeverfahren (-) *admission procedure*

der Asylant (-en) *asylum seeker*

das politische Asyl (no plural) *political asylum*

der Ausländer (-) *foreigner*

der ausländische Arbeitnehmer (-) *foreign worker*

die Ausländerfeindlichkeit (-en) *hostility towards foreigners*

das Ausländerwohnheim (-e) *hostel for foreigners*

der Ausreisewillige (-n) *person wanting to emigrate*

die Auswanderung (-en) *emigration*

auf der Durchreise *passing through*

der Einwanderer (-) *immigrant*

die Einwanderung (-en) *immigration*

die Freizügigkeit (no plural) *freedom of movement*

der Fremde (-n) *stranger, foreigner*

der Gastarbeiter (-) *foreign worker in Germany*

der Gewaltakt (-e) *acts of violence*

der Gewaltausbruch (-e) *eruption of violence*

das Ghetto (-s) *ghetto*

aus politischen Gründen *for political reasons*

das Herkunftsland (-er) *country of origin*

die Integration (no plural) *integration*

die Integrierung (no plural) *integration*

die Minderheit (-en) *minority*

das Mißverständnis (-se) *misunderstanding*

das Notaufnahmelager (-) *reception centre, transit camp*

der Umsiedler (-) *(German speaking) migrant*

die Ungleichheit (no plural) *inequality*

ärmliche Unterkunft (-e) *poor accomodation*

die Schwierigkeit (-en) *difficulty*

mangelnde Sprachkenntnisse *poor command of language*

die doppelte Staatsbürgerschaft (-en) *dual nationality*

das Visum (plural: Visen) *visa*

das Vorurteil (-e) *prejudice*

ändern *to change*

anwerben (wirbt an, warb an, angeworben) *to recruit*

sich auflehnen gegen *to rebel against*

Flüchtlinge aufnehmen (nimmt auf, nahm auf, aufgenommen) *to admit/absorb refugees*

begreifen (begreift, begriff, begriffen) *to understand, grasp*

beseitigen *to abolish*

der Immigration Einhalt gebieten *to stop immigration*

in Grenzen halten *to limit*

sich in die Lage hineindenken *to put oneself in someone else's shoes*

Viele können sich nicht in die Lage der Gastarbeiter hineindenken. *Many cannot put themselves in the shoes of the foreign workers*

hinweghelfen über (+ Acc.) *to help over* (hilft hinweg, half hinweg, hinweggeholfen)

integrieren *to integrate*

protestieren gegen (+ Acc.) *to protest against*

repatriieren *to repatriate*
den Zuzug sperren *to stop the influx*
verfolgen *to persecute*
verschärfen *to tighten up*
vorbeugen *to prevent*

elend *squalid*
erbärmlich *squalid*
schlechtbezahlt *badly paid*

b) Rassismus *racism*

Zeichen der Solidarität mit Ausländern
    setzen *to indicate solidarity with
    foreigners*
Sie bekunden ihren Abscheu für
    Gewalttaten *They demonstrate their
    disgust for acts of violence*
Die Schatten der Vergangenheit ziehen
    am Horizont auf *the shadows of the
    past appear over the horizon*
Die Zuwanderung von Menschen aus
    weniger wohlhabenden Ländern
        *The immigration of people from less
    wealthy countries*

die Anschläge auf Ausländer (plural)
    attacks against foreigners
die gewalttätige Ausschreitung (-en)
    violent attack
der Asylbewerber (-) *asylum seeker*
die Feidseligkeit (-en) *hostility*
der Halbstarke (-n) *thug*
der Kulturkreis (-e) *cultural background*
das Mißtrauen (no plural) *mistrust*
der Neo-Nazismus (no plural) *neo-
    nazism*
die Rassendiskriminierung (-en) *racial
    discrimination*
die Rassenunruhen (plural only) *racial
    disturbance*
die Rechtsextremisten (plural) *right
    wing extremist*
das Recht auf politisches Asyl *the right
    to political asylum*
das Wiederaufleben (no plural)
    resurgance

den Groll anfachen *to fuel resentment*
wieder auftauchen *to resurface*
ausnutzen *to exploit*
diskriminieren gegen (+Acc) *to
    discriminate against*
leiden unter (+Dat) (leidet, litt, gelitten)
    to suffer from
schikanieren *to harass, bully*
terrorisieren *to terrorise*
zusammenschlagen *to beat up*

7. Die dritte Welt

Es gilt, den krassen Unterschied
    zwischen Arm und Reich
    abzubauen. *The task is to reduce the
    great gulf between the poor and the
    rich.*
80 Prozent aller Krankheiten sind auf
    schlechtes Wasser
    zurückzuführen *80 % of all diseases
    can be traced back to dirty water*
gleiche Verteilung der vorhandenen
    Güter *equal distribution of the
    available goods*
die dringendsten Bedürfnisse des Lebens
    the absolute necessities of lifer
das Nord-Süd-Gefälle *the economic
    difference between northern and
    southern countries*
die Besserung der Lebensbedingungen
    improvement of living conditions

der Analphabet (-en) *illiterate person*
die Armut (no plural) *poverty*
die Bakterie (-n) *bacteria*
der Berater (-) *advisor*
der Brandt-Report *report on third world
    countries by former German
    chancellor Willi Brandt*
die Dürre (-n) *drought*
das Elend (no plural) *misery*
die Entwicklungshilfe (-n) *aid for
    development*
der Entwicklungshelfer (-) *person
    working on third world projects*
das Entwicklungsland (-er) *developing
    country*
die Erosion des Ackerlandes *erosion of
    farmland*
der Fortschritt (-e) *progress*
die Geburtenregelung (-en) *family
    planning*
die Hungersnot (-e) *famine*
mangelnde Hygiene *lack of hygene*
das Industrieland (-er) *industrialized
    country*
die Kindersterblichkeit (no plural)
    infant mortality
die Krankheit (-en) *disease*
niedrige Lebenserwartung (no plural)
    low life-expectancy
die Nahrung (no plural) *nutrition*
eigenständige Nahrungsmittelproduktion
    independent production of food
die Not (-e) *need*
das Projekt (-e) *project*
die Rohstoffpreise (plural only) *price for
    raw materials*
die Selbsthilfe (-n) *self-help*
die Sicherung der Grundbedürfnisse
    *securing the basic requirements of
    life*

die Spende (-n) *donation*
der Spender (-) *donor*
die Südhalbkugel (no plural) *southern hemisphere*
das Trinkwasser (no plural) *drinking water*
das Trockengebiet (-e) *dry land, area of drought*
der Tümpel (-) *water hole*
der Überfluß (no plural) *abundancy*
die Überschwemmung (-en) *flood*
die Überbevölkerung (no plural) *overpopulation*
die Unterernährung (no plural) *malnutrion*
der krasse Unterschied (-e) *the huge difference*
die Verminderung der Abhängigkeit *reduction of dependence*
die Wasserverseuchung (-en) *contamination of water*
die dritte Welt *third world*
die Weltgesundheitsorganisation *world health organization*
das Wirtschaftswachstum (no plural) *economic growth*

aufbauen *to build up*
ausbilden *to train, educate*
beitragen (trägt bei, trug bei, beigetragen) *to contribute*
entwickeln *to develop*
fördern *to support, aid*
gezielte Hilfe leisten *to give targeted aid*
organisieren *to organize*
schicken *to send*

8.Krieg und Frieden

a) Das Militär *the armed forces*

im Heer dienen *to serve in the army*
ein guter Schütze *a good shot*
außer/in Schußweite *out of/within range*
Der General steht an der Spitze der Streitkräfte *The general is at the head of the forces*
ein Lager aufschlagen/ schlägt auf, schlug auf, aufgeschlagen/ abbrechen bricht ab, brach ab, abgebrochen *to pitch/break up a camp*

die Abteilung (-en) *detachment*
der Admiral (-e) *admiral*
die Atombombe (-n) *nuclear bomb*
der Atomsprengkopf (-̈e) *nuclear warhead*
die Ausrüstung (-en) *equipment*
der (Ober-)Befehlshaber (-) *commander (in chief)*
die biologische Waffe (-n) *biological weapons*

die Brand-/Sprengbombe (-n) *incendiary/explosive bomb*
die Bundeswehr (no plural) *German armed forces*
die chemische Waffe (-n) *chemical weapons*
das Dienstgradabzeichen (-) *badge of rank*
der Düsenjäger (-) *jet fighter*
die Einberufung (-en) *call up/draft*
die Einheit (-en) *unit*
die Entwarnung (-en) *the all clear*
der Exerzierplatz (-̈e) *parade/drill ground*
die Fahne (-n) *flag, colours*
der Fallschirm (-e) *parachute*
der Fallschirmspringer (-) *paratrooper*
der Feldwebel (-) *sergeant*
der Fliegeralarm (no plural) *air-raid warning*
der Flottenstützpunkt (-e) *naval base*
der Flugplatz (-̈e) *airfield*
die Flugzeugabwehr (no plural) *anti-aircraft defence*
die Flugzeughalle (-n) *hangar*
der Flugzeugträger (-) *aircraft carrier*
der Freiwillige (-n) *volunteer*
die Garnison (-en) *garrison*
die Gasmaske (-n) *gas-mask*
das Geschwader (-) *squadron*
das Gewehr (-e) *rifle*
die Granate (-n) *shell*
der Hubschrauber (-) *helicopter*
die Infantrie/Artillerie (no plural) *infantry/artillery*
das Jagdflugzeug (-e) *fighter aircraft*
die Kaserne (-n) *barracks*
die konventionelle Waffe (-n) *conventional weapon*
der Kreuzer (-) *cruiser*
der Kriegshafen (-) *naval port*
die Kriegsmarine (no plural) *navy*
das Kriegsschiff (-e) *warship*
die Kugel (-n) *bullet*
die Langstreckenwaffe (-n) *long-range-weapon*
der Luftangriff (-e) *air-raid*
die Luftbrücke (-n) *air-lift*
der Luftschutz (no plural) *air-raid protection*
der Luftschutzkeller (-) *air-raid shelter*
die Luft-/Seeschlacht (-en) *air-/sea battle*
der Luftstützpunkt (-e) *air base*
die Luftwaffe (no plural) *air force*
die Luftwarnung (-en) *air-raid warning*
der Major (-e) *major*
die Mannschaft (-en) *crew*
das Manöver (-) *manoeuvre*
der Marschflugkörper (-) *cruise missile*
das Maschinengewehr (-e) (MG) *machine gun*

das Minensuchboot (-e)   *minesweeper*
die Munition (no plural)   *ammunition*
der Notruf (-e)   *S.O.S.*
der Oberleutnant/Leutnant   *first/second lieutenant*
der Oberst (-en)   *colonel*
der Panzer(kampfwagen) (-)   *tank*
die Patrone (-n)   *cartridge*
die Patrouille (-n)   *patrol*
die Pioniere (-)   *engineers*
die Pistole (-n)   *pistol*
das Regiment (-er)   *regiment*
die Rakete (-n)   *rocket*
der Rekrut (-en)   *recruit*
die Reserve (-n)   *reserves*
der Scharfschütze (-n)   *sniper*
der Scheinwerfer (-)   *searchlight*
das Schulschiff (-e)   *training ship*
die Schußwaffe (-n)   *firearm*
der Schützengraben (-)   *trench*
die Sirene (-n)   *siren*
der Soldat (-en)   *soldier/private*
der Splitter (-)   *splinter*
der Stahlhelm (-e)   *steel helmet*
die Streitkräfte (plural only)   *armed forces*
der Tornister (-)   *kit bag*
das U-Boot (-e)   *submarine*
der Unteroffizier (-e)   *corporal*
der Wachposten (-)   *sentry*
die Werft (-en)   *shipyard*
die allgemeine Wehrpflicht (no plural)   *general conscription*
die Verdunkelung (-en)   *black-out*
der Zerstörer (-)   *destroyer*

*ab*feuern   *to fire off*
Anker werfen/lichten   *to cast/to weigh anchor*
*aus*bilden   *to drill train*
*aus*rüsten   *to equip*
*ein*berufen (beruft ein, berief ein, einberufen)   *to call up/to draft*
explodieren   *to explode*
grüßen   *to salute*
schießen (schießt, schoß, geschossen)   *to shoot*
in die Luft sprengen   *to blow up*
*unter*gehen (geht unter, ging unter, untergegangen*)   *to go down*
*unter*tauchen   *to dive/submerge*
verwüsten/verheeren   *to devastate*
*(an)*werben (wirbt an, warb an, angeworben)   *to recruit, to enlist*

bombensicher   *bomb-proof*
luftdicht   *airtight*
wehrlos/schutzlos   *defenceless*

b) der Konfliktfall   conflict

am Rande eines Krieges stehen   *to be on the verge of war*

im Kriegsfalle   *in the case of war*
der Ausbruch von Feindeseligkeiten   *outbreak of hostilities*
den Krieg in Feindesland tragen   *to take the war to the enemy*
die feindlichen Stellungen wurden im Sturm genommen   *the enemy's positions were taken by assault*
den Sieg davon tragen   *to win the day*
Schon zweimal ist dieses Land gegen seine Nachbarn in den Krieg gezogen. (ziehen, zieht, zog, gezogen*)   *This country twice went to war against her neighbours*

die Abschreckung (-en)   *deterrent*
der Angreifer (-)   *aggressor*
das Atominferno (no plural)   *nuclear holocaust*
die Aufrüstung (-en)   *armament*
die neutrale Auslandspresse   *the neutral foreign newspapers*
die Besatzungstruppen (-)   *occupying forces*
das Blutvergießen (no plural)   *bloodshed*
das Bündnis (-se)   *alliance*
der Bürgerkrieg (-e)   *civil war*
der Einfall (-e)   *invasion*
die Eroberung (-en)   *conquest*
der Eroberer (-)   *conquerer*
die Explosion (-en)   *explosion*
das Feldlazarett (-e)   *field hospital*
der Feldzug (-e)   *campaign*
der Friedensvertrag (-e)   *peace treaty*
der Flüchtling (-e)   *refugee*
die Gefangenschaft (-en)   *imprisonment*
der Held (-en)   *hero*
die Heldentat (-en)   *heroic deed*
der Kampf (-e)   *combat*
die Kapitulation (-en)   *surrender*
die Genfer Konventionen (plural)   *Geneva convention*
der Kalte Krieg   *Cold War*
der Krieger (-)   *warrior*
der Kriegsgefangene (-n)   *prisoner of war*
der Kriegsschauplatz (-e)   *theatre of operations/of war*
das Kriegs-/Standrecht (no plural)   *martial law*
der Kriegsverbrecher (-)   *war criminal*
die kriegführende Macht (-e)   *belligerent power*
die Neutralität (no plural)   *neutrality*
die Niederlage (-n)   *defeat*
der Radar (no plural)   *radar*
der Rückzug (-e)   *retreat*
die Salve (-n)   *volley*
der Sieger (-)   *victor*
die Schrecken des Krieges (plural only)   *the horrors of war*
die Sturmangriff (-e)   *assault*

der Straßenkampf (-e) *fighting in the streets*

die alliierten Truppen (plural only) *the allied forces*

der Verbündete (-n) *ally*

die Verfolgung (-en) *pursuit*

die Verluste (plural only) *casualties*

der Verrat (no plural) (der Hochverrat) *treason*

der Verräter/in (plural: Verräter/innen) *traitor*

der Waffenhandel (no plural) *arms trade*

der Waffenstillstand (no plural) *cease-fire, armistice*

Verhandlungen *auf*nehmen/*ab*brechen/ *wiederauf*nehmen *to enter into/ break off/resume negotiations*

besiegen *to vanquish*

*ein*kreisen *to encircle*

entwaffnen *to disarm*

sich ergeben *to surrender*

*gefangen*nehmen *to take prisoner*

Widerstand leisten *to offer resistance*

einen Überfall machen auf (+Acc) *to raid*

plündern *to plunder*

in die Flucht schlagen *to put to flight*

Frieden schließen mit (+ Dat) (schließt, schloß, geschlossen) *to make peace with*

an Zahl überlegen sein *to outnumber*

im Krieg sein mit (+ Dat) *to be at war with*

in Brand stecken *to set on fire*

auf Widerstand stoßen (stieß, staß, gestoßen*) *to meet with resistance*

sich verbünden *to ally*

verraten (verrät, verriet, verraten) *to betray*

verwüsten *to lay waste*

in den Kampf ziehen (zieht, zog, gezogen*) *to go into action*

sich *zurück*ziehen (von + Dat) *to withdraw*

bedingungslos *unconditional*

beunruhigend *disturbing*

blutig *bloody*

entscheidend *decisive*

gefangen *captive*

kriegerisch *warlike*

siegreich *victorious*

ungleich *unequal*

vermißt *missing*

verzweifelt *desperate*

c) Der Friede

die Abrüstung (no plural) *disarmament*

der Abrüstungsvertrag (-̈e) *disarmament treaty*

die Beschwichtigung durch Zugeständnisse *appeasement*

der Blauhelm (-e) *blue berêt*

die Entspannungspolitik (no plural) *policy of reducing tensions between countries*

die Ethik (no plural) *ethics*

die Friedensbewegung (-en) *peace movement*

die Friedenssicherung (no plural) *peace-keeping*

aus Gewissensgründen *for reasons of conscience*

der Kriegsdienstverweigerer (-) *conscientious objector*

der Pazifismus (no plural) *pacifism*

der Truppenabbau (no plural) *reduction of troops*

die Vereinten Nationen (plural only) *United Nations*

der Zivildienst (no plural) *community service*

der Zivildienstleistende (-n) *person doing community service (instead of military service)*

Truppen *ab*ziehen *to withdraw troops*

wirtschaftliche Sanktionen *auf*stellen gegen (+ Acc) *to set up sanctions against*

Friedensverhandlungen führen *to conduct peace negotiations*

diplomatische Beziehung herstellen *to establish diplomatic relations*

Schwerter zu Pflugscharen schlagen (schlagen, schlägt, schlug, geschlagen) *to beat swords into ploughshares*

den Wehrdienst verweigern *to refuse to do military service*

---

1. Technologie und Gesellschaft

a) Im Büro

die Arbeit vereinfachen *to make work easier*

Zeit sparen *to save time*

Die Angestellten werden für andere Aufgaben freigestellt *The employees are freed for other tasks*

Routinevorgänge übernehmen (übernimmt, übernahm, über-nommen) *to take over routine processes*

qualifiziertes Personal benötigen *to need skilled staff*

die Büroarbeit rationalisieren *to make office work more efficient*

Aufträge werden per Telefonleitung übermittelt *Orders are transmitted by telephone line*

ein Dokument per Telefax schicken   *to fax a document*
an das Telefonnetz angeschlossen   *connected to the telephone network*
den Arbeitsplatz zu Hause haben   *to have one's work place at home*

die Akte (-n)   *file*
der Aktenschrank (-e)   *filing cabinet*
der Bildschirmtext (no plural)   *teletext*
die Datenübertragung (-en)   *data transmission*
die Datenvermittlung (-en)   *data transfer*
das Ferngespräch (-e)   *long-distance call*
das Glasfaserkabel (-)   *optical fibre cable*
das Ortsgespräch (-e)   *local telephone call*
die elektronische Post (no plural)   *electronic mail*
der Telefax (no plural)   *fax*
das Telefaxgerät (-e)   *fax-machine*

archivieren   *to store*
entlasten   *to free from*

b) In der Industrie

neue Arbeitsplätze schaffen   *to create new jobs*
besser ausgebildete Arbeiter   *more skilled workers*
Menschen werden durch Industrie roboter ersetzt   *people are being replaced by industrial robots*
monotone Arbeiten vermeiden   *to avoid monotonouos work*
vollautomatische Fertigung   *fully automated production*
Arbeitsplätze wegrationalisieren   *to cut down on the number of jobs*
Maschinen gefährden Arbeitsplätze   *machines put jobs at risk*
es unterliegt einem schnellen Wandel   *it is undergoing rapid changes*
Zeit- und Kostenaufwand verringern   *to reduce costs and time*

die Fertigungstechnik (-en)   *production technology*
der Technologiepark (-s)   *science park*

beschleunigen   *to accelerate*
ersetzen   *to replace*
verringern   *to reduce*

2. Die neue Technologie/Informatik

Komputer dringen in fast alle Lebensbereiche ein   *computers are entering into almost all areas of life*
In den Schulen wird computerunterstütztes Lernen betrieben   *Schools use computer-assisted learning.*

fast korrespondenzfähige Druckqualität   *Near Letter Quality (NLQ)*
Sie verbrachten viel Zeit dabei, Fehler zu beseitigen   *They spent a lot of time debugging*

nur zum persönlichen Gebrauch gespeicherte Daten   *data stored only for personal use*
die Ablage (-n)/   *file*
die Ausgabe (-n)   *output*
die Bearbeitung/Gestaltung des Textes (-en)   *editing*
der Bildschirm (-e)   *screen*
der Bug(s)   *bug*
die Datei (-en)   *file*
die Datenbank (-en)   *database*
das Datenschutzgesetz (-e)   *data protection law*
die Datenverarbeitung (no plural)   *data processing*
die Diskette (-n)   *floppy disc*
das Diskettensystem (-e)   *Disc Operating System (DOS)*
der Drucker (-)   *printer*
die Eingabe (-n)   *input*
die Graphik (-en)   *graphics*
die Hardware/Software (no plural)   *hardware/software*
die Hervorhebung (-en)   *highlighting*
die Informatik (no plural)   *information technology*
die Informationsgesellschaft (-en)   *information technology based society*
der Komputerfehler (-)   *computer error*
der Komputerterminal (-s)   *computer terminal*
das Komputerzeitalter (no plural)   *computer age*
das Laufwerk (-e)   *disc-drive*
der Mikrochip (-s)   *microchip*
das Netzwerk (-e)   *network*
der Positionsanzeiger (-)   *cursor*
ein fehlerhaftes Programm (-e)   *programme with faults*
die Sicherheitskopie (-)   *back-up*
der Speicher (-)   *memory*
das Spielprogramm (-e)   *games software*
die elektronische Stimme (-n)   *voice synthesiser*
das Tabellenkalkulationsprogramm   *spreadsheet*
die Taste (-n)   *key*
die Tastatur (-en)   *keyboard*
die Textverarbeitung (-en)   *word processing*
das Verbrauchsmaterial (-ien)   *consumable (paper etc)*
die Wissensexplosion   *the information explosion*
die Zugriffszeit   *access time*
der Komputervirus   *computer virus*

anzeigen *to display*
auflisten *to list*
bearbeiten *to edit*
löschen *to delete*
speichern *to save*

fett (gedruckt) *bold*
komputergesteuert *computer-controlled process*

3. Medizin und Forschung

a) Forschung allgemein

ein ressortübergreifendes Programm *an inter-disciplinary programme*
durch Ausprobieren *by trial and error*

die Abhandlung (-en) *treatise*
der Befund (-e) *result*
der Entdecker (-) *discoverer*
der Erfahrungswert (-e) *figures arrived at by experience*
das Ergebnis (-se) *result*
die Erkenntnis (-se) *insight/knowledge*
das Experiment (-e) *experiment*
der Fachausdruck (-̈e) *technical term*
der Fachmann (-̈er) *expert*
der Forscher (-) *researcher*
die Forschung (-en) *research*
der Fortschritt (-e) *progress*
das Gerät (-e) *apparatus*
das Labor (-s) *laboratory*
das Meßgerät (-e) *apparatus used for measuring*
die Messung (-en) *measurement*
die Methode (-n) *method*
das Reagenzglas (-̈er) *test tube*
das Resultat (-e) *result*
das Risiko (-en) *risk*
die Theorie (-n) *theory*
die Untersuchung (-en) *examination*
das Verfahren (-) *procedure*
der Versuch (-e) *experiment*
das Wissen (no plural) *knowledge*
der Wissenschaftler (-) *scientist*

bestätigen *to confirm*
bewältigen *to overcome*
eine neue Phase einleiten *to mark the beginning of a new phase*
einzeln angeben, (gibt an, gab an, angegeben) *to specify*
entwickeln *to develop*
erforschen *to investigate*
forschen (über + Acc) *to research into*
Pionierarbeit leisten *to pioneer*
ein Problem lösen *to solve a problem*
nutzbar machen *to utilize*
Abhilfe schaffen *to take remedial action*
an der Spitze stehen *to be in the lead*
verbessern *to improve*

Wirklichkeit werden (wird, wurde, geworden*) *to become reality*
zurückliegen (liegt zurück, lag zurück, zurückgelegen) *to be behind in something*

b) Medizinische Forschung

an die Grenzen des Wissens stoßen *to reach the limits of knowledge*
sich einer Organverpflanzung unterziehen *to undergo organ transplantation*
die Risiken vermindern *to reduce the risks*
moralisch und ethisch vertretbar *morally and ethically justifiable*
als Versuchskaninchen verwenden *to use as a guinea-pig*
zur Routine werden *to become routine*

die Behandlung (-en) *treatment*
das menschliche Erbgut (no plural) *human genetic make-up*
die Erbkrankheit (-en) *hereditary disease*
die Gen-Verpflanzung (-en) *genetic transplant*
die Heilung (-en) *cure*
die pharmazeutische Industrie (-en) *pharmaceutical industry*
die Wohlstandskrankheit (-en) *illness caused by affluence*
die Nachweismethode (-n) *detection technique*
die Nachwirkung (-en) *after-effect*
die Nebenwirkung (-en) *side-effect*
die Operation durch's Schlüsselloch *key-hole surgery*
die Operationstechnik (-en) *operation techique*
die Organverpflanzung (-en) *organ transplant*
das Retortenbaby (-s) *test-tube baby*
der Tierversuch (-e) *experiment on animals*
die Überlebensrate (-n) *survival rate*
der Ultraschall (no plural) *ultra-sound*
die Vorsorge (no plural) *prevention*

das Organ abstoßen (stößt ab, stieß ab, abgestoßen) *to rejct the organ*
ausmerzen *to eradicate*
einsetzen *to use*
einstellen *to stop*
die Genauigkeit erhöhen *to increase accuracy*
ein Organ ersetzen *to replace an organ*
genehmigen *to permit*
manipulieren *to manipulate*
jemanden quälen *to cause pain to somebody*

rechtfertigen   *to justify*
steigern   *to raise*

4. Der Verkehr

sich an den Baukosten beteiligen   *to share the cost of building*
den Individualverkehr auf öffentliche Verkehrsmittel umstellen   *to transfer private transport users onto public transport*
die Verkehrspolitik richtet sich nach dem Auto   *the traffic policy is oriented towards the car*
verkehrsberuhigende Maßnahmen   *traffic-calming measures*
die Beförderung (-en)   *movement of goods or people*
der Fernverkehr (no plural)   *long distance traffic*
die Grenze (-n)   *limit, border*
der Individualverkehr (no plural)   *individual traffic (i.e. car, moped, etc)*
der Nahverkehr (no plural)   *short distance traffic*
das Schienennetz (no plural)   *rail network*
die Sicherheit (no plural)   *safety*
der Straßenbau (no plural)   *road building*
das Straßennetz (no plural)   *road network*
die Strecke (-n)   *route*
der Ärmelkanal-Tunnel   *Channel Tunnel*
die Umweltbelastung (-en)   *pollution of the environment*
der Verkehrsminister (-)   *secretary of state for transport*
die öffentlichen Verkehrsmittel (plural only)   *public transport*
die Verkehrsplanung (-en)   *traffic planning*
die Verkehrsprobleme   *traffic problems*
die Verkehrssicherheit (no plural)   *safety of traffic*
der Zeitgewinn (-e)   *time-saving*

a) Die Eisenbahn   *railway*

das Abteil (-e)   *compartment*
der Anschluß (-sse)   *connection*
der Bahnsteig (-e)   *platform*
der Bahnwärter (-)   *signalman*
die Elektrolok (-s)   *electric engine*
die Entgleisung (-en)   *derailment*
das Fahrgeld (-er)   *fare*
der Fahrkartenschalter (-)   *ticket office*
der Fahrplan (-e)   *timetable*
finanzielle Hilfen (plural)   *subsidies*
das Gepäcknetz (-e)   *luggage rack*
der Gepäckwagen (-)   *luggage van*

der Güterwagen (-)   *truck*
der Güterzug (-e)   *goods train*
die Hauptstrecke (-n)   *main line*
die Hauptverbindung (-en)   *main line*
der Knotenpunkt (-e)   *junction*
die Lokomotive (-n) /Lok (-s)   *engine*
der Lokomotivführer   *engine driver*
die Nebenstrecke (-n)   *branch line*
die Notbremse (-n)   *emergency brake, communication cord*
die Oberleitung (-en)   *overhead cable*
der Personenzug (-e)   *slow train*
der Schlafwagen (-)   *sleeper car*
die Schranke (-n)   *barrier*
der Speisewagen (-)   *dining car*
die Streckenstillegung (-en)   *line closure*
die Subvention (-en)   *subsidies*
die Unterbrechung (-en)   *break (of journey)*
der Zugführer (-)   *guard*
das Zugunglück (-e)   *railway accident*
der Zusammenstoß (-sse)   *collision*
das Defizit abbauen   *to reduce the deficit*
entgleisen   *to derail*
verunglücken   *to have an accident*

besetzt   *occupied*
regelmäßig   *regularly*
überfüllt   *crowded*

b) der Flugverkehr   *air traffic*

der Flug muß wegen Nebel umgeleitet werden   *the flight has to be diverted because of fog*
den Flugverkehr lahmlegen   *to paralyse air-traffic*
lange Wartezeiten bei der Abfertigung   *long waiting times when checking in*

der Absturz (-e)   *crash*
die Bruchlandung (-en)   *crash landing*
das Cockpit (-s)   *cockpit*
das Düsenflugzeug (-e)   *jet-plane*
die Einflugschneise (-n)   *route taken by approaching aircraft*
das Fahrgestell (-e)   *landing-gear*
der Fallschirm (-e)   *parachute*
der Fluggast (-e)   *air passenger*
die Fluggesellschaft (-en)   *airline*
der Flughafen (-)   *airport*
der Fluglärm (no plural)   *air traffic noise*
der Fluglotse (-n)   *air-traffic controller*
der Fluglotsenstreik (-s)   *air-traffic controllers' strike*
die Flugroute (-n)   *flight path*
der Flugschreiber (-)   *black box, flight recorder*
der Hubschrauber (-)   *helicopter*
der Jet-lag (no plural)   *jet-lag*
der Luftraum (no plural)   *air space*
die Notlandung (-en)   *emergency landing*

die Pilotenkanzel (-n)   *cockpit*
der Rumpf (-̈e)   *fuselage*
das Segelflugzeug (-e)   *glider*
die Sichtweite (-n)   *visibility*
die Startbahn (-en)   *runway*
der Tiefflieger (-)   *low flying aircraft*
das Transportflugzeug (-e)   *cargo aircraft*
die Überschallgeschwindigkeit (no plural)   *supersonic speed*
das Verkehrsflugzeug (-e)   *commercial aircraft*
der Zeitunterschied   *time difference*

abstürzen   *to crash*
auftanken   *to refuel*
landen   *to land*
schweben   *to hover*
starten   *to take off*
steuern   *to pilot*

sichtbar   *visible*
zerschmettert   *smashed*

c) Die Schiffahrt

der Anker (-)   *anchor*
das Backbord (no plural)   *port (side)*
die Boje (-n)   *buoy*
der Bug (-e)   *bow*
das Bullauge (-n)   *porthole*
das Deck (-s)   *deck*
mit Dieselantrieb   *diesel-powered*
der Dampfer (-)   *steamer*
der Fischkutter (-)   *trawler*
die Flagge (-n)   *flag*
die Fracht (no plural)   *cargo*
der Frachtkahn (-̈e)   *barge*
das Frachtschiff (-e)   *freighter*
die Hafenanlagen (plural only)   *docks*
das Handelsschiff (-e)   *merchant ship*
das Heck (-s)   *stern*
der Kai (-s)   *quay*
die Kajüte (-n)/die Kabine (-n)   *cabin*
das Kielwasser (no plural)   *wake*
die Koje (-n)   *berth*
der Kran (-e)   *crane*
der Laderaum (-̈e)   *hold*
die Landungsbrücke (-n)   *landing-stage*
der Laufsteg (-e)   *gangway*
das Leck (-s)   *leak*
der Leuchtturm (-̈e)   *lighthouse*
der Lotse (-n)   *pilot*
die Mannschaft (-en)   *crew*
die Motoryacht (-en)   *motor yacht*
der blinde Passagier (-e)   *stowaway*
das Rettungsboot (-e)   *lifeboat*
der Rettungsring (-e)   *lifebelt*
das Rettungstau (-e)   *lifeline*
die Ruderpinne (-n)   *tiller*
der Schiffbruch (no plural)   *shipwreck*
der Schlepper (-)   *tug*
der Schleppzug (-̈e)   *train of barges*

die Schleuse (-n)   *lock*
die Schwimmweste (-n)   *lifejacket*
der Seeweg (-e)   *seaway*
das Segelboot (-e)   *sailing boat*
das Steuerbord (no plural)   *starboard*
der Tanker (-)   *tanker*
der Taucher (-)   *diver*
die Untiefe (-n)   *shallows*

ankern   *to anchor*
anlegen, landen, einlaufen (läuft ein, lief ein, eingelaufen*)   *to dock, to reach port*
sich einschiffen (nach) (+Dat)   *to embark (for)*
kentern   *to capsize*
auf Grund laufen   *to run aground*
vor Anker liegen (liegt, lag, gelegen)   *to ride at anchor*
in See stechen (sticht, stach, gestochen)   *to put to sea*

schiffbar   *navigable*
seetüchtig   *sea-going*
stürmisch   *stormy*
wellig   *wavy*

d) Straßen

eine Straße vierspurig ausbauen *to widen a road to four lanes*
die Auffahrt (-en)   *slip-road (to enter motorway)*
die Ausfahrt (-en)   *slip-road (to leave motorway)*
die Autobahn (-en)   *motorway*
das Autobahndreieck (-e)   *motorway junction*
das Autobahnkreuz (-e)   *motorway junction*
die Baustelle (-n)   *road works*
die Bundesstraße (-n)   *A-road*
die Durchgangsstraße (-n)   *through road*
die Einbahnstraße (-n)   *one-way street*
der Engpaß (-̈sse)   *bottle-neck*
der Feldweg (-e)   *farm track*
die Fernverkehrsstraße (-n)   *trunk road*
die Hauptstraße (-n)   *main road, high street*
die Landstraße (-n)   *country road*
die Linkskurve (-n)   *lefthand bend*
die Nebenstraße (-n)   *minor road*
das Pflaster (no plural)   *cobble stone*
die Ringstraße (-n)   *ring road*
die Sackgasse (-n)   *cul-de-sac*
die Schnellstraße (-n)   *express road*
der Straßenbau (no plural)   *road building*
die Straßendecke (-n)   *road surface*
der Teer (no plural)   *tar*
die Umgehungsstraße (-n)   *by-pass*
die Umleitung (-en)   *diversion*

der Umweg (-e)   *detour*
der direkte Weg   *direct route*

reinigen   *to clean*
teeren   *to tar*
eine Straße verbreitern   *to widen a road*

kurvenreich   *with many bends*
zweispurig   *with two lanes*

e) Fahrzeuge

der Auspuff (-e)   *exhaust*
das Auto (-s)   *car*
das Automatikgetriebe (-)   *automatic gear box*
der Autoreifen (-)   *car tyre*
der Benzintank (-s)   *petrol-tank*
der Blinker (-)   *indicator*
die Bremse (-n)   *brake*
das Ersatzteil (-e)   *spare part*
das Fahrzeug (-e)   *vehicle*
die Feder (-n)   *spring*
der Gang (-e)   *gear*
das Gaspedal (no plural)   *accelerator*
der Gebrauchtwagen (-)   *second-hand car*
die Hupe (-n)   *horn*
der Katalysator (-en)   *catalyst*
der Kindersitz (-e)   *child seat*
der Kofferraum (-e)   *boot*
der Kombi (-s)   *estate car*
der Kühler (-)   *radiator*
die Kupplung (no plural)   *clutch*
der Lastkraftwagen (LKW) (-)   *lorry (official term)*
der Lastwagen (-)   *lorry*
die Lenksäule (-n)   *steering column*
der Lieferwagen (-)   *van*
das Moped (-s)   *moped*
das Motorrad (-er)   *motorbike*
die Motorhaube (-n)   *bonnet*
der Personenkraftwagen (PKW) (-)   *car (official term)*
der Rennwagen (-)   *racing car*
der Rücksitz (-e)   *rear seat*
der Rückwärtsgang (no plural)   *reverse gear*
der Schalthebel (-)   *gear lever*
der Scheibenwischer (-)   *windscreen wiper*
der Scheinwerfer (-)   *head light*
der Sicherheitsgurt (-e)   *seat belt*
das Schlußlicht (-er)   *rear light*
der Sportwagen (-)   *sports car*
das Steuerrad/Lenkrad (-er)   *steering wheel*
die Stoßstange (-n)   *bumper*
der Tacho(meter) (-s/ -)   *speedometer*
der Türgriff (-e)   *door handle*
der Vordersitz (-e)   *front seat*
der Wagenheber (-)   *jack*

das Warnblinklicht (no plural)   *hazard warning lights*
die Windschutzscheibe (-n)   *windscreen*
die Zündkerze (-n)   *spark-plug*

abblenden   *to dip the headlights*
abschleppen   *to tow*
sich anschnallen   *to fasten one's seatbelt*
aufpumpen   *to pump up*
beschleunigen/Gas geben   *to accelerate*
hupen   *to honk*
vorsichtig fahren (fährt, fuhr, gefahren*)   *to drive carefully*
gründlich nachsehen (sieht nach, sah nach, nachgesehen)   *to overhaul*
schleudern   *to skid*
einen Helm tragen (trägt, trug, getragen)   *to wear a helmet*
überholen   *to overtake*
umstürzen   *to overturn*

schlauchlos   *tubeless*
verkehrssicher   *roadworthy*

f) Der Straßenverkehr

der Auffahrunfall (-e)   *hitting the back of another vehicle*
der Führerschein (-e)   *driving licence*
die Fahrerlaubnis (-se)   *driving licence (official term)*
die Fahrschule (-n)   *driving school*
die Fahrprüfung (-en)   *driving test*
die Glasscherben (plural only)   *broken glass*
die Geldstrafe (-n)   *fine*
die Geschwindigkeitsbegrenzung (-en)   *speedlimit*
das Halteverbot (-e)   *no waiting zone*
die zugelassene Höchstgeschwindigkeit   *permitted top speed*
die Karambolage (-n)   *pile-up*
der Parkplatz (-e)   *car parking space*
das Parkverbot (-e)   *no parking area*
die 0,8 Promillengrenze   *permitted level of blood alcohol when driving*
rechts vor links   *traffic from the right has priority over that coming from the left*
die Radarkontrolle (-n)   *radar speed trap*
die Richtgeschwindigkeit (-en)   *advised speed on motorways*
der Strafzettel (-)   *parking ticket*
der Straßenverkehr (no plural)   *road traffic*
die Straßenverkehrsordnung (no plural)   *highway code*
mit 130 Stundenkilometern (km/h)   *at 130 km/h*
die Tiefgarage (-n)   *underground car-park*
die Trunkenheit am Steuer   *drink driving*

das Überholverbot (-e) *no overtaking area*
der Unfall (⁺e) *accident*
das Verkehrsopfer (-) *road casualty*
das Verkehrszeichen (-) *traffic sign*
die Vorfahrt (no plural) *priority over another car*
der Zusammenstoß (⁺sse) *collision*

zu dicht auffahren (fährt auf, fuhr auf, aufgefahren) *to drive too close to another car*
ins Schleudern geraten (gerät, geriet, geraten*) *to get into a skid*
Abstand halten (hält, hielt, gehalten) *to keep one's distance*
ein Verkehrshindernis sein *to cause an obstruction*
jemanden überfahren *to run someone over*
die Geschwindigkeit überschreiten (überschreitet, überschritt, überschritten) *to exceed the speed limit*
frontal *zusammen*stoßen (stößt zusammen, stieß zusammen, zusammengestoßen*) *to collide head-on with someone*
für alle Fahrzeuge gesperrt *closed to all vehicles*

5. Verbindungen

das Autotelefon (-e) *car phone*
der Empfänger (-) *receiver*
die Fax-Maschine (-n) *fax*
der Fernschreiber (-) *telex*
der Funker (-) *wireless-operator*
das Funkgerät (-e) *walky-talky*
der Funkspruch (⁺e) *radio message*
die Kommunikation (-en) *communication*
das Komputernetzwerk (-e) *computer network*
das Komputerzeitalter (no plural) *computer age*
der Nachrichtendienst (-e) *news-service*
die Nachrichtenübermittlung (-en) *news-transmission*
die Post (no plural) *post office, mail*
der Programmierer (-) *programmer*
der Sender (-) *sender*
das Telefon (-e) *telephone*
das drahtlose Telefon *cordless telephone*
das Telefongespräch (-e) *telephone-call*
das Telegramm (-e) *telegramme*

empfangen (empfängt, empfing, empfangen) *to receive*
in Verbindung stehen mit (steht, stand, gestanden) *to be in touch with*
übermitteln *to transmit*

drahtlos *wireless*

6. Die Raumfahrt

die Abgelegenheit (no plural) *remoteness*
die Abschußrampe (-n) *launching pad*
das All (no plural) *space*
die Antenne (-n) *ariel*
der Astronaut (-en) *astronaut*
die Ausdehung (-en) *dimension*
die Bodenstation (-en) *earth-station*
die Daten (plural only) *data*
die Dreistufenrakete (-n) *three-stage rocket*
das äußerste Ende *extremity*
der Kontrollraum (⁺e) *control-room*
der Fernsehsatellit (-en) *TV-satellite*
die Fläche (-n) *expanse*
die Flugkontrolle (-n) *flight-control*
die Forschungsgeräte (plural only) *research equipment*
die Grenze (-n) *frontier*
der Kontakt (-e) *contact*
die Landung (-en) *landing*
die erste Landung auf dem Mond *the first landing on the moon*
der Lotse (-n) *pilot*
die Mondlandefähre (-n) *lunar module*
die Rakete (-n) *rocket*
der luftleere Raum *vacuum*
der Raumanzug (⁺e) *space suit*
die Raumfahrt (no plural) *space travel*
das Raumfahrzeug (-e) *space-vehicle*
die Raumkapsel (-n) *space capsule*
das Raumschiff (-e) *space ship*
die Raumsonde (-n) *space probe*
der Raumtransporter (-) *space shuttle*
die Reichweite (-n) *range*
der Satellite (-en) *satellite*
die Schwerelosigkeit (no plural) *weightlessness*
das Signal (-e) *signal*
der Start (-s) *start*
die Sternwarte (-n) *observatory*
das Teleskop (-e) *telescope*
der Treibstoff (-e) *fuel*
die Umlaufbahn (-en) *orbit*
das Vacuum (no plural) *vacuum*
der Weltraum (no plural) *space*
die europäische Weltraum-Organisation *European Space Agency*
das Weltraumrennen *space-race*
die bemannte Weltraumstation (-en) *manned space station*
die Weltraumwaffe (-n) *space weapons*
das Weltraumzeitalter (no plural) *space age*
der Wettersatellit (-en) *weather satellite*

absteigen (steigt ab, stieg ab, abgestiegen*) *to descend*
*aus*dehnen *to expand*
erforschen *to explore*

neue Erkenntnisse gewinnen (gewinnt,
  gewann, gewonnen)   *to gain new
  knowledge*
*hinauf*steigen   *to go up (into the air)*
Proben sammeln   *to take samples*
schweben   *to hover*

ausgedehnt   *extensive*
zentral gelegen   *centrally located*
umfangreich   *voluminous, bulky*
umfassend   *comprehensive*
weit verbreitet   *widespread*
weitreichend   *far-reaching*

**CULTURE AND
GEOGRAPHY**

1. Die deutschsprachigen Länder

a) Die Schweiz

der Kanton (-e)   *Canton, district in
  Switzerland*
der Eidgenosse (-n)   *Swiss citizen*
die Eidgenossenschaft (no plural)
  *confederation by oath (Swiss
  constituion)*
die Neutralität (no plural)   *neutrality*
die Unabhängigkeit (-en)   *independence*
die Unabhängigkeitserklärung (-en)
  declaration of independence
der Staatenbund (-̈e)   *confederation of
  states*
die Bundeshauptstadt (-̈e)   *federal
  capital city*
der Bergbauer (-n)   *mountain farmer*
die Alm (-en)   *alpine pasture*
die Sprachenvielfalt (no plural)   *variety
  of languages*

b) Österreich

das Kaffeehaus (-̈er)   *cafe*
die Habsburger   *name of the last dynasty
  of Austrian monarchs*
die Donau   *Danube*

c) Liechtenstein

der Zwergstaat (-en)   *small country*
das Fürstentum (-̈er)   *princedom*
unter schweizer Verwaltung   *under
  Swiss administration*
von der Schweiz vertreten   *represented
  by Switzerland*

2. Geographie

a) Flüsse

der Bach (-̈e)   *stream*
der Binnenhafen (-)   *riverport*
das Binnenschiff (-e)   *riverboat*
die Fahrrinne (-n)   *deepest part of a river
  which is used for navigation*
die Flußmündung (-en)   *estuary*
das Flußufer (-)   *river bank*
die Furt (-en)   *ford*

der Kanal (-̈e)   *canal*
der Nebenfluß (-̈sse)   *tributary*
die Quelle (-n)   *source*
die Schiffahrt (no plural)   *shipping*
die Schleuse (-n)   *lock*
der Strom (-̈e)   *big river*
die Strömung (-en)   *current*
der Strudel (-)   *whirlpool, eddy*
der Sumpf (-̈e)   *bog, marsh*
die Talsperre (-n)   *dam*
stehendes Wasser   *stagnant water*
der Wasserfall (-e)   *waterfall*
die Überschwemmung (-en)   *inundation*
die Wasserscheide (-n)   *watershed*

*hervor*sprudeln   *to burst forth*
überfließen (überfließt, überfloß,
  überflossen)   *to overflow*
überfluten   *to submerge, flood*

schiffbar   *navigable*
seicht   *shallow*
sumpfig   *marshy*
trübe   *muddy*

b) das Gebirge

der Abhang (-̈e)   *slope*
die Anhöhe (-n)   *rise*
die Bergkette (-n)   *mountain range*
der Bergrücken (-n)   *ridge*
die Bergschlucht (-en)   *ravine*
der Erdrutsch (no plural)   *landslip*
der Gipfel (-)   *summit*
der Gletscher (-)   *glacier*
der Hang (-̈e)   *slope*
die Hochebene (-n)   *plateau*
das Hochland (-̈er)   *upland area*
die Höhle (-n)   *cave*
die Lawine (-n)   *avalanche*
der Paß (-̈sse)   *pass*
die Schlucht (-en)   *gorge*
der Steinblock (-̈e)   *boulder*
das Vorgebirge (-)   *foothills*
der Vulkan (-e)   *volcano*

abrutschen   *to slide down*
bergsteigen (only used in the infinitive
  and the past participle:
  berggestiegen*)   *to mountain climb*

steil   *steep*
erloschen   *extinct (of a volcano)*

c) Die Meere

die Brandung (-en) *breakers*
die Bucht (-en) *bay*
der Deich (-e) *dyke*
die Düne (-n) *sandhill, dune*
die Ebbe (no plural) *low tide*
das Festland (⸗er) *mainland*
die Flut (no plural) *high tide*
die Gezeiten (plural only) *tides*
die Halbinsel (-n) *peninsula*
die Insel (-n) *island*
das Meer (-e) *sea*
die Meerenge (-n) *strait*
der Meeresspiegel (no plural) *sea-level*
das Kap (-s) *cape*
die Klippe (-n) *cliff*
die Küste (-n) *shore*
die Küstenwache (-en) *coast guard*
die Landenge (-n) *isthmus*
die Sandbank (⸗e) *sand-bank*
der Strand (⸗e) *beach*
die Sturmflut (-en) spring tide

d) Allgemeine Begriffe

der Äquator *equator*
die Ebene (-n) *plain*
das Erdbeben (-) *earthquake*
die Halbkugel (-n) *hemisphere*
die Heide (-n) *heathland*
der Horizont (-e) *horizon*
der Kontinent (-e) *continent*
die Lichtung (-en) *clearing*
das Moor (-e) *swamp, fen*
der Nordpol *north pole*
die Oase (-n) *oasis*
der Südpol *south pole*
die Weide (-n) *pasture*
die Wüste (-n) *desert*

e) Ländernamen

Land Nationalität Adjektiv Meaning
Afrika Afrikaner/in afrikanisch
    Africa
Amerika Amerikaner/in
    amerikanisch *America*
Asien Asiate/in asiatisch *Asia*
Australien Australier/in
    australisch *Australia*
Belgien Belgier/in belgisch *Belgium*
China Chinese/in chinesisch
    China
Dänemark Däne/in dänisch
Denmark
Deutschland Deutsche/r deutsch
    Germany
England Engländer/in englisch
    England
Europa Europäer europäisch
    Europe

Frankreich Franzose/in
    französisch *France*
Griechenland Grieche/in
    griechisch *Greece*
Großbritannien Brite/in britisch
    Great Britain
Holland Holländer/in holländisch
    Holland
Indien Inder/in indisch *India*
Italien Italiener/in italienisch *Italy*
Ireland Ire/in irisch *Ireland*
Israel Israeli israelisch Israel
Japan Japaner apanisch *Japan*
die Niederlande/ Niederländer/in
    niederländisch *Netherlands*
Neuseeland Neuseeländer/in
    neuseeländisch *New Zealand*
Norwegen Norweger/in
    norwegisch *Norway*
Österreich Österreicher/in
    österreichisch *Austria*
Polen Pole/in polnisch *Poland*
Rußland Russe/in russisch *Russia*
Schottland Schotte/in schottisch
    Scotland
Schweden Schwede/in *schwedisch*
    Sweden
die Schweiz Schweizer/in
    schweizerisch *Switzerland*
Spanien Spanier/in spanisch *Spain*
Ungarn Ungar/in ungarisch
    Hungary
die Vereinigten Staaten (von America)
    The USA
Wales Waliser/in walisisch *Wales*

f) Geographische Bezeichnungen

die Alpen *the Alps*
der Ärmelkanal *the English Channel*
der Atlantik *the Atlantic Ocean*
der Bodensee *Lake Constance*
die Donau *Danube*
die Irische See *Irish Sea*
das Mittelmeer *Mediterranean Sea*
die Nordsee *North Sea*
der Nahe Osten *Middle East*
der Ferne Osten *Far East*
die Ostsee *Baltic Sea*
der Pazifik *Pacific Ocean*
die Pyrenäen *the Pyrenees*
der Rhein *Rhine*
Siebenbürgen *Transylvania*
die Themse *Thames*

g) Städtenamen/Ländernamen

Aachen *Aix-la-Chapelle*
Bayern *Bavaria*
Bern *Berne*
Bozen *Bolzano*
Brüssel *Brussels*
Den Haag *The Hague*

Edinburg *Edinburgh*
Genf *Geneva*
Hanover *Hannover*
Köln *Cologne*
Kopenhagen *Copenhagen*
Lüttich *Liège*
Mailand *Milan*
Moskau *Moscow*
München *Munich*
Neapel *Naples*
Niedersachsen *Lower Saxony*
Rheinland-Pfalz *Rhineland- Palatinate*
Rom *Rome*
Schlesien *Silesia*
Straßburg *Strasbourg*
Thüringen *Thuringia*
Venedig *Venice*
Warschau *Warsaw*
Wien *Vienna*

3. Essen und Trinken

a) Die Ernährung

der Appetit (-e) *appetite*
der Bluthochdruck (no plural) *high blood presure*
der Blutfett (Cholesterin-)Spiegel (no plural) *cholesterol level*
der Braten (-) *roast meat*
die Diät (no plural) *diet*
das Eingemachte (no plural) *preserves*
die Energiezufuhr (no plural) *energy intake*
die Ernährung (no plural) *nutrition*
die Ernährungsgewohnheit (-en) *eating habit*
das Fett (-e) *fat*
das Geflügel (no plural) *poultry*
die Getreideflocken (plural only) *cereals*
die Gewichtskontrolle (-n) *weight control*
das Gewürz (-e) *spice*
die Grundnahrungsmittel (plural only) *basic food stuff*
das Hammelfleisch (no plural) *mutton*
das Kalbfleisch (no plural) *veal*
die Karies (no plural) *tooth decay*
die Kilokalorie (-n) *kcal*
die Kohlenhydrate (plural only) *carbohydrates*
das Kotelett (-s) *chop*
die Magersucht (no plural) *anorexia*
die Nahrung (no plural) *food*
die Nahrungsmittel (plural only) *foodstuff*
die Pflanzenfaser (-n) *fibre*
das Rheuma *rheumatism*
das Schweinefleisch (no plural) *pork*
die Soße (-n) *sauce*
das Übergewicht (-e) *excess weight*

der Pro-Kopf-Verbrauch (no plural) *consumption per head*
der Verbraucher (-) *consumer*
die Verstopfung (-en) *constipation*
der Verzehr (no plural) *consumption (of food)*
die Zusammensetzung der Nahrung *composition of food*
die Zuckerkrankheit (no plural) *diabetes*

auspressen *to squeeze*
backen *to bake*
sich bemühen *to make an effort*
braten *to roast*
dünsten *to steam*
drosseln *to reduce*
kochen *to boil*
rösten *to toast*
schälen *to peel*
schlucken *to swallow*
schmoren *to fry*
verschlingen *to devour*
verzehren *to consume*
würzen *to flavour*

künstlich *artificial*
lecker *tasty*
magersüchtig *anorexic*
saftig *juicy*
schmackhaft *tasty*
übermäßig *excessive*
umsetzbar *convertible*
unausgewogen *unbalanced*
verfault *rotten*

b) Die Getränke

Sie löscht ihren Durst *She quenches her thirst*
Die Soldaten trinken auf die Gesundheit der Königin *The soldiers drink to the health of the queen*
Er trinkt viel *he is a heavy drinker*

der Alkohol (no plural) *alcohol*
der Branntwein (-e) *brandy*
das Getränk (-e) *drink*
das alkoholfreie Getränk (-e) *soft drink*
der Korken (-) *cork*
der Punsch (no plural) *punch*
der Qualitätswein (-e) (mit Predikat) *wine of (high) quality*
die Trunkenheit (no plural) *drunkenness*
die Überproduktion (-en) *over-production*
der Weinbau (no plural) *wine farming*
der Weinberg (-e) *vinyard*
die Weinprobe (-n) *wine tasting*
der Weinsee (no plural) *wine lake*
der Winzer *wine-producer*

aromatisch   *aromatic*
herb   *dry*
lieblich   *sweet*
vollmundig *rounded*

4. Literatur und Theater

a) Literatur allgemein

Forssetzung folgt   *to be continued*
das Buch ist soeben erschienen   *the book has just come out*

die (kurze) Abhandlung (-en)   *essay*
die Abkürzung (-en)   *abbreviation*
der Abschnitt (-e)   *paragraph*
der Ausdruck (-̈e)   *phrase*
die Ausdrucksweise (-n)   *style*
die Ausgabe (-n)   *edition*
die gebundene Ausgabe (-n)   *hardback edition*
die Aussprache (-n)   *pronunciation*
der Auszug (-̈e)   *extract*
die Autobiographie (-n)   *autobiography*
der Band (-̈e)   *volume*
die Begebenheit (-en)   *event, incident*
die Belletristik (no plural)   *fiction and poetry*
der Bildungsroman (-e)   *novel about the development of a character*
der Charakter (-e)   *character of a person*
die Dichtkunst (no plural)   *the art of poetry*
das Drama (-en)   *drama*
die Druckspalte (-n)   *column*
der Eindruck (-̈e)   *impression*
die Einfachheit (-en)   *simplicity*
die Einleitung (-en)   *introduction*
die Einzelheit (-en)   *detail*
die Erläuterung (-en)   *comment*
die Erzählung (-en)   *tale, story*
das Exemplar (-e)   *copy*
die Flüssigkeit (no plural)   *fluency*
die Frauenliteratur (no plural)   *books by women*
die Gattung (-en)   *genre*
das Gedicht (-e)   *poem*
der Gemeinplatz (-̈e)   *commonplace*
die Geschmacksache (-n)   *matter of taste*
die Gruselgeschichte (-n)   *horror story*
der Herausgeber (-)   *editor*
die Handlung (-en)   *plot*
der Höhepunkt (-e)   *climax*
das Hochdeutsch (no plural)   *standard German*
der Inhalt (no plural)   *contents*
die Inhaltsangabe (-n)   *resume, precis*
das Inhaltsverzeichnis (-se)   *table of contents*
das Kapitel (-)   *chapter*

die Komödie (-en)   *comedy*
die Kurzgeschichte (-n)   *short story*
der Kriminalroman (-e)   *detective story*
die (negative) Kritik (-en)   *(adverse) criticism*
die Lebenserinnerungen (plural only)   *memoirs*
der Leser (-)   *reader*
die Literatur (-en)   *literature*
die Lösung (-en)   *dénouement*
das Märchen (-)   *fairy tale*
die Novelle (-n)   *short story*
die Person (-en)   *character in a novel or play*
die Phantasie (n)   *imagination*
die Prosa (no plural)   *prose*
der Reim (-e)   *rhyme*
die Rezension (-en)   *review*
der Roman (-e)   *novel*
die Romanliteratur (no plural)   *fiction*
das Schauspiel (-e)   *play*
der Schriftsteller (-)   *writer*
das Sprichwort (-̈er)   *proverb*
der Stil (-e)   *style*
die Strophe (-n)   *verse*
das Taschenbuch (-̈er)   *paperback*
die Tatsache (-n)   *fact*
der Tatsachenbericht (-e)   *factual report*
der Text (-e)   *text*
das Thema (-en)   *theme, subject*
der Tonfall (no plural)   *intonation*
die Tragödie (-en)   *tragedy*
die Trümmerliteratur (no plural)   *literature of the immediate post war era*
der Überblick (-e)   *survey*
der Verlag (-e)   *publishing house*
das Verlagsrecht (-e)   *copy right*
der Vers (-e)   *verse*
die Veröffentlichung (-en)   *publication*
das Vorwort (no plural)   *preface*
der Vortrag (-̈e)   *lecture*
das Werk (-e)   *work*
die Widmung (-en)   *dedication*
das Wörterbuch (-̈er)   *dictionary*
die Zeile (-n)   *line*
das Zitat (-e)   *quote*
die Zusammenfassung (-en)   *summary*
der Zusammenhang (-̈e)   *context*

ausdrücken   *to express*
sich kritisch äußern über (+Acc)   *to comment (on)*
beeindrucken   *to impress*
drucken   *to print*
herausgeben (gibt heraus, gab heraus, herausgegeben)   *to edit*
kritisieren   *to criticise*
nachschlagen (schlägt nach, schlug nach, nachgeschlagen)   *to consult*
rezensieren   *to review*
veröffentlichen   *to publish*

*vor*lesen (liest vor, las vor, vorgelesen)
    to read aloud
widmen *to dedicate*
zitieren *to quote*

vergriffen   *out of print*

b) Literaturkritik

es setzt sich kritisch mit ... auseinander
    it takes a critical look at ...
ein starkes gesellschaftliches
    Engagement   *a strong social
    conscience*
eine moralisch fundierte Sozialkritik
    social criticsm with a moral base
die Nöte und Sorgen der kleinen Leute
    *the problems and worries of
    ordinary people*
der Schauplatz der Erzählung   *the
    setting of the story*
ein Roman in der Ich/Er-Form   *a novel
    in the first/third person*
es stellt hohe Ansprüche an den Leser
    *it makes great demands on the
    reader*
man bekommt dadurch einen Einblick in
    menschliche Beziehungen   *it gives
    an insight into human relationships*

der Aufstieg (no plural)   *rise*
das Bild (-er)   *figure of speech*
der Dialog (-e)   *dialogue*
die Einfühlung mit (+ Dat)   *empathy with*
der Erzähler (-)   *narrator*
der Ideenreichtum (-er)   *richness of ideas*
das Klischee (-s)   *cliché*
die Metapher (-n)   *metaphor*
der Verfall (no plural)   *fall*

abgedroschen   *commonplace*
anspruchsvoll   *demanding*
aufregend   *thrilling*
aufrüttelnd   *stirring*
ausdrucksvoll   *expressive*
ausführlich   *detailed*
bildlich   *metaphorical*
buchstäblich   *literal*
dunkel   *obscure*
dichterisch   *poetical*
dürftig   *insubstantial, slight*
erfunden   *fictituous*
erschreckend   *frightening*
fesselnd   *absorbing*
gefühlvoll   *sensitive*
gekünstelt   *affected*
geschmackvoll   *tasteful*
glänzend   *splendid*
humorvoll, heiter   *humorous*
ironisch   *ironic*
komisch   *comic*
langweilig   *tedious*
lebendig   *vivid*

lebenswahr   *true-to-life*
leicht verständlich   *easily understood*
leicht zugänglich   *easily accessible*
sehr lesenswert   *worth reading*
literarisch   *literary*
packend   *gripping*
realistisch   *realistic*
reichlich   *copious*
rührend   *moving, touching*
sorgfältig ausgearbeitet   *elaborate*
spannend   *fascinating*
trist   *drab*
unglaubwürdig   *unbelievable*
unterhaltend   *entertaining*
unwahrscheinlich   *implausible*
weitschweifig   *long-winded*
wirklichkeitsfliehend   *escapist*
witzig   *witty*
wohlklingend   *melodious*
wortreich   *wordy, copious*
zusammenhanglos   *disjointed*

c) Das Theater

die Aufführung (-en)   *performance*
die Beleuchtung (no plural)   *lighting*
die Besetzung (-en)   *cast*
das Bühnenbild (-er)   *scenery*
die Bühnenrequisiten (plural only)
    stage properties
die Dekoration (-en)   *scenery*
die Drehbühne (-n)   *revolving stage*
der Erfolg (-e)   *success*
das Foyer (-s)   *foyer*
das Freilichttheater (-)   *open-air theatre*
der Gang (-e)   *aisle*
die Garderobe (-n)   *cloakroom*
die Generalprobe (-n)   *dress rehearsal*
die Inszenierung (-en)   *production*
das Kabarett (-e)   *cabaret*
die Kulisse (-n) (usually plural)   *wings*
das Laientheater (-)   *amateur dramatics*
die Loge (-n)   *box*
erster Rang   *dress circle*
zweiter Rang   *balcony*
der dritte Rang, die Galerie   *gallery*
das Parkett (-e)   *stalls*
der Platzanweiser/in (plural:
    Platzanweiser/innen)   *usher*
die Posse (-n)   *farce*
das Publikum (no plural)   *audience*
der Regisseur (-e)   *stage-manager/
    director*
die Rolle (-n)   *part*
der Schauspieler (-)   *actor*
der Souffleur (-e)   *prompter*
der Sitzplatz (-e)   *seat*
der Sperrsitz (-e)   *stalls*
der Spielplan (-e)   *repertory programme*
die Theaterkasse (-n)   *box-office*
die Uraufführung (-en)   *world première
    (of a play)*

der Zauberer (-) *magician*
der Zuschauer (-) *spectator*

*auf*führen *to perform*
applaudieren *to applaud*
auf die Bühne bringen (bringt, brachte,
    gebracht) *to put on stage*
schwärmen für (+ Acc.) *to enthuse about*

5. Kunst und Musik

a) Die Musik

das Akkordeon (-s) *accordion*
die Aufnahme (-n) *recordings*
die Baßgeige (-n) *double bass*
die Becken (plural only) *cymbals*
der Begleiter (-) *accompanist*
die Blaßkapelle (-n) *wind band*
das Blechinstrument (-e) *brass
    instrument*
die Bratsche (-n) *viola*
der CD-spieler (-) *CD-player*
der Chor (-e) *chorus*
der Compactdisc (-s) *CD*
der Dirigent (-en) *conductor*
der Dudelsack (-e) *bag-pipe*
das Fagott (-e) *bassoon*
die Flöte (-n) *flute*
der Flügel (-) *grand piano*
die Geige (-n)/Violine (-n) *violin*
das Geräusch (-e) *noise*
der Gesang (-̈e) *singing*
die Gitarre (-n) *guitar*
die Harfe (-n) *harp*
die Hifi-Anlage (-n) *hi-fi system*
die Hintergrundsmusik (no plural)
    background music, muzak
der Hit (-s) *hit song*
der Jazz (no plural) *jazz*
das Kammerorchester (-) *chamber
    orchestra*
der Kapellmeister (-) *bandmaster*
die Kassette (-n) *audio cassette*
der Kirchenchor (-̈e) *choir*
die Klarinette (-n) *clarinet*
der Komponist (-en) *composer*
die Komposition (-en) *composition*
das Konzert (-e) *concert*
der Konzertsaal (-̈e) *concert hall*
die Langspielplatte (-n) *long play record*
der Lärm (no plural) *noise, din*
volkstümliche Lieder *traditional
    popular songs*
die Melodie (-n) *melody*
die Mundharmonika (-s) *mouth organ*
die zeitgenössische Musik (no plural)
    contemporary music
der Musikautomat (-en) *juke-box*
der Musiker (-) *musician*
das Musikfest (-e) *music festival*
das Notenblatt (-̈er) *sheet of music*

der Notenständer (-) *music stand*
die Oper (-n) *opera*
das Orchester (-) *orchestra*
die Orgel (-n) *organ*
die Partitur (-en) *score*
der Plattenspieler (-) *record player*
das Saiteninstrument (-e) *string-
    instrument*
der Schall (no plural) *sound, resonance*
das Schifferklavier (-e) *accorieon*
die Schlagerparade (-n) *hit parade*
der Schlager (-) *pop song (usually in
    German)*
das Schlagzeug (no plural) *percussion
    instruments*
die Stereoanlage (-n) *stereo-system*
der Straßenmusikant (-en) *busker, street
    musician*
die Symphonie (-n) *symphony*
der Takt (-e) *beat*
die Taste (-n) *key on an instrument*
der Ton (-e) *individual sound, note*
die Tonart (-en) *key of a piece of music*
die Tonhöhe (-n) *pitch*
die Trommel (-n) *drum*
die Unterhaltungsmusik (no plural)
    light music
der Verstärker (-) *amplifier*
der Virtuose/in (-n) *virtuoso*
das Waldhorn (-̈er) *French horn*
die Ziehharmonika (-s) *concertina*

*auf*nehmen (nimmt auf, nahm auf,
    aufgenommen) *to record*
dirigieren *to conduct*
ins Konzert gehen (geht, ging,
    gegangen*) *to go to a concert*
in die Oper gehen *to go to the opera*
klingen (klingt, klang, geklungen) *to
    sound*
komponieren *to compose*
musizieren *to make music*
vom Blatt spielen *to sight-read*
stimmen *to tune*
üben *to practise*
vertonen *to set to music*

begabt *gifted*
musikalisch *musical*
talentiert *talented*

b) Die Kunst

Die Figur im Vordergrund hebt sich gut
    gegen das Blau des Himmels ab.
    *the figure in the foreground stands out
    well against the blue of the sky.*

die Ausstellung (-en) *exhibition*
das Aquarell (-e) *water colour painting*
die Baukunst (no plural) *architecture*
der Bildhauer (-) *sculptor*

die Bildhauerei (no plural) *sculpture*
das Bildnis (-se) *portrait*
der Bogen (·) *arch*
der Buntstift (-e) *coloured pencil*
das Gewölbe (no plural) *vault*
die Grafik (-en) *graphic art*
der Halbkreis (-e) *semi-circle*
der Holzschnitt (-e) *wood cut*
die bildenden Künste *fine arts*
der Künstler/in *artist*
die Kunstgalerie (-n) *art gallery*
das Kunstwerk (-e) *work of art*
der Kupferstich (-e) *engraving*
die Landschaft (-en) *landscape*
die Malerei (no plural) *painting*
das Meisterwerk (-e) *master piece*
die Ölfarbe (-n) *oil paints*
das Ölgemälde (-) *oil painting*
die Plastik (-en) *sculpture*
der Pinsel (-) *brush*
das Porträt (-s) *portrait*
die Radierung (-en) *etching*
der gute Ruf *good reputation*
die Schnitzerei (-en) *carving*
die Skizze (-n) *sketch*
die Staffelei (-en) *easel*
das Standbild (-er) *statue*
der Stil/Malstil (-e) *style (of painting)*
das Talent für (+ Acc.) *talent (for)*
die Tubenfarben (plural only) *paints in a tube*

die Vernissage (-n) *opening of an exhibition*
der Vordergrund/Hintergrund (no plural) *foreground/background*
die Zeichnung (-en) *drawing*

abändern *to modify*
sich abheben gegen (hebt ab, hob ab, abgehoben) *to stand out against*
aushauen *to sculpture*
blühen/gedeihen *to flourish*
darstellen *to represent*
entwerfen (entwirft, entwarf, entworfen) *to design*
malen *to paint*
nachahmen *to imitate*
schnitzen *to carve*
skizzieren *to sketch*
verfallen (verfällt, verfiel, verfallen*) *to decay*
zeichnen *to draw, sketch*

architektonisch *architectural*
bemerkenswert *notable*
gewölbt *arched*
hervorragend *eminent*
kitschig *tasteless, trashy, kitsch*
kreisförmig *circular*
künstlerisch *artistic*
künstlich *artificial*
zierlich *graceful*

APPENDIX

BOARD BY BOARD SYLLABUS DETAILS

AEB

NEAB

NISEAC

OCSEB

ODLE

UCLES

WJEC

GETTING STARTED

This appendix will give you the opportunity of checking the assessment requirements for your syllabus. You can further check these by contacting your own Examination Board (see p. iv). It is worth doing this as syllabuses do change from time to time. When contacting the Examination Boards you will need to ask for the publications Department and request an order form to be sent to you. On the order form indicate exactly which syllabus you are studying and be prepared to send a cheque or postal order with your order.

The way in which each Examination Board tests whether students have achieved the *aims* outlined in Chapter 1 varies somewhat in detail. I have therefore listed each A Level syllabus in outline below, so that you can check what **you** will be asked to do. The information refers to 1993 and 1994 syllabuses. The detail does change from time to time, and you should check the current position. I have not listed 'set books' or 'set topics' for the same reason—it is vital to check the current requirement with your teacher.

If you are taking AS Level German, in broad terms, you will take identical Speaking and Listening papers to A Level candidates doing the same board. The Reading paper will be broadly similar, too, but there will in most be some adaptation to allow you to do some simple writing. Don't worry—the writing required is usually very similar in standard to that required for GCSE. But do check the exact details with your teacher.

If you are taking the COSSEC AS Level German, it is based on the OCSEB A Level.

THE ASSOCIATED EXAMINING BOARD (AEB)

Speaking 20% (20 minutes)

(a) Discussion of material of contemporary interest prepared in the 20 minutes before the exam.
(b) Discussion on a topic chosen by the candidate from a list of 20 provided well before the exam.
(c) General questions suitable for candidates at A Level.

Listening 20% (1 hour)

Candidates listen to:
(a) six or seven short items—news items, advertisements, conversations,
(b) a longer interview or discussion.

Reading 20% (2 hours)

Candidates do:
(a) a translation of about 300 words from German into English,
(b) a reading comprehension, including partial summary, of a passage of 700–800 words.

Writing 20% (2 and a half hours)

Candidates

(a) Answer questions in German on a passage in English. This may include translation of parts of it.
(b) Study two passages in German and write 250 words in German in response to one of them.

Civilisation, Literature and Culture 20% (2 and a half hours)

Two essays of not less than 350 words in German on set topics.

NORTHERN EXAMINATIONS AND ASSESSMENT BOARD (NEAB)

Speaking 20% (15 minutes)

(a) Role-play: one task prepared immediately before the exam.   (4%)
(b) Reporting: Candidates have to convey information given to them in written or visual form before the start of the exam. It might include a newspaper article, or information on British customs.   (4%)
(c) Conversation:
  (i) everyday topics,
  (ii) discussion of one of two books of 50+ pages; the examiner decides which one of the two.
Candidates can expect to have their ability to express and defend and opinion tested.   (12%)

Listening 20% (one hour)

Candidates hear a number of shorter items and one longer item. There are questions in English, multiple-choice questions, and summaries. Occasionally candidates may be required to write down in German what was said.

Reading and Writing 35% (three hours)

Candidates study two German texts of different linguistic registers and answer questions arising from them. The questions will always include:
(a) translation into English,
(b) translation into German of about 80 words related to one or both of the texts,
(c) free writing of 250 words of German which may or may not be loosely related to the text,
(d) other questions, including comprehension with answers in German.

Literature/Coursework 25% (three hours)

EITHER:

Candidates answer questions on 4 set books:
(a) questions on two 20th century texts to be answered in German,
(b) questions on two texts which may be answered in English or German. Only the content of the answer is marked (i.e. there are no marks for the quality of the German).

OR

Candidates submit three essays totalling 2500 words in German. The work is usually based on works of fiction or non-fiction in German, but one essay may be based around a study visit to a German-speaking country.

NORTHERN IRELAND SCHOOLS EXAMINATION AND ASSESSMENT COUNCIL (NISEAC)

Speaking 20% (20 minutes)

(a) Candidates discuss stimulus material from a choice of two topics determined by the visiting examiner. They read part of the material aloud, and discuss it with the examiner.
(b) A conversation with the examiner about the candidate's life and times, and current affairs or events at home.
20 minutes' preparation time is allowed, during which a German–English dictionary is available.

Listening 20% (45 minutes)

Questions in English on 4—6 passages in German, based on the topics in the topic list.

Reading 20% (2 hours)

(a) Reading comprehension, with questions in English.
(b) Two 100 word passages of contrasting styles to be translated into English.
All material is based on the topic list.

Writing 20% 2 hours (30 minutes)

(a) A passage in English, with questions in German.
(b) 150 words to be translated into German.
(c) 250 word essay in German, choice of title, with some accompanying stimulus material in German.

Literature and Culture 20% (2 hours 30 minutes)

Three questions in English. Candidates must answer at least one literary and one background question.

OXFORD AND CAMBRIDGE SCHOOLS EXAMINATION BOARD (OCSEB)

Speaking 20% (various times—see below)

Either: 25 minutes with either your own teacher or a visiting examiner consisting of:
(i) two role-plays chosen by the candidate involving some negotiation (5 minutes),
(ii) discussion of interests of current concern based on one of three articles available for candidates to choose from (10 minutes).
All the materials for (i) and (ii) are given to candidates 2—7 days beforehand.
(iii) Discussion of a cultural topic originating in a German-speaking country. Candidate's choice (10 minutes).

Or: 5 short assessments are made by your teacher during the A Level course, two in the Lower Sixth and three in the Upper Sixth. In addition, a visiting examiner visits the class to observe the general standard of oral work and to check on your teacher's judgement.

Listening 20% (approx 1 hour)

A selection of news items, dialogues and interviews with questions in English or multiple-choice type. Dictionaries are allowed.

Responsive Reading 20% (2 hours 30 minutes)

Three passages drawn from contemporary journalism, brochures, advertisements or literary works are set. The first passage is used to test comprehension of detail, by one or more of questions in English or summary. The second one has questions in English and is in a contrasting register of German. The third passage—which carries half the marks—is for translation into English.

Writing 20% (2 hours 45 minutes)

Candidates choose two of the following options:
(a) Essay in German (250—350 words).
(b) Translation into German (Prose).
(c) Use of German—a series of exercises which test vocabulary, syntax and idiom.

Literature and Civilisation 20% (2 hours 45 minutes)

Three questions on literary text or civilisation issues. There is a choice of questions on each text or topic. The list of set books and set topics varies from time to time. Answers may be written in English or German, but answers in German are only really expected from native speakers.

Personal Study

In place of one question on the Literature and Civilisation Paper, candidates may submit a piece of coursework 2000—2500 words long, in German or English. Titles have to agreed with the board.

UNIVERSITY OF OXFORD DELEGACY OF LOCAL EXAMINATIONS (ODLE)

A German–German dictionary is allowed throughout the examination.

Speaking 30% (30–35 minutes with a visiting examiner or your own teacher)

(a) Role play given to the candidate 35–40 minutes in advance (10 minutes).
(b) (i) Introductory presentation of a topic from the Writing paper list (3 minutes).
    (ii) Discussion of the topic presented, and possibly a second one. Candidates give the examiner a list of headings in German relating to the topic, which they are prepared to discuss (15–20 minutes).

Listening 20% (1 hour)

A range of items and questions are set. The questions are usually set and answered in German, but the German candidates writing is only assessed for 'the ability to transmit the correct information', not for accuracy of the language.
Candidates have a cassette each, and headphones, and can play the tape as often as they wish. Some centres will use a language laboratory for this test.

Reading 25% (2 hours)

Shorter and longer extracts of German, with answers usually to be written in German. For the longer passages there nay be some use of language exercises.

Writing 25% (various times–see below)

There are five options, ranging from 100% coursework to 100% examination, with combinations of the two. Also possible is a Viewing Test (2–3 minutes of video played four times as a stimulus to a longer piece of written work) taken in combination with either coursework or an examination.
Examination questions and the Viewing Test require 350–400 words of German as an essay. There is some choice of question.
The Coursework option requires three pieces of written work of 500–700 words each per topic, or twice that amount if 100% coursework is selected. Some of the work has to be completed by 15th January, the remainder by 30th April. The topic list has literary and non-literary titles. The literary topics allow a wide choice of text, but the non-literary topics are somewhat more specific.

UNIVERSITY OF CAMBRIDGE LOCAL EXAMINATIONS SYNDICATE (UCLES)

Speaking 25% (various times–see below)

Either:
(a) 20 minutes with a visiting examiner consisting of:
(i) a pre-prepared sustained speech on a topic chosen by the candidate (3 mins),
(ii) a discussion of the topics raised in the sustained speech (7–8 mins),
(iii) general conversation discussing topics of personal interest and current affairs.

Or:

(b) Continuous assessment (15%) and a short test with a visiting examiner (10%). The continuous assessment element consists of assessment of a variety of classroom exercises including presenting material and discussing with others. The visiting examiner conducts a shorter version of the test in (a).

Listening 20% (approx 1 hour)

There are two sorts of passages:
(a) A selection of news flashes, advertisments, announcements, etc., ending with a longer passage such as a longer news item or anecdote. (7%)
(b) Two extended interviews or discussions invloving two or more speakers. (13%)
Some questions will be in English, some in German, some mere gap-filling, others requiring longer answers.

Reading and Writing 25% (2 hours 30 minutes)

There are two sorts of passages:
(a) Two passages in German on the same theme, with a variety of tasks in English and German (guide time: 1 hour).
(b) A text or texts in English about a topic of current interest. Candidates respond in German, either writing a guided composition, or answering questions about the passage (guide time: 1 hour).

Essay in German 10% (1 hour 30 minutes)

Candidates write an essay in German on one of the topics studied. Centres are told in March which topics will come up (but not what the exact titles would be). This procedure is currently under review.

Coursework 20%

Four items of coursework totalling about 3000 words of German are submitted. Two of them (400–500 words) are done by the whole class, the others (800–1000 words) allow more individual choice.

Thematic Studies 20% (3 hours)

Set books are arranged in groups of four by theme. Candidates need to prepare three themes, and should have read at least one text from each theme. The texts can be taken into the exam room. Questions are set and are answered in German.

UNIVERSITY OF LONDON EXAMINATIONS AND ASSESSMENT COUNCIL (ULEAC)

Speaking 20% (20 minutes)

(a) Candidates have 20 minutes to study an extract before spending 10 minutes discussing it and issues arising from it.
(b) 10 minutes general conversation on a variety of topics, which may include those areas chosen for Literature/Civilisation/Coursework.

Listening 20% (45 minutes)

Up to 25 questions in English on recordings in German.
(a) 3–4 short items including newsflashes, public announcements, advertisements.
(b) 2 more substantial pieces including reviews, interviews, discussions, conversations or current affairs broadcasts.

Reading 20% (2 hours)

(a) Translation into English of a 200–word passage of contenporary German.
(b) Comprehension questions in English on a 700–800-word passage of contemporary German.
The passages for (a) or (b) may be narrative, descriptive, or dialogue or a mixture of these.

Writing 20% (2 hours 30 minutes)

(a) Two guided writing tasks based on stimulus material in German.
(i) Writing 150 words of German in respose to the stimulus material.

(ii) Translation 100 words of English into German.

(b) Essay of 250 words in German. Choice of 6 titles, at least one of which will relate to the material in (a).

Literature/Civilisation/Coursework 20% (2 hours 30 minutes)

ONE of these options may be chosen.

(a) Literature: Questions in English on 3 set books. On at least one of the books candidates have to do either a commentary or a structured question. On the other two they have a choice of two essays.

(b) Civilisation: candidates answer questions on two topics reating to 20th century Germany and Austria, or Mozart. Candidates write two 350-word essays.

(c) Coursework: Candidates submit two 1200 work pieces of German during the Upper Sixth year.

WELSH JOINT EDUCATION COMMITTEE/CYD-BWYLLGOR ADDSYG CYMRU (WJEC)

Speaking 20% (15–20 minutes)

(a) Role-play.

(b) Candidates talk with the visiting examiner about their life and times.

(c) Discussion of an issue related to the set topics.

Listening 20% (1 hour)

Questions are answered in the mother tongue (English or Welsh).

(a) Questions on up to four short informal situational dialogues. (6.7%)

(b) Questions on up to 5 short news items. (3.3%)

(c) Questions on an interview or more formal talk. (10%)

Reading 20% (2 hours 30 minutes)

Questions are answered in the mother tongue (English or Welsh).

(a) Comprehension qwuestions on 2/3 items of journalism. (7%)

(b) Questions about a longer text, which may be narrative, interview, an information piece or an argumentative article. (8%)

(c) Translation of selected sentences from the texts used for (a) and (b) into English or Welsh. (5%)

Writing 20% (3 hours)

German–English dictionaries may be used.

(a) Candidates write a letter of 150 words in German in response to stimuli. (5%)

(b) A 250-word essay in German – choice of titles. (8%)

(c) Either (i) a 150-word précis in German of an English or Welsh text

or   (ii) translation of 120 words of English or Welsh into German

or   (iii) a 150-words report in German using information from tables, diagrams, survey results, etc. (7%)

Literature, Extended Language or Project (20%)

Candidates choose *one* of:

Either **Literature** (2 hours 30 minutes)

Three questions in English/Welsh, one commentary and two essays, on set texts

Additionally two pieces of work (commentary or essay) done during the Upper Sixth are assessed.

Or   **Extended Language** (1 hour 30 minutes)

(a) 120–150-word answers in German on each of two set texts.

(b) Oral exposé plus discussion with the visiting Speaking examiner (10 minutes).

(c) Two pieces of coursework (essays in German or oral exposé) done during the Upper Sixth are assessed.

Or   **Project** – 1500 words in one, two or three pieces of work on a topic agreed by the WJEC. Titles are decided by late October, and work completed by the end of May.

Index

Abgeordnete 238
Ablehnen 204
Abwägen 205
Accusative 129
active and passive, verbs 157
adjective ending tables 124
adjective, definition 121
adjectives 9–22, 123–126
advantage, expressed by dative 130
adverb, definition 121
adverbs 126–128
AEB, syllabus outline 263
agent in passive 166
agreement 204
agreement, definition 121
Aids 216
alcohol 216
Alles Klar 9, 154
Alter, das 217
als ob + subjunctive 173
Anschluß 118
Arbeit 226
art 260
ärztliche Behandlung 215
assignments 1
Authentik 7, 11
avalanche rule 153

Bildwörterbuch, Duden 4
body 214, 219
body language 75
Bundesrepublik Deutschland 118

Cambridge Local, syllabus outline 266
capital letters 149
case, definition 121
cases, use 128 –131
checking adjectives 86
checking cases 86
checking genders 86
checking punctuation 87
checking spelling 86–87
checking verbs 86
checking word order 86
checking writing 9
checking, systematic 9, 10
cinema 224
citizen's movement 243
civil law 234
classroom phrases 5
clause, definition 121
clauses anticipated by *es* 191
clichés 29
command forms 175–176
commas 149
communicating 7
comparatives, definition 121
comparisons 131–132, 206
compound nouns 27, 28
compound words 26–28
compound words, gender 136
comprehension questions, reading, answers 42–44
comprehension questions, reading, examples 35–41
comprehension questions, reading, method 30
comprehension questions, reading, worked examples 32–33
conditional perfect, definition 157
conditional, definition 157
conditions 172–173
conflict, armed 247
conjugation, definition 122
conjunctions 132–134
connections 254
countries, German-speaking 255
countries, names 256
country 231–232
coursework 93, 112–117
crime 233
current affairs 235–241

DAN 154
dates 151–152
dative 130–131
days 151
DDR, ehemalige 242
DDR, former 242
definite time 129
demonstrative pronouns 148
Deutsche Demokratische Republik 118
dictionary work 2
direct speech, punctuation 150
disadvantage, expressed by dative 130
disagreement 204
distances 129
Dreißigähriger Krieg 117
drink 257
Dritte Welt 245
Drogen 216
drugs 216
du and *Sie, ihr* and *Sie* 145
dürfen 177

economic policy 241
economics 239
education 206–210
Ems-Depesche 118

Endlösung 118
energy 230
environment 228, 230
er, sie and *es* 145
Erklären 205
Ernährung 257
es gibt 189
es ist 189
es, anticipating clauses 191
essay writing in German 87–89, 100–104, 107–112
Essen 257
etwas 126
Europe 241
exam preparation 12, 13, 14
exam techniques 14
exams 208
exclamation marks 150
exclamations 129
explanations 205

Fahrzeuge 253
family 212
fashion 221, 222
Fernsehen 223–224
finance, personal 242
financial institutions 240
Flugverkehr 251
Flüsse 255
food 257
fractions 140
Frauenfragen 213–214
free time 221
Fremdwörter 3, 28
Friedrich der Große 117
future perfect tense 157, 162
future tense 156, 158–159

GCSE German – Your Speaking Test Guide 7
GDR, former 242
gender 134–137
genitive 129–130
geographical terms 256
German History – brief review 117–119
glossary of grammatical terms 121–123
Grammar 1 120–154
Grammar 2 155–200
greetings 129
GROLPEO 154
Großhandel 239
gute Eigenschaften 219
Gute Literaturnoten 119
Gutenberg 117

haben or *sein* in the perfect 160
Hapsburg 117
Hauptschwierigkeiten, Duden 4
health 214–217
Herz 139
History, German, brief review 117–119

illness 215
immigration policy 244
imperatives 122, 175–176
imperfect tense 156, 161
impersonal verbs 189–191
indefinite time 130
industrial technology 249
-ing 187–188
infinitives 122, 181–185
informatik 249
information technology 249
inseparable prefixes 23–24
interrogative pronouns 122, 147
introduction 206
irgend- 127
irregular verb table 197–200
irregular verbs, definition 122
it – see er, sie and *es* 145

journalism 28–30, 235
Jugend 210–211
Junker 117
justification 206

Karl der Große 117
Konjunktiv I 167
Konjunktiv I for instructions 174
Konjunktiv I in wishes 174
Konjunktiv II 167–168
Konjunktiv II for softening the tone 174
können 178
legal expressions 233
legal framework 234
Lehrer 208
Leisure 221–225
listening 7, 8, 49–70
literary criticism 259
literary texts 104–105
literature 258
Literature, Civilisation & Coursework 99–119
Luftverschmutzung 229

Machtergreifung 118
making admissions 205
Männerfragen 211–213
marriage 211–213
measurements 129

media 223–224
medical treatment 215
medicine 250
Medizin 250
Meere 256
men's issues 213–214
Militär 246
mixed verbs, definition 157
modal verbs 176–181
Mode 221
mögen 178
months 151
moods, definition 157
mountains 255
MP 238
music 8, 260
müssen 179

NEAB, syllabus outline 263
new technology 249
newspapers 11, 235
nichts 126
nirgend- 127
NISEAC, syllabus outline 264
Nominative 128–129
nouns 16–19, 134–139
numbers 139, 140

oceans 256
OCSEB, syllabus outline 265
öffentliche Recht 234
office technology 248
old age 217
open conditions 172
opinions 204
Österreich 255
Oxford & Cambridge, syllabus outline 265
Oxford Local, syllabus outline 265
PAD 154
PADAN 154
parents 211
parliament 238
participles 185–188
parties, political 238
passive 163–166, 181
past participle 122, 185–186
peace 246
perfect infinitive 181
perfect tense 156, 159–161
personal pronouns 144
Personenbeschreibungen 219–220
persons of verbs, definition 156
pluperfect tense 156, 162
plural forms 4, 137
politics 237, 239
possibilities 172
prefixes 16, 24–26
prepositions 122, 141–144
present participle 122, 186–187
present tense 156, 158
Privatrecht 234
pronouns 122, 144–148
psychology 218–219
punctuation 149

question words 128
question-spotting 12

racism 245
Radio 223
Rassismus 245
Rauchen 216
Raumfahrt 254
re-unification 242, 243
reading 10, 11
reflections 205
reflexive pronouns 144
reflexive verbs 123, 193
regrets 205
regular verb list 196–197
Reisen 225
relative pronouns 123, 146
Religion 217–218
reported speech, colloquial usage 171–172
reported speech, formal usage 169–171
research 250
revision planning 12
revision technique 13
rewards 13
rivers 255
roads 252
roots of words 16

sagte, alternatives 30
Saxon Genitive 130
Schiffahrt 252
schlechte Eigenschaften 220
school 207
Schüler/Schülerin 207
Schweiz 255
seas 256
semi-colon 150
senses 219
separable prefixes 22
sequences 206
set text, study method 104
set topic, study method 104
simple past tense, definition 156

Sinne 219
smoking 216
Social issues 225–235
sociology 225
sollen 179
speaking 5, 6, 7, 73–82
spelling 148–149
ss or *ß*? 148
Städtenamen 256
Stadtprobleme 232
Stasi 119
statistics 225
Straßen 252
strong verbs 157, 197–200
subjunctive 166–175
suffixes 16
suggestions 204
summary, answer 45–46
summary, example 42
summary, method 31
summary, worked example 34
summing up 205
superlative sentence patterns 132
superlative, definition 123

teachers 208
technology 248
tenses, definition 123, 156
Theater 258
Third World 245
time, definite and indefiniote 152
times 150–151
times of the clock 150
TMP 153
town 231–232, 256
trade 239, 241
training 209
transcripts 7
transitive and intransitive verb pairs 192
translation during your course, method 91
translation in an exam, method 92
translation into English 30–31, 33–34, 41–42, 44–45
translation into German 90–93
translation 90–93
travel 225, 251–254
Treuhand 118
Trinken 257
triple consonants 149
Tugenden 219
TV 7, 223–224

UCLES, syllabus outline 266–267
ULEAC, syllabus outline 267
Umlaut 74, 148
Umwelt 228
Umweltprobleme 228
Umweltschutz 230
unemployment 226
university 209
UODLE, syllabus outline 265

vehicles 253
verb forms 4, 158–163, 167–169
Verbindungen 254
Verbrechen 233
verbs 188–189, 194–196
verbs with prefixes 22–24
verbs with suffixes 26
verbs, common regular 196–197
verbs, definition 156
verbs, impersonal 189–191
verbs, irregular verb table 197–200
verbs, moods, definition 157
verbs, reflexive 193
verbs, transitive and intransitive pairs 192
Vergleichen 206
Verkehr 251
vices 220
virtues 219
vocabulary 4, 201–261
Völkerschlacht 118
Vorschläge 204

war 246
Wasserverschmutzung 229
weak verbs, definition 157
weather 236
wie wenn + subjunctive 173
Wiedervereinigung 118, 242–243
Wiener Kongreß 118
wishes 129, 174
WJEC, sylllabus outline 268
wollen 180
women's issues 213–214
word formation 16
word order 152–154
work 226
writing 8, 9, 10, 85–93

youth 210–211

Zeitenfolge 206
Zollverein 118
Zugeständnisse machen 205
Zusammenfassen 205
Zustimmen 204